The Diary of Hannah Callender Sansom

The Diary of Hannah Callender Sansom

SENSE AND SENSIBILITY IN THE AGE OF
THE AMERICAN REVOLUTION

EDITED BY
SUSAN E. KLEPP AND KARIN WULF

CORNELL UNIVERSITY PRESS
ITHACA AND LONDON

First published 2010 by Cornell University Press
First printing, Cornell Paperbacks, 2010

Printed in the United States of America

Library of Congress Cataloging-in-Publication Data

Sansom, Hannah Callender, 1737–1801.
    The Diary of Hannah Callender Sansom : sense and sensibility in the age of the American Revolution / [edited by] Susan E. Klepp and Karin Wulf.
       p. cm.
    Includes bibliographical references and index.
    ISBN 978-0-8014-4784-6 (cloth : alk. paper) — ISBN 978-0-8014-7513-9 (pbk. : alk. paper)
    1. Sansom, Hannah Callender, 1737–1801—Diaries.   2. Quakers—Pennsylvania—Philadelphia—Diaries.   3. Women—Pennsylvania—Philadelphia—Diaries.   4. Philadelphia (Pa.)—Social life and customs—18th century.   5. Philadelphia (Pa.)—History—18th century.
I. Klepp, Susan E.   II. Wulf, Karin A., 1964–   III. Title.

    F158.9.F89S26 2009
    974.8'1102092—dc22
    [B]

2009016844

Cornell University Press strives to use environmentally responsible suppliers and materials to the fullest extent possible in the publishing of its books. Such materials include vegetable-based, low-VOC inks and acid-free papers that are recycled, totally chlorine-free, or partly composed of nonwood fibers. For further information, visit our website at www. cornellpress.cornell.edu.

Cloth printing   10 9 8 7 6 5 4 3 2 1
Paperback printing   10 9 8 7 6 5 4 3 2 1

Contents

Preface

The diary of Hannah Callender Sansom offers readers a compelling new look at how a woman in eighteenth-century British America lived and observed the world around her. In more than two hundred pages over thirty years, HCS kept note of her daily life, her courtship, her reading, her religion and philosophy, and above all her family. The diary was preserved by generations of HCS's granddaughter's family, the Vauxs. In 1888 George Vaux published selected portions of the diary, but only those of "general interest," by which he meant of largely public and political interest. Until the early 1990s the original diary rested in the vault of a later George Vaux; he then donated it to the American Philosophical Society, where it is now archived.

The manuscript diary begins on January 1, 1758, with the first entries on separate sheets of paper. She then probably used multiple booklets that were bound together in the nineteenth century in a single large volume, 9 inches by 12 inches, with a stippled yellow and brown board cover and handsome leather spine and corners. Paper was expensive, and HCS took care to write on the entire surface of each page, leaving little in the way of margins. Her penmanship, although somewhat crabbed, is usually clear except when she tried to squeeze in an extra line or two at the bottom of a page. The ink has faded to a soft brown color but is almost always legible. There are a very few places where passages have been cut out of the diary, perhaps by HCS herself or by a descendant. A few items have been placed in the pages of the diary, such as a cutout of a reindeer (see page 94) that look to have belonged to HCS; these placements are noted in the edition.

One striking aspect of the diary is its gaps. HCS put away her diary during periods of intense family obligation, such as the births of her children and the ill-

A Memorandum Book, from the 1 Day of the Year 1758,
1th of the first M.° and 1 of the Week, for my own Satisfaction, and to
try if a Retrospect of my time, may not make me husband it more.

1 M. 1 Day Morn: went to Meeting, B. Trotter spoke, too loud. S. Stanton prayed,
did not go in the after noon, see a great many People walking out, wish people
would think it more their duty, to go to some place of Worship that day,
went in the evening, S. Stanton, S. Tasher, spoke.

2 Morn: at work. afternoon, with B. Ritchie went to N. Gibson's spent it in
agreable Conversation.

3 Morn: went to meeting, a rainy Day, stayed at home the rest of it.

4 Morn: at home busey, afternoon went to B. Rawles.

5 Morn: Ironing, afternoon, my two little Cousins Lightfoot to see me.

6 Morn: three O Clock waked, by S. Flower calling Mamme to, with him
to Caty, mamme a bad cold did not go, after break fast went to see her
found her brave, a fine Girl, called Caty, went from there to bechy's to talk
about some irregularities in the conduct of Neighbour B. wished her to
grow better, came home and worked till after Diner, then went there
again, staid to supper.

7 all the day agreably spent in work and talk with my Parents.

1 Day Morn: went to meeting, B. Trotter spoke, S. Stanton prayed, afterward
gave us some good advice on keeping the hour, and presenting ourselves to
worship, the obligations on our side for Health and its adequate blessings
being beyond our comprehension, as much as the benignity of God.
afternoon, at meeting S. Tasher spoke, came hear afterwards with several
other friends, evening went to meeting, S. Tasher, S. Churchman spoke, S.
Churchman prayed, (am affraid we have some young Coquets)

2 Morn: at work, afternoon the same, evening some advice given me by Daddy,
not to spend my sentiments too freely, either on men or things, but let Judgement
ripen, a resolution for the futer to try for amendment. A. James there.

3 Morn: some things not very agreable, went to meeting, S. Churchman spoke, after
ward a letter from D. Smith comical enough, company in the afternoon, Bet
and I thought to have translated in the evening but company hindered, wish
our design of improveing one another in the french may not drop.

4 Morn: wrote to D. Smith, a poor miserable creature came hear for Chari
ty, How thankful I thou Being Omnipotent, am I that thou has
cast the Lot of my humanity in a sort so much better, give me a heart
susceptable of others woe: wrote to Sally rest of the day hard at work.

5 Morn: at meeting D. Stanton A. Mulford M. Emlen S. Churchman
spoke, Sukey Loyd much too fligant, afternoon a Neighbour Warner hear,
finished my green Chair Cushin. 10 O Clock evening. a fine night the
moon just appearing in the horrison glances into my Chamber, the even
ing star sparkling above it. serenity inclines me to think of its Author, and
those admirable luminaries, made, like him, to shine on the evil and on
the good. At this teach us compassion on our fellow creatures who have fal
len thro' folly or inadvertancies, keep me as in the hollow of thy hand O Lord.

nesses of her parents. The imperial crisis that led to the Revolutionary War forced another gap in diary keeping. The editors have interspersed the diary sections with chapters that emphasize the thematic development of the period and of HCS's life.

In preparing the diary for publication, the editors have been conservative in their decisions. The document is close to a precise transcription, while keeping an eye toward aiding readers by silently expanding some opaque abbreviations and adding punctuation (HCS used very little at all), inserting full names where known or relevant, and clarifying obscure terms. A few of HCS's writing habits have not been corrected to accommodate modern style. She wrote, for example, of having "tead" when she had tea with someone. She usually wrote B———n for Burlington, New Jersey. Quoted extracts of prose or verse which HCS set off with irregular spacing have been regularized by centering and italicizing the text. Footnotes reference where possible specific material HCS cites, such as Biblical passages and literary works. We cannot know, of course, what editions HCS consulted and the editors have often simply attributed the passages she cites or confirmed her attribution using available editions as close as possible to the diary dates. The notes also identify select contemporary political or diplomatic events, terms typical of the time, and some of her closest family and friends. Some of these draw from information provided in HCS's descendant George Vaux's published excerpts of her diary. Not all of the hundreds of people with whom HCS came into contact have been identified in the notes. Interested readers may wish to consult the extensive biographical directory in the three-volume *The Diary of Elizabeth Drinker,* edited by Elaine Forman Crane (Boston: Northeastern University Press, 1991), written by HCS's contemporary and friend.

For the diary, HCS used a system of dating that may be unfamiliar to some. She numbered the days of the week according to Quaker practice, beginning with Sunday. Sunday was "1 day" or "first day," Monday "2 day" and so on. She sometimes, but not always, numbered the months beginning with January. In the final section of the diary she shifted to listing the numbered day of the week and the month. The editors have inserted the months and years in brackets throughout the edition to help orient readers, although date attributions, particularly in the last secton of the diary where HCS misnumbered or miscounted days of the month, cannot be precise.

Readers should note that women's names were often abbreviated or shortened, and HCS regularly referred to her closest friends and family by these nicknames. Although there was no common nickname for Hannah, and some nicknames may seem obvious (such as Becky for Rebecca, Caty or Katy for Catherine or Katherine, and Betsy or Eliza for Elizabeth), others may seem more obscure. Thus Fanny was short for Frances, Hessey for Hester, Hetty for Mehitable or Esther, Jenny for Jane, Molly or Peggy for Margaret, Nancy or Nanny for Anne, Nelly for Eleanor, Patty for Patience, Polly for Mary, Sally for

Sarah, and Susie or Sukey for Susannah. HCS was not always referring to young women when she used such nicknames; even older women could be known by diminutives.

The editors have chosen to refer to the diarist herself, Hannah Callender Sansom, as HCS. "Hannah" seemed too familiar and too informal, "Sansom" too curt and too awkward given the state of her marriage and the fact that even her son and her nineteenth-century descendants preferred to call her "Hannah Callender." Another option would have been to use HCS's nickname for herself, employed a few places in the diary, "Hallender." Charming, but again, too familiar. So HCS she is, for the purposes of this book.

Acknowledgments

We started talking about an edition of Hannah Callender Sansom's diary more than fifteen years ago, and we are grateful to the many friends and colleagues who have helped us along the way. An early invitation from Richard S. Dunn to give the end-of-year seminar at the McNeil (then the Philadelphia) Center for Early American Studies was very useful in pointing us toward the literary elements of HCS's narration of her life and in highlighting the contentious issues of gender that the diary raises. Mary Maples Dunn was a particularly supportive contributor to that discussion. Elaine Forman Crane's work on Elizabeth Drinker's diary made our tasks much easier; her support and early comments were also very helpful. Patricia Keller gave us substantial help on the details of quilting and on HCS's quilt in particular. Craig Harle and Jean Soderlund offered helpful information from their own extensive knowledge of eighteenth-century Pennsylvania. Sarah Knott and Mary Beth Norton provided extremely valuable readers' reports on the manuscript, and we appreciate, too, their enthusiasm for the project. A number of graduate student assistants helped us through the years we worked with HCS's diary. Two were indispensible to this project: Diana Reinhard for her extraordinary research assistance and Christina Gessler for her contributions to the transcription process and the diary edition. And of course we are very grateful to the American Philosophical Society for permission to publish, and to the wonderful staff there for answering our many questions about the diary and its provenance. Lastly, we thank the late George Vaux for donating the diary to the APS, and Judy Van Buskirk for, long ago, suggesting we contact Mr. Vaux to see if that old manuscript was still hanging around in his family collection (it was).

Thanks to Peter Potter for his faith in the project, as well as for steering us through the submission process at Cornell University Press. Michael McGandy has been very helpful in the final stages of bringing this book into print; we also thank Karen Laun and Martin Schneider for their careful attention to this tricky manuscript.

Susan E. Klepp thanks Karin Wulf for discovering this long hidden record and Temple University's History Department and School of Liberal Arts for providing research assistance. Thanks also to Stevie Wolf for generously underwriting a research fund that was supposed to be anonymous. Our research assistant Diana Reinhard, Purchase College, SUNY, went above and beyond the requirements of a research assistantship. And special thanks to my family of Rushes and Divver—Phil, Ben, Emily, Karen, and grandbaby Jackson—for all their support.

Karin Wulf also thanks Susan Klepp, for signing on to this in the first place, and hanging in there for so long; American University for graduate research assistance funding; my mom, Dixie Swenson, for a very helpful reading of the manuscript at a critical juncture; Christopher Grasso for comments on the manuscript, as well as so much more; and Jack and Ethan, for nothing much to do with this book.

Abbreviations

APS	American Philosophical Society
B——n	Burlington, New Jersey
Crane, Drinker Diary	Elaine F. Crane et al., eds., *The Diary of Elizabeth Drinker* (Boston: Northeastern University Press, 1991), 3 vols.
GSP	Genealogical Society of Pennsylvania
GV	George Vaux, "Extracts from the Diary of Hannah Callender," *Pennsylvania Magazine of History and Biography* 12 (1888), 432–56.
HCS	Hannah Callender Sansom
HSP	Historical Society of Pennsylvania
PMHB	*Pennsylvania Magazine of History and Biography*
WMQ	*William and Mary Quarterly*

The Diary of Hannah Callender Sansom

Hannah Callender Sansom
and her World

Hannah Callender sat down to begin a journal on New Year's Day 1758, when she was twenty-one years old. In the preface to the first entry, she explained that she wrote "for my own satisfaction, and to try if a retrospect of my time, may not make me husband it more." Did this daily practice of writing really encourage her to manage her time more efficiently? The diary seemed to play a very different role in its author's life. HCS wrote in her diary for months and sometimes years at a time, with a few short and some quite lengthy stretches of silence. The diary starts when she was single and continues through her courtship and marriage to Samuel Sansom, the births of her five children, and her daughter's controversial marriage, until she was fifty years old. The diary entries were the repository of minutiae about the weather as well as details about activities such as her artistic needlework. Social visits are a prominent feature. But in the diary HCS also shared her internal life, her deep convictions, fears, and emerging ideas about the significance of relationships and of spirituality. She wrote about her friends and family, the trips she took, the books she read and discussed, her views on politics, religion, and society. She returned to the diary again and again over thirty years to narrate the developing story of her life, leaving us a remarkable record, and a marvelous reflection, of a woman's life in an extraordinary time.

The diary reflects not only HCS's life as a woman of the eighteenth century— most starkly in the ways that the entries and significant gaps highlight important events like childbirth, the marriages of acquaintances, and the deaths of friends—but also many of the changing patterns and experiences of life in the eighteenth-century Atlantic world. The American Revolution produced one of the longest breaks in HCS's journal writing, although she later recorded sharp comments about the outcome of the Revolution and about the nature of post-

Revolutionary America. But there were other revolutions in the last half of the eighteenth century: revolutions in modes of thought and expression swept across the Atlantic, both contributing to and taking energy from the military and political actions that created the young United States. These revolutions shaped HCS's life, particularly how she interacted with others and how she interpreted those interactions.

A move from sociability toward an embrace of sensibility shaped her diary. Sociability—a mode of enjoying company and of being entertaining—was a product of an urban economy that could support some leisure time for the wealthier segments of society. Well-off Quakers did not attend balls or the theater but, like others of their financial means, gathered for festive weddings and funerals and, most commonly, at tea tables for afternoons of pleasant social interaction. At the tea table, conversation ranged from domestic issues of childrearing, sickness, and weather to abstract moral, philosophical, and theological inquiries to pragmatic economic concerns and local and imperial politics. These gatherings might consist of women only, women and men, young adults, or a mix of young and old. Variety was a key to sociability.

Sensibility was the capacity for feelings of sympathy and empathy; it could be refined but not taught and was increasingly a quality that literate English men and women and their colonial counterparts valued as a mark of human distinction and moral excellence. Sensibility became intensely prized in the middle and later years of the eighteenth century. The cultural uses of sensibility were widespread: military heroes were celebrated for their selfless manly feelings that provided evidence of sensibility—George Washington was said to have dropped tears of humility when sworn in as the nation's first president. Human relationships were to be based on companionate, affectionate ideals rather than traditional hierarchical and rigid power relations. Parent and child, husband and wife, neighbors and friends were to be connected by feelings of mutual concern, not by authoritarian dictates of a master to subordinates.[1]

One consequence of the prominence of sensibility was the greater influence accorded women's opinions at social gatherings, where social talk, even simple gossip, shaped the reputations of men and women, and in the family, where women assumed more authority. Social gatherings also provided opportunities for women, whose formal education was often limited, to expand their mental horizons and engage in self-education projects. But the cultivation and expression of sensibility were not necessarily empowering for women. Women's sensi-

---

1. Historians and literary scholars have paid close attention to the emergence of specific forms of sociability and the value accorded sensibility in the mid- to late eighteenth century. A foundational work on these topics that contends with the gendered language of sensibility is G. J. Barker-Benfield, *The Culture of Sensibility: Sex and Society in Eighteenth-Century Britain* (Chicago: University of Chicago Press, 1992); an account that expands both the chronology and the political importance of sensibility—and insists on its inherently masculine origins and dimensions—is Julie Ellison, *Cato's Tears and the Making of Anglo-American Emotion* (Chicago: University of Chicago Press, 1999).

bility was alternately praised, feared for its potency in disrupting social order, or described as a natural consequence of the supposed emotional frailty of females. HCS, both as a young woman and, later, as the mother of a young daughter, wrote in ways that reflected these tensions between the emerging centrality of sensibility and the tug of more traditional expectations of duty and obedience.

THE DIARY

Since the 1888 publication of a small portion of the earliest parts of the diary, historians have cited HCS's opinions on those few subjects deemed of interest to her late Victorian descendant and first editor, George Vaux. His short selections from the diary stress politics and war, elite culture, and genealogy. In his introduction to those brief excerpts, Vaux dealt dismissively with the remainder: "It is mostly personal in its character, and the parts of general interest are not numerous, and are scattered at wide intervals from each other."[2]

Though Vaux did not think that the full diary would be of interest to his Victorian-era readers, students and scholars of the twenty-first century will find much in HCS's absorbing work that addresses topics and questions of importance—gender, race, religion, consumerism, and reading are among the issues raised. The tasks, obligations, and diversions of diurnal time—morn, afternoon, and evening—are regularly and sometimes monotonously noted. Clock time governed more notable events. Interspersed within this chronological structure are longer passages on a wide variety of topics that caught her interest: subjective musings, religious meditations, descriptions of people and places—all obviously recorded for HCS's "own satisfaction" (language she repeated later in the diary). She made regular entries from 1758 until January 2, 1760, when she stopped writing as she left Philadelphia for Burlington, New Jersey, to attend to her ill mother, who suffered from the first of what may have been several strokes that would leave her partially paralyzed for the rest of her long life. This break in the diary was the first of several. All came at times of great stress and change in HCS's life: family obligations, marriage and children, and aging. On July 14, 1760, perhaps urged on by friends, HCS again took up her pen. But by New Year's, her mother

---

2. George Vaux, ed., "Extracts from the Diary of Hannah Callender," *PMHB* 12 (1888): 432–56. Some sources utilizing the published diary excerpts are Mary Sumner Benson, *Women in Eighteenth-Century America: A Study of Opinion and Social Usage* (1935; repr. Port Washington, NY: Kennikat, 1966), 265, 294–95; Carl Bridenbaugh, *Cities in Revolt: Urban Life in America, 1743–1776* (New York: Oxford, 1955); Carl Bridenbaugh and Jessica Bridenbaugh, *Rebels and Gentlemen: Philadelphia in the Age of Franklin* (New York: Oxford, 1965), 115, 162, 214–19; Frederick Tolles, *Meeting House and Counting House: The Quaker Merchants of Colonial Philadelphia, 1682–1783* (New York: Norton, 1948), 130, 134–35; and Elva Tooker, *Nathan Trotter: Philadelphia Merchant, 1787–1853* (Cambridge, MA: Harvard University Press, 1955), 34–47, 235–42, esp. 240n37. An indication of how dated the published version has become is that the encyclopedic anthology, *American Women Writers to 1800,* ed. Sharon M. Harris (New York: Oxford, 1996), mentions it in passing but finds nothing worth reprinting.

once more needed her constant attention, and she stopped writing. Eight months later, on August 26, 1761, she wrote five long entries as a "Journal of my Journey to Bethlehem." This seems to have been a brief respite in an otherwise difficult time. Not only was her mother in poor health but her father's health was beginning to deteriorate as well. As her parents' only child, HCS bore particularly heavy responsibilities for her elderly parents' well-being.

The diary was not a private document at this early stage: we know that HCS shared it with her good friends and former classmates Betsey and Polly Sandwith. She lent it to them on June 2, 1760, and Betsey later spent a whole morning reading it.[3] It inspired Betsey (known to later audiences by her full, married name, Elizabeth Sandwith Drinker) to begin her own daily account. The diary was also not the only book HCS composed. Simultaneous with her diary-keeping, she kept a commonplace book, a series of notes of her reading that probably included excerpts from poetry and other writings she encountered. That book apparently has not survived. And although she maintained a steady correspondence with family and friends, only one of her letters still exists. Thus, from the pen of this prolific woman, only the diary remains.

It was the approach of her marriage to Sammy Sansom that compelled her to begin the second major section of the diary on March 26, 1762, this time "for my own Satisfaction, or some of my friends, if I should think fit in future Time, to leave it for their perusal, or otherways destroy it." HCS's entries subsequently became more personal and private as she struggled to adjust to the elaborate public requirements of a Quaker marriage and then to her condition as a married woman. Several entries in this section were later excised, probably by HCS herself once she decided not to destroy the entire book. The onset of labor the day before the birth of her first child on June 2, 1763, just a month after the death of her father on May 2, was more than enough reason to lay the diary aside once again.

Almost five years later, when her first three children were older—William was five, Sarah (Sally) three, and Joseph ten months old and out at a wet nurse's—she felt ready to begin again. The date was May 6, 1768. It was no longer her own satisfaction that compelled her to write; rather, she explained, the diary would be an extended epistle to Sally. "My daughter," she wrote, "it may be, will look in this with some pleasure, as I hope to be a humble Instrument in fixing her mind to the path of Virtue." The remainder of the diary sputtered along at significant intervals. HCS only wrote for a few weeks in 1768, when the death of her cousin Betsey Smith Allinson plunged her into despair. She wrote again from November 1 to December 29, 1769; from February 11 to July 3, 1770; and from January 5 to November 24, 1772. Then the Revolutionary War intervened, causing HCS "more of anxiety . . . than I wish to recolect." The Revolution remained a closed chapter in her life, and it commenced the longest period of the diary's silence.

---

3. Crane, ed., *The Diary of Elizabeth Drinker* (Boston: Northeastern University Press, 1991) (hereafter Crane, Drinker Diary), I:60.

Figure 2 Two sketches of Hannah Callender's husband, Samuel Sansom, as an elderly man. These were probably drawn by Joseph Sansom. A fragment of George Vaux's late nineteenth century genealogical research is above. Courtesy American Philosophical Society.

On November 1, 1784, watching once again at her mother's sickbed, HCS began the third major section, a more intensive period of writing. This segment ended with her husband's severe illness on August 13, 1786, but it also saw a successful conclusion to her daughter's courtship with a non-Quaker: his conversion and a proper marriage within the rules of the Quaker faith. On New Year's Day 1788, she began what would be the diary's final segment. The last entry in HCS's extraordinary diary was dated October 29 of the same year. Those last ten months seem to have been the happiest of her recorded life. HCS had fulfilled all of her hopes for her daughter and remedied some of the disappointments in her own experience. Like the novels she so admired, the last chapter of her diary tied up the loose ends of her life as they were fulfilled in the respectable romance and contentment of her daughter's marriage.

THE SETTING

The city of Philadelphia was still a small town of only about 7,300 residents when HCS was born in 1737.[4] Founded a half century earlier as the capital of Pennsylvania, William Penn's holy experiment in Quaker governance, the town had gotten off to a slow start. Political conflict, the Keithian schism among Quakers, and several severe epidemics were among the factors that hindered the colony, although in comparison to other colonial ventures Pennsylvania fared quite well, particularly since careful diplomacy, first by the original Swedish colonists and then by founder Penn, helped prevent protracted warfare with native peoples, at least until the 1750s. The promise of religious freedom in Pennsylvania's charter and Penn's active recruitment of settlers produced a varied population of English, Scots, Irish, German, and other European ethnicities and ensured religious diversity; the colony included not only many Protestant sects but a small Roman Catholic and Jewish presence as well. Not all arrivals were voluntary, of course: enslaved people from Guinea, Angola, and other places in west and central Africa were a source of exploitable labor for European colonists. Quakers in particular struggled with the ethical quandaries produced by forced labor and the market in human beings. In the 1730s Philadelphia still had traces of a frontier town near the outer edge of the British Empire: it was raw, ramshackle, and provincial. The city could boast of a newspaper, Benjamin Franklin's *Pennsylvania Gazette,* and a modern statehouse, but it offered few other urban amenities apart from the plentiful taverns.

---

4. General introductions to eighteenth-century Philadelphia and Pennsylvania can be found in Richard Dunn and Mary Maples Dunn, *The World of William Penn* (Philadelphia: University of Pennsylvania Press, 1986); Susan E. Klepp, "Colonial Pennsylvania," in *Pennsylvania: A History of the Commonwealth,* ed. Randall M. Miller and William Pencak (University Park: Pennsylvania State University Press, 2003), 47–100; and Billy G. Smith, ed., *Life in Revolutionary Philadelphia, 1775–1806* (University Park: Pennsylvania State University Press, 1995), 155–74.

By the time of HCS's marriage in 1762, Philadelphia was a much more impressive city, with close to 20,000 inhabitants. It was the largest city in British North America and the rival of provincial English cities such as Bristol or Newcastle. The major conflict known variously as the Great War for Empire, the French and Indian War, or the Seven Years' War brought trade and war contracts to the city but devastated the western part of the colony. If the frontier was engulfed in violence, Philadelphia was itself a very unhealthy place, as HCS's diary attests. Garbage and offal lay thick in the streets intermixed with the dust and mud of unpaved cartways. Water supplies were often polluted. Both endemic and epidemic diseases were common. Epidemics frequently followed the arrival of immigrants, soldiers, and forced laborers. Ill health was common among the young and the poor, but even wealthy adults could do little to avoid disease. Life expectancy was low, death rates high.

Still, the town now offered a college, a hospital, an almshouse, and many fashionable churches in addition to bookstores and libraries. Trade with the Atlantic world increased. Ships brought both luxuries and necessities, and shops were becoming more specialized. Wealthy families lived in modern townhouses furnished with elaborate tea and dining tables, chairs, high chests, silver plate, and imported china. The well-to-do dressed in silks, satins, and brocades. Merchants, lawyers, and land speculators were acquiring great wealth that supported, among these other luxuries, country estates that allowed them to avoid the stench of city summers. The risks of trade and the volatility of prices, however, meant frequent anxiety and insecurity even for the wealthy. Like many residents, HCS took considerable pride in her hometown. Yet social inequities were growing, and within a couple of years rebelliousness against the strictures of empire would challenge loyalties and raise questions about the meaning of liberty, freedom, and equality.[5]

Philadelphia was the capital of the recently victorious United States at diary's close in 1788, and despite losses and hardship during the Revolutionary War when the city came under first British and then American military control, the population stood at 42,000. While still an important commercial center, manufactures were expanding rapidly and so, despite a postwar recession, were markets. Philadelphians could speculate in Caribbean, European, and Chinese goods and hoped to supply the new settlements in the Ohio Valley. The city was healthier and cleaner than it had ever been, although the wealthy still preferred to move to the country during the hot and humid summers. The wealthy built their townhouses on the broad streets of the city while the poor were increasingly confined to filthy alleys. Epi-

5. Thomas M. Doerflinger, *A Vigorous Spirit of Enterprise: Merchants and Economic Development in Revolutionary Philadelphia* (New York: Norton, 1986); Richard Alan Ryerson, *The Revolution Is Now Begun: The Radical Committees of Philadelphia, 1765–1776* (Philadelphia: University of Pennsylvania Press, 1976); and Billy G. Smith, *"The Lower Sort": Philadelphia's Laboring People, 1750–1800* (Ithaca: Cornell University Press, 1990).

demics were much rarer than they had been at midcentury but no less awful when they did occur.[6] The diary ends before the deadly yellow fever epidemics of the 1790s. Once the war had ended, entrepreneurial Philadelphians created many cultural institutions: a theater, a circus, a museum, beer gardens, a pleasure garden, newspapers, magazines, and various clubs and literary societies. Philadelphia was described as a center of learning. It was the "Athens of America."[7]

An essential aspect of Philadelphia's growth and development and a central feature of the elite circles in which HCS moved was Quakerism. The Friends of God, as they originally called themselves, or the Society of Friends, their official name today, originated in England during the religious turmoil of the middle of the seventeenth century. Their enemies called them Quakers but they soon adopted the derogatory name as a badge of honor. The sect began as a critique of Puritan theology, which held that the majority of mankind would be condemned to eternal torment in hell, while only a small elite (the "elect") were offered eternal salvation. The Friends, for their part, imagined a loving God, not a harshly judgmental deity. Central to their belief system was the concept of the light of Christ within, the "inner light," a reflection of God that resides within all people. To find salvation, one need only look within. Quakers found priests, theology, rituals, sermons, and the entire formal apparatus of most other Christian sects unnecessary: the truth was easily accessible to those who would seek it. Certain social distinctions were considered impediments to the truth because they denied the basic equality among souls. Quakers refused to take off their hats, to bow, or to use "you" and "your," in the seventeenth century a common form of address to one's superiors (instead they used "thee" and "thou," a more egalitarian form).

In HCS's lifetime the meaning of equality was hotly disputed, and slavery was a central issue in this ongoing debate. Gradually and often reluctantly, the Quakers disavowed the buying and selling of slaves; in 1775, they finally foreswore owning of slaves outright. In 1776, they founded the Pennsylvania Abolition Society, the first antislavery society in the western world. They actively supported many other charitable enterprises such as hospitals, almshouses, and schools, particularly because they had lost control of the Pennsylvania Assembly in 1756 and were therefore no longer as active and influential in politics. Quakers were pacifists who abhorred the killing of their fellow men. But as events in the New World lurched toward the French and Indian War, those Quakers serving in the colonial legislature, including HCS's father, found themselves in an agonizing bind: voting against war preparations exposed settlers on the frontier to Indian attack but preserved pacifist principles, but voting for war materiel might saved the lives of Pennsylvanians but killed native peoples and violated core Quaker be-

6. Susan E. Klepp, *Philadelphia in Transition: A Demographic History of the City and Its Occupational Groups* (New York: Garland, 1980).

7. Gilbert Stuart, quoted in Edgar P. Richardson, "The Athens of America, 1800–1825," in *Philadelphia: A 300-Year History,* ed. Russell F. Weigley, et al. (New York: Norton, 1982), 208.

liefs.[8] Abandoning governmental participation, Quakers took their political agenda, organizational skills, and funds elsewhere, into voluntary societies. This way, they felt, they could maintain the Quaker "peace testimony."

The loose organizational structure of the Quakers was centered on the local meeting for worship. Men and women would gather several times a week, usually on Sundays and one other day, Tuesdays or Wednesdays, and often in the morning and again in the afternoon and evening. The place of worship was meant to be a simple structure without stained glass, pulpits, or altar. The meetinghouses in Philadelphia were simply constructed but graceful and lovely. Usually women would sit on one side of the main room, men on the other. Acknowledged "weighty friends," those who spoke regularly during meeting or had been recognized as ministers by their peers, might sit at the front. A member of the congregation might be moved to speak for a brief or lengthy period, and then someone else might speak. Possibly the meeting would be silent. A traveling minister, a "Public Friend," might be passing through the area and appear for an extemporaneous talk. At some point, the attendees would nod to one another and get up to leave.

Each local meeting also incorporated a monthly meeting intended for business. Here the secular concerns of the meeting were addressed by a separate women's meeting and men's meeting. The women's meeting supervised the behavior of members, investigated courtships, and approved marriages and met the charitable needs of the women (and some men) in their jurisdiction. The men's meeting did the same for their male peers and also was the venue for maintaining the meeting's property and for considering major issues and controversies such as the place of slavery within the Society. Representatives were sent from the Monthly Meeting to a larger group of local meetings, the Quarterly Meeting, and from the Quarterly Meeting to a regional Yearly Meeting. Whole families of New Jersey and Pennsylvania Quakers, not just the business representatives, gathered alternately in Burlington and Philadelphia for the week-long Yearly Meeting.

In the early decades of Quakerism, the faith readily accepted new members. By the middle of the eighteenth century, Quakers increasingly discouraged converts, preferring to confine themselves to birthright members, those who had grown up as Friends. This inward turning of the faith was based on several interrelated beliefs. Quakers rejected the idea of original sin, holding that children were born innocent. Evil entered through selfishness and willfulness as the child matured. It was therefore very important to Quakers that children be reared by

8. This section draws on J. William Frost, *The Quaker Family in Colonial America* (New York: St. Martin's, 1973); Barry Levy, *Quakers and the American Family: British Settlement in the Delaware Valley* (New York: Oxford, 1988); John M. Moore, ed., *Friends in the Delaware Valley* (Haverford, PA: Friends Historical Association, 1981); and Jean R. Soderlund, *Quakers and Slavery: A Divided Spirit* (Princeton: Princeton University Press, 1985). The importance of Quaker antislavery activism in America and elsewhere is a subject of recent scholarly attention, including Christopher Leslie Brown, *Moral Capital: Foundations of British Abolitionism* (Chapel Hill: University of North Carolina Press, 2005).

godly Quaker parents who would take care to preserve their offspring in their original innocence. A "convinced" Friend, that is, a convert, would not have the benefit of careful, tender upbringing by birthright members—or so Quakers began to think. They would be more prone to non-Quakerly behavior, to violence, to selfishness, to distraction by the things of this world. Good parenting would result from carefully monitoring marriages, so Friends of the eighteenth century made marriage a centerpiece of the faith. A couple wanting to marry had to be clear of other romantic obligations, had to have their parents' consent, and had to be members of the meeting in good standing. In addition, they should have the financial resources necessary to live independently. To ensure that couples who wanted to marry met these requirements, they had to stand up in the local meeting for worship on three separate occasions to announce their intentions. The women's meeting would send a committee to investigate the prospective bride, while the men's meeting would do the same for the groom. The women's meeting would then report to the men's meeting. After receiving final approval from the men's meeting, the marriage could take place. If only approved marriages were likely to produce godly children, and if only godly children would grow up to be good marriage partners and good parents, there was little place for outsiders. The Quakers had become quite insular.[9]

Not only did the Friends increasingly discourage converts, starting in the mid-1750s they began to disown (expel) large numbers of wayward members. A stricter enforcement of the lived practice of Quaker ideals developed in part as a reaction to the need to maintain their peace testimony during the Seven Years' War (1756–1763), in part from their increasingly marginal status in society and government, and in part from what they saw as the ill effects of the temptations and distractions of refinement, fashion, and luxury in an increasingly prosperous society. Local meetings took an active role in seeking out backsliders. Common reasons cited for disownment included marrying out of meeting and walking in the way of the world, that is, not acting like a Quaker. Those described as "marrying out of meeting" included Quaker couples who did not follow all the rigorous steps of notification, consultation, and confirmation mandated by the faith. A man or woman who married someone of another faith could also be disowned, even if that person had indicated a desire to convert. Thus, though they had been at the forefront of Pennsylvania's founding and leaders in Philadelphia for most of its history, by the mid–eighteenth century Quakers increasingly defined themselves as a distinct group, detached from the rest of society. By the late eighteenth century, the neutrality of a majority of Quakers during the Revolution (again, out of pacifist principles) helped to foster anti-Quaker sentiment among the victors and only added to the Quakers' isolation.[10] Even so, the intermarriage of Quakers

9. On Quaker domestic and economic lives, see Frost, *Quaker Family in Colonial America;* Levy, *Quakers and the American Family;* and Tolles, *Meeting House and Counting House.*

10. Jack Marietta, *The Reformation of American Quakerism, 1748–1783* (Philadelphia: University of Pennsylvania Press, 2007), x.

with men and women of other religions, their advocacy of philanthropic endeavors, their influence on public and private education, and their longstanding position in Pennsylvania made them still an important social presence and cultural force—even many of the disowned remained committted to the tenets of the faith.

The Society of Friends was exceptional for its support of gendered equity.[11] Women had their own meetings for business, handled their own finances, and made their own decisions. Women could speak in meetings for worship, could be appointed to committees, and could be designated as Public Friends (traveling ministers). But the larger legal culture of the British Empire supported none of these opportunities for women. By custom women were expected to marry, and most did. Once married, women were considered *femes covert,* "covered women," whose very identities were subsumed under those of their husbands. Like children and the mentally incompetent, married women were considered irresponsible, irrational, and properly dependent. They were to obey their husbands, the heads of household. A wife had virtually no control over her residence, her body, her children, her clothing, or, in most cases, her property or wages, if any. Quaker women lived in two worlds: a religious world that allotted them some authority and autonomy within the meetinghouse and a legal world that denied their independent existence. This disparity could be, as this diary makes very clear, a source of considerable tension.[12]

Quakerism shaped Philadelphia as it also shaped the life and experiences of HCS. The prominence of Quakers, including her father, in public affairs, considerations of wealth and status, the difficulty of putting a belief in equality into practice, the importance of the meeting (in which both her parents were very active), the ban on marrying non-Quakers, all of these would play a significant part in her life and in the diary.

The Principal Characters

Hannah Callender was born in 1737, the only surviving child of her parents, William and Katherine Smith Callender. She was named after her father's

11. Mary Maples Dunn, "Saints and Sister: Congregational and Quaker Women in the Early Colonial Period," *American Quarterly* 30 (1978): 582–601.

12. On Quaker women in early Pennsylvania, see Susan B. Forbes, "Quaker Tribalism," in *Friends and Neighbors: Group Life in America's First Plural Society,* ed. Michael Zuckerman (Philadelphia: Temple University Press, 1982), 145–73; Margaret Morris Haviland, "Beyond Women's Sphere: Young Quaker Women and the Veil of Charity in Philadelphia, 1790–1810," *WMQ* 51 (1994): 419–46; Joan M. Jensen, "Not Only Ours But Others: The Quaker Teaching Daughters of the Mid-Atlantic, 1790–1850," *History of Education Quarterly* 24 (1984): 3–19; Jean R. Soderlund, "Women's Authority in Pennsylvania and New Jersey Quaker Meetings, 1680–1760," *WMQ* 44 (1987): 722–49; Nancy Tomes, "The Quaker Connection: Visiting Patterns among Women in the Philadelphia Society of Friends, 1750–1800," in *Friends and Neighbors,* ed. Zuckerman, 174–95; and Karin Wulf, *Not All Wives: Women of Colonial Philadelphia* (Ithaca: Cornell University Press, 2000). An uncritical view of Quaker women in America is Margaret Hope Bacon, *Mothers of Feminism: The Story of Quaker Women in America* (San Francisco: Harper and Row, 1986).

mother. Because the Callenders, like many other Quaker families, did not record the births and deaths of their children with the meeting, we do not know how many siblings she had or when they died; we only know that there was at least one brother, who died before she was born, and perhaps some sisters. On October 6, 1758, she noted the eighth anniversary of her recovery from smallpox, "then my God see fit in Mercy to spare me! to my Parents prayers," she wrote. It may have been during this 1750 epidemic that she became the only surviving child, but she did not elaborate. By the time she began writing her diary on New Year's Day 1758, her cousins Caty, Betsey, and Sarah Smith filled the dual roles of sisters and confidants in her life.

We know very little about her childhood, although she remembered it, in the conventional language of the mid-eighteenth century, as a happy time. There is a brief glimpse of her at age eleven riding out to the Burlington countryside one Sunday afternoon with Nanny Smith and her older cousin, twenty-six-year-old John Smith. At the end of the day John wrote "returned safe" in his diary, perhaps because he took his responsibility for the girls to heart, perhaps because the girls had been rambunctious.[13]

She was certainly well-educated by the standards of the day, far surpassing her mother in penmanship and spelling. She attended Anthony Benezet's school, one of the many Quaker schools in the city, along with Elizabeth Drinker and other well-to-do Quaker girls. She also studied under a French schoolmistress, Maria Jeanne Reynier (see entry for March 18, 1788), and French studies would remain a passion for the rest of her life. She had access to the Library Company of Philadelphia, a private subscription library that both her father and husband had joined, and she was an avid reader. She had a lifelong interest in the fine arts: painting, prints, sculpture, architecture, and landscaping. These were somewhat unusual for a Quaker, since simplicity, plainness, and spirituality were emphasized over decoration, elegance, and aesthetic pleasure.[14] Here she seems to have been self-taught, seeking out local art collections and fine houses and collecting prints—mostly, it seems, European landscapes. She would later encourage her son Joseph's artistic interests. In addition, she was a highly skilled needleworker. The elaborate embroidery, quilting, knitting, and tailoring skills that she had mastered by her early twenties could only have come from years of instruction,

13. Albert Cook Myers, ed., *The Courtship of Hannah Logan: A True Narrative* (Philadelphia: Ferris and Leach, 1904), 174. On women in eighteenth-century Philadelphia, see Elaine Forman Crane, ed., "The World of Elizabeth Drinker," special issue of *Pennsylvania History: A Journal of Mid-Atlantic Studies* 68, no. 4 (2001): 408–506; Susan E. Klepp, "Revolutionary Bodies: Women and the Fertility Transition in the Mid-Atlantic, 1760–1830," *Journal of American History* 85 (1998): 910–45; Marylynn Salmon, "Equality or Submersion? Feme Covert Status in Early Pennsylvania," in *Women of America: A History,* ed. Carol Ruth Berkin and Mary Beth Norton (Hopewell, NJ: Houghton Mifflin, 1979), 92–113; and Wulf, *Not All Wives.*

14. For example, Haverford College, the first Quaker college, did not have a Fine Arts Department until 1971. See Emma Jones Lapsansky, "Past Plainness to Present Simplicity: A Search for Quaker Identity," in *Quaker Aesthetics: Reflections on a Quaker Ethic in American Design and Consumption,* ed. Lapsansky and Anne A. Verplanck (Philadelphia: University of Pennsylvania Press, 2003), 1–15.

probably acquired through specialized schooling. Obituaries are not always trust-worthy sources, but one line in hers does seem to capture these intellectual and artistic aspects of her life: "She was a woman endowed with superior under-standing and many talents."[15]

As an adult, HCS described herself as occasionally sharp-tongued and argu-mentative, with "a hasty quick forward temper [that] I have to gain the mastery over" (March 1, 1759). An angry and outspoken tendency seemed to run in the family. Particularly in the months around her marriage to Sammy Sansom in 1762, disputes of unknown origin occurred frequently involving her father, her mother, and herself. Throughout her life she sometimes offended friends and rel-atives—always unintentionally, she thought. Her tendency to use exclamation points at the end of her sentences, unusual in eighteenth-century women's diaries, is another indication of her strong opinions, quickly adopted. Her temper and headstrong attitude set her apart from most other Quaker women whose records have survived. Whether nominal Quakers like Elizabeth Drinker, who as an adult rarely attended meeting, or convinced Friends like Elizabeth Ashbridge, who converted to the faith, or weighty Friends like Susanna Morris, Elizabeth Hudson, or Ann Moore, these Quaker women diarists did not seem to struggle with the quietist requirements of the faith as HCS did throughout her life.[16] A pacific spirituality, an easy selflessness, an automatic turning of the other cheek did not come naturally to HCS, and she labored to conform throughout her recorded life. But where she felt she could not or should not adapt to certain im-posed standards, she could be a formidable opponent.

Anger was only one facet of her personality. HCS had a good sense of humor, delighted in mirth, read satires with relish, and wrote ironic, even sarcastic, ac-counts of people and places in her diary. Conversations over tea, during walks in the countryside, or at dinner cemented her many friendships with fellow Quak-ers and with neighbors. She enjoyed travel and new experiences. Before her marriage she traveled to New York City as well as Long Island, Wilmington, Bethlehem, Shrewsbury, and Princeton. She could only take shorter trips after her marriage, but her creation of a suburban retreat for her family at Parlaville on the banks of the Schuylkill River gave her an ever-changing vista of water and sky, while her garden provided seasonal variety. These seem to have satisfied her desire for change and novelty. The second half of the diary is filled with her ro-mantic depictions of nature as found in her front yard.

Physical descriptions of contemporary women were commonplace, because then as now, women were often judged in terms of their appearance. HCS's

---

15. Poulson's *American Daily Advertiser,* March 10, 1801, vol. 30, no. 7563.

16. Crane, Drinker Diary; Daniel B. Shea, ed., "Some Account of the Fore Part of the Life of Eliza-beth Ashbridge," in *Journeys in New Worlds: Early American Women's Narratives,* ed. William L Andrews, et al. (Madison: University of Wisconsin Press, 1990), 117–80; Margaret Hope Bacon, *Wilt Thou Go On My Errand? Three 18th Century Journals of Quaker Women Ministers* (Wallingford, PA: Pendle Hill Publica-tions, 1994).

mother was remembered as "remarkably handsome" and her friend Elizabeth Drinker as possessing "uncommon" personal beauty, but there are no recorded depictions of HCS.[17] The only clue to her appearance comes in the poem she wrote about her bout with smallpox, indicating that she had been permanently scarred during that ordeal (October 6, 1758). Her silhouettes, taken during her fifties by her son, show a plump, matronly woman. As a young woman, she did not have throngs of suitors seeking her hand, although for a few weeks the recently widowed Henry Drinker called often.

In 1762, she married Samuel Sansom Jr. It was not a love match. She was probably urged into the marriage by her dying father, since her mother, widowed a year later, moved out of town and required HCS to visit her rather than set foot in the same house as Sammy. In agreeing to marry Sammy Sansom, HCS retreated from her belief that "I dislike much haveing any thing to do with match making, I would have People always chuse for themselves" (December 20, 1758). Yet it was certainly a logical match. Both the Callenders and Sansoms were wealthy mercantile families. Although the Sansoms had more money than the Callenders, HCS was able to bring a sizable dowry of household goods, land, and cash into the marriage, and she stood to inherit the whole of her father's estate after the parental generation was gone. The two families were equally active in meeting and were longtime neighbors. HCS and Sammy had visited, "tea'd," and dined in company for many years, and they shared an interest in French and the fine arts as well as in the nascent antislavery movement. Their political beliefs were apparently similar. Neither is known to have had other love interests. But the marriage, particularly in the earliest years, was not a mutually supportive relationship. There would be five children: William (Billy), born in 1763; Sarah (Sally), in 1764; Joseph (Josey), in 1767; Catherine (Kitty), in 1769; and Samuel (Sammy), in 1773. Catherine died in 1770 of smallpox, but all the rest reached adulthood; of these, all but Sammy married. In 1769, HCS described her family thus: "its beloved Master, my little dear Billy, Sally, Josey, and the last come Kitty, who is with her Nurse Wood, Dicky Vaux, Eliza Montgomery, Mary Shingleton, G: Shofts" (November 1, 1769). So it was an affectionate family when the children were growing up, if not an affectionate marriage. Sammy Sansom relished the title of master, which he used on other occasions as well. He was not described by HCS as *my* beloved master, nor did she use other terms of endearment commonly found in the diaries of Quaker women.

In the Sansom's world, the notion of family generally encompassed one or more household servants and other employees, some of whom stayed for years, while others rotated in and out the household rapidly. Eliza Montgomery was one servant who would cause HCS particular concern when she was seduced and rejected by the son of a neighbor. George Shoft was a longtime employee who

---

17. Joseph Sansom Jr., quoted in George Hood, *Family Record of Charles Poultney Perot* (Chester, PA: Joseph Sansom Jr., 1870); Crane, Drinker Diary, I:xv.

managed their suburban house. Dicky Vaux was an Englishman apprenticed to Sammy Sansom. His son would marry the Sansom's granddaughter; it was they and their descendants who would preserve HCS's diary.[18] Other employees came into the household. When the children were newborns they were sent out to wet nurses, as was customary among the wealthy. HCS also hired mantua makers, seamstresses, gardeners, and washer women to assist her in various household tasks but did much of the sewing, ironing, planting, and other domestic chores herself. The Sansoms all engaged in some physical labor, which their wealth might have led them to avoid, but they also had considerable leisure time to attend meeting, visit, read, and write.

Over the course of HCS's life, domesticity came to crowd out other interests. She came to prefer her suburban house away from the constant sociability of the city. She may have anticipated the resolution of the Women's meeting of 1792, when urged by "Men friends and united with [them] by the Women," they reproved "the unnecessary visiting on the occasions of Births and Marriages also formal visits at other times apprehending it to be an unprofitable custom."[19] Religion and domesticity intertwined and increasingly circumscribed her world, but she was not unhappy about these developments—she had come to focus on those areas of life where she might have the most influence. Her family noted that "her benevolence . . . was universal, and extended to all things within her sphere." The construction of that sphere is another of the themes of her life.

HCS was a devout Quaker. She generally attended meeting on Sundays and Wednesdays, and sometimes on other days as well. She went to the Quarterly and Yearly Meetings whenever she could. She and her parents were particularly close to Anthony and Joyce Benezet and shared their concerns with education and antislavery. When her children were older, she became involved in charitable projects. She visited the sick poor in the Pennsylvania hospital, provided Bibles to the needy, and took an interest in the condition of African Americans, the French refugees in the 1790s, and the foundation of a "select" school—a school devoted solely to the teaching of Quaker children. While she was not called to the ministry, she was active in the religious and charitable activities of the Friends, although to a substantially lesser degree than her parents or in-laws. Her mother, in particular, had taken a very public role in the Friends. HCS retreated to a domestic setting.

Still, despite her attachment to the Quaker faith, there were two moments in her life when her relationship to the meeting became deeply troubled. The first was during the early stages of the American Revolution, when she and Sammy were more in favor of Revolution than was usual among wealthy Quakers, albeit not to the point of renouncing pacifism and joining the Free Quakers, a break-

18. George Vaux VIII, "*Pedigree* showing ten Persons named George Vaux, in ten successive Generations," *Journal of the Friends Historical Society* 6, no. 1 (1909): 186.

19. Women's Monthly Meeting, Philadelphia, August 31, 1792, microfilm Swarthmore College, pp. 420–21.

away sect that supported the war. In 1772, her diary, which had been so full and varied, abruptly switched to a singleminded focus on her attendance at one religious meeting after another. It was not doctrine that absorbed her here; in retrospect it seems to have been a repetitive, ritualized enactment of affiliation consistent with a crisis of faith or fellowship. In November 1772, she stopped writing in her diary and did not pick it up again until the year after the war's end. Her last sustained contact with her old friend Elizabeth Drinker came in September 1777, after Drinker's husband was arrested by the revolutionaries as an enemy to the revolution. While HCS visited Drinker to offer her condolences during the early stages of that crisis, the two met only a handful of times over the next two decades, and then only briefly. The Sansom family was not suspected of treasonable activities by the revolutionaries, as the Drinker family and many others were. After the war, her whole family idolized George Washington as the father of his country, and HCS heartily approved of the Constitution of 1787, but, as before, in very domestic terms.

Her second crisis of faith occurred when she encouraged the courtship between her daughter and Elliston Perot, then a non-Quaker. She risked disownment from the meeting for this breach of Quakerly precept. She worked for Perot's conversion to Quakerism, saw him accepted by the meeting and then by her husband, and witnessed the marriage of Sarah and Elliston. It was a defining moment in her life. Because her own marriage had been such a disappointment, all her energy and courage went into assuring a different fate for her beloved only daughter.

While HCS was devout, she does not conform to our stereotypical images of early Quaker womanhood. She enjoyed her wealth and fine furnishings, she noted, somewhat warily, the latest fashions, and she appreciated the fine arts, music, plays, formal gardens, and elaborate architecture that most Quakers condemned as worldly. Her friendships crossed denominational boundaries. Her travels and her love of all things French made her more cosmopolitan than many wealthy Quaker women. While she enjoyed the genteel pleasures of the tea table, she also relished a cup of "Sangree" at the local tavern. She strove to submit in a meek, godly spirit to her condition as daughter and wife as these roles evolved toward genteel domesticity, but her first impulse was always to be independent, assertive, and argumentative. Conforming to Quakerly precepts required constant struggle against other, more secular attractions.

HCS's father, *William Callender,* was born in Barbados in 1703. His parents were Scottish Quakers long resident in the islands. He first traveled to the Delaware Valley in 1727, where he met Katherine Smith of Burlington. They were married in 1731 and moved to Philadelphia two years later. Callender was a merchant engaged in the West Indian sugar trade, which also included commerce in slaves: he imported seven adults in 1729 and seven children in 1731, all from Barbados.[20] By the 1750s, he had experienced a change of heart and was ac-

20. Darold D. Wax, "Negro Imports into Pennsylvania, 1720–1766," *Pennsylvania History* 32 (1965): 263, 265.

tive in "monthly meeting committees to labor with Friends who bought or sold slaves."[21] Yet in 1762, he advertised in the *Pennsylvania Gazette* for Joe, "a Negroe Man" who had absconded in Kingston, Jamaica, offering 40 shillings for his return. It is not clear whether Joe was a slave hired or transported by Callender or owned by one of his Barbadian relatives; it is also possible that he was an indentured servant.[22] Callender remained in the Caribbean trade even though by the end of his life, activists like John Woolman were beginning to criticize trafficking in slave-produced goods as well as the trade in enslaved peoples.[23] Callender also profitably bought and sold Philadelphia real estate during his lifetime.

William Callender pursued the life of a Quaker gentleman. His various dwellings on Front Street were recalled as "Callender's grand houses." His summer retreat was "Richmond Seat," eventually consisting of seventy acres near the estates of other wealthy Philadelphians in the Point-No-Point neighborhood, located north of the city on the Delaware River, an area now called Port Richmond.[24] He helped found the Fellowship Fire Company and the Library Company of Philadelphia. He was an overseer of Penn Charter School from 1751 to 1763, and he was very active in the Monthly Meeting.

Callender was elected a tax assessor in 1747 and was a county commissioner from 1748 to 1751; he served in the Pennsylvania Assembly between 1753 and 1756. Callender was a pacifist as a matter of faith and practice. In 1747, he was one of four men appointed by the monthly meeting "to deal with such persons as refused to acknowledge their fault in joyning to fit out a Ship of War &c."[25] In the mid-1750s, war was breaking out on the Pennsylvania frontier. As an active member of the Pennsylvania Assembly, Callender was caught between his pacifist principles and his responsibility to protect settlers in the west from violent incursions by the French and their allies among the native peoples. Several times he changed his position on whether to authorize funds that would be used, directly or indirectly, for the defense of the western frontier. But in the spring of 1756, as the war intensified, he and five other members of the Assembly (James Pemberton, Joshua Morris, William Peters, Peter Worrall, and Francis Parvin) decided that the actions of the government did contravene their religious principles. They resigned their positions, and thus Quakers lost political control of the colony they had founded.

21. Much of the following discussion is dependent on Jeffrey L. Scheib, "William Callender," in *Lawmaking and Legislators in Pennsylvania: A Biographical Dictionary, Volume 2: 1710–1756,* ed. Craig Horle et al. (Philadelphia: University of Pennsylvania Press, 1997), 253–61, quotation 254.

22. Advertisement for September 2, 1762, in Billy G. Smith and Richard Wojtowicz, eds., *Blacks Who Stole Themselves: Advertisements for Runaways in the Pennsylvania Gazette, 1728–1790* (Philadelphia: University of Pennsylvania Press, 1989), 58.

23. Frederick B. Tolles, ed., *The Journal of John Woolman and A Plea for the Poor* (Secaucus, NJ: Citidel, 1961), 179.

24. John F. Watson, *Annals of Philadelphia and Pennsylvania in the Olden Time* (Philadelphia: Stuart, 1899), III:225–26.

25. Myers, ed., *Courtship of Hannah Logan,* 125.

After leaving the government Quakers tried to influence governmental policy from outside, rather than inside, the institutional structure of the empire. William Callender was soon a founder and was subsequently elected one of the sixteen trustees of the Friendly Association for Regaining and Preserving the Peace with the Indians by Pacific Measures. HCS served as his secretary, reading letters and copying replies in this attempt to prevent war. The Friendly Association sought peace by dealing directly with Native American leaders and by providing a neutral and pacifist presence at treaty negotiations. The governments of Pennsylvania and Great Britain, having committed to a war that was becoming a contest between the world powers of France and Great Britain, saw the Association as at best naive and at worst traitorous. Officials and western settlers did not appreciate what they deemed Quaker interference. Tensions ran high. The Meeting for Sufferings, organized to protect the civil liberties of Quakers in the face of this official hostility, drew Callender's support.

As a politician, Callender was both contentious and volatile, leading some opponents to call him "sour and ignorant" and one of the Quaker "stiffrumps."[26] His daughter's diary also hints at his fiery temper, which she inherited. What little we know of his personality comports with contemporary analyses of the children of slaveowners, especially in the Caribbean: they were presumed to be passionate, mercurial, and imperious from their early lessons in absolute power over other human beings. Callender seems to have been true to type in this regard, even if he did come to renounce enslavement.

William Callender's last years were marked by near-constant physical suffering; he died in 1763, just a month before the birth of his first grandchild. In his will, he left his daughter valuable property in the heart of the commercial district and confirmed her marriage portion of furniture, valued at £400. His wife received his personal estate of £1,255 and real estate, which she liquidated for £3,700.[27] He was a moderately wealthy man.

Katherine Smith Callender, HCS's mother, was the youngest daughter of Daniel and Mary Murfin Smith, born in Burlington in 1711. Her extensive network of Quaker kin and friends in Burlington would remain important to her throughout her life; it would provide her daughter with an extended family. Still, she dutifully moved across the river to Philadelphia after her marriage to William Callender in 1731. Her few surviving letters indicate that she was barely literate. She used inconsistent and sometimes nearly indecipherable spellings, even of her own name, and wrote in a cramped, inelegant hand. She was, however, active in the family's mercantile business, keeping many of the financial records for her husband during their married life. Years later she could recall precisely that "there are entries of My Husbands & mine" in an account book.[28]

26. Thanks to Craig Horle for directing us to these quotations from Richard Peters and Benjamin Franklin in Scheib, "William Callender," 254, 258.

27. Scheib, "William Callender," 260.

28. Katherine Callender to James Pemberton, December 16, 1774, Pemberton Papers, HSP.

Katherine Callender was very active in the Women's Monthly Meeting of Philadelphia before the death of her husband, twice serving as overseer and three times as representative to the Quarterly Meeting. In March 1755, she was one of the participants in the Philadelphia Yearly Meeting of Ministers and Elders who successfully urged Quaker lawmakers, including her husband, to withdraw from the legislature because of the war. She served on thirteen disciplinary committees and twenty-six other committees in the 1740s and 1750s.[29] She was later active in the Burlington Monthly Meeting.

"Katy" Callender was also independent. In 1742, she left her family behind and went with cousins John Smith and Benjamin Smith and Benjamin Smith's wife on a week-long trip to New York City. They enjoyed the sights, climbed the steeple of the "new Dutch Church" for the view, and judged Philadelphia to be superior, on the whole. They survived an upset carriage and a near-drowning on the way home. Callender would later allow her daughter to take a similar trip.[30]

Beginning in the late 1750s, when she was in her forties, Katy Callender was bedridden with what may have been a series of strokes, frequently compounded by other ailments. The details of her health have not survived, but at several points she appeared near death. It is possible that not all of her ailments were as serious as she insisted and that she sometimes used her health problems to draw her daughter away from Philadelphia and by her side. Jemmy Pemberton wrote to her in 1775 that "I did not hear of thy horceness until Coz[n] Hannah Sansoms return from her visit to thee and [I am] pleased to hear of thy being in a favorable way of Recovery."[31] Whether real or perhaps occasionally exaggerated, her invalid status kept her only daughter in a constant state of anxiety and necessitated many emergency trips to Burlington.

No surviving documents reveal HCS's mother's thoughts and hopes, although her actions clearly indicate that she despised her son-in-law. She did not move in with her daughter after her husband's death in 1762 but instead retreated to Burlington. There she lived in the houses of various relatives with the nurses and servants her daughter had hired to attend to her. She maintained this semi-nomadic life for twenty-six years until her granddaughter Sarah, who married Elliston Perot in 1788, had a household of her own. Callender almost immediately moved in with the newlyweds and happily spent the last year of her life back in Philadelphia with family. She left an estate of £2,459, most of it placed in trust for her daughter and grandchildren, firmly out of Sammy's control.[32]

The *Smith Cousins* were like sisters to HCS. We know little about them be-

29. Scheib, "William Callender"; many thanks to Jean Soderlund for her correspondence with Susan Klepp, August 8, 1996.

30. Myers, ed., *Courtship of Hannah Logan,* 335.

31. James Pemberton to Katherine Callender, March 1775, Pemberton Papers, HSP.

32. Will of Katherine Callender, Quaker Collection, Haverford College. New Jersey Archives, First Series: *Documents Relating to the Colonial History of the State of New Jersey,* vols. 1–13, *Abstracts of Wills,* ed. A. Van Doren Honeyman (1918), 8:x.

yond the bare outlines of their lives and what appears in HCS's diary. Catherine Smith the daughter of Robert Smith and Elizabeth Bacon Smith, was born in 1741. She died unmarried in 1783. Sarah Smith, a daughter of Daniel Smith of Burlington, married the reluctant James Pemberton in 1768. They had one child before she died in 1770. Betsey Smith was born in 1738 and married Samuel Allinson in 1765. She bore two children before dying in 1768.[33] So while the cousins were close during the early years of HCS's diary, two died young, and even Catherine Smith died before HCS.

Sammy Sansom remains an enigma. He kept a diary, which he sometimes read to the Drinkers, but his audience recorded no comments and his descendants did not preserve it. His business records do not survive, nor, with one exception, do his letters. HCS only once recorded anything he had to say, and Elizabeth Drinker, who found him a persistent visitor, only once commented on the substance of his conversation. The most his children and business associates could find to praise in his obituaries was that he had "regular and temperate habits."[34] He described himself as painfully shy; "the Diffidence of my Nature," he wrote to James Pemberton, "is such as effectually to prevent me from speaking my Sentiments in Public."[35]

Sammy was the son of Samuel Sansom (1707–1774), a Quaker merchant who immigrated to Philadelphia from London in 1732, and Sarah Johnson Sansom (1706–1768), an "innofensive" woman born in Philadelphia.[36] Sammy was the second child and first son of the seven children born between 1738 and 1749. Only he and his brother survived to the early days of the diary, and Josey died in 1764 at age seventeen. The elder Samuel Sansom made his money in importing English cloth and hardware and Chinese tea and porcelain. Rather than maximize his income, he retired from business when he had achieved a competency. He "used to say that he had enough," which apparently referred to his very large estate of £92,060.[37]

Sammy began business in 1759 with a trip to London and Liverpool with his business partner, Benjamin Swett Jr. He did more than work on that trip. On November 8, he, his business partner, and Dr. William Shippen, then a young medical student, had dinner with Benjamin Franklin at his London house.[38] He took the time to buy many prints, "perspective views" that attracted HCS and Elizabeth Sandwith to his house for several visits when he returned.[39] This trip was

33. Crane, Drinker Diary, 3:2213–14.

34. "Obituary," *Poulson's American Daily Advertiser* (vol. 53, no. 14,714), January 24, 1824, 3, and (vol. 53, no. 14,782), February 14, 1824, 3.

35. Samuel Sansom to James Pemberton, 11 mo. 5 1774 (Pemberton Papers, HSP).

36. For this description of Sammy's mother, see HCS, November 1, 1769.

37. Obituary from the *Pennsylvania Gazette,* March 2, 1774, quoted in Tooker, *Nathan Trotter,* 37. Estate valuation (including real estate) from 1780, ibid.

38. Betsy Copping Corner, *William Shippen, Jr.: Pioneer in American Medical Education* (Philadelphia: American Philosophical Society, 1951), 28, 45.

39. Crane, Drinker Diary, I:56–57.

his sole venture away from his birthplace. Like his father, he and Swett special-ized in wholesaling British cloth and hardware, saving money by renting cargo space in ships rather than building and maintaining their own commercial fleet. By the late 1760s the partnership had dissolved and Sammy was in business for himself in a combination store/warehouse on Front Street, near the docks. Later, Sammy invested heavily in real estate, both in the city and its hinterland. He was a creditor by the 1790s, if not earlier, lending Robert Morris substantial sums and taking a sizable plot of city land when Morris defaulted.[40] Apparently his busi-ness did not require much effort, and his income from the ground rents on his city properties provided a steady income. He was left with plenty of time on his hands.

By the late 1770s Sammy was moderately active in the business affairs of the Philadelphia Monthly Meeting.[41] He began serving as treasurer of the Library Company and of the Philadelphia Contributionship for the Insurance of Houses from Loss by Fire in 1776. He served in the latter position for thirty-one years without pay, but he allowed unpaid interest payments of between £900 and 1,900 to accumulate. His successor was left with the task of pressing for repayment, "in-creas[ing] the efficiency of the Company's routine."[42] A concerned George Vaux wrote to a friend in 1768 that "the only one I have heard of that wants an ap-prentice is Saml Sansom Junr. He is a sober man and as I am Informed does his business methodically but I am afraid has not quite business enough to keep a Lad fully Emply'd."[43] Vaux finally did send his son to apprentice with Sansom.

Sammy apparently had too little to do during the Revolution as well. Early in February 1781, he began hanging around twenty-three-year old Anna Rawle, in-sisting she meet with him for hours every day in order to learn French. Rawle was living without parental supervision while her mother and stepfather, both staunch Tories, were refugees in New York City. She soon tired of his constant attention, writing to her mother on February 19 that "I have said a great deal about taking up his time and proposed, as it is a matter of very little consequence, to go seldomer." It was of no little consequence to Sammy: "he says we must not forget that he is master and must do as he directs." In April, Rawle noted wearily that "our master here as usual of this day." She finally broke off the exclusive lessons two weeks later, substituting group lessons with both HCS and Sammy every Thursday evening.[44] This episode is more transparent than any other sim-ilar event in Sammy's life, but from the early days of his marriage he frequently

40. Bessie Sansom-Wilson (Saltsburg, Pennsylvania) mentions a block of city property acquired for a debt of £40,000, mss. letter dated February 6, 1939 in Sansom Family Genealogy, Genealogical Society of Pennsylvania. See Tooker, *Nathan Trotter,* 237n22.

41. Correspondence from Jean R. Soderlund, August 8, 1996.

42. Nicholas B. Wainwright, *A Philadelphia Story, 1752–1952: The Philadelphia Contributionship for the Insurance of Houses from Loss by Fire* (Philadelphia: Philad. Contributionship, 1952), 75, 84, 91.

43. Dr. George Vaux of London to Edward Pennington, quoted in Tooker, *Nathan Trotter,* 38.

44. Anna Rawle diary transcripts in Pemberton Papers, HSP, passim, but esp. Feb. 19, Apr. 16, Apr. 29, 1781; and Jan. 24, 1782. See also letter from Rebecca Rawle Shoemaker, Aug. 28, 1781.

spent evenings and sometimes whole nights away from home, causing HCS great distress.

Sammy appears to have been isolated during the revolution because of his political beliefs. Like most merchants in the city, he signed the non-importation agreement on November 7, 1765. But in 1770, he was not among the prominent merchants, including John Reynall, Abel James, Henry Drinker, Jeremiah Warder, Thomas Fisher, and Clement Biddle, whose petition for a revival of trade caused "much resentment among the non-mercantile classes."[45] It seems that unlike most other prominent Quaker merchants, he was willing to continue the American boycott of British goods. In 1774, Sammy wrote an uncharacteristic letter to James Pemberton, clerk of the Yearly Meeting, mildly rebuking the Friends for being unduly antagonistic to "the general Proceedings of the People" and praising the intention of the Continental Congress to abolish the slave trade, arguing, "Who is there among us who can say that the Hand of Providence is not in these Things?"[46] He appears to have spoken for many moderate Quakers. In 1776, he joined the Society for Assisting Distressed Prisoners, which included more than a few members of radical committees, including Christopher Marshall, who was later disowned for his support of the revolutionaries.[47] He was not among the prominent Quakers arrested by the revolutionary government in 1777, he did not have his property confiscated, nor was he among the "Tories, Quakers, and non-combatants remaining in Philadelphia during the British occupation."[48] While Sammy Sansom was moderately active in the Philadelphia Monthly Meeting from his marriage in 1762 to 1771, the meeting did not once call upon him for service between 1771 and late 1777. Sammy apparently decided to cast his lot with mainstream Quakers after September 1777, but he remained sympathetic to revolutionary causes for the rest of his life. After one visit by Sammy, Elizabeth Drinker observed, "I could not have believed he was so much of a Democrat as he shows himself to be."[49]

So Sammy was a contradictory figure: a democrat and antislavery activist who liked the title of master, a wealthy businessman who may have been rather incompetent but still grew wealthier, a shy man who challenged authority. He was a man of apparent probity whose routines included forcing his attentions on

45. Sharf and Westcott, *History of Philadelphia,* I:284.

46. Saml Sansom to James Pemberton, May 11, 1774, Pemberton Papers, HSP. This episode is discussed in Arthur J. Mekeel, *The Relation of the Quakers to the American Revolution* (Washington, DC: University Press, 1979), 90; and Richard Bauman, *For the Reputation of Truth: Politics, Relision, and Conflict among the Pennsylvania Quakers, 1750–1800* (Baltimore: Johns Hopkins University Press, 1971), 150–52. See also Steve Rosswurm, "Class Relations, Political Economy, and Society in Philadelphia," in *Shaping a National Culture: The Philadelphia Experience, 1750–1800,* ed. Catherine E. Hutchins (Winterthur, DE: Winterthur, 1994), 69n19.

47. Notice of Meeting, *Pennsylvania Gazette,* Feb. 14, 1776. Richard Ryerson, *The Revolution is Now Begun: The Radical Committees of Philadelphia, 1765–1776* (Philadelphia: University of Pennsylvania Press, 1978).

48. Sharf and Westcott, *History of Philadelphia* I:365–66.

49. Crane, Drinker Diary, 1406.

young women and spending frequent nights on the town. His descendants remembered his sons and son-in-law, his parents and parents-in-law, but found nothing about him to commemorate either during his lifetime or thereafter. And when his great-grandson published excerpts from his wife's diary, it was under her maiden name only.

Sarah "Sally" Sansom Perot was born on November 11, 1764, and from her early years was the center of her mother's attention, a focus expressed in the diary written after 1768 for Sally's perusal and instruction. Sally was well educated, well trained in domestic skills, and occasionally indulged with presents. Because few other records of Sally Sansom Perot survive, it is her mother's voice that dominates. There is only one reference to Sally's rebelling against her mother's agenda for her: in 1781 Sally went off with her friends, insisting that her mother remain behind even though her mother "had sent word she was coming too."[50] It was a small act of rebellion. As is the case with most women of the period, the surviving records capture her husband's experiences, not hers.

The man Sally would marry was *Elliston Perot,* born in 1747 of French Huguenot parents on the island of Bermuda. After various mercantile ventures in New York, St. Eustatius, Bermuda, and London, he settled in Philadelphia in 1784 with his brother John, where he continued as a merchant, invested in real estate, and served as president of the Philadelphia and Lancaster Turnpike Company and manager of the Pennsylvania Hospital from 1787 to 1804.[51] He achieved some local renown for developing Long Branch, New Jersey, as a family seashore resort after 1788. By the 1820s summer vacations of a week or more at the shore attracted thousands of Philadelphia families, and not only the rich.[52] It seems appropriate that Perot achieved local attention for his family resort since he was a family man himself. He established his townhouse next door to his brother's family: the two brothers remained inseparable. Sally's grandmother was welcomed into his and his wife's household, and Katherine Callender "had much satisfaction" in Sarah's "affectionate husband."[53] As long as HCS was alive, he and Sally moved to Parlaville for the summer. After her death in 1801, he and Sally and his brother and family summered at 4782 Germantown Avenue (proudly remembered by the family as George Washington's residence during the yellow fever epidemic of 1793). Apparently he couldn't abide his father-in-law, still living at Parlaville, any more than other members of the family.

50. Rawle/Shoemaker Collection (HSP, typescript), Anna Rawle Diary, May 9, 1781, pp. 95–96.

51. George Hood, *Family Record of Charles Poultney Perot* (Chester, PA: Published by the author, 1870), photonegative, GSP. based on the reminiscences of Samuel B. Morris (1834) and Joseph Sansom Jr. (undated).

52. Watson, *Annals of Philadelphia,* II:464; and Crane, Drinker Diary, III:2053n48.

53. Joseph Sansom Jr., quoted in Hood, *Family Record,* photonegative, GSP.

PART I

Sociability

Chapter 1

Talk, Travel, and a Couple of Murders

Hannah Callender's Sociable, Venturesome Life

In 1758 Hannah Callender was twenty-one years old. She lived in her parents' home within a busy community of economically comfortable to wealthy families, many of them Quakers like herself. She spent her days alternating between the solitary, quiet pursuits she loved, such as reading and needlework, and the highly sociable environment that she also enjoyed. Some readers will marvel at the intensity of her sociability, the nearly constant round of tea, talk, travel, and news; others may find it faintly exhausting. Whether at home or visiting others, most days found HCS surrounded by people and talk.

Her sociable world was an artifact of a particular place and time. Sociability was the quality of being inclined to keep company with others of like mind, to polish manners, to expand knowledge and sympathy, and to practice an easy and "natural" sincerity. Sociability was emerging as a vital element of the eighteenth-century urban milieu. Literary historian David Shields notes that sociability developed as a new form of social encounter in the late seventeenth century, distinct from the more stiffly formal, traditional, and more exclusively masculine venues that preceded it. Embracing sociability as "friendship, mutual interest, and shared appetite" did not imply a casualness about these new forms of social interaction.[1] Eighteenth-century European societies were still quite formal and hierarchical, and HCS and her family and friends were conscientious about how they exchanged spoken and epistolary conversation, who they communicated with, where, and in what circumstances. Reciprocity in visits and correspondence was carefully calculated—one of the purposes of the journal was to keep track of

---

1. David S. Shields, *Civil Tongues and Polite Letters in British America* (Chapel Hill: University of North Carolina Press for the Omohundro Institute of Early American History and Culture, 1997), 31.

social obligations. But sociability eased the intermingling of middling and elite people in a realm where status was not predicated quite so directly on the rigid, inherited hierarchies of nobility, for example, that had long dominated the early modern world. Gendered inequalities moderated because sociability allowed genteel men and women to interact as near equals. As merchants and other professionals expanded both their financial and cultural capital in the eighteenth century, they moved into these new social spaces that bespoke their ability to enjoy leisure time and to afford the comforts made available by commercial and imperial expansion.[2]

For young men and women, sociability was often experienced and practiced as friendship with other young people and as a prelude to courtship. In a city such as Philadelphia, with houses built close together and densely developed networks of affiliation, friendship was a feeling and a connection that could be shared with kin or non-kin and was demonstrated through time spent in company. Some of HCS's closest friends were her cousins. A letter from Sarah ("Sally") Smith caused HCS to remark that "great is the joy, or innate satisfaction in hearing from a friend one loves."[3] It was a sentiment both heartfelt and formulaic, found in magazines and novels as well as personal diaries. Such ideals saturated the conversations and writings of the literate, tying together a supportive community of near equals. Female friends visited one another at home, read together, strolled and shopped together along the city streets, attended to the sick or pregnant among their compatriots, and paid close attention to one another's ideas, health, behavior, and reputation. Together men and women drank tea, conversed on a wide range of subjects, and took in the city's amusements and educational opportunities—even traveling outside the city to emerging tourist destinations, such as Bethlehem, the Moravian community north of Philadelphia.

Yet social engagement was never intended to be self-indulgent or unproductive—those were qualities associated with an indolent aristocracy. Sociability encouraged other qualities. A broad reading in philosophy, literature, history,

---

2. Many scholars have explored the complex interplay of new political and economic forms with the new cultural, particularly expressive, modes of the eighteenth century. For a review of some of this literature pertaining to Britain from one its influential authors, see Lawrence Klein, "Politeness and the Interpretation of the British Eighteenth Century," *Historical Journal* 45, no. 4 (December 2002): 869–98.

3. HCS, February 21, 1758, 6. The number of people who passed through HCS's life and the pages of her diary is vast. Some people appear frequently. Close neighbors in Philadelphia, the set of young men and women with whom HCS went to meeting and socialized with, her Burlington relatives, particularly the young people, were important stock characters. HCS characterized the connection of kinship to friendship among this latter group in this way: after a Burlington dinner at her uncle's home, she remarked on the cousins gathered around the table, their evening "spent in friendship as the children of one father." That these were, in fact, her *mother's* relatives is an indication of the pull of patriarchal convention. HCS, April 22, 1759, 49. For a useful study of the importance of friendships, the narrow definitions of family, and broad notions of kin, see Naomi Tadmor, *Family and Friends in Eighteenth-Century England: Household, Kinship, and Patronage* (Cambridge, U.K.: Cambridge University Press, 2001). For a study of the social networks of Elizabeth Drinker, one of HCS's friends in the early part of her diary, see Elaine Crane, "The World of Elizabeth Drinker," *Pennsylvania Magazine of History and Biography* 57 (January 1983): 3–28.

politics, and the arts was expected, as was the ability to conduct witty, refined, and enlightening conversations that enhanced the understanding of all attending. These acquired, cultivated attributes of participants, rather than birth rank or raw wealth, became marks of distinction and helped create a public sphere, a place where public opinion was formed and where citizen-subjects of the crown might bring their interests to the attention of policy makers. Sociability therefore was not simply about social pleasure but also served several community and cultural functions.

Sociability was a key mechanism for political exchange and for the management of social crisis. In the mid-1750s and early 1760s, HCS and her extended social network deployed sociability to determine and to express social and moral values, often through commentary on the course of acquaintances' courtships and marriages. That network also depended on sociability to address and to contain various kinds of threats to order and comity, including the violence in their midst. Everyone knew that war with France was in the offing. Ever-increasing rounds of violence among and between the Delawares, Shawnees, and Iroquois and the encroaching colonists finally led to war in 1754. The first section of the diary is as much about the context of the French and Indian War and its terrible toll in Pennsylvania and elsewhere as it is about polite tea parties and conversation. Indeed, to understand HCS's sociable world, it is important to see the relationship between those two seemingly disparate forces.[4] Conversation and pleasure-seeking helped create and cement the ties that would be necessary to contain the kinds of violent disruption that swept in from the battlefields, the hostilities of the backcountry settlements, and the divisive politics of the war years. The direct and indirect impact on the city and the community of neighbors and friends with whom HCS spent most of her time can be traced in her diary.

TALK

A fascinating aspect of HCS's diary, intimately connected to sociability, is her emphasis on "talk." Not simply formal greetings or ritual communications, talk represented the deeper exchanges of information, ideas, and feelings that formed a kind of glue connecting people, reinforcing reputations, and shaping opinions. HCS describes valued conversations with her parents, cousins, many friends, other Quakers of varying ages, ministers, and others. In the first weeks of the di-

---

4. On the ways that sensibility, sociability's close cultural cousin, became essential to the conduct of war, see Sarah Knott, "Sensibility and the American War for Independence," *American Historical Review* 109, no. 1. Knott argues in her recent book, *Sensibility and the American Revolution* (Chapel Hill: University of North Carolina Press, 2009), that sociability was the essential proving ground for sensibility. For an analysis of the role of emotion in mediating conflicts, including asymmetries of power even to the point of war, see Nicole Eustace, *Passion is the Gale: Emotion, Power, and the Coming of the American Revolution* (Chapel Hill: University of North Carolina Press, 2008).

ary, for example, she described an evening conversation with her father: "Some advice given me by Daddy, not to spend my sentiments too freely, either on men or things, but let Judgement ripen."[5] William Callender may have been suggesting that his daughter temper her enthusiasm for a particular young man while also warning that in general, it was good practice to take time before forming opinions about people. Her reaction to this exchange and many others suggests both that she respected her father and that theirs was a warm and open, if unequal, relationship.

Some conversations seemed more idle than others. After spending the day at her cousin's house with other young women, HCS noted that the "conversation run on Courtship and the ridiculous behavior of some People in it."[6] Even humorous gossip could help instruct in appropriate conduct, but discussions with her peers could be serious as well. Within a few days of the courtship chat, HCS and her friends conducted "a great deal of talk on liars and calumniators." And in this, as so much else in her life demonstrated, the effect on the community was of paramount concern: "Individuals constitute a whole," she wrote.[7] Sociable behavior was the mechanism by which individuals contributed to the making of a community.

This sort of talk required a suitable environment. Middling and well-off families expected to equip their homes to welcome guests for parties and informal visiting. They purchased tea tables and teapots, teacups and saucers (tea was sweetened and stirred in cups, but sipped out of the saucer, hence having a "dish" of tea), sugar tongs and sugar cutters (sugar came in solid loaves), and teaspoons and slop bowls (for any remaining tea, tea leaves, or dregs from the pot). The tea table was set in the middle of sofas and chairs in a room designed, principally, for sociable occasions. A servant was kept busy refreshing the teapot with boiling water. In the Callenders' comfortable home on Front Street or their later apartment on Market Street, Hannah could welcome her friends in a front room or upstairs in a more private chamber.[8]

And welcome her friends she did. A close look at the first month of HCS's diary reveals important patterns in the life of a young, marriageable woman—a young woman who was not only very sociable but also acutely aware of the necessity of sociability. In the thirty-one days of January 1758, HCS visited out on at least twelve days. Some of those days included multiple activities, and a varied cast. On Tuesday, January 17, for example, HCS went first to Quaker meeting and then she and Anna Pole went shopping together and to see another friend,

---

5. HCS, January 9, 1758.
6. HCS, January 12, 1758.
7. HCS, January 15, 1758.
8. Those rooms were well positioned to observe and interpret news as will be seen below. On the use of sociable space, see Shields, *Civil Tongues and Polite Letters;* Jessica Kross, "Mansions, Men, Women, and the Creation of Multiple Publics in Eighteenth-Century British North America," *Journal of Social History* 33, no. 2 (1999): 385–408; and Bernard Herman, *Town House: Architecture and Material Life in the Early American City, 1780–1830* (Chapel Hill: University of North Carolina Press, 2005).

Polly Pemberton. At the Pembertons they not only found Polly and her sister, but also "king Tedeuskung," a prominent Delaware leader who had come to Philadelphia, probably at the behest of the Friendly Society. What a pity that HCS did not record the nature and substance of their conversation. That evening she took Polly along to visit Patsy Hill, a sick friend. So a single day involved several different places, talking and socializing with a varied group of people for a variety of purposes. On at least ten days in the month, friends came to the Callender home. On January 16, for example, HCS simply noted that she had "afternoon and evening Company."

Although HCS claimed that she wanted to write her diary in part to ensure that she would "husband" her time more carefully, her comments about the events of each day suggest that from the start she was aware of the personal, familial, and communal value of cultivating an extensive circle of amiable friends. On January 25, she finally recorded a very different sort of day. "The day spent agreably at home with work, I am thankful, that I am not so great a burthen to myself, as that I cant enjoy myself alone." On this rare day in January, HCS attended to her needlework, as she often did, and probably to her reading as well as her writing. She treasured time alone; though she clearly reveled in her social whirl, she appreciated its costs. She commented on "visits of form" (formal visits required at marriages, burials, and births) and the obligations they incurred, "which will take up more of one's thoughts than perhaps we are aware of at the time."

Sociability was an obligation, but HCS was discerning and discriminating about conversation. She seemed to enjoy most aspects of her social life, but she also elevated some experiences above others.[9] For example, when HCS met "Rich: Footman's wife . . . a Woman of Sense," there was no "'Scandel over the Tea'" sort of discussion, there were "no base Innuendues hinted at," but rather they pursued "the true desighn of Conversation" which was "mutual Pleasure." And how was this achieved? "We talked of authers," HCS wrote, and the new arrival was found to be "well versed, in Books of good repute."[10] As HCS remarked some weeks later, "A good memory is a help to Conversation, makes people able to intersperce it, with Incidents from History, or Books and things from knowledge or observation of Men."[11] An impressive public figure, an accomplished Quaker minister, a very close friend, or an interesting new acquaintance could, when intermingled with insights from books, produce an inspiring

9. HCS was constantly assessing the value of conversation and social encounters. For just one among many, many examples, see February 28, 1759, in which HCS noted in passing that during a visit to Caty Howel's house with Polly Sandwith, she enjoyed "some wholesome and agreeable conversation." In other passages she described the quality of a friend's reading and ability to analyze and extrapolate from text as a precondition for a good conversation. She also appreciated an ability to speak wisely about contemporary politics or issues of moral urgency.

10. HCS, December 16, 1758.

11. HCS, January 8, 1759.

conversation that would provide food for thought and, usually, inspiration for a diary entry on contemporary moral and political matters.[12]

Talk and reflection were mutually reinforcing. After what may have been a particularly busy day, HCS paused to ponder this connection: "I am noteing those trite amusements of mine, as I pass through the busy herd, it often brings me with satisfaction to my home, as the place of more cool reflection."[13] Those reflections were a cherished result of talking with friends and family. A few months after she began the diary, for instance, HCS remarked that there was "no part of our Lives so critical for our behaviour, as the point of time between Girl and Woman." As was often the case, this sort of contemplation followed a conversation, this time with Abby Smith, and HCS followed reflection with a verse: "Send the fluttering soul abroad, / praised for her shape, her mien, / the Little Goddess and the queen."[14] She then returned to her own thoughts and conclusions: "All the follies of one without the prudence of the other. Then is the time we have need of the Maternal care."[15] Youth was treacherous, especially for women.

HCS probably considered herself well advanced into womanhood at the age of twenty-one. It was the later teen years when so many young women in her favorite novels, as well as young women of her acquaintance, seemed particularly vulnerable to false steps and loss of reputation. The theme of a critical period was a recurring one in this first section of the diary, circling through many conversations and recorded contemplations. HCS regularly remarked on the qualities she saw in friends, strangers, and people she had only just met. These remarks reveal something of her emphasis on the social vulnerability of young, unmarried women. In September she described a new acquaintance, Betsy Brook, with whom she confessed she found herself "delighted." Brook, a Quaker from Maryland, seemed to have all the requirements of modesty and presentation most becoming in a young woman. Her appearance ("tall and genteel") and clothing ("plain, and . . . with a little black silk hood, graced as Innocent a face, as I ever see") were perfectly complemented by her comportment; she "engaged your attention before she spoke, then, though not brought up in a City, delivered herself with ease and becoming freedom."[16] These were qualities that HCS's world most valued in a woman of her age—beauty and fashion, certainly, but self-confidence and public presence as well.

Contrasting examples were provided by countless characters in the novels

---

12. Again, among many examples, see HCS's appraisal of the young, "convinced" (meaning converted) Quaker Rebecca Jones, and her prospects as a minister (which HCS correctly judged to be bright). HCS, January 20, 1759. Or HCS's report of the company's discussion about the life and death of Benjamin Lay, an early abolitionist who chose to live as a hermit ("his passions so strong that they incapacitated him for argument.") HCS, February 14, 1759.

13. HCS, November 20, 1759.

14. Henry Brooke, "Love and Vanity," in volume IV of his *Poetical Works* (1792), lines 167–68.

15. HCS, March 20, 1758.

16. HCS, September 19, 1758. Nearly a year later, HCS reported: "Poor Betsy Brooks thy joys nipt in the bud of Prospect." Her fiancée, John Hopkins, had died. HCS, August 15, 1759.

HCS read, whose sense of virtue was weak, who followed passion instead of reason, or whose circumstances drove them into situations which damaged their
character, virtue, and reputation. Real-life characters reinforced the novel's messages.[17] HCS relayed the sorry tale of Betty Shirley, whose "misfortunes were so
great as to carry the air of Romance" but who ended up in Philadelphia with her
illegitimate child and nothing else to her name. True to romantic tragedy, Shirley
died shortly thereafter. HCS's conclusion from this drama? "Misfortune's are easier brought on, than they are born. The Sexes [are] made for each others aid, [but
then] employ deceitfulness of there hearts to ruin each other."[18] If only Shirley
had followed the path of virtue. There were plenty of other examples of female
vulnerability among HCS's acquaintances, especially because of the presence of
British Army officers during the war. These were cosmopolitan, sophisticated
young men, free from parental oversight and experienced in the arts of seduction.
Not all the dangers they posed were on the battlefield.

The moment in their lives when women were marriageable but still unmarried
required a delicate balancing act. Women were to attract men but not to succumb
to passion. They were to marry out of affection but also to consider the financial
prospects and social status of their suitors. Women from families like HCS's had to
pretend that men admired them—and not merely their dowries. Parental approval
still mattered and had to be taken into account, even though HCS's generation had
more freedom in choosing partners than their parents had. Feminine ploys such as
teasing, flirting, or encouraging several men at a time were condemned, but so was
pedantry, coolness, or haughtiness. Courtship required women's resolute attention
to manners, deportment, and expression. This period before marriage was no less
important for young men, though they had greater latitude in all these areas. HCS
was attuned to the complexities of navigating this system and its inequities. As
much as she chided women's poor choices, she clearly regretted the unfairness of
the high-stakes game in which they found themselves.[19]

17. Among many examples of HCS's references to the lessons of popular novels, see November 18 and
December 30, 1758, on Samuel Richardson's heroine, Clarissa Harlowe, whom HCS refers to by name
rather by reference to the book (*Clarissa*). See also her note on January 28, 1759, about her father's reading
aloud from "extracts out of different Authors, all tending to compose the Mind, to think on the important
task assigned to all human Beings. 'Work out your own Salvations with diligence.'" In this instance, HCS
knew that seeking salvation had a social element as well, and required behavior toward others as well as
toward one's inner spiritual condition. William Callender knew this as well. This reading of her father,
HCS reported, "was for ought I know, a prepareative to a friendly visit . . . from Sam: Spavol. with Betty
Morris." Numerous scholars have addressed the significance of Richardson's novel for colonial readers, and
particularly for female readers—many of them in the broader context of so-called sentimental fiction more
generally. For an important statement on the subject of women's novel reading in eighteenth-century
America, see Cathy N. Davidson, *Revolution and the Word: The Rise of the Novel in America* (New York:
Oxford University Press, 2004). For a recent analysis of how female readers assessed *Clarissa*, particularly
with regard to the themes of romance, seduction, and love, see Katherine Binhammer, "Knowing Love:
The Epistemology of Clarisa," *English Literary History* 74 (2007): 859–79.

18. HCS, December 6, 1759; April 1 and 12, 1759.

19. On the importance of courtship and women's behavior see Eustace, *Passion is the Gale;* and Martha
Blauvet, *The Work of the Heart: Young Women and Emotion, 1780–1830* (University of Virginia Press, 2007).

Travel

HCS's sociable venues were not confined to home, Quaker meeting, shops, and visits. Between late January 1758 and August 1761, the nearly three years of the diary's first section, she also traveled frequently. Some of that travel encompassed simple commutes between her father's new country house, Richmond (or Richmond Plantation, at Point-No-Point), and Philadelphia. In the late summer of 1759, William Callender purchased this rural retreat on the Delaware River, but only in July of the next year did he sell his Philadelphia house on Front Street with an eye to being at Richmond more regularly. As HCS explained, "We removed to Richmond Seat, having apartments, at our good Cousin Sam: Noble's to be at when in town."[20] Having urban and rural residences allowed an expansion of the Callenders' social life. In addition, the Yearly Meeting, the annual gathering of Quakers throughout the region held alternately at Philadelphia and Burlington, New Jersey, brought reunions with distant friends and relatives and introduced new people into their realm.

Trips long and short incorporated the values and functions of sociability: traveling to interesting places gave HCS an opportunity to learn (which could be translated into knowledgeable conversation) and to encounter new people and surroundings. Explorations in and around town provided a change from the formality of the tea table. HCS described several day trips to places such as the "Schulkill Fishing house" or a "ride up Wisehicken" (a local scenic creek) that altered her daily routine. Longer trips brought curious new sights, sounds, and sensations. These expeditions excited the mind and the senses, engaging HCS and her friends with new acquaintances, strange customs, and what seemed to be exotic locales.

HCS considered Burlington, New Jersey (about twenty miles northeast of Philadelphia across the Delaware River) a second home, and she visited there often. There her Smith aunts and uncles, relatives on her mother's side, were an intimate part of her family. She was particularly close to her female cousins. Between 1758 and 1762 she made at least five trips to Burlington, staying with the Smiths for several weeks at a time. She clearly felt at home, attending the Quaker meeting, visiting kin and other neighbors, and generally enjoying her time with "an agreeable Company of young folks."[21] Sociable outings included walks to sites of local interest such as the barracks, the "London" bridge, and the churchyard to "read the tombstones."

HCS took more extended trips from Burlington, one to Shrewsbury, about forty-five miles away, and an extensive journey to New York and Long Island that followed several day trips, including a visit to Princeton, where she "walked round the Colledge, and the presidents House." These trips were lively parties of

20. HCS, August 1, 1759 and July 14, 1760.
21. HCS, April 27, 1759 (?).

young adults (and a few, barely visible older chaperones), which HCS described at great length. In 1759, HCS wrote that she had "some thoughts of taking a journey to Newyork & flushing" and, after permission arrived from her parents, she, her cousins, and some friends started out. To go, even with approval, necessitated that she carefully place herself "under the Care of Jane Burling," an older woman. Being in Burling's "care" did not mean much in practical terms—HCS even traveled separately from her—but it did safeguard the reputations of the young women, always something to consider, even away from home. HCS stayed in New York for the month, taking trips out to see Long Island and other places of local interest. She also availed herself of New York's urban amenities, such as bookshops, reporting that she purchased copies of Seneca's *Morals,* James Thomson's *Seasons,* and Edward Young's *Night-Thoughts,* all recognized and praised as high-minded literature for young women.[22]

In her travels, HCS was consistently interested in learning about local customs and diverse social practices. Religious pluralism in New York City offered multiple perspectives on faith. The Friends' practice was to sit quietly until someone of the congregation was moved to speak—it was their proof that it was the living spirit of God governing the worship. Thus, for a Quaker, other formal, ritualized worship services were contrary to true religion, and they elicited HCS's disdain. She visited a synagogue, where she found both the service and the people stiff and formal. The experience did not call forth the religious toleration that William Penn had promoted: HCS condemned Jewish belief and prayed that she might never find herself bound to the "Slavery of Tradition." HCS also visited Anglican and Dutch churches in New York City, though seemingly more for the architecture than for an exploration of their theology.

In HCS's diary there is also a record of a trip to the Moravian town of Bethlehem, Pennsylvania. HCS marked out this section of her journal distinctly, titling it as her "Journal of Journey to Bethlehem in 1761." Setting the scene for the journey, HCS described the departure on August 26: "Parents consenting, Anna Pole, Betsey Bringhurst, Hallender, Jemmy Bringhurst, and Sammy Sansom, set out for Bethlehem and the Country adjacent." There were three young women and two young men on this trip, including Hannah's future husband, Sammy Sansom. On her major trips HCS referred to herself as "Hallender" an amalgam of "H. Callender," perhaps an indication of the freedom from social or familial constraints that she felt when traveling. Before the trip, she had only mentioned Sammy Sansom a few times, beginning the previous fall, though her diary entries lapsed for the first eight months of 1761, when she might have begun spending more time with him. Now they were obviously spending much more time in each other's company.

Bethlehem is about sixty miles due north of Philadelphia, along the Lehigh River. The travelers spent three days getting to Bethlehem and then about three

22. HCS, April 27, 1759.

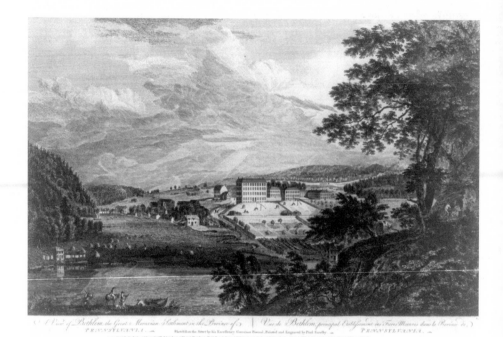

Figure 3 A view of Bethlehem, Pennsylvania, 1761. Courtesy Library of Congress.

days visiting the town. Bethlehem was a fascinating place for Philadelphians and had become something of a tourist attraction.[23] The Moravian settlement was part of a communal, somewhat mystical, religious order that traced its origins to fifteenth-century Moravia and Bohemia, today in the Czech Republic. Revitalized early in the eighteenth century by Count Nicolaus Zinzendorf of Saxony, Germany, Moravians were committed to evangelizing. They founded Bethlehem in Pennsylvania in 1741 as a base for their missionary work to Native Americans. While nuclear families prevailed among missionaries, those living in Bethlehem resided in "choirs," with married women in one building and married men in another. The same separation prevailed for the single men and women, while children were raised communally. HCS knew several of the Moravian sisters, some of whom were converts.

More than anything else, HCS used her time in Bethlehem to learn about, and to comment on, Moravian life. She was intrigued by the ritual structures of work and worship that organized the Moravians' days. HCS and her companions took part in some of this ritual, including the sex-segregated "Love feast," where each participant was served bread and chocolate. No more tolerant of Moravian worship than she was of Jewish worship, HCS noted that she could not comprehend

23. On touring in Bethlehem, see Karin Wulf, *Not All Wives: Women of Colonial Philadelphia* (Ithaca: Cornell University Press, 2000), 77–81.

how "persons of good understand[ing] could imagine themselves paying real worship to the deity in [such] unsubstantial forms."[24] Religious concerns aside, Bethlehem offered an alternative vision, a place where marriage and childrearing were not women's sole options.

These years as a young, wealthy, unmarried woman gave HCS unusual access to worlds beyond her own. She never again had such freedom to travel once she became a wife and mother. HCS's traveling life was an opportunity for her to consider the kinds of life that might be led beyond the confines of her social circles, even if her travel was carefully bounded by the extended and extensive networks of family and friends. Thinking through the possibilities, the potential for tragedy and for success, imagining what others experienced and valued, offered HCS a contrast to her own experience. All of this travel, literal and internalized, drew on and contributed to the sociability underpinning the life she knew best and to which she remained committed.

MURDER

Although HCS's diary is a record of much sociable pleasure, it also speaks loudly and persistently of the trauma and violent realities of life in the colonies of the mid-eighteenth century. The Seven Years' War, and the threatened violence that preceded and followed it, was a near-constant presence in HCS's life—even in her father's parlor. Just as Americans are now all too accustomed to news of wartime atrocities arriving in their homes via television or the internet, HCS and her family found that the war came in by multiple means. Newspapers, of course, carried some local and regional news, particularly sensational stories about those who were taken captive by Indians, the scattering of refugee families, and murderous raids. These plunged Quakers in particular into despair over the fate of "Penn's colony." But the war came in person, too. Important Indian leaders, Quaker politicians, and British soldiers passed through the Callenders' doors or at least by their front windows. Though she only occasionally mentioned the horrifying violence that marked the Pennsylvania backcountry, evidence of the war's omnipresence and the culture of violence the war spawned saturates the first part of the diary.

The Great War for Empire, as the British called it, was a global war, and recently historians have argued that it shaped America's future as no war before or since—including the American Revolution.[25] The political and territorial consequences of the war were great, including Great Britain's eventual acquisition of most of France's holdings on the North American continent. For Pennsylva-

---

24. HCS, May 16, 1759.
25. Fred Anderson, *Crucible of War: The Seven Years' War and the Fate of Empire in British North America, 1754–1766* (New York: Knopf, 2000).

nia the war also frayed political alliances and necessitated the creation of new ones. The Quakers' opposition to war cost them political influence within the colony, while backcountry settlers' frustration with Philadelphians' seeming lack of sympathy for their plight pushed Quaker policies and plans even further to the political margin.

But Quakers wanted to be back in the middle of things. In 1756 Quaker politicians, including William Callender, left their positions in the Pennsylvania Assembly rather than continue to vote for funding the war, even while they sympathized both with the settlers in the backcountry and the Indians and agonized over the devastating violence on all sides.[26] They formed the Friendly Association for Regaining and Preserving Peace with the Indians to try to encourage diplomacy. Using their political energies and skills to push for negotiations did not endear the Friendly Association to the governor or his council or the British officials prosecuting the war (though none minded taking advantage of the Quakers' gifts to the Indians as a diplomatic tool now and again). Even within the Quaker group, disagreements developed. HCS refers to the tension that she and her friends, the Pemberton women, were feeling because their fathers were in dispute. Political fragmentation led to violent rhetoric that threatened civil society.

By the fall of 1758, if not earlier, HCS could not help but be deeply aware of the politics of war. She helped her father make copies of letters and documents for the Friendly Association; on one afternoon, for example, she described "copying letters for Daddy to send to England, concerning Politicks."[27] In the space of a couple of weeks she not only read the journal of Frederick Post, the Moravian missionary who was deployed by the Pennsylvania government to negotiate with the Delawares and Susquehannocks, but she then read aloud to her father the tract by Charles Thomson, *An Enquiry Into the Causes of the Alienation of the Delaware and Shawnese Indians from the British Interest.* Post's journal and Thomson's essay were published together in London in 1759. HCS must have had access to a manuscript version in late 1758. A couple of weeks after reading Post's journal, he dined and, a few days later, breakfasted with the Callenders. HCS applauded him in ways that convey her political and communal values: "I have a respect for the man as a good Commonwealth's man. the man who does no hurt to society, is a good Citisen, but the man who for the good of his fellow citisens, will go there errands with his Life as in his hand. this man is worthy the public thanks, and the joy which he must feel on so laudable an action."[28] A "Commonwealth's

---

26. Appraisals of the Friendly Association's efforts were mixed; the governor and many in the legislature were sharply critical of what they deemed the Association's interference in diplomacy. On the changes in Native/settler relations over the eighteenth century and the culmination of the Seven Years' War, see Jane Merritt, *At the Crossroads: Indians and Empires on a mid-Atlantic Frontier, 1700–1763* (Chapel Hill: University of North Carolina Press, 2007).

27. HCS, October 23, 1758.

28. On reading Post and Thomson, then meeting Post, see HCS, October 23, November 25, December 12, 15, 18, 1758, and February 15 and 21, 1759.

Pemberton's

AN

Anthony Benezet's /

E N Q U I R Y

INTO THE

Caufes of the Alienation

OF THE

Delaware and *Shawanefe Indians*

FROM THE

B R I T I S H I N T E R E S T,

And into the Meafures taken for recovering their
F R I E N D S H I P.

Extracted from the PUBLIC TREATIES, and other Authen-
tic Papers relating to the Tranfactions of the Government of *Penfilvania* and the faid *Indians*, for near Forty
Years; and explained by a M A P of the Country.

Together with the remarkable JOURNAL of *Chriftian Frederic Poft*,
by whofe Negotiations, among the *Indians* on the *Ohio*, they were
withdrawn from the Intereft of the *French*, who thereupon
abandoned the Fort and Country.

With Notes by the EDITOR explaining fundry *Indian* Cuftoms, &c.

Written in *Penfylvania*.

by Charles Thompson

afterwards Secretary to Congress,

L O N D O N:

Printed for J. WILKIE, at the Bible, in St. Paul's Church-yard.
MDCCLIX.

man" links Post to the anti-monarchical, radical Protestant cause of the English Civil War, more than a century earlier. Those same months she described news of various military maneuvers, diplomatic efforts, and rumors about the wretched state of humanity in the backcountry. In mid-December, for example, she wrote eloquently of the French abandonment of Fort Duquesne and the reputed horrors that ensued there: "Oh War! horrid War; how does it make human Nature, act derogatory to the first Principles of it instilled by the Divine Dictator."[29]

In the late summer and early fall of 1760, another kind of violence intruded. Homicide indictments more than doubled in the city, rising from 3.1 per 100,000 to 7.0 between 1750 and 1770, at least in part because during the war "violent speech and the possibility of violent action were usually close at hand."[30] Within the space of a month, two murders occurred within HCS's circle of Philadelphia acquaintances. Her response, along with newspaper articles about these events, illustrates how important the language of sentiment was becoming, in this case for expressing, understanding, and containing violence among intimates. HCS's response also reveals the tensions that developed in a city living through a war whose harshest effects were felt elsewhere, but whose consequences were driving politics and altering personal relationships.

On August 27, HCS was enjoying a day of visiting. She and Nancy Gibson had just settled in "my chamber, for Conversation." Suddenly, seen from the windows looking onto Front Street, someone rode by "post haste" to collect Dr. William Shippen. A young man named Robert Skull had been shot at the Centre House tavern.

The assailant was a "Broken Officer," John Bruleman. Bruleman was probably a Pennsylvanian and served in the Royal American Regiment, a British regiment that had been raised from among the Germans living near Philadelphia. He had served as an officer but had recently been dismissed (thus "broken"). Newspapers later speculated that he had been a silversmith and a counterfeiter and that, having been discovered, he was forced to relinquish his commission. Whether that loss of position or the accusations of crime provoked his violent behavior was, of course, unclear. Reports agreed that Bruleman left his lodgings on Wednesday, August 27, looking for a fight.

Several accounts, including the one in HCS's diary, reported that Robert Skull made a good shot at billiards, whereupon Bruleman declared "I will show you a fine stroke" and, pulling out a pistol, fired twice.[31] Skull lingered for several painful days, during which he reportedly forgave his attacker. Bruleman said that he "had been tired of his life for some time, but could not kill himself, and so chose that way . . . knowing blood would be required for blood." HCS's diary indicates

29. HCS, December 10, 1759. The title "Dictator" did not then have the negative connotations the term acquired in the twentieth century.

30. Jack D. Marietta and G. S. Rowe, *Troubled Experiment: Crime and Justice in Pennsylvania, 1682–1800* (Philadelphia: University of Pennsylvania Press, 2006), table 2.2, 36, quotation 170.

31. HCS, August 27, 1760; *The Pennsylvania Gazette,* September 4, 1760.

that he asked men on the scene to kill him with his own pistol, but they took him to the jail instead. Bruleman was reputed to have said to Skull after the shooting, "Sir, I had no malice no ill-will against you, I never saw you before, but I was determined to kill somebody, that I might be hanged, and you happen to be the man.... I am very sorry for your misfortune."[32] Self-murder by the authorities was his goal. This is the practice now colloquially known as "suicide by cop."

HCS was much affected. She wrote of seeing Bruleman brought to jail, "bound like a Malefector." To think that he had been "some parent['s] early hope but now, alas, there latter grief."[33] More than a month later, on October 8, Bruleman was executed. He got his wish. By that time the horror of his crime had been surpassed by another.

Not four weeks after Skull's murder, another homicide occurred, this one in the bosom of the Quaker community. HCS spent September 22 much as she had many days—in visiting and, she reflected, "in Innocense of Conversation, and that blindness which Gracious Providence has been pleased to afford poor Mortals with regard to the events of futurity!" Friends had just left the Callenders' house when "Jos: Howell come in haste & enquired for Israel Pemberton telling Daddy that Joseph Jordan had stabed Thomas Kirbride in the belly, and he was dead." Dramatic details followed. Jordan had "come home very drunk and abusive" while everyone but Sarah Pemberton was out. She quickly fled. Thomas Kirkbride was persuaded to enter the house to entreat with Jordan. The two men struggled and Jordan stabbed Kirkbride. "Thus," wrote Hannah, "in one moment fell the flower of our City."[34]

Kirkbride's death was stunning, and "Josey" Jordan's actions more so. Shocking as the fatal Bruleman-Scull encounter was, this murder hit much closer to home. HCS had socialized with both Kirkbride and Jordan. The developing relationship between Jordan and HCS's good friend Sarah ("Sally") Pemberton seemed to suggest that they would marry. Discussions of Jordan's reputation for temper and bad behavior indicated, however, at least some hesitancy—though it was unclear whether it was Sally's family or Sally herself who was concerned.[35]

War and murder in the 1760s further shattered hopes for a Quakerly peaceable kingdom in Pennsylvania, but the language of sensibility and the bonds of sociability helped HCS and others through these crises. Unknown to HCS and her fellow Quakers, these events in 1760 only served as prologue to the prolonged violence, conflicted loyalties, and loss of influence of the American Revolution.

32. *Boston Evening Post,* November 3, 1760.

33. HCS, August 27, 1760.

34. September 22, 1760 (old doc).

35. In 1762 Mary Pemberton married Samuel Pleasants; her sister Sarah married Samuel Rhoads in 1765. *Diary of Elizabeth Drinker,* 3:2197. These two young women were the daughters of Israel and Sarah Kirkbride Pemberton.

The Meaning of Sociability in an Often Violent World

For HCS, sociability came as naturally as breathing. Scholars of the eighteenth century have seen the emergence of sensibility, a new way of articulating social concerns and social relationships, as a critical aspect of a developing modern world that was increasingly individualistic, urban, commercial, and governed by complex class divisions. We will learn, in the chapters to come, how deeply HCS invested in the ethos of sensibility. But sociability was a necessary precursor to sensibility. The premium placed on ways of encountering others appropriately gave HCS and the people around her a purchase on themselves and their world, a world filled with political, military, social, and personal dangers. Sociability was not just a way of navigating tea parties and conversation, it was also the engine for political and intellectual exchange as well as for courtship. Further, in the especially heated and violent environment of the 1758–1760 period, it provided a mechanism for discussing and coping with the nature and the parameters of community.

Chapter 2

The Diary: January 1758–August 1761

[January 1, 1758]

A Memorandom Book, from the 1ˢᵗ Day of the Year 1758, 1ᵗʰ day of the first Month and 1ˢᵗ of the Week,[1] for my own Satisfaction, and to try to see if a Retrospect of my time, may not make me husband it more.

1 Mo.	1 Day Morn: went to Meeting, Benjamin. Trotter spoke, too loud, Daniel Stanton prayed, did not go in the after noon, see a great many People walking outside, wish people woud think it more their duty, to go to some place of Worship that day. went in the evening, D. Stanton, J. Tasker spoke.
2	Morn: at work, afternoon, with P. Ritche went to N. Gibson's, spent it in agreable Conversation.
3	Morn: went to meeting, a rainy Day, stayed at home the rest of it.
4	Morn: at home busey, afternoon went to B. Rawles.
5	Morn: Ironing, afternoon, my two little Cousins Lightfoot to see me.
6	Morn: three O Clock waked, by J. Howel calling on Mamme to go with him to Caty,[2] but mamme had a bad cold and did not go, after break fast I went to see her and found her brave,[3] [she had] a fine Girl, called Caty, went from there to Becky's, talked about some irregularities in

---

1. Sunday. HCS employed the Quaker system of numbering the days of the week beginning with Sunday. She also often preceded the day of the week with the month of the year. Thus, "1 mo. 2 morn." would be a Monday morning in January.

2. Caty Howell, who was in labor.

3. *Brave* or *bravely* meant well, healthy, strong.

the conduct of Neighbour Ritchie. wished her to grow better, came home and worked till after Diner, then went there again, staid to supper.

7   all the day agreably spent in work and talk with my Parents.

1 Day   Morn: went to meeting, B. Trotter & E. White spoke, and D. Stanton prayed, afterward gave us some good advice on keeping the hour, and presenting ourselves to worship, the obligations on our side for Health and its adequate blessings, being beyond our comprehension, as much the benignity of God. afternoon, at meeting J Tasker spoke, come hear afterwards with several other friends, evening went to meeting, J. Tasker, and J Churchman spoke, J. Churchman prayed, (am affraid we have some young Coquets)

2   Morn: at work, afternoon the same, evening some advice given me by Daddy, not to spend my sentiments too freely, either on men or things, but let Judgement ripen, a resolution for the futer to try for amendment, Able. James there.

3   Morn: some things not very agreable, went to meeting. J. Churchman spoke, after ward a letter from D Smith comical anough, company in the afternoon. Elizabeth Sandwith and I thought to have translated in the evening but company hindered, wish our design of improveing one another in the french may not drop.

4   Morn: wrote to D Smith, a poor miserable creature came hear for Charity! How thankful. O thou Being Omnipotent, am I, that thou has cast the Lot of my humanity in a sort so much better, give me a heart susceptable of others woe: wrote to Sally rest of the day hard at work.

5.   Morn: at meeting D Stanton, H Hulfered, M Emblen, and J Churchman spoke. Sukey Loyd much too flipant, afternoon Neighbour Warner hear, finished my green Chair Cushin.————7 O Clock evening. a fine Night the Moon just appearing in the horrison— glances into my Chamber, the evening star sparkling above it. serenity, inclines me to think of its auther, and those admirable luminaries, made, like him, to shine on the evil and on the good. let this teach us compassion on our fellow creatures who have fallen thro' folly or inadvertancies. keep me as in the hollow of thy hand O Lord.[4]

6   Morn: at Work, afternoon and evening at Catys, P. Howel there, conversation run on Courtship and the ridiculous behavior of some People in it.

7   Morn: Work and wrote to B. Smith by her Brother Bobby, afternoon at Becky's.

---

4. Isaiah 40:12.

1 Day. Morn: at meeting B.T. and J Tasker spoke, A. Pole dined with me, afternoon at meeting DS preached and prayed. afterward some talk of Anna's unhappy Brother.

2 Morn: at work. a rainy Day, afternoon and evening Company, a great deal of talk on liars and calumniators, wish there were fewer, Individuals constitute a whole, a resolution to avoid those evils.

3 Morn: at meeting H. Williams and —————Easter spoke. afternoon with anna Pole at some shops, afterward at P Pemberton's: the three girls, king Tedeuskung,[5] and myself, all the company. evening Polly and I to see P Hill, found her very poorly.

4 Morn: at work, afternoon P Ritche hear, talked of the inconstancy of female friendships. 7 O'Clock evening, just returned from a walk to Nan Gibsons, thought on the many visits of form,[6] they lay under a sort of obligation (in their opinion) to pay, which will take up more of one's thoughts than perhaps we are aware of at the time.

5 Morn: at meeting M. Emblen, E Steavens, H Hulfred spoke. afternoon PP. and myself to see the hills, a fine company of Girls, It must be very agreable s[ight] so many of them together. evening at Catys.

to day 6 Morn: very agreably spent in work, and conversation with mamme. afternoon the same.

7 Morn: Riche Smith hear, or one that calls himself so: all day at work at my Piece.[7] Evening Betsey hear translateing the Oeconemy of human life.[8]

1 Day Morn: at home, employed in writing and reading. afternoon at meeting W Brown prayed.

2 Morn: at the Burial of Becky Lewes. younger than myself afternoon at work at my peice.

5. Teedyuscung was the head of an important Delaware clan that had originally lived on the edge of the Kittatiny Mountains, near what is now Nazareth and Bethlehem, but had moved west to the Susquehanna River. He had been baptized by the Moravians in 1750 but by 1756 "had little trust 'in the words of white people.'" In early 1758, he was engaged in diplomacy among the English, the Delaware, the Ohio peoples, and the Iroquois. William Callender, as a trustee of the Friendly Association for Regaining and Preserving Peace with the Indians by Pacific Measures since its founding in December 1756, was another component of these negotiations. See Jane T. Merritt, *At the Crossroads: Indians and Empires on a Mid-Atlantic Frontier, 1700–1763* (Chapel Hill: University of North Carolina Press, 2003), passim, quotation 210; Jeffrey L. Scheib, "William Callender," in Craig Horle et al., *Lawmaking and Legislators in Pennsylvania: A Biographical Dictionary, Volume Two, 1710–1756* (Philadelphia: University of Pennsylvania Press, 1997), 259; and Anthony F. C. Wallace, *King of the Delawares: Teedyuscung, 1700–1763* (1949; repr. Syracuse: Syracuse University Press, 1990).

6. Visits of form: according to etiquette, most formal visits generated an obligation to return the visit, which often became quite time-consuming. Part of the function of this diary was to keep track of who visited whom.

7. HCS's "piece," an elaborate embroidered portrayal of a lion, has apparently not survived.

8. Robert Dodsley, *The Oeconomy of Human Life. Translated from an Indian manuscript, written by an ancient Bramin* (1751)

3 Morn: at work at my peice. afternoon, Becky, her mother, Spouse and child, an agreable afternoon. 6 O'Clock evening just set down to read and work.

4 the Day spent agreably at home with work, I am thankful, that I am not so great a burthen to myself, as that I cant enjoy myself alone.

5 all Day at work at my peice. evening at Catys. Jos: at New York, memorable events at the State House.

6 at Work at my peice.

7 at Work at my peice. evening at Warners, translateing with Betsey.

1 Day Morn: at meeting, B T. spoke, afternoon at meeting, afterward at Catys with Company, evening at meeting S Morris, H Williams spoke.

2 all day at work at my Peice. evening at Beckys spent pleasently in work & talk.

3 at Work at my peice, evening writeing.

[February 1, 1758]

2 Mo 4 Morn: at Work, afternoon Polly Shoot hear, this day some disagreable accidents happened in a branch of the Smith family that I much respect. Learn to bear all things with acqueasence. says some auther. evening writeing Copy of a letter from Ireland giving an account of the Death of Molly Peasely Who as she lived a Christian life, departed in a well grounded expectation of the Crown of Christian warfare, Life eternal.

[In margin: "the first Spring Month."]

5 at Work at my piece.

6 at Work at my peice, evening at Work, wrote to P Morris.

7 at Work at my peice. an agreable surprise in the sight of Polly M. evening at Warners translateing l'Economie de la Vie Humaine.

1 Day Morn: just now gone, by James Hambleton for New York thence to England. at meeting H Williams spoke. P Morris dined with me. afternoon at meeting, HW. and DT spoke, with Nancy Gibson at her Mamme's, talk on various branches of female folly, evening at meeting HW. Spoke, A Widdow Feild spoke

2 at Work at my peice, evening at Beckys, read in the first mag: that S——h[9] began to show himself in.

9. *The American Magazine, or Monthly Chronicle* (October 1757–October 1758) was edited by the Rev. William Smith. He was extremely critical of the Quakers and of the French. See Frank Luther Mott, *A History of American Magazines, 1741–1850* (Cambridge, MA: Harvard University Press, 1939), vol. I, 80–82.

3   morn: at meeting, it being youths meeting, SM, J Tasker, DS, WB. spoke, went home with AP, we spent the afternoon pleasently, evening at Catys, PH there, Conversation, work and book, an agreable evening

4   at Work at my peice, and now evening writeing ————and so my days pass swift as a weavers shuttle,[10] our Time (when truly understood)

Is the most precious earthly good.[11]

5   Morn: at Work at my peice, apres midi:[12] Betsey Sandwith hear, drawing some things for me, evening translateing. she is a girl of good sense: on the choice of Company, in all ages, there has been great stress laid, I think some auther says: something like this, on the choice of thy company depends thy good or bad conduct in life.

6   All day at Work at my peice, evening reading to Daddy & Mamme some of S: Crisps sermons,[13] I think them very good ones,

7   Morn: at Work at my peice, afternoon the same, wrote to Sally, evening at Warners very pleasent a good many of the family there.

1 Day   Morn: at home on account of family: A beautiful day: in thy mercy give us hearts to deserve thy manifold favours. ————afternoon at meeting, evening at meeting DS prayed, JT spoke.

2   at Work at my piece.

3   at Work at my peice. Sally Morris hear at dinner. a worthy woman:

4   at Work at my peice.

5   at Work at my peice.

6   Ironing.

7   Morn: wrote to Sally, at work, afternoon work, evening read to mam.

1 Day   Morn: at home, afternoon at meeting, Thomas Bullard spoke, When the Judgements of the Lord are in the Earth, the inhabitents thereof learn Righteousness,[14] went to Catys, company there, conversation on politicks, evening at meeting, T B., HW., ————Easter, and D Stanton spoke, the latter desired us on a very good manner, to think of mortality, none being; to there knowledge, exempt from the sudden stroke of it:

2   Morn: at Work with my Mamme. afternoon at Work at my peice.

3   Morn: a letter from Sally, great is the joy, or innate satisfaction in hear-

---

10. Job 7:6.
11. Written over erasure.
12. Apres midi: Fr., afternoon.
13. Samuel Crisp, *Christ Alone Exalted in Dr. Crisp's Sermons* (1693).
14. Isaiah 26:9.

ing from a friend one loves. went to meeting DS., ME., HH., & James Tasker spoke, all in an extraordinary manner, James, gave a sermon, the Truth & sentiments, of which I hope, the curtain of my last hour may be drawn up by: went to the interment of an honest man, our neighbour at point[-no-point]: every honest man is a loss to the community; where of he is: afternoon, Dr Evans hear, talking of england, a place for which I seem to feel a sort of filial reverance: my mother Country! evening at Caty's, none but she and I, "the Conversation of a friend brightens the eyes" a pretty metaphor, intimateing that when the heart is glad it cant but brighten the countenance of the person.

4   Morn: at Work, afternoon agreable, with Molly Foulk & her Daughter. 'tis in part as the saying is: education makes the man, or in the younger years however, it is in the power of parents to do a great deal for their childrens benifit when older. see Ned Phisick wished him joy ie Ab: Sing.[15]

5   Morn: received a letter from Betsey, some thoughts of going to B——n.[16] poor girl I wish it was, more than it is, in my power to console her! at meeting, B T., H H., DS., H W., & Easter spoke. afternoon at Sally Stanton's. from that house, has dropt one of my youthful Acquaintance. evening, at Anna Poles, Hannah Hudson there; too much of the family failing, a certain stifness, or form, not agreable in —————— when it enters, either, in company or conversation.

6   Morn: at Work, afternoon, A. James hear, some men take great liberty in laughing at the Women, however, not being clear of failings themselves, and in a general way, we getting the right side of them; make me think of an old saying "let them laugh that Wins."

7   morn: at Work at my peice, afternoon at Becky's, E——d P——k there, talk of dispariety of years, in relation to marriage, such as 25 to 40, unanimus 15 too much: it was occasioned by the proposeals of marriage made yesterday between B.S. & SB.[17]

1 Day   Morn: at meeting, DS. and BT. spoke. afternoon, at meeting H W. ——sharp evening at: meeting, DS. spoke and prayed for our gracious King George.

2   Morn: at work at my peice, see the disconsolate Widdow of melchor, afternoon Neighbour Stiles & Polly hear,

3   Morn: at Work at my peice, read in Pope's Letters,[18] afternoon, went

15. Abigail Syng and NP are to be married.
16. B——n is HCS's shorthand for Burlington, New Jersey, home of many of her mother's family and site, every other year, of the Friend's regional Yearly Meeting.
17. She was twenty-six and he forty; see entry of May 1, 1758.
18. Anon., *A Collection of Letters, Never Before Printed; Written by Alexander Pope, Esq; and Other Ingenius Gentlemen* (1751).

to Sam Noble's, the Barracks a fine Building, raised by Loyal Subjects. yet cant help wishing there had never been occasion for them, thinking it a most glorious and precious Proclamation, given at the comeing of the greatest Prince on earth, "glory to God on high, peace on earth and good will towards all men."[19]

[March 1, 1758]

3 Mo 4   Morn: at Work, went to Stiles, got a new recruit of that fine invention Pens, heard of the Death of the Arch Street Beauty! been married about a year, with her first child, supposed to be fright, for as soon as she was taken in Labour, was taken in convulsion fitts, held till she died. this afternoon have thoughts of setting out for B——n. Anna Watson and I had a pleasant Passage, arrived at Burlington eight o'Clock in the evening; walked by myself uptown. I have seen in part, and heard of quieter days, nights of peacefuler slumbers; hear in B——n, as well as the rest of my poor Country! War. tis one of the Almighty's smaller chastisements.

5   Morn: hear have my Ancestors lived in quiet, hear part of them lie, "in the House appointed for all liveing."[20] went to Meeting. afternoon, at work at my Peice, took a run with Edward to Cousin John's, found a full Councel: in that House, I have past many happy hours; in my Peruile amusements. Elizabeth Smith, Daughter of the Worthy Rich: Smith, a Woman of great Sweetness of Temper, and Affability of Manners, sobriety, blest with Good sense, Religion without sourness, or austerity, now a Maiden about thirty, always has been, and still remains to be, of use in the Creation, by reason of a Prudent Conduct, with her I had the Happiness, of passing some of my youthful days, and the pleasure of seeing, still at times may heaven Continue the blessing.

6   Morn: Breakfasted with Unkle Joseph & family. at Work at my Peice, afternoon, Dan: come from Phila:, Daddy and Mamme well, evening Seaman, hear, a Gentleman that remembers the transactions of his youth so well, as to repeat them over and over, occasioned by a defect in his memory.

7   Morn: an agreable Walk with Sally, all nature carries a sort of solemn Gaiety in Her aspect: afternoon, Cousin Betty called for us, and we went down to Edward Cathrels, an agreable Conversation enjoying and enjoyed by one another, one of the most exalted faculties of the Human Nature giveing and receiveing Pleasure.

1 Day   Morn: at Meeting A. Large spoke, dined at Edwards, afternoon at Cousin Sam: Smith's, Jenny Burlen there, lately left a Second time a

19. Luke 2:14.
20. Job 30:23.

Widow, and in a suden manner, Death often surpries us, by the fall of those in the nearest connections to us:

2   Morn: at Meeting Two Couple passed, one Stacia Potts: John Churchman spoke, Sally and I at home.

3   Morn: worked dilligently at my Peice, afternoon, went to see Nanny French.

4   Morn: at Work at my Peice, poor Unkle Robert hear, strugling under difficulties. afternoon, at Work at my Peice.

5   Morn: at Meeting A L. spoke, went home with Cousin John, Caleb Barker there, 'Tis a most melancholy thing, the Sight of a Person robed of his Reason,

All Death's all Tortures in one pang combined,
Are gentle to the Tempest of the mind.' Thompson[21]

to Day 6   Morn: a Letter from Mamme, at Work at my Peice, afternoon, part out, in a Walk with Cousin Mary Noble, to some poor Folks houses, in one Four old Women, who put me in mind of that paper of the Spectator,[22] which treats of them, in the Vulgar notion, of age and infirmity constituteing them Witches but in reality the time when, "the Grasshopper shall become a burthen, and desire shall fail, because Man goeth to his long home, and the mourners go about the Streats."[23]

7   At work at My Peice, evening wrote to Mamme.

1 Day   Morn: a very fine one, worship thou the Deity, in holy Truth, for his manyfold Favours to thee. went to Meeting, AL. spoke. Sally and I spent the Afternoon, agreably with Cousin Jenny Burlen. evening at home, Sally read in the *Art of Contentment.*[24]

2   Morn at Work at my Peice, afternoon, Hannah Cathrel come to see us, much diverted with some insidents that happened. took a run in the evening.

3   Morn: at Work at my peice, afternoon R: Smith gave me an account of the strange perfidy of John Wormly to Polly Peck.

4   Morn at Work at my Peice. afternoon at Eliza: Barker's, the time spent in pleaseing talk of our Childish amusements: happy days when, nor care for to morrow, nor deep sorrow at today, touches the heart! the least bittered part of Life, tho' perhaps, it may not have so refined a relish of enjoyments as riper years.

5   Morn: at meeting, dined at JN, see the utmost stupifaction in a branch

21. James Thompson, *The Tragedy of Sophonisba* (London, 1730).
22. Joseph Addison, "A Village Witch," *The Spectator,* no. 117, July 14, 1711.
23. Ecclesiastes 12:5.
24. Possibly John Pulleyn, *The Art of Contentment. A Sermon Preached at St. Swithen's Church* (1701).

of the Family. (JS) spends his days ingloriously with a Woman of no Character, without any other care, but to please her; at the expence of his Friends esteem, and the Worlds respect.

6   Morn: a Walk to hinder our seeing the execution of cruelty on two Soldiers, Afternoon Company, evening a walk, Abby Smith with us, no part of our Lives so critical for our behaviour, as the point of time between Girl and Woman.

> *send the fluttering soul abroad,*
> *praised for her shape, her mien,*
> *The Little Godess and the queen.*

all the follies of the one without the prudence of the other. Then is the time we have need of the Maternal care.

7   Morn at Work at my Peice, afternoon Company, John Lawrence is a good humoured man but was not bred at Court, Complasency and an easey behaviour in company is a great addition to a Person.

1 Day   Morn: at Meeting Sam: Notingham spoke. I was almost ready to think, to some of my Cousins, "scease to do Evil, and thou shalt Learn to do well."[25] afternoon Company.

2   Morn: out paying several Visits, wrote to Mamme by Isreal Pembertons express. afternoon Unkle Robert and Danny come to town, who' ne'ar new affliction hardly knows deeply enough to simpathise with the afflicted, one of the most exalted Capacities of the Mind.

3   Morn: Eight O'Clock. Edward Cathrel and I set out on Horseback for Phila:d got to Coopers by Eleven, there took my leave with thanks, to him for as pleasent a jant, as I have had, crossed the River, and was again happy in the sight of my Parents, may Heaven continue the Blessing long as the breath they gave. afternoon Ironing. evening. Ben: Sweat hear, passed in talk of the Religion; Heaven born Maid that only sooths the Soul to Peace, amid the rufling tumults of a vain vexing World:

4   Morn: at Work, afternoon bought Silk for a Watch String for Edward Cathrel, went to Becky Rawle's, left Mamme alone—wont do so again. This Night between ten and Eleven a small Shock of an Earth quake, how awful O Death is the thought of thee! at short warning, to us poor Mortals. leave not thy self at his mercy, but prepare thyself for the final hour.

5   day. Busy.

6   Day. Busy. evening Cousin Betty come from Burlington.

25. Isaiah 1:16–17.

7   Morn: finished Edwards Watch String and presented it to him. after-
           noon Company from Shrewsbury. Cousin Molly Brown. (note mamme
           says my Letters to her shoud be wrote with more ease.)

1 Day   Morn: our Spring Meeting. at Meeting Eliza: Morris and Eliza: Shiply
           spoke, the latter in a an extraordinary manner, she is a Person of a fair
           Character, and acquits herself well in the Ministry, afternoon, at meet-
           ing James Tasker spoke, some friends from Egg Harbour, Ann Gant a
           fine Woman, shines in the Neighbourly and Domestick Sphere.
           evening Zachary Faress spoke.

2   Morn: at meeting William Horn spoke, afternoon at home with my
           Friends

3   Morn: at meeting JT: spoke, Thus ended our Spring meeting, in a peace-
           able manner, afternoon to see Nancy Drinker, Betsey Sandwith and I
           [had] some talk about the King of Prussia, a greater Hero than history
           affords an account of, and our Royal Family, the Princess Caroline dead!
           eveing Polly Morris & I spent very agreably with Pope's translation of
           the *Satires of Horace,*[26] "and beguiled the hours" with further talk

4   Morn: Company, afternoon Polly Morris and I, Docter Moor's, Peggy
           Hill surpriseingly recovered, from a consumption by Sucking of Breast
           Milk,[27] a large Company of us, one of them the Widow Richardson.
           a little time with Caty, returned home spent the evening agreably with
           mamme and Cousin Betty.

5   Morn: at Meeting Sally Morris spoke, Abby Smith come home with me
           and spent the rest of the day, evening, Fire, an awful Cry.

6   Morn: at meeting Cousin Betty Smith spoke, Beulah Shoemaker, passd
           the meeting the 2nd time with Sam: Burge. afternoon Cousin Johan-
           nah Brooks, Lidia Noble, and Patty Noble drank Tea with me.

[April, 1758]

4 Mo 7   Morn: out a walking, noon cousin Hannah Smith and Betty left us for
           Burlington, Abby and I went to see the State House thence to Nancy
           Gibson's, some talk of Petit Maitres,[28] called to see Mary Armitt.

1 Day   Morn: some Items from Daddy to kirb my spirit, went to meeting B T.
           spoke, afternoon went to meeting BT. spoke. went to see my early
           Friend and youthful Companion Grace Allison who had just come to
           town. evening at meeting, BT & DS. spoke.

---

26. Alexander Pope, *The First Satire of the Second Book of Horace* (1733), and related publications.

27. Breastmilk was sometimes used as a medicine. Margaret Hill Morris would become widely known for her medical skills; see Margaret Morris, *Private Journal Kept During the Revolutionary War* (1838; repr. New York: Arno, 1969); and Margaret Morris, *Gardening Memorandum,* ed. Nancy V. Webster and Clarissa F. Dillon (Chillicothe, IL: American Botanist, 1996).

28. "Little masters," that is, haughty men.

2 Morn: writeing, Sally Pemberton, ~~and~~ ———— Abby Smith, and
    I, at Shops, SP a talkative Girl. afternoon at Work at my Peice, Neigh-
    bour Brooks hear, evening Grace & Polly Allison hear.

3 Morn: at meeting BT & DS spoke, a weding, afternoon Patty Noble
    hear. evening at JH.

4 Morn: writeing, wrote to Betsey, afternoon at G. Allison's, a Coxcomb
    there, one of the most disagreable things in nature.

Monkeys in action, Peroquets in talk
They are crowned with feathers like the cock a too
And like camelions daily change there hue.

5 Morn: 8 O'clock mamme set out with a fair Wind for Burlington, rest
    of the day at Work. evening Nancy Gibson and Polly Ritchie.

6 day at work at my peice. afternoon Becky Rawles come for me to go
    home with her. went. Becky Cooper is a good humoured, sensible girl,

7 Morn: at Work wrote to mamme, Betsey Sandwith, afternoon Polly
    Ritchie, Nancy Warner drank tea with me.

1 Day Morn: at meeting W: Brown spoke, Company at Diner, afternoon at
    meeting

2 Morn: paid several running visits. afternoon Jos: Noble from Burling-
    ton. a letter from Mamme. at Work at my peice. Polly Sandwith hear.
    the Men as soon as married seem as tho' they had got rid of a heavy
    burthen, and in short some think they may take greater Liberties in
    Conversation than before. evening began the History of England by
    Rapin.[29]

3 Morn: out on business, went to meeting, HW. DS spoke. afternoon
    Widow Ball and Nancy Gibson to see me. evening read in the *History.*

4 Morn: at Work, went to see Nancy Drinker. noon Mamme and Cousin
    Sally arrieved from B———n. Anna Pole hear.

5 Morn: talk of going to Duck Creek. went to Chester on our way, in
    company with Dan: Ofly and his wife, Will: Cliften, Jos: Fisher [and]
    his Daughter, and John Loydd & Sally dined at Bivens that night went
    as far as Wilmington at Jos: Littlers, lodged at D Faress.

6 Morn: as far as the Red Lyon Tavern, dined and Just after we had set
    out again, fell into a small run of Water off my horse, but did myself
    no damage, except the spoiling of my new gown. a great Mercy as I
    think, got within twelve miles of Duck creek. lodged at Dan: Corbet's.
    see the Widow Dyers house but coud not go to see her.

7 Morn: rode to Duck Creek Monthly Meeting, Mary Emblen spoke,

29. M. Paul Rapin de Thoyras, *The History of England, as well Ecclesiastical as Civil* (1730).

went to Michael Ofley's. good livers for that part of the country, and cleaver sort of people, was at Thomas Hammon's too.

1 Day	Morn: rode to meeting. Thomas Reynolds, Mary Emblen, and John Loyd spoke, went home with Michael.
2	Morn: rode to meeting. see a young woman I knew in Philadelphia, Peggy Emson, went to William Phersons, lodged there.
3	Morn: went with Sally some miles below Duck creek to See her Aunt Jude Chicken, an ancient Woman. passed thro a town called the cross roads return to Mich: Ofly's and lodged.
to Day 4	Morn: set out on our way home with DO and Wife, WC, Sally and I. went over Apoquimony bridge, a beautiful prospect of the country from the adjacent Hills, baited at Skulls, dined at the Red Lyon, rid thro' New Castle, see the girls of my acquaintance there, got to Wilmington. lodged at Faress's, see and had some conversation, with a woman friend who had been to Winchester, on a visit to the Soldiery, Martha Harress, and some miles further back, in the Country, where she met with a People hardly having, a knowledge of the Deity or Jesus Christ his son, but before she left them, they seemed to be engaged in a search after eternal Life.
5	Morn: rode to Chester Dined at Copeland's, on the road met with a poor Sailer that had been pressed on board a sloop of war, that lay at the capes, who seemed almost affraid of his own shadow. John Armit come with us from chester. in the evening see myself safe arrived in my fathers house.
6	Agreably spent at Plantation with Daddy, Mamme, and Sally
7	Morn: busy. after Diner Sally, Bil Morris, and I, set out for John Morris's, arrived there, just in the evening, all nature mending on us as we come along, made the surprise of Seeing that Earthly Paradise rather less strikeing to us. the situation naturally is so fine that what little helps it may have received from art and culture has made it, perhaps as fine a plain gentleman's country seat as any extent in our Province.
1 Day	Morn: rode to meeting spoke. dined at JM where there was a chearful friendly welcome, which made our time agreable, till three O'Clock, when we set out for Philadelphia, but half past 5, went to meeting, Ann more, and Samuel Spavald spoke.
2	Morn: writeing, went to see Nancy Drinker, and helped her down stairs the first time, for 5 weeks, having had a tedious illness. afternoon Grace Allison and I spent in agreable work and talk, went to Sally at DO's, to tommy lightfoots, and at home the rest of the evening,
3	Morn: at Meeting SP and AM spoke, Company at Diner, afternoon

Sally and I at Becky's, Caty moveing into Front Street, an agreable evening at home.

4   Morn: 9 O'Clock. Tommy and Sally set out for B——n, at Work at my Piece, SP and Joshua Emblen hear. afternoon at Work at my Peice. John Reynold.

5   Morn: at meeting SP spoke, "beware of the leven of the Pharisse, which is Hypocrisy."[30] afternoon at Nancy Mitchels, evening at Catys.

6   Morn: at Work at my Peice, reading in the History, finished my Strawberry Poket book. drank Tea with Nancy Drinker. evening read in the Histo: coud wish with all my heart the sex gave less proofs of there passion, for Red coats.[31] as far as I have observed, people seldom take warning, by anothers harms, thinking bought experience is the best. but it may be bought too dear.

7   at Work at my Peice, evening Polly Morris hear, a sorrowful accident happened to the Syng family, John Syng going into a valt with a lighted Candle, it catched fire, to a vapour, which flew up and burnt his face, and disordered his senses!

1 Day Morn: at home, Company to Diner, afternoon at meeting, Eliza: Morgan, and SP, spoke, drank tea at Catys with Polly Morris and Anna Pole, evening at meeting Ellis Hugh John Loyd, and D Stanton spoke,

[May 1, 1758]

5 Mo 2 Morn: at meeting Mary Lightfoot, Ellis Hugh, and Sarah Morris spoke, news of Abraham Farington's decease in London, from Jersey on a visit to England, afternoon at the Widow Edwards to see Betsey, called at Bekys, just come from paying a bride visit to Beaulah Burge, just entering on the Scene of Life, he at forty, she Six & twenty.

[In margin: "the first summer month:"]

3   Morn: youths meeting Ellis Hugh, Sam: Spavald, and D Stanton spoke. afternoon at Warners, Rachel and Peggy Hill there, an agreable time,

4   day at Work at my Peice,

5   Morn: at meeting BT, and Joice Benezet spoke, afternoon at A P and N Gibson's. gave her my Strawberry poket book, evening read in Crisp.

6   Morn: makeing a bonet for Mamme, afternoon, Polly & Betsey Sandwith and Rachel & Peggy Hill drank Tea with me. poor Nancy Drinker

---

30. Luke 12:1.
31. British Army officers.

in a low condition. the lot of some Peoples Humanity much harder to bear than others, one of the Blessing's, "Blessed are they that comfort the Afflicted."[32] John Syng dead.

1 Day	Morn: at meeting DS spoke, Edith Doughty hear, a letter from Sally, afternoon, at home, went to Neighbour Samsons, a good old friend there, Mary Night who gave Polly, Betsey, and I some salutary advice, evening went to meeting SP spoke, very well on the government of the Tongue, and prayed in as strong terms for us, as I ever remember to have heard,
2	Morn: at work at my Peice, afternoon Mamme went to plantation, Anna Pole hear, went to Polly Shoots. these wretches, the Men, say we are like the Mackerel caught by a red rag![33] evening Company.
3	Morn: at meeting BT, SP spoke. afternoon at Work, Cousin John, wrote to Sally by him. afternoon at work.
4	Morn: Daddy and I, went to Point-no-point, a very pleasent day there, mam come home in the evening,
5	day Ironing,
6	Morn: Ironing, afternoon, walking and reading, Daddy come for me and we went in the evening.
7	Morn: at Work, a good old Woman dined hear, Ann Scofeild, afternoon at Becky's, several Vessels from England, called at Catys.
1 Day	Morn: at meeting, Mary Night spoke, afternoon at meeting S:P Spoke, come hear after meeting with Is: Pem: great differences now about among friends, as well as others, Oh my poor Native Land! how art thou torn and rent by Civil Commotions.[34] evening at meeting, where SP took leave of us for his eastern Journey, desireing us to repeat no greviences, forget all that was past and come to a reconsiliation. I think he seems to be a man sent us with invitations of Peace and Reconsiliation, to God, and one another.
2	Morn: at Work at my Peice, afternoon at Mary Armitts with Mamme. evening at Catys, English Mag: the Princes Caroline's Will,[35] short and so well done as I coud have wished, an English Princes's.

32. Matthew 5:7.

33. The red coats of British Army officers.

34. Israel Pemberton and William Callender were usually allies, having both served in the Pennsylvania Assembly and having resigned together in protest of the war. They cofounded the Friendly Association for Regaining and Preserving Peace with the Indians by Pacific Measures in December 1756. By the late 1750s, factions had formed within the organization, with Pemberton was on one side and Callender on the other (see entry of January 2, 1759). By 1758, Pemberton and Callender would also split over the issue of slavery. Pemberton "had less interest in abolitionism," while Callender was an associate of radical abolitionist Anthony Benezet. Jean R. Soderlund, *Quakers and Slavery: A Divided Spirit* (Princeton: Princeton University Press, 1985), 140, 170.

35. Princess Caroline of Great Britain died December 28, 1757.

3   Morn: at Work at my peice, Ann Scofeild hear, went to meeting, Alex: Seaton, DS, HW, and A Scofeild spoke. afternoon, Ann relateing some of her Travel's in New England, to mamme and I, there must be something which the World knows not of, to bear peoples minds up in difficulties so great, as those traveling friends sometimes go thro'. wrote to betsey. at Work, evening stept to see Jos: Stiles [who has] got the gout badly, talked of Sir Charles Grandison, Harriot and his Sisters, three fine Characters.[36]

4   Morn finished grounding my Lyon Peice, the Weather and the human Frame, somewhat resemble one another, at morn. the Sun shone fine and clear, before noon interveaning Clouds, rain, and Sun Shine. ———————— afternoon, finished flowering my flowered queen stich poket book, Nancy hear.

5   day Morn: at Work, and reading in the History, afternoon at Catys,

6   Morn: little Work, out at shops, bought me a China sugar dish, a couple of little stoneware plates, afternoon at Becky's, evening reading,

7   Morn: at Work, finshed the first Vol: of the History, rest of the Day at Work, evening begun the second Vol: of the History.

1 Day   Morn: at meeting Mary Night spoke, afternoon Nancy Drinker brought abed of a dead child, evening Betsey Sandwith hear, moral discourse, on several points:

> *What'er your Age would reap, your youth should sow,*
> *For the great sead time of your Life is now;*[37]

to Day 2 Morn: at Work, and reading in the History, afternoon at Work, poor Nancy Drinker, they say women have nine lives, but it seems as if she must almost have the tenth, to live.

3   Morn: at Nancy's and home the day, out in the evening at 8 O'Clock she departed, after a long and tedious illness, thro' which she behaved with great calmness, and resignation. in the bloom of her days, Three & Twenty years and Three months, lacking some days, she was of a mild disposition, had a guard on her tongue, that it uttered not folly, this was her whole conduct since an acquaintance with each other, of almost half our age, it gives me a satisfaction, in the full assurance and hope of Jesus Christ, that she is ever lastingly Happy.

4   Morn: at Nancy's, the scene how different from about this time last year, married. (the fourth of this month,) receiving the gratulations of her Acquaintance! now a cold corps, with them weeping round her. Oh Time, how thou shifts thy scenes,

36. Samuel Richardson, *The History of Sir Charles Grandison. In a Series of Letters* (1753).
37. Samuel Wesley, "A Letter from a Guardian to a Young Lady," (Cambridge, 1743).

The Pleasures which the smileing day,
With large right hand bestows,
Shortly, her left conveys away, and shuffles in our woes. [38]

5   Morn: Ten O'Clock just returned from the interment of Nancy Drinker. which was solemn: when the prepared go, those that are behind, shoud weep for themselves, in that they have lost one of the lights which the just man's path, is said to be, "a shineing light." [39] afternoon, Joshua & Caty drank tea with us,

6   Morn: wrote to Sally and Betsey Smith, and Polly Morris. afternoon, Anna Pole and Grace Allison drank tea with me, Danny Smith from B——n, all my friends well there,

7   Morn: out at shops, afternoon at Neighbour Warners.

1 Day   Morn: at meeting. afternoon at meeting Marget Ellis, Eliz Morris spoke, at Catys with Polly & Betsey. evening at meeting D Stanton and B Trotter spoke,

2   Morn: at home, afternoon Peggy Leech hear, one of my school mates. Nancy Pole.

3   Morn: at work, afternoon at becky's.

4   day at work.

[June 1, 1758]

6 MO 5   Morn: at meeting John Scarborough, John Wolman & William Ricketts spoke. afternoon at Anna Pole's, the anniversery of her birth, and her twenty first year, Polly Rhodes there, rained. staid all Night; Aunt Sarah Smith from New York, Widdow of my mother's brother Benjamin. she is under affliction, one part or branch of a family cant fall without hurting the rest, or seldom does, for drowning men will catch at a straw.

6   Morn: at home by five O'Clock. at Work, W: Ricketts dined hear.

7   Morn: at Work, bad news from Wioming. [40] afternoon the same. E Cathrel hear.

1 Day   Morn: at Meeting Ester White spoke, afternoon at home, a Neighbour of ours, a thorough belle, [because] the admiration of the Men, is as good as meet and drink to her. when alas! 'twill by and by be.

38. Isaac Watts, "To John Hartopp, Esq. Casimire, Book I. Ode 4, imitated 'vive, jucande, me tuens juventae' & C," in *The Poetical Works of Isaac Watts and Henry Kirke White,* by Sir Harris Nicholas (Boston, 1831), 231–32.

39. Proverbs 4:18.

40. The Wyoming Valley was a disputed territory claimed by Pennsylvania, the Iroquois, the Shawnee, and settlers from Connecticut. Violence in the region would last into the 1780s, and the various claims to the territory would not be settled until the early nineteenth century. Wilkes-Barre and Scranton are now the major cities in the area.

"deef the praised ear, and mute the tunefull."[41]

read in the Bible, Polly & Betsey drank tea with us, evening at meeting DS, BT & William Rickets spoke.

2   Morn: at Work, Aunt Sarah went to B——n on her way to New York. wrote to Sally. afternoon at Gracy Allison's very pleasently spent. a West India woman there, one Lowrie. called at Nancy Gibson's. they make me think of the old song, for I think them a painstakeing happy Couple, How easey was Labour, how patient was toil,

When kindly rewarded, repaid with a smile.

3   Morn: at meeting, Alex: Seaton, Benjamin Trotter, and William Rickets spoke, afternoon Polly & Betsey Sandwith and I drank tea with Rachel Drinker, the rememberance of the just is as a sweet savour, to there remaining friends. spent the evening at Caty's. this day landed the High land reigements, consisting of 110 Men, besides too many Women.[42]

4   Morn: busy white washing,[43] wrote to Aunt Sarah.

5   Busy.

6   Busy. evening a walk with Becky, vast crouds of People comeing from the High landers Camp. Curiosity excessively prevalent in mankind.

7   Morn: blacked and reded[44] and one of the Women's tedious jobs over, Witewashing. afternoon at Work.

1 Day   Morn: at home reading, got a bad cold. afternoon at meeting, evening Nancy Warner hear, Abel James says her features resemble the Worthy Mary Peasely.

2   Morn: at Work. afternoon Daddy & Mamme went Point-no-point, Sally Dugdill come to see me, had a bad toothake, sent for Jacob and pulled it out. Mamme come home with a hot fevour and great oppression at her breast. how dreadful is the appearance of Sickness, in a beloved friend.

3   Morn: Mamme better, at Work. she assigns the returning health, to her takeing, 8 drops of spirit Turpetine, (very good for wind or stiches.)

4   Mamme very poorly yet, afternoon Neighbour Warner hear.

41. Alexander Pope, "Elegy to the Memory of an Unfortunate Lady," in *The Oxford Book of English Verse, 1250–1900,* ed. Arthur Quill-Crouch (1919).

42. Regiments employed women to cook, clean, sew, and carry baggage from one encampment to another. These women were sometimes soldiers' wives and sometimes prostitutes. In both cases, they were poor, disheveled, and tough.

43. This involved the application of a lime and water mixture on interior walls and ceilings; whitewashing walls and ceilings was usually done once a year.

44. Meaning polished iron and copper.

5   with Mamme, afternoon friend Coleman hear, at Work.

6   day Mamme very bad. how serviceable and always to be valued is a good Neighbour. Becky Rawle hear.

7   Mamme better, afternoon Sarah Samson drank tea with us. evening finishd the 2 Vol: of the history

1 Day   with Mamme, afternoon Debby Morris was here to drink Tea.

2   busy.

3   day Ironing, Amelia Williams dead. heard from Sally, by Sally Davis. Mamme got quite brave again.

4   Morn: at Work, afternoon Mary Armitt, a woman of an affable disposition, esteemed and respected by me, as the particular friend of my mother. 6 O'Clock paid several short visits to divers of my Acquaintances. Polly Ritchie married to Jacob Bryant.

5   Morn: at meeting Robert Jones, William Rikets spoke, afternoon at Caty's, company there. evening with Grace Allisson, she informed me of her intended marriage. I wish her well. as I do the rest of my Sex, in that engagement. and her in particular.

6   Morn: at work, afternoon Sally Raper hear, went to G: Allisson's. took a ride, was caught in a shower, lost a gold button.

to day 7   at Work, drank tea With Neighbour Warner.

1 Day   Morn: at meeting BT: and Robert Jones spoke, afternoon at meeting Robert Jones spoke. company, evening at meeting Will Riketts, DS spoke.

2   Morn: at work, heard from Barbados, by a letter from my Cousin I Callender, afternoon at becky's. becky Cooper there.

3   Morn: went to Darby with F Brawle and wife. Becky Cooper Dined and spent the Day at Doc^t Paschal's, a fine company of Girls there. 5 grown up.

4   Morn: at Work, afternoon the same, evening an agreable hour with Caty Howel, Oh Life how chequered are thy scenes, how great had been the avenues for joy, if pain had never found them.

5   Morn: at meeting, BT. and Wil: Riketts spoke, Cousin Pole hear, afternoon at Becky Cooper's on a visit. evening went to Capt Mase's, found Grace Allisson married and gone for Lancaster, the gentleman's name————Caldwell.

6   Morn: at home, afternoon on a visit to the Widow Mifflin & Sally.

[July 1, 1758]

7 Moth 7   Morn: went to Plantation with Daddy and Mamme, poor Neighbour Oldman has accomplished what has long been her design. afternoon, company Jos: Morris, and his Sister Sally Griffitts.

1 Day   Morn: at meeting BT. Spoke, afternoon at meeting, went to Ann Pole's, called at Neighbour Carney's, a most beautiful woman, puts me in mind of Milton's description of our common mother Eve.

Grace was in all her steps
Heav'n in her eye, in every Gesture dignity and Love.[45]

2   Sally Holloway hear, Taylorising[46]

3   Sally and I at work. evening Tommy Lightfoot, returned from a journey of 2 hundred miles, to the back parts of Virginia, where the poor inhabitents, witness the terror of desolation, an Indian War!

4   Sally and I at Work.

5   Morn: at Work. wrote to Sally, afternoon at Susey Worrell's with Mamme, cant but say we women are hardly to be trusted with Liberty.

6   Morn: at Work. and reading, got a New recruit of Pens. afternoon to see Sally Penington, a great deal of talk on the actions of Neighbour Ritchie. the Character of a fine Lady is by no means to be envied, a life full of disappointments and chagreens,[47] which appear to them as bad as real Misfortunes.

7   Morn: at Work, afternoon agreably with Daddy, evening Dan: Smith.

1 Day   Morn: at Meeting DS. spoke, afternoon at meeting, Will: Rikets spoke. Betsey Sandwith drank tea with me, evening at meeting, Sarah Morris and Will: Riketts spoke:

2   Morn: at Work. afternoon at mary Armits. Widow Loydd and Hannah there, in bodily affliction when the Almighty enables the mind to bear it with resignation, it must be vastly to the satisfaction of the friends of the person, to see them prepare for another life in this.

3   Morn: wrote to Gracy Caldwell, at meeting BT and DS spoke. Company at diner, afternoon at Esther Fishers, a good deal of talk concerning the single state. resolved that elderly maidens, are of service in the creation, notwithstanding Calumny.

4   busy. Young says "some surprise us by their death."[48] it seems as tho' it made our standing shake, Will: Clark at the Indian treaty a 7 day[49] and now, a Corps:

---

45. John Milton, *Paradise Lost* (London, 1821), 241.

46. Cutting, fitting, and sewing tailored clothing, a complex task that required professional assistance, in this case from Holloway.

47. Chagrins, regrets, embarrassments.

48. Edward Young, *The Complaint; or, Night-Thoughts on Time, Death, Friendship* (London, 1743). HCS quoted Young often.

49. Meaning the previous Saturday. The treaty was signed at Easton in October 1758, after contentious negotiations.

5	Morn: Ironing. afternoon the same
6	Morn: busy afternoon, at Plantation with mamme.
7	Morn: at Work, afternoon Tommy Lightfoot. evening at the funeral of a child. death lays his Iron hand on all.

1 Day	Morn: at meeting, afternoon at home reading in Crisps Sermons. poor distressed B__n_j Sweet hear
2	busy, makeing Current Jelly, Elixer and bitters.[50] afternoon Company Hannah & Betsey Morris, Becky Rawle,
3	Morn: at meeting. BT: and DS: spoke, afternoon agreably with ma ———————— mamme, evening at Becky's. the news of our having lost the brave Lord Howe, and divers other officers,
4	Morn: cutting out Shirts, afternoon Molly Brown and Sally Penington drank tea with me, evening betsey Sandwith and I, admireing the beauties of the evening. some one likens hope to "the Fair Summer evening mild and sweet."
5	Morn: fixed my three Peices in the Frames. at meeting Hannah Smith, Alex: Seaton, Jane Hoskins, and Grace Fisher spoke, afternoon at Nancy Gibson's agreably spent in work and talk with her, and her mother, Docter Shipy[51] drank tea with us, talk: on the Carthagean dominions, a larger place than I imagined, to hear of People Whose understandings are so clouded and benighted as to Worship Images, and Gold for God, out ———————— ought to make us more thankful, that Providence has cast our lot in a land frought with Blessings, double Liberty, Liberty, and Liberty of Consience, which we ought to Prise, not abuse.
6	Morn: Mamme, Anna Pole and I went to Plantation, the diversities of Town and Country, make each the more agreable.
7	Morn: rose with the Sun, to walk the dew bespangled Lawn, afternoon, Daddy and Mamme, heightened the pleasure by there Company, we returned in the evening. Caty Smith came from burlington very agreably to me, and I hope will stay with us some time

1 Day	Morn: at meeting Rebecka Jones,[52] Hesekiah Williams, and Hannah Smith spoke, Cousin Hannah come home with us, afternoon Caty and I at meeting, a violent Gust, Thunder and Lightening, dreadful Artillery of the Sky. evening at meeting WB.

50. Elixirs and bitters were often taken for stomach complaints.

51. Shippen.

52. "Rebecca Jones became an eminent minister in the Society of Friends. . . . Her conversion to Quakerism is supposed to have been largely due to the influence of Hannah Callender's mother. . . . Her memoirs were published . . . under the editorial pen of the late William J. Allinson." GV.

2   day agreably at home with Caty, evening a walk, begun a Shirt for Daddy. gave Caty my white mounted Ivory fan, and a silk Lace,

3   Morn: at meeting W: Riketts and Joice Benezet spoke, afternoon at home, Daddy is but in a poor state of health, at Mary Armitt's a bit, continual mementos of mortality, yet the eye of mens minds is not sufficiently opened, the building still is hear as tho' for an habitation eternal, beneath the heaven, but God has provided hearafter.

4   day at Work, Mamme and Friend Worrell rode out, evening Becky Rawle and I went to Neighbour Ritchie's child's funeral, the behaviour of some of the Ladies, made me think of a Satire, cast on the Sex, by the famous Law,[53] who says, the Generallity: are pretty triffling Gew gaw things, entirely wronged in their education, made to believe they were formed for Man, when in fact they are formed for a purpose of their maker's Glory as well as he.

5   day at Work, Neighbour Wall hear in the afternoon, Daddy very poorly.

6   Morn: finished my Shirt, Hannah Moor. Peggy Hill, Rachel Hill, and Polly Morris, called hear in there way from meeting, where Peggy had been publishing her intensions of marriage, with Billy Morris, afternoon at Katy and I at Warner's, Nancy and we took a walk as far, as the Hospitol, Joined Company with With Polly Pemberten and Jordan, ("[54] with a sickly mien.")

7   day at Work. finished the 3 Vol: of the History, Daddy very poorly with the flux,[55] which is bri[sk] at present, numbering many of the Children to there Graves. Evening Anna Pole.

today 1 Day   Morn: at meeting, BT: and DS spoke, afternoon at meeting Mary Emblen, and Will: Brown spoke. Caty and I at Polly Shoots a little, Daddy unwell still.

2   day, Daddy no better. begun a Shirt.

[August 1, 1758]

8 MO 3   day, with him.[56]

4   day, Ironing, Daddy no better.

5   day, with Daddy,

6   day, with Daddy,

53. Possibly William Law, *An Appeal to All who Doubt, or Disbelieve the Truths of the Gospel whether they be Deists, Arians, Socinians, or nominal Christians* (1742).

54. Two illegible erased words, first possibly "afflict." Polly Jordan had been treated with a double dose of emmenagogues, drugs designed to restore menstruation, on July 19. Thomas and Phineas Bond Co-Partnership Ledgers, vol. 3, p. 94, College of Physicians of Philadelphia.

55. Diarrhea.

56. Nursing her father.

7   day, with him, a little easier, a most sharp disease full of excruciating
           pain. a good nurse, is a great matter, as well as a, skilful Physition, my
           dear mother a faithful one. Mary Noble, Hannah Cathrel, and Anna
           Pole hear.

1 Day   with Daddy, wrote a line to Sally.
2   Morn: Quarterly meeting, at meeting Margaret Ellis, B Trotter, and
           Mary Emblen spoke. ME spoke exceeding well on brethren's bearing
           and forbearing with one another, to shew it was the sum total of Reli-
           gion, brought the instance of the two mothers contending for the
           Child, before King Soloman, who when he orderd the Child to be split
           in half, soon found the true mother, who had rather loose her right,
           than the Child should be killed.[57] so every member of the Church
           should sacrifice pecuniary motives, to general good, Daddy better. af-
           ternoon Neig. Warner, Polly & Sally Lightfoot.
3   Morn: Youth's meeting. Caty and I went to meeting, William Horn,
           D Stanton, and James Tasker, spoke. afternoon at Work. Gracious be-
           ing: well may thou be called "Parent of Good" who gives us blessings,
           and that we maynt forget ourselves, sometimes takes them to thy self,
           in mercy to us, at others lets us see how soon 'tis in thy power so do:
4   day. finished my shirt, Daddy better,
5   day. began a shirt. afternoon Cousin Rachel and Anna Pole hear.
           Martha Barker from Burlington, a letter from Sally full of Cordial
           Friendship. which Love, David said, exceeded all other.[58]
6   day. agreably at Work, in Company of my Parents, Martha and Caty,
           Industry, as Thomson says, has indeed furnished us with

                    "Joys which the rugged Savage never felt"
                    "His days roll heavy, dark and uninjoy'd along"
                         "A waste of time. —————"

7   Morn: at Work, afternoon, at Work, and finished the 4 Vol: of the his-
           tory of England.

1 Day   Morn: at meeting John Pemberton spoke, afternoon at meeting, Com-
           pany to drink Tea, evening at meeting BT and DS spoke,
2   Morn: finished a shirt, afternoon began a Shirt. Anthony Benezet,
           drank tea with us, talked of some persons who had been searching for

---

57. 1 Kings 3:16–28.
58. HCS has reversed genders here; see 2 Samuel 1:26: "my brother Jonathan: very pleasant hast thou
been to me: thy love to me was wonderful, surpassing the love of women."

a place to dwell in where the Devil had not been, but alas! he is as hear to fore, "walking too and fro in the Earth."[59]

3   Morn: at meeting, DS and Hezikiah Williams spoke. afternoon agreably at work with Mamme and Caty. evening took a run to Caty's, some talk on pretenders to religion, hateful in my eyes.

4   Morns at Work. afternoon at Work, Henry Groth an english man drank tea with us, gave an account to what a prodigious height the Pantoons[60] were carried in England. shows Custom and fashion to be things, that ought to be nipt in the the bud. Evening Caty and I took a walk.

5   Morn: finshed my shirt, Nancy Gibson brought a bed, this day 2 weeks, have not been to see her, afternoon Caty Howel set a bit ~~and~~ ——— eat some water million[61] and went away. went with Caty to see the valt and interment of Tench Frances.

6   day mantua making with Sally Holloway.

7   day. the same, Company at tea.

1 Day   Morn: Mamme and I at the funeral of Elizabeth Rawle, at meeting, HW: and Eliza: Stevens spoke, afternoon at meeting Eliza Morris spoke. Caty and I drank tea at Caty Howel's. evening at meeting DS. and [a] stranger from Virginia spoke, warned us greatly to take heed to our ways, or destruction would be the Consequence.

2   day. Sally Holloway and I at Work. evening took a walk, news of Cape Breton surrender, the 26th of this month,[62] the noise of the Mob upon such occasions rather proceeds from a dissolute propensity in the minds of men, to take all allowed oppertunitys, for I was going to say acting the part of brutes, as in reality, the annoyance and disturbance of their Neighbours, drinking and ranting, is [never] kin to the rational mind.

3   day. at work, evening a distant relation arrieved from Barbados, James Mayres.

4   day Ironing. evening a grand Illumination for Cape Breton for which the Quakers paid, broke 20 pains of Glass for us, at John Reynolds house the Windows in general, and some window shutters were shattered to peices.[63]

---

59. Job 1:7.

60. Headdresses.

61. Watermelon.

62. The recapture of Fort Louisburg had occurred the previous month. The mouth of the St. Lawrence River was now under British control.

63. Philadelphia residents would set candles in all their windows to mark military victories and to light the streets at night for the crowds of joyous and rowdy revelers. The Quakers, as pacifists, did not participate and as a result had their darkened windows broken by the celebrants.

5   Morn: went [to] meeting, DS, Hannah Hulford, Rebeca Jones, HW, and Will: Brown spoke, DS extraordinary on our distressed circumstances, saying in stillness is your greatest safety, you shall know that I am God.[64] afternoon Polly & Betsey Sandwith, Anna Pole and James Mears drank tea with me, worked at my Purse,

6   Morn: at meeting Peggy Hill passed the second time, diner Joseph Noble, Edward Cathrel. the latter come down to be at meeting with his Son Isaac and Hannah Coffin. afternoon Joice Benezet and Ann Thornton to see Mamme, evening Caty and I took a walk exceeding Pleasent. worked at my purse to Day. also.

7   Morn: at Work at the Purse, a present of Sweetmeats[65] from W Mears. afternoon Daddy and Mamme rode out, Caty and I worked and read, in the second Vol: of the Iliad, the first of which I have read.

1 Day   Morn: at meeting Will: Brown spoke, Daddy and Mamme went by water to burlington, afternoon at meeting, evening at meeting DS and BT spoke.

2   Day Sally Holloway at work, afternoon at work at my purse. evening Neighbour Warner, Polly and betsey.

3   Morn: at meeting DS & BT spoke. afternoon Sally holloway at Work with her. seven o Clock evening a letter from Daddy, wrote to him again. they had a fine passage up.

4   Morn: at market, see different figures of undress,[66] Sally holloway at work. afternoon the same

5   Morn: at meeting BT, Sarah Morris, becky Jones spoke. mears went to diner at Carneys, afternoon Caty and I at Work, evening Henry Drinker hear just returned from new york, a pleasant place but not so pleasent as Philadelphia.

[September 1, 1758]

9 Mo   Morn: Tommy Pryor from burlington, informs me daddy & mamme
today 6 set out yesterday for Burden town, with Dan and Sally. afternoon at Caty howell's, Neighbour Warner, Becky, Polly and Betsey there, a very pleasent dish of tea, Isarel Pemberton there,

[In margin: "the first Fall Month"]

7   Morn: sent a letter to Daddy by Wollard, and presently after by benny Cathrel, word of mouth, afternoon Caty and I took a ride to Skylhill

---

64. Psalms 46:10.
65. Candy.
66. Models or drawings of less formal clothing meant to be worn at home.

fishing house, walked a bit among the rocks, found it very pleasent, thence across the Country to frank fort, drank tea at Abel James place, who accompanied us home.

1 Day   Morn: at home, mears very unwell, John Hauxworth hear, afternoon, at meeting Polly & Betsey Sandwith, with Nancy Warner, drank tea with me.

2   Morn: at Work at my purse. afternoon Sally, Nancy & Debby Mitchel, also Sally Dugdil drank tea with me. evening a Fire works played off, on account of Cape breton's surrender.

3   Morn: at Work at my knot purse, went to meeting, Martha Harress, the worthy friend, who I see at Wilmington, spoke, also, Grace Fisher, ———————— Easter, and James Tasker. I sent Word by Abra: Carlisle, to burlington, that I coud be easey with dady & mamme's longer stay. if they thought fit. afternoon Caty and I at work evening——————— Caldwell hear, brought me a letter from Gracy.

4   Morn: at market. wrote to Gracy Caldwell. afternoon at Work at my purse,————————Caldwell drank tea with us, an agreable polite Gentleman. evening Nancy Warner eat some water melon with us.

5   Morn: Daddy and Mamme come from burlington by ten O'Clock, Anna Pole hear, at Work at my purse. Anna Staid with us all day, evening walked out, went round by the barracks,

6   Morn: at work helping Caty, afternoon, at Nancy Gibson's a most agreable afternoon, Friendship's the sovereign balm of Life, evening very agreably spent with Caty Howel.

7   Morn: at work for Caty, went to the Widow Balls, there concluded upon a party to bush hill. Widow Ball and mamme, Nancy and I, John Gibson and Billy Ball, in the afternoon, a fine house and gardens, with Statues, and fine paintings. particularly a picture of Saint Ignatius at his devotions, exceedingly well drawn, and the rape of Proserpine,[67] where the grim god of hell, seems to exult with horrid joy, over his prey, who turns from him with[68] a dread and loathing such as fully pictures, the horrors of a loathed embrace.

1 Day   Morn: wash to morrow, and after my good mamme's custom reckoned the cloaths, at meeting BT spoke, after diner wrote in my place book,[69] afternoon at meeting Martha Harress, DT, and HW spoke,

67. Persephone: Greek goddess of spring, abducted by Pluto to serve as the queen of Hades.
68. illegible word crossed out.
69. HCS's "place book" was a commonplace book, a collection of excerpted writings, usually including poetry and prose, but sometimes correspondence. Given her literary tastes, and her tendency to quote in the diary, she probably copied from whatever she happened to be reading. For an example of a woman's commonplace book that included some work with which HCS would have been familiar, see Catherine La Courreye Blecki and Karin Wulf, eds., *Milcah Martha Moore's Book: A Commonplace Book from Revolutionary America* (University Park: Pennsylvania State University Press, 1997).

2   Morn: at Work at my purse, Jem Logan hear, says the people at burlington, have been prepareing this month past for the Carnival, he had need of 2 months preparation if he intends to have a part in it: evening at becky's with several of the family.

3   Morn: Ironing. evening news of the takeing of fort fronteneac.[70]

4   Morn: a fruitless attempt to go to Burlington, with Caty. finished the Fifth Vol: of the history of England. set an hour with Caty Howel in conversation.

5   Morn: at Work for Caty, afternoon John and Molly With there. Sister Groth drank tea with us, went to Capt Sibbald's child's funeral.

6   Morn: a second resignation of burlington, because mamme has a bad cold. at Work at my purse all day and reading Pope's Essay on Man,[71] to Caty.

7   Morn: at Work at my purse. found thrown down on the flat a Libel called Labour in vain, or washing the black moor white, a spirited thing, with a picture of those concerned in the fruitless attempt, placed in the face.[72] afternoon finshed Mamme's Knot purse,

1 Day   Morn: reading in the Bible, at meeting DS spoke well on worship to God, in the words of the salmest "stand open ye everlasting gates, and let the King of glory in"[73] afternoon at meeting, James Tasker and some other friends drank tea hear, evening at meeting JT spoke.

2   Morn: at Work, friend Tasker dined hear, afternoon flowered a side of a pin cushen.

3   Morn: grounding, went to meeting, becky Jones spoke, 6 Couple passed, among them Jonathan Miflin to his third venture. afternoon went to see a poor woman at the Hospital,[74] at Anna Pole's and Molly Allisson's, evening finished the 2 Vol: of the Iliad.[75]

4   Morn: took some care about the poor woman in the hospital: 12 O'Clock noon, a nother attempt to go burlington but failed. Evening at becky Rawle's.

5   Morn: Caty and I at meeting, William Morris married to Marget Hill, the whole conducted with the utmost decency. Samuel Spavald and

70. August 27, 1758.

71. Alexander Pope, "Essay on Man" (1733–34).

72. "Labour in Vain: or, an attempt to wash the Black-Moor white. Humbly inscrib'd to the author of the Chronicle." A versified satire on prominent local Quakers and others. Available on the Library of Congress website at www.memory.loc.gov. William Logan wrote to John Smith, HCS's uncle, on October 13, 1759, "Sometime since I sent thy Bro Sammy the pce called *Washg the Black Moore White* with a promise It should be returned but it never was. I wish thou wouldst get it & send it." John Smith Correspondence, 1740–1770 (nineteenth-century transcription), Historical Society of Pennsylvania.

73. Psalms 24:7.

74. Pennsylvania Hospital for the Sick Poor, founded 1751–56.

75. Homer, "The Iliad."

Daniel Stanton spoke. afternoon Neighbour Warner drank tea hear, evening spent at Caty Howels, with Kilby—— MacAdam and his Wife, she gave us no very favourable account of the conduct of the new york Ladies. Kilby is an elderly Gentleman who from knowing how to talk well, has got a continual faculty of talking. Mac Adam married his daughter for a living. I know not what's the matter with the Sex, they cant reconcile themselves to a single state, I think she woud have been better without him. appearing a woman of a prety good under-standing till you see her choice.

6   Morn: busy, afternoon Neighbour Warner, Mamme, Polly Sandwith and I had a pleasent passage to B——n, where we drank an agreable dish of tea, with Katy Lightfoot, Unkle and Sally, evening wrote to bet-sey Sandwith, went to see Unkle R

7   Morn: agreable with those my friends, afternoon Company comeing into town from all quarters, to be at our yearly Meeting which began on

1 Day   Morn: when William Brown spoke, afternoon Samuel Spavald, eve-ning Sam: Spavald. crouded Audiences, being as large a meeting, as could be remembered.

2   Morn: at meeting John White, and Peter Andrews helped an extraor-dinary meeting, by speaking well, on the text "he that brideleth not his Tongue, his Religion is vain."[76] in the afternoon, Sally and I went to meeting, soon after observeing a young [woman] who we knew to be a stranger, and had thought a lovely girl, to go out with Phebe Brown, as if unwell. we followed, Phebe haveing an inclination to go into meet-ing again, we begged her to go with us to my Unkle's where she might a little recover herself, she with an engageing sweetness went, where after reposeing a little, she sat up in the chamber, and we engaged in a most agreable conversation concerning each others stations in life, her name was Betsey Brook, Just turned of Seventeen, her Person tall and genteel, her Complexion fine, features admirably well proportioned, engaged your attention before she spoke, then; tho' not brought up in a City, delivered herself with ease and becomeing freedom, as though she had been used to Company, and addorned her Parents care in her Education, as well as shewed it not labour lost. one observation more, I never see a more engageing manner, than She was mistress off: when addressed by a Stranger. her dress was plain, and something particular from us: yet coud not be altered in her, without robing her of a beauty, which seemed intirely her peculiar. a cambletee rideing gound, sto-merger[77] of the same, a white silk lace x and x before it, a peek cor-

76. James 1:26.
77. Stomacher: a bodice.

nered sinkle hankercheif tucked in it, a round eared cap, with a little black silk hood, graced as Innocent a face, as I ever see, when a walking she wore a Plat bonnet: she lived in Mary land some where near West River, to which yearly meeting she said she belonged. we were all three, lone Sisters, she had lost her Mother about a twelve month before; of whom she spoke in a dutiful manner, saying altho it was hard for her to bear yet she thanked Providence, for enabling her to attend her in a long illness, and the Grace to keep, from offending her, in word or deed. we drank tea by our selves, and Sally and I were delighted with her:

3   Morn: Tommy Lightfoot brought Robert Pleasent to see us, a hansome and Accomplished Gentleman, a Virginian. Polly and I went to meeting. Joseph White and Phillip Dennis spoke. a great deal of company, dined at my Unkle's, Polly Pusey, Phebe Bayley a young woman from chester county, Betsey Brook, Phebe Brown. Robert Pleasent, John Hopkins, Isaac Webster, and Jemmy Brook, (betsey's brother), Marylanders. afternoon a Women's meeting, where in, the Love of god, shone forth with great warmth and tenderness, a Pathetick and worthy to be remembered, exortation; to the young Women, by one of their own age, ie between 16 & 17, Polly Pusey lately come forth in the Ministry, from chester County. also becky Jones said a little, a nother young woman lately come forth in the Ministry, may Providence prove a stay to their feet, and a guide to their Paths; for the love he was pleased to show to us thro' them in that meeting, toward evening went down to Joshua Raper where I spent the evening with Patience Gray, Elizabeth Stevens, and Betsey Brook, they were her relations.

4   Morn: drest and went to Eliza Barkers, found Polly Pusey there. Phebe bayly and more, after a while went to Raper's, found betsey Brook there, the time passed very agreably till meeting time. went to meeting, Ann Scofeild and Sarah Marcy spoke. Polly Sandwith and I dined at John Smith's. afternoon, a women's meeting meeting, Sam: Spavald come and set among us, and gave some Wholesome Advice. evening run to betsey Smith's.

to day 5   Morn: agreably surprised by a visit from betsey Brook, Robert Pleasent there, went to meeting. James Tasker, Sarah Morris spoke. Polly Rhodes, Anna Pole, Phebe Lewes, Sally Yarnel, Hannah Zane dined at my Unkles, also, Cousin Phebe Pell from new york, Unkle Benjamin Smith's Wife's Sister. afternoon went to meeting Eliza: Smith, Mary Emblen, becky Jones spoke, Betsey Mood, Polly Polly Pemberton, Polly Sandwith, beulah Coat, Abby Moot, Sally Holloway, Betsey Brook drank tea at Unkle's. wrote to Father, and Betsey Sandwith.

6   Morn: Mary Armitt, Neigbour Warner, Joseph Jacobs, a stranger from long Island, Polly Sandwith and I, walked to Tommy Weatherils, and breakfasted, then went to meeting. ann Scofield and Ann Moor spoke,

and the yearly meeting concluded well: afternoon Sally Hawkshurst, a young woman from new york, spent with us.

7   Morn: Seemed melancholy by reason of so many "fare well"s, among them went, with the good will of all, the amiable Betsey Brook. afternoon Polly Sandwith, Sally Hawkshurst, Sally & betsey Smith, and I walked round the Point, looked at the barracks, thought them a compleat thing for so small a place. we returned and drank tea with Scamon & Sam: Rodman, Rich: & Dan: Smith, then took the Windmill walk, set down in the Porch of Connore's house,[78] certain it is that the dwelling of riot and licentiousness, shall become the dwelling of the Screech Owl and the Bittern: even there the Swine shall wallow in mire:[79]

[October 1, 1758]

1 Day   Morn: Neighbour Warner, Polly Sandwith, Phebe Pell, Sally Hawk and Mamme set out for Phila:——————— read in no Cross no Crown,[80] 11 O'Clock went to meeting, dined at Sammy Smith's, afternoon Sally, Abby Smith and I spent to gether. evening set a while with betsey Smith.

[In margin: "10 Mo."][81]

2   Morn: Monthly Meeting Peter Fern and John Sleeper spoke, several Couple's passed, one James Kinsey with Hannah Decow, dined at Edward Cathrel's, afternoon Sally come to us, spent tolerably.

3   Morn: at Work at my flowered Poket book, afternoon went to Unkle Robert's, evening agreable at home.

4   Morn: at home, Sally and I at work at the Poket book, afternoon the same,

5   Morn: at meeting Peter Fern, Cousin Hannah Smith, afternoon Ironing.

6   Morn: Betsey Smith and I at work at my worsted gown, afternoon the same, an agreable day.

7   Morn: Sally and I walked out to the barrack viewing Nature's works, gathered Mock's store of blackberrys for Winter, afternoon took a ride to Plantation with unkle, come round by Ben: Merrits house, the dwelling of Poverty:

78. A tavern.

79. Isaiah 13:21, 14:23.

80. William Penn wrote *No Cross, No Crown* about the power of the cross and of human self-denial, while in a London prison as a Quaker martyr.

81. Someone later penciled in "1 mo," "2 mo,' and so on, but in this case "10 Mo." seems to be in HCS's hand.

1 Day   Sally and I in our Chamber reading, 11 O'Clock went to meeting. Peter Fern spoke, afternoon Sally and I spent at Cousin Johns, to wards evening, Phebe Pell, Sally Hawkshurst, and Caty Smith, come from Phila:, evening down at Unkle Roberts, Sally Raper and Eliza Barker there.

2   Morn: went to Unkle Roberts, worked at my Poket book, dined at Abenezer Large's, spent the afternoon there with Phebe Pell, Sally Hawkshurst, Jenny Burlen, and Anne Rodman.

3   Morn: busy. Sally Hawkshurst spent the day with us.

4   Morn: at Work. afternoon betsey and Caty Smith.

5   Morn: parted with Phebe Pell, and Sally Hawkshurst for New york, went to meeting Peter Fern spoke, Afternoon drank tea with Caty weatheril.

6   Morn: betsey and I at Work at the Gound, afternoon Caty there, finished our work:

7   Morn: at Work. afternoon Joseph Noble's. evening agreable with Unkle and Sally[82]

1 Day   Morn: reading in Laws appeal:[83] went to meeting Peter Fern, Han: Hartshorn, and Benaja Andrews, spoke. afternoon Mary Noble and Caty Weatherill drank tea with us. evening the Council met. John & Sam: Smith, Joseph Noble and my Unkle's.

2   Morn: at Work. afternoon at Cousin Samy Smith's, Joseph Jacob drank tea there.

3   Morn: at Work. afternoon Sally, Betsey, Caty, and I at Rapers, towards eveing we took a walk,

4   Morn: Sally and I rode out, a round about way to Docter Rodman. spent the day with Anne.

5   Morn: 9 O'Clock Caty and I set out for Phila: arrieved about noon. afternoon and evening rectifying my Diary. found my Parents In good health. see Polly & betsey Sandwith, heard my Acquaintance in general well. this evening died Atwood Shoot.

6   Morn: Caty and I out at shops. afternoon set with Molly Allison and Grace Caldwell. she is very unwell. evening wrote to Sally.

7   Morn: at Work, afternoon at Grace Caldwell's, she misscarried a quarter of an hour after I left her last night, but is like to do well: the Indian Treaty[84] began 2 weaks ago, no nigher finishing than at first. evening began a cushin for an Arm Chair in double cross stich.

---

82. Erased: "————finishe"; in margin, erased: "1 Day."

83. William Law, *An Appeal to All that Doubt, or disbelieve the Truths of the Gospel, whether they be Deists, Arians, Socinians, or nominal Christians* (1742).

84. The negotioations produced the Treaty of Easton in October 1758, in which, among other things, Ohio Indians agreed not to enter the French and Indian War on the side of the French. The provisions of the treaty were not honored—on all sides.

1 Day Morn: at meeting Becky Jones spoke, after diner reading in Laws appeal; went to meeting, Grace Fisher spoke, a kind repremand from my dear friend Caty Howel, evening Caty and I went to meeting: I think I have sometimes seen the goodness of God in a very conspicuous manner, to such children, as he has pleased to rob of their parents when young. turning their feet, and giveing them cause, to call him Father; and bless his name: BT: and DS: spoke, and 'twas a good meeting:

2 Morn: eight years, to day, as near as we can remember, since I had the small Pox, a memorable event to me, as then my God see fit in Mercy to spare me! to my Parents prayers. and prolong a life then thought in manifest danger.

> *May I return the Blessings lent!*
> *May the Presentments in my Breast*
> *Inspired by this Salvation, Last,*
> *Till on my Skin the marks imprest*
> *By the distemper are eraz'd.*

all the day, and evening, Copying letters for Daddy to send to England, concerning Politicks.[85] Sally Cathrel from B——n, all well there.

3 Morn: Ironing. Abby Raper at diner, staid all night,

4 day most part writeing for daddy. Caty and I put mammes black russel quilt[86] in the frame.[87] —————————I hate the Sly provokeing hint, in Conversation, robing my Neighbour of his reputation under the artful guise, of not designing it.

5 Morn: quilting, afternoon a kind Visit from Neighbour Warner, Polly & Sally Lightfoot here,

6 Morn: Writeing in my place book, Caty and I went to meeting, DS, Sarah Morris, and Hannah Hulford spoke, Jona: Copeland & Polly Nichols passed. Hannah Hulford dined hear, and gave me some very wholsome advice, thy ways are ways of wonder O Providence, and all thy paths, are paths of light, 'tis not the Wise by natural Wisdom, that thou chusest to declare thy truths. but the simple honest mind, thou gives tounge and Utterance too. ——drank tea with Caty Howel, staid the evening, becky there, a good deal of conversation concerning some matches and talked of, Joshua, of popes opinion

> *Every Woman is a Rake at heart.*[88]

85. The Friendly Association was attempting to influence treaty negotiations.
86. Russell: a ribbled or worsted cotton and woolen fabric.
87. Three or four words crossed out, "evening" perhaps one of them.
88. "Men, some to Business, some to Pleasure take; / But ev'ry Woman is at heart a Rake." Alexander Pope, "Moral Essays, II, To a Lady," Epistle ii, Lines 215–16 (1743).

7   day. Caty and I quilting, Tommy Lightfoot here, says that my beauties
       are all gone home, evening Abel James, says that Women generally
       take care to place their Love discretionally. Caty & I read in the Spec-
       tator Ann Bullen's letter to Harry 8th,[89] who I make no doubt will in
       her own words be convinced of his mistake:

> When Bones sepulcred leave there narrow rooms,
> And hostile Kings rise tumbling from there tombs;
> When nor your heart, nor mine, can lye conceal'd,
> But every secret motive stands reveal'd,
> Stands full reveal'd, that God, and Man, may see,
> How fate has err'd, and you have Injured me.

[In margin: "Susy Wrights translation of Ann Bullens letter into verse."]

1 Day   Morn: writeing in this and my place book. went to meeting, DS. and
           Hez: Williams spoke, between meetings reading in Laws appeal, af-
           ternoon BT, drank tea at Neighbour Warners with Frances and becky
           Rawle, evening went to meeting with becky, Polly, and Betsey Sand-
           with, Hez: Williams, & DS spoke. Nanny Rakestraw suped hear.
2   Morn: sorted the family Stockings, put the Winter ones for ware, pre-
           served some Crabapples. afternoon see a good many of my acquain-
           tance, drank tea with Grace Allison, found Polly Pemberton at Anna
           Pole's, from thence we proceeded to Nancy Mitchels, where we spent
           an agreable hour, with four Charming Sisters. Isaac Parish come home
           with me, and is like to succeed with the second, Sally Mitchel. there can
           be no greater felicity on this side the grave than that of a Man who has
           a good Wife and large family of Promiseing children, to think that he
           has been one means of fitting so many inhabitents for the region of
           Eternal Happiness.
3   Morn: quilting, Caty and I went to meeting, DS, Becky Jones, Eliz:
           Morris, and BT, spoke. this day Ann Rawle a twelve month old, after-
           noon Mary Amitt, Mamme and I at Docter Caldwaleder's, no other
           company but his Wife and Daughter.

[November 1, 1758]

11 Mo 4   Morn: quilting. afternoon Neighbour Warner, Mamme, and I at Neigh-
           bour Fishers, he is just returned from Boston, says it is larger than

---

89. Anne Boleyn's letter to Henry VIII in Joseph Addison, *The Spectator,* June 5, 1712. For Susannah
Wright's full poem and a discussion of the circulation of such manuscript poetry among a Quaker circle
in Pennsylvania and New Jersey, see Blecki and Wulf, *Milcah Martha Moore's Book,* 121–24.

Phila: but not so regular. he called at B——n and Sally sent me her green and blue Cushen to look at. with notice of their health.

5 Day Caty and I quilting till four O'Clock, C: read an hour to me in my Exercise book, then Martha Barker from B——n, all well. I went to becky Rawle, becky Cooper and I spent the evening there, Poor Nancy Gibson has lost her baby.

6 Morn: Caty and I quilting till ten O'Clock, then I went down to Nan: Gibson's, found her in trouble, but bearing it with Christian fortitude. she is a woman of a fine person, and good understanding, capable of nice sensibillitys,————How blest the lovely Pair,

Beyond Expression, if well mingled Loves
And woes well mingled could Improve our Bliss!
————Thrice happy Man, if Pleasure only knew
These Avenues of Love to reach our Souls,
And Pain had never found 'em! Watts.[90]

afternoon I went to the funeral, Ann Scofield hear. evening Caty and I set together, I read Watts Peice to his friend Mitio.

7 Day Caty and I quilting, evening kniting.

1 Day Morn: at meeting, Mary Kirby, a friend from Staffordshire in England, Sarah ashton and Grace Fisher spoke. It is our quarterly meeting, Several friends dined hear, afternoon at meeting Ellis Hugh and Jane Ellis spoke. evening Mamme, Martha Barker, Caty, and I spent together, the old folks, turning living histories, and recounting things past, in the dear land of our Ancestors B——n.

2 Morn: Caty I got mamme's black russel quilt out of the frame. wrote in my place book. 11 O'Clock went to meeting, Mary Kirby, Sam: Spaval, and Betty Morris spoke. it held till 2, afternoon some young Visiters: Sarah Logan Smith, daughter of John Smith of B——n, Nancy Dylvin, and Patty James.

3 Morn: Youth meeting. Caty and I went to meeting, Hannah Hulford, Mary Kirby, Ann Scofeild, Jane Hoskins, Sam: Spaval, and D: Stanton spoke. Cousin Hannah Smith and her daughter Sally dined hear. did something towards turning my bonnet, 3 O Clock Caty & I went [to] becky Rawles. Flattery exceding pernicious to youthful minds.

4 Morn: finished my Bonnet. noon Cousin betty smith and Jos: Smith from b——n, also Jos: Noble. eveing writeing for daddy.

5 Morn: at meeting Jonathan Mifflin and Sarah Powel took one a nother for better, for worse, Sam: Spaval preached a thorough weding sermon,

90. Isaac Watts, "To Mitio, My Friend," in *The Poetical Works,* Nicholas, 238–39.

Jos: White spoke. dined with Anna Pole. drank tea with my old friend Anna Gibson. we were pleasently without intruders, or the busy tongue of sensure, enjoying one anothers converse, on things moral and eternal. evening agreable with Mamme, Cousin Betty, Caty, & Josey Smith.

6   Morn: Cousin betty & Josey set out for concord quarterly meeting, 2 gentlemen from boston, Howel and Jos: Noble dined hear. one of a corrispondent of my late Cousin John Pole's, Will: Whitwell, and has showed himself to be an honest man, and a good Christian with regard to his Orphans. this day our Gracious king George entereth his 75 year. may the day when he shall quit time for eternity, be suspended till mature age, may with divine assistance have fitted his grand Son, for the sacred seat. Tommy Lightfoot suped hear.

7   Morn: out at shops. began to turn my Camblet[91] long cloak. finished the fifth Vol. of the History of England. afternoon bettsey Warner hear.

1 Day   Morn: went to meeting BT spoke. after diner read to mamme and Caty in the Bible. at meeting, drank tea at becky Rawle with Will Fisher and Wife, evening Caty and I went to meeting, Joseph White spoke. Benj Sweet seems to be quite got over his malady, he and henry drinker suped hear.

2   Morn: busy, Becky Rawle and Debby Morris hear a bit. Writeing to Hannah Callender daughter of Richard Callender second son of my grand father William Callender in Barbados. evening set an hour with Mamme, in silence where the Soul communes with it self and is still.

3   Day: Ironing. Will: Whitwell and ————————Hill drank tea hear. evening read part of Cato[92] to Caty.

to day   Morn: puting up the wash. burnt my letter to hannah some things be-
4   ing not quite to mammes mind. Anthony Beneset[93] breakfasted hear, the poor Newtrals[94] in a bad situation, suffering great hard ships even unto death. at work at my cloak. evening finished reading Cato to Caty. began a pair of Stockings.

5   Day: at work on my Cloak, evening Wrote to hannah Callender again, this is my birth day where I am One and Twenty years of age. more than likely I have passed the better half [of] my days,

6   Day: at work on my Cloak and finished it. Jemmy Mears surprised us

---

91. A heavy woolen fabric with a ribbed texture.

92. Josept Addison, *Cato: A Tragedy* (1714).

93. Anthony Benezet was an early, internationally prominent abolitionist and educator.

94. Poor neutrals: French Acadians forcibly removed from Nova Scotia. Many came to Philadelphia where, they were not treated well, mistrusted as enemies and Catholics, except by Anthony Benezet and a few others. See Christopher G. Hodson, "Refugee Acadians and the Social History of Empire, 1755–1785" (PhD diss., Northwestern University, 2005).

by a short visit, evening I run over to Neighbour Warners a bit and set
with betsey Sandwith, come home and read to Mamme and Caty in
Isaac Peningtons Works.[95]

7   Morn: busy, my Cousin Caty's being hear is very agreable to me. after
diner wrote in my place book till three o'Clock. drank tea at Neighbour Warners. began my queen stich thread case. evening at beckys, I
worked at it and she read in Clarissa.[96] a fallen woman is the more in-
excusable as from the cradle the Sex is warned against them.

1 Day   Morn: read in the third Volume of Pope to Caty. went to meeting.
H: Williams and BT spoke. Ben: Sweet dined hear, afternoon at meeting H.W: spoke. Mary Emblen, Mamme and I drank tea at Mordeica
Yarnel's with his Wife. he has a large family of Children, and he is
pretty capable when at home of going in and out aright before them.
Caty and I went to meeting BT:, HW:, H: Hulford, and John Hawksworth spoke. two celebrated beauties set near me, Patty Loyd and a
Daughter of Docter Shippen. Shippen far exceed Patty, who has been
brought up to think she can have no action or gesture that looks amiss.
when on the contrary:

> *I hate the Face however fair,*
> *That carries an affected air,*
> *The lisping tone, the shape constrain'd,*
> *Are fopperies which only tend,*
> *To injure what they strive to mend.*[97]

2   Morn: tacked my ten stich peice in the frame, did a little tea carnation,
went to pay a morning Visit or two, Caty Lightfoot and Grace Caldwell, afternoon Mamme and I went to see Nancy Gibson. Polly Donalson, and the Widow Ball there, the universal topic of the Town now,
is a French Frigate that lies off the Capes and annoys the shiping much,
has taken from New york and this place 21 Vessels. Women either by
conections of Husband or Father &cc cant help interesting themselves
in Politics. I woud always avoid it, and think that the duties of our Station would be much more agreable Conversation. evening at Work.
3   Morn: at meeting BT: spoke, our Cousin Jemmy Mears come and took

---

95. Isaac Penington, *The Works of the Long, Mournful and Sorely Distressed Isaac Penington, whom the Lord in His tender Mercy at length visited and relieved by the Ministry of that Despised People called Quakers* (1681).

96. Samuel Richardson, *Clarissa; or, The History of a Young Lady* (1748).

97. Edward Moore, "Fable VII. The Goose and the Swans," in *Fables for the Ladies* (Philadelphia, 1789), 27. HCS missed a line from the first stanza, which should read "I hate the face however fair / that carries an affected air; / The listing tone, the shape constrained / The study'd look, the passion feigned / Are fopperies which only tend, / To injure what they strive to mend.'"

leave of us for Barbados. Eliza Bud from Hampton Hanover, the place where my Unkle Robert lived, called to see us. afternoon Polly and Betsey Sandwith drank tea with us. evening Joseph Gibons hear, Caty and I retired, I read to her, in the 3 Vol: of Addison.

4   Morn: Worked at my Carnation, received a Letter from Sally. William Clothier dined hear, an Englishman with whom Edward Pole, the eldest Son, now living of Cousin John Pole, goes home to England, to the care of his Unkles, Poor Caty seems dull, but her separation from her friends, is not made more disagreable by being hear. I hope. evening arrived Cousin Betty and Josey Smith with John Jones and his Sister Susey Mason from there Journey to Chester quarterly meeting, which they think to be larger than Burlington yearly meeting.

5   Morn: at meeting BT: and DS: spoke. Jonathan Copeland & Polly Nichols were married: and he spoke badly, afternoon I drank tea with Francis and Becky Rawle. evening worked at my crosstich cushen.

6   Morn worked at the Carnation. Cousin Rachel and Anna Pole, with myself went on board Capt Richy, to see Neddys accomodations, afternoon I went to see Hannah Cathrel, evening Josey Smith from B——n and says Unkle Daniel's house has been broke open, but no great loss. evening wrote to Sally Smith.

7   Morn: went to market with Caty, at work read the journal of Frederick Post to the Ohio, among the Indians in July 1758.[98] who went as with his Life in his hands and was in Jopardy every moment, to Mamme & Caty. Cousin Betty and Josey Smith with Tommy Lightfoot set out for B——n. afternoon finished the Carnation, evening worked on my Cushin, and read in Addison.

1 Day   Morn: went to meeting. Will: Brown, Eliza: Stevens, and becky Jones spoke. Caty read in Pope. afternoon at meeting Sarah Morris spoke, on the Important duty of Praise to God, none being able to fit us fort it but himself. "Quicken thou me, O Lord and I will Praise Thee."[99] went home with Caty Howel, evening Joshua went to meeting and left us, she has now three fine Children, Girls, Anne, Sarah, and Cathrine, we diverted our selves a while with them, Caty, is a woman fearing God, and valueing his blessings. she read to me in the Art of Contentment, and we had a Satisfactory evening, the Pleasures of a Friend are great, Jonathan valued them before Life:

98. First published as an appendix to [Charles Thomson], *An Enquiry into the Causes of the Alienation of the Delaware and Shawanese Indians from the British Interest* (London, 1759), according to Reuben Gold Thwaites, ed., *Early Western Travels,* vol. I (Cleveland: A. H. Clark, 1904), 328. Available at www.alexander street2.com/EENALine/eena.toc.sources.html. The Callenders must have had access to an earlier manuscript version.

99. Perhaps an amalgam of Psalms 119:37 and 119:7.

2   Morn: busy, afternoon at Docter Moor's on a Visit to Peggy Morris and Rachel Hill, Betsey Meredith and Godfry Leacock there, a gentleman from Lancashire in England. evening at work on my Cushen.

3   Morn: at Work on my Yellow ten stich Flower, at meeting Eliza & Sarah Morris spoke, Anna & Neddy Pole dined hear, afternoon Caty and I drank tea at Abraham Mitchels, with Nancy, Sally, Debby, and Hetty mitchel, began me a pair of White silk mittins in a sort of Crown work, but mamme does not quite like of it so I dont know wether I Shall go on with them, evening worked at my Cushen.

4   Morn: worked at my yellow flower. afternoon the same, note I bought the day I was at mitchels [bought] one shillings worth of white silk.

5   Morn: worked at my yellow flower. Anna Pole come hear, a while after Neddy, William Clothier and they dined hear, at 2 o'Clock Neddy took leave of us, and went on board Capt Williams Richy for Bristol in England. I wish the poor little fellow a safe passage and well thro' Life. I went home with Anna, did not stay Long, called at Grace Caldwells, drank Tea at Joshua's with F & B Rawle, Whitwell & Hill, and Polly & Betsey Sandwith, spent the evening very agreably there, with Caty, Polly, & Betsey.

[December 1, 1758]

6   Morn: worked at my yellow flower, afternoon mamme and I drank tea with Neighbour Wall, evening worked at my cushin

12 Mo 7   Morn: finished the Yellow flower, afternoon Caty and I at Work to gether, talk on Burlington, and our friends there. my Nurse Peggy Gregory called to see me, she nursed me in the small pox and I have a great affection for her. evening mamme, Caty & I at Work, and Conversation.

[In margin: "first Winter month."]

1 Day   Morn: at meeting Daddy read the London yearly meeting Epistles. Mary Emblen, Eliza: Stevens, and B:T: spoke, read in the Bible, towards the latter end of Deuteronemy, the Benedictions of that excellent Ancient Poet Moses, to the Tribe of the children of Israel, when about to Die on mount Nebo, Israel then shall dwell in safety alone. the Fountain of Jacob shall be upon a land of Corn and Wine, also his Heavens shall drop down dew. Deu: C23.V28. at meeting Nanny Emblen, and her Daughter Peggy, with Joseph Fox drank tea with us. Caty and I went to meeting, HW: and BT spoke,

2   Morn: Tommy Lightfoot breakfasted hear, when all manner of Wickedness is perpetrated by our Army, even to starveing their Horses by hundreds, so that the people cannot bring their Waggons back, but

are obliged to leave them behind to ruin in the woods. what construction seems most natural to put on this "what have you done with my Wool, Flax, Oyl, & cc that I entrusted you with."[100] sorted the Glove drawer, made me a Needle Book,

3   Morn: up early and to sprinkling cloaths, Ironing afternoon. Joshua and Caty, with their Daughter Anna drank tea hear. Neighbour Ritchie went by with that young Fop, West.[101] no wonder the men laugh at the Sex, when some of them are so fond of encourageing the race of Petit Maitres. Whitwell and Hill suped hear,

4   Morn: at Work on my blue Flower Pot, afternoon Caty and I went down to Poles. Cousin Molly Wethrel there, Cousin John Murfin Lodged hear, a relation of mamme side,

5   Morn: worked at my blue flower pot, Caty and I went to meeting. Mary Emblen spoke, concerning the Joy and Satisfaction to be felt some times in a good meeting, "is there not a Book of Rememberance Written."[102] BT: and DS: spoke. Afternoon Neighbour Wall mamme and I drank tea with neighbour James, evening worked at my Cushin,

6   Morn: a Visit to Becky & Caty: sticking mamme a pair of Shoes. afternoon read in the 4 Vol: of Pope to Caty, Whitwell drank tea hear. evening Worked at my Cushin.

7   Morn: at Work on the Cloath Shoes. afternoon finished them. evening William Morris of Trentown suped hear.

1 Day   Morn: at meeting Becky Jones and BT spoke. Nancy Pole dined hear. afternoon at meeting John Pemberton and DS: spoke, evening Caty and I went to meeting John Hawksworth, HW:, DS, and BT: spoke.

2   Morn: News of fort Du Quesne's being forsaken by the french who blew up most part of it,[103] with the Poor English sick and wounded Prisoners, that they had in their Possesion, Oh War! horrid War; how does it make human Nature, act derogatory to the first Principles of it instilled by the Divine Dictator. they found odds of a Hundred of the Poor Highlanders lying above ground, with pokets not so much as picked, but some of their english money, which they changed our paper for, not thinking it money till they had it in Coin: which proved no safegaurd to them, against the Wild Beasts of the feild, who mangled their Carcases! the Army, passed by the dreadful feild of Slaughter the remaining Bones of Bradoak's Army. and desently Intered them, no

100. Possibly a loose reconstruction of portions of Matt. 25.

101. Probably Benjamin West, then a young painter who already commanded five guineas for a portrait. He was courting Elizabeth Steele at about this time. Robert C. Alberts, *Benjamin West: A Biography* (Boston: Houghton Mifflin, 1978), 24–25.

102. Malachi 3:16.

103. Fort Duquesne (now Pittsburgh) was set on fire by fleeing French troops, November 24, 1758.

doubt but there was them, who wept there, for near Relations and Friends! Forbes has called the Indians in to have a treaty, and has leave of them to repair the fort and calls it by the Name of Pitts burg. finished the 4 Vol: of Addison. Tommy Lightfoot dined hear, run the heels of a Pair of Daddy's Stokings. evening Worked for Caty.

3   Morn: Worked for Caty, afternoon Cousin Lydia Noble hear, evening Worked for Caty.

4   Morn: John Hoskins hear from B———n. wrote to betsey Smith. afternoon worked for Caty, she takes in sowing and when hurried, I help her. evening reading to daddy, in the Indian Enquiry.

5   Morn: at work for Caty, Sammy Noble hear, afternoon mamme and I at Mary Armits, William & Hannah Logan there, evening I went see Betty Stretch who is in a very poor way and not like to live long. evening at Work for Caty, Cousing Anthony Sikes and Joshua Morris suped hear.

6   Morn: at Work for Caty. afternoon Whitwell, becky Rawle and her Child, Nancy and betsey Warner, drank Tea hear. evening Samy Noble and Samy Wethrel, Anthony Sikes and Daddy setling differences, Discord is every where a troublesome Companion, but When it is shut up within a family and happens amongst relations that cant easily part 'tis harder to deal with.

to day 7   Morn: at Work for Caty. Mamme drawed some of her quince wine made at home. afternoon Worked for Caty. I went with her to Mary Armitts, for some work. evening much displeased with the Librarian; who hinders me from going on with the History: read in the Indian Enquiry to Daddy.

1 Day   Morn: at meeting, DS: and Grace Fisher spoke. afternoon at meeting Sam: Spavol, spoke according to my Mind he spoke to the true State of the meeting, our Intestine divisions had much weakened us, and would still more, if we sought not for Grace, The Fear of God, and Learned to Live in Love, and mutual forbearance. Sam: Spavol, Joshua Emblen, Peter Worrel, and Anthony Benezet hear. evening I went not to meeting, wrote in this book and read:

2   Morn: Worked at my flower Pot, afternoon Mame and I at Neighbour Samsons, Friend Samsom, his Wife and Son, Daddy, Mamme, Henry Drinker, and myself drank tea. evening at becky Rawle's, Peggy & Polly Paschal. Becky Cooper.

3   Morn: at meeting Mary Emblen, ————— Easter, and BT: spoke, afternoon at Caty Howels in Company with Sally Smith, and Rich: Footman's Wife, an English man, and a Woman of Sense and though we talked of the Gentry of the Town, yet twas not "in Scandel over the Tea," no base Innuendues hinted at, but the true designh of Conversa-

tion, was endeavoured at, mutual Pleasure. we talked of Authers, and I found her a woman well versed, in Books of good repute. a pleasent afternoon. evening, read in the Indian Enquiry to Daddy.

4   Morn: Friend Footman sent me Ayre's Comments on Pope's Life and writeings,[104] Whitwell and Hill dined hear, afternoon 3 O'Clock I took a most agreable walk, round the out side of the City, along third street, by Willings, so to Vine Street, and called at Pole's. evening finished the Indian Enquiry to Daddy. I dislike much having any thing to do with match making, I woud have People always chuse for themselves.[105]

5   Morn: 7 O'Clock rejulateing this Book, worked for Caty, afternoon she and I at Neighbour Warners, Rebeca Coleman (her mother, about 80 years of age, who can remember when a child, rideing on the boughs of the trees cut down in the clearing of Front Street, and but two or three houses, in the now famous city of Philadelphia, (verily in blessing God, God had blessed thee, O Pensylvania:) herself and Nancy Warner, Polly & Betsey Sandwith all the company. evening Becky Rawle and Caty Howel come there. the Anniversiry of Becky's marriage, this time 2 years. and as I think them a good sort of family, and much respect them, may there Prospects never ware a worse face than at Present, but that they may more and more abound.

[In margin: "in grace and good Works."]

6   Morn: Worked for Caty, afternoon at Polly Parrocks, a good deal of talk about Polly Parker of Chester, a person of 20 thousand pound fortune, but no other accomplishment either of body or mind. has had a great many Admirers, but cant think of marrying, among others 'tis said Charles Norris, which is not much to his honour.[106]

---

104. William Ayre, *Memoirs of the Life and Writings of Alexander Pope, Esq.* (1745).

105. This is a rather daring statement. Assertive women were objects of derision, and the idea that they might make their own choices could be considered absurd. A fictional letter to the editor from nineteen-year-old Charlotte Wilful, concerns her three suitors. "The first is 'squire *Scrape,* who has 1200 l. [pounds] *per annum,* which he keeps in his own hands and farms himself, and therefore is favour'd in his pretentions by her father. Mr *Myrtle,* her mother's favourite, is the other, who, by his own account is near 40, by that of his acquaintance 10 years older, has squander'd away a good estate, but by the death of an uncle is now worth 1000 l. *per annum,* and is a perfect humourist. But to both these she prefers Mr *Plume* of the *Inner-Temple,* [an attorney,] who has no estate, but is of a sweet temper. [She] Concludes with desiring [the editor] to declaim on parents making choices for their Children, with a stroke on antiquated beaus, and rural animals, and to recommend a fine gentleman with no fortune. [She] Desires, by way of postscript, that [the editor] would not delay publishing her letter, because Mr *Plume* and she had agreed to run away together on *Tuesday* next." *The Gentleman's Magazine,* I (January, 1731), 15.

106. Mary Parker did marry Charles Norris less than a year later, as HCS noted, in June of 1759. She spent much of her married life, however, still in Chester caring for her ailing father, the source of her fortune.

7   Morn. worked for Caty, afternoon she and I went of some errends. evening Sammy Shoemaker hear. who I think answers my Idea of a Gentleman.

1 Day   Morn: at meeting. William Brown, BT: spoke, afternoon read in the Bible went to meeting Hezi: Williams and DS: spoke. Edward Brooks and his Wife, and Peter Worrell drank tea hear. evening William Fisher and Abel James.

2   Morn: Neddy Penington breakfasted hear, worked at my thread case. afternoon Widow Scatergood hear. from B——n, Caty Hartshorn married to a Soldier,

3   Morn: unwell, read in Pope's Life, afternoon at Work, evening our agreable Neighbours Sam: Shoemaker, and Neddy Penington

4   Morn: Cutt out cloath shoes for Caty and myself, a violent stomach ake,

5   Day also a violent Stomack ake, worked at my shoes. read in Pope's Life

6   Day took Physick, finished stiching my Shoes, anna Pole hear

7   Day took Physick, read to Caty in the 4 & 5 Vol:s of Clarissa, betsey Sandwith hear an hour in the afternoon, agreable conversation: evening I read to Caty again, where I find this remark on her, (made by a brother Rake, Lovelace's friend Belford,) dislike of Double Entredres: the disgrace of Conversation.——"Not Poorly, like the generality of her Sex, affecting Ignorance of meaning too obvious to be concealed; but so resenting, as to shew each Impudent laugher, the offence given to, and taken by a Purity, that had mistaken its way, when it fell into such Company."

1 Day   Morn: at home writeing, in this and my Place Book. Mary Emblen dined hear, afternoon reading in the Independant Reflector, a public Spirited paper, printed at New York, wrote in a good Stile, by the Worthy Levingston, a Gentleman, the growth of our Infant Colony.[107] Widow Scattergood drank tea hear, my dear Friend Caty Howel come to sit an hour with me, the Friend of my Youth, with whome I have passed many happy Hours. till distrust, that enemy to friendship and not opening our minds, clouded a Friendship that was the joy of our hearts. but it now shines again, tho' not with that unsullied lustre I once knew. I have a profound respect for her. and let changes happen as they may, I trust shall love her till my dissolution

---

107. William Livingston, *The Independent Reflector; or, Weekly Essays on Sundry Important Subjects More Particularly Adapted to the Province of New York and Others* (1752/53).

[January 1, 1759]

The First Day of the Year 1759

1 Mo 2   Morn: our Standing in Time, makes us candidates for Eternity! It pas-
seth away as a Weaver's Shuttle,[108] at Work, Jos: Morris hear, hasty
People make work for themselves and others, great dissensions now
among friends, which cant but concern, every Individual as Individuals constitute a whole; afternoon Nancy Carlise here. evening Becky
Rawle hear, agreable talk between Mamme, Caty, Becky and I,

3   Morn: at meeting Sarah Morris, DS: and Sam: Spavol spoke, Polly
Pemberton and I had a little sort of renewal, to our Early acquaintance,
but the difference of our fathers sentiments, I plainly see creates a distance between us.[109] afternoon Ironing, Danny Smith from B——n, a

---

108. Job 7:6.

109. Pemberton was accusing HCS's father and others of malfeasance in the course of this dispute.
One letter on the subject survives:

> "Philadᵃ, 1ᵐᵒ· 26ᵗʰ 1759.
> Friend Israel Pemberton,
> Thy Letter of the 15ᵗʰ Insᵗ. Directed to William Callender, Owen Jones, Jacᵇ. Shoe-
> maker, junr, Jacᵇ. Lewis, Richd Wistar, Peter Worral, Thos. Say, Jos. Morris, Abel James
> & John Reynell, came to our hands, which we have read & seriously considered, wherein
> thou acknowledges the receipt of the Trustess of the Friendly Association Letter on the 25ᵗʰ
> of the last Month (at Lancaster [two short words illeg.] art pleased to distinguish us in the
> Manner thou do'st from that Board, We think it necessary to observe that we have not given
> thee any Delay in the Release of our Captive fellow subjects, nor in the restoreing & con-
> firming the Peace of our Country in making Presents of thy Goods to our Indian allies, for
> the Truth of this, we refer thee to the Trustees Letter, but that we did desire thee not to
> prosecute thy Intentions of Fixing a Licensed Trade with Indians in the manner thou
> propos'd, taken fro [some letters illegible] own words at the Head of the Invoice, & in thy
> Letter to the Commissioners for Indⁿ Trade, and as great Care was taken to avoid all Re-
> flection, and to write thee in the most affectionate & kind Manner, we are not Conscious of
> giving thee any just Cause of offence, or being unable to justify our selves in any part of our
> Conduct, yet it gives us Consern to find that after all our tendʳ regard for thee, and Care
> to prevent any Act, that in its Consequences might have brought on thy Self or the Society
> of Friends with whom thou art in Religious Fellowship; just Cause of Reflection. Thou art
> pleas'd to say many harsh and unkind things of us, which at present we shall Wave answer
> as we are desirous of not entering into any Disputes with thee, but as we are all members
> of the Board of Trustees of the Friendly Association, and the Letter wrote thee was from
> that Board, We think it best thou wilt Call a Meeting of the Trustees, and there let them
> know how farr thou hast Comply'd with their Friendly advice—that we may still retain
> that noble Title of Friendly association hopeing these considerations may have their due
> weight with thee—We are thy truly Loveing Friends
>
> > *Wᵐ Callender*
> > Jos Mason
> > John Reynell
> > Jacob *Lewis*
> > *Owen Jones*
> > Rich Wistar
> > Jacob Shoemaker, jun.
> > *Thoˢ Say*"

Pemberton Papers, Quaker Collection, Haverford College.

letter <u>from</u> Sally, more robberies commited. Tommy Lightfoot drank tea hear, evening Danny, Tommy, and Abel James.

4   Morn: folding cloaths. afternoon Jos: Morris drank tea hear, evening Abel James, and Sam: Shoemaker. D Smith, descants, on Public affairs.

5   Morn: read a little in Clarissa, wrote to Sally Smith, by Danny, afternoon Ironing. evening at Work.

6   Morn: at Work, afternoon Friend Coleman, and Neighbour Warner, evening reading to Mamme and Caty in the Reflector.

7   Morn: at Work, afternoon at Work, on my Rose Poket book, when People once give way to bad Cources, the Path is dreadfull to tread back again, and good Name sooner lost than got: in a censorious World. Frances Rawle hear, Mordecai Yarnell arrived from England.

1 Day   Morn: some things in the Family much disturbed me, Oh that I was Mistress of more stediness, Life thou art a chequered Scene————— at meeting, BT: and John Hawksworth spoke, afternoon wrote in this. went to meeting. Sam: Spavel spoke, afternoon Caty and I went to Caty Howels, Sammy Howel there, evening we went to meeting, Sally Morris, BT: and John Hawksworth spoke.

2   Morn: wrote in my Place book, afternoon, Mamme and I went to see Hannah Shoemaker, Tommy Carpenter there, family Punctilio, often Causes family differences, evening being fine Caty and I walked up to Poles. Polly Rhodes there, an agreable hours Chat. a good memory is a help to Conversation, makes people able to intersperce it, with Incidents from History, or Books and things from knowledge or observation of Men. began the Sixth Vol: of the History of England.

3   Morn: at Work went to meeting DS: and Mor: Yarnell, spoke, how often have Women to repent at Leisure for things Committed in Haste.[110] Sally Morris dined hear, drank tea with Becky Rawle, William Brown & Frances Rawle, staid the evening there, reading Venice Preserved,[111] to becky.

4   Morn: at Work, rainy bad day out doors but passed agreably. afternoon at Work, I read some of Lovelace's mad letters, to Caty.

5   Morn: at Work, Caty & I went to meeting, Mary Emblen, Eliz: Stevens, and DS: spoke, see Tommy Prior from B——n. Cousin Jenny Burlin has lost her little Girl Amelia, gave Caty a Bath mettle[112] Thimble, afternoon at Work,

110. Richard Saunders [pseud. Benjamin Franklin], *Poor Richard's Almanack for 1734.* "Wedlock, as old Men note, hath likened been, / Unto a publick Crowd or common Rout; / Where those that are without would fain get in, / And those that are within would fain get out; / Grief aften treads upon the Heels of Pleasure, / Marry'd in Haste, we oft repent at Leisure; / Some by Experience find these Wrods misplac'd, / Marry'd at Leisure, they repent in Haste."

111. Thomas Otway, *Venice Preserved; or, A Plot Discovered. A Tragedy.* (1755).

112. Bath metal: an alloy of zinc and copper.

to Day 6   Day, at Work, read a little to Caty in Clarissa, reading is one of my most pleaseing amusements, I had some years ago a sort of viciated taste, in books, but I have done with the fulsome Romance now, my Dear Mother, often was displeased at me about them, which at that time only learnt me the more industriously to conceal them from her. I hope they corrupted not my Morals, for as I grew in years I began to discern the Folly of Chemeracal notions. and distinguish the fitt and the unfitt. evening our agreable Neighbour Sam: Shoemaker.

7   Morn: at Work, wrote a little in my Place Book. afternoon run a pair of Stockings for Daddy, Anna Pole and Molly Parrock hear, some cautions given to us Girls to take care of what Company we keept, for tho' ill habitts may be hartily detested, yet often seeing of a thing, we become more hardened to it, feel less of those checks, the glory of the human mind, which preserves us from the bane of Evil Communication, that corrupts good Manners. evening reading to mamme & Caty in the history of England.

1 Day   Morn: at meeting, Betty Morris, Becky Jones, and David Easter spoke. afternoon Caty and I at meeting Sam: Spavol spoke, evening Caty & I at meeting Sam: Spavol spoke.

2   Morn: finished my blue tenstich flower pot, Neighbour Warner called in, the rest of the day very busy Copying for Dadddy, Abel James, Docter Evans drank tea hear, some passages of Ben: Franklins droll humour related, in a letter to his Sister in New England, a strong Presbeter, "I am glad to hear of the reduction of Cape Breten, when it was taken before, 'twas taken by prayer, now by fight and I desire you will pray, that it may never be given up again, which was omitted before." another, "your religion leads you three stories high: Faith, hope, and Charity, but before I go any further, I wish to the lord, I coud turn the house bottom up wards, and put Charity at the bottom,"[113] evening knit

3   Morn: my dear mamme has always used me to rise at an early hour,

---

113. Benjamin Franklin, London, to Jane Mecom, Boston, September 16, 1758. This letter is now lost, but it was reproduced in the nineteenth century as: "I congratulate you on the conquest of Cape Breton, and hope as your people took it by praying, the first time, you will now pray that it may never be given up again, which you then forgot." "You are to understand then that faith, hope, and charity have been called . . . the three stories of the christian edifice. . . . *Faith* is then the ground floor, hope is up one pair of stairs. My dear beloved Jenny, don't delight so much to dwell in those lower rooms, but get as fast as you can into the garret, for in truth the best room in the house is *charity*. For my part, I wish the house was turned upside down; 'tis so difficult (when one is fat) to go upstairs; and not only so, but I imagine *hope* and *faith* may be more firmly built upon *charity,* than *charity* upon *faith* and *hope.*" In Charles Van Doren, ed., *The Letters of Benjamin Franklin and Jane Mecom* (Princeton: Princeton University Press/Memoirs of the American Philosophical Society, 1950), 65–68. This is one of many examples in the diary of the circulation of manuscript literature, as well as an example of the relatively rapid spread of information within the empire.

by which I often enjoy the Beauties of the morn, 7 O'Clock. henry Drinker brought Caty a Peice of linnen to make up for him. she and I at meeting, James Tasker spoke, and to a very large audience, much to the purpose, on our differences with one another, biding us to pray for Charity which hopeth all things,[114] mentioning where our Lord tells Peter, Saten has desired to have you that he may sift you as wheat.[115] Beware of knowledge wich puffeth up.[116] let your Brethren see with their own Eyes. drank tea with Becky Rawle, spent the evening agreably with my early friend Caty.

4   Morn: at Work, Grace Beaucannon from B——n hear, all our friends well, afternoon at Work, evening Owen Jones hear, I read a little in the history of England

5   Morn: writeing for Daddy, mamme very unwell. I went to meeting, Sam: Spavol took his leave of us, in a very pathetic manner. finally Brethren let no false Coverings appear among you, nothing but the covering of the holy Spirit of God, fear, reverance, and adore him, he will protect you, even from your selves. from the heat and animosity of your own spirits.

afternoon, Caty and I went to some shops, come home fatigued and we went to work at our Needle, in the Company of our Dear Mamme, rejoiced that we had a home to sit and take a Solemn pause in, and learn caution by the harms of other unwary Youth, the which a great City generally furnishes instances anough, evening I read to Caty in the History of England.

6   Morn: at Work, Mary Lightfoot Relict[117] of Michael Lightfoot a worthy Minister of the Gospel among friends, agreably surprised us by a Visit. She is upwards of 80, yet of a sound mind and memory of good things. their Son Tommy, Married my Unkle Dan: Smith's 2ᵈ daughter Mary, who died about 8 years ago, and left 2 girls, who will experience a loss of her in their education. afternoon to see Polly & Betsey Sandwith, Peggy Parr there, evening read in the history of England to Mamme and Caty.

7   Morn: at Work, afternoon agreably at Work with Mamme and Caty, note when I come to read this over, (though to another Person, there often Mentioning of my home Conversations with mamme and Caty, might appear as Tautology) but to myself they will be looked on with the greatest Pleasure, as the earnest of my having enjoyed in part, one of the greatest sublunary enjoyments, home felt Satisfaction, afternoon and evening diligent at Work.

---

114. 1 Corinthians 13:7.
115. Luke 22:31.
116. 1 Corinthians 4:6.
117. Widow.

1 Day   Morn: half an hour of meditation, went to meeting BT:, DS:, and HW: spoke, John Hawkworth dined hear, he is a Country man of my fathers and Daddy loves every thing that comes from Barbados. afternoon Caty and I at meeting, Becky Jones, and BT: spoke, becky Jones, is the daughter of a poor Widow not of our persuasion, but had got unhinged in her mind by Whitfield,[118] and went no where, by which reason her Daughter was left in a manner to do as she pleased, and [since] the bank meeting house was hard by[119] woud often step in there, till she began to give friends a preference, tho' her mother took not much care of her religion, she gave her as good an Education others ways as her abilities woud afford. which joined to a good Natural Capacity, has opened her understanding, and Enlarged her Ideas, till by divine assistance she became Convinced of Truth, and if she continues her Integrity, by the fittness and well adapting of her words, will be a good Minister. evening Caty and I at meeting. John Hawksworth, John Churchman, and DS: spoke.

2   Morn: began the first of eight shifts for mamme, Tommy Lightfoot dined hear, after diner, my beloved friend Nancy Gibson come hear, and we went on some poor visits, a benevolent mind is an inestimable favour from heaven, I drank tea with Becky Rawle, in Company with Peggy Paschal, Hannah Hicks, and Polly & Betsey Sandwith. evening I wrote in this Book.

3   Morn: Caty and I at some shops, I went to meeting, BT: and Sam: Spavol spoke, Let the Fear of God be your shield and Buckler.[120] Saml: is detain'd by stress of wether, Mary, Caty and Polly Lightfoot dined hear. afternoon Capt Sibald his Wife and Daughter, with Neighbour Carney spent the afternoon with us. Cousin John Smith & Edward Cathrel from B———n.

4   Morn: Docter Evans breakfasted hear, at Work, afternoon Jos Morris, and Grace Caldwell here, a pleasent Conversation with my early friend, evening very agreable with Cousin John, Edward, Mamme, and Caty, there is that certain Je ne seai qui,[121] often found in a select Company, which a larger seldom finds. note a great many men Visitors backwards and forwards to Day.

5   Morn: at Work, afternoon Copying for Daddy, evening a large Councel of Gentlemen in the Parlour, very merry and facitious, John Smith, Edward Cathrel, Sam: Shoemaker, Edward Penington, and Abel James.

6   Morn: at Work, drank Tea with Becky Rawle in the afternoon, Con-

---

118. George Whitfield, an English evangelical preacher who preached throughout the colonies in 1739–41, generating tremendous religious enthusiasm. Many people were, as was HCS, critical of his methods and suspicious of his converts.

119. Near, close by.

120. Psalms 91:4.

121. "Je ne sais quoi," meaning "I do not know what," an intangible.

versation on some more effects of female frailty, all stand or fell to themselves, and we must have Charity for all, even for the worst.

7   Morn: wrote largely to Sally, scenes of distress in the family yet, John & Edward went home, Afternoon Caty and I went to some shops, thence to Becky Rawles where with Joshua & Caty Howel we spent some pleasent hours.

1 Day   Morn: went to meeting BT: and HW: spoke, after dinner Daddy read some extracts out of different Authors,[122] all tending to compose the Mind, to think on the Important task assigned all human Beings. "Work out your own Salvations with dilligence." this was for ought I know, a preparetive to a friendly visit of a quarter of an hour from Sam: Spavol. with Betty Morris, at meeting BT: and Sam: Spavol spoke. evening Caty and I at meeting, Sam: Spavol spoke to Libertines; what can your serving the wicked Power do for you after breaking a Constitution given you for better purposes, in his service, can he restore it again, or even enable you to bear it Patiently, In famine can he raise a grain of Corn, because the Judgements of God are not immediately inflicited, will you go on in sin.

2   Morn: busy in the family, afternoon folding Cloaths.

3   Day Ironing. Poor John Groves is suddenly departed this Life, left a poor Widow and orphan Children. evening I read to Caty In Clarissa.

4   Morn: Tommy Lightfoot breakfasted hear, busy in the family. afternoon Polly Sandwith and I went to Hannah Peters's funeral, and had a solemn walk in the Grave Yard.——————— I drank tea at Neighbor Warners and had a pleasent Hours Conversation with the family.

[February 1, 1759]

2 Mo 5   Morn: at meeting, BT: and James Tasker spoke: afternoon mending up the Glove Drawer, evening reading to mamme and Caty in the history of England

6   Morn: a glorious Day, began my blue ten stich flower, worked at it all the Day, in Company of mamme and Caty. evening I finished the 6 Vol: of the History of England.

7   Morn: worked at the blue flower. these extracts from Clarissa, with regard to her Conduct in Life to herself and others. I have made as worthy memento for us all. Persons of accidental or shadowery merit may be Proud: but in born worth must be always as much above conceit as arrogance. Who can be better, or more worthy, than they should be? and, who shall be proud of talents they give not to themselves? The darkest and most contemptable ignorance is that of not knowing one's self; and all that we have, and all that we excell in, is the Gift of God.

122. Perhaps an earlier edition of Anon, *Extracts from Different Authors on Christian Union* (1777).

All human excellence is but Comparative. There are persons who excel us, as much as we fancy we excel the meanest. In the general Scale of beings, the lowest is as useful, and as much a link of the great Chain, as the highest.[123] The grace that makes every other grace amiable is Humility. There is but one pride pardonable; that of being above doing a base or dishonourable action. she used to say, It was a proof that a Woman understood the derivation as well as sense of the Words she used, and that she stopt not at sound, when She spelt accurately. afternoon finished my blue ten stich flower. evening at Work.

1 Day	Morn: at meeting Becky Jones. John Churchman spoke. James Tasker, John Armit, and Joshua Emblen dined with us. Sam: Spavol set out for England. Went to meeting. Marget Ellis spoke. James Tasker, Jeremy Elfreith, David bacon, Docter Moor, and Sally Dugdill drank tea hear. evening Caty & I at meeting, James Tasker spoke. the meeting held till ten O'Clock.
2	Morn: began my yellow edged blue flower. Jos: Lynn hear, a Widower that wants a Wife. I went to meeting. BT. Marget Ellis, James Tasker, Sarah Morris, and DS. spoke. afternoon very agreable with my friend Grace Caldwell. a young gentleman there, on the latter part, behaved pretty tolerable, tho' plain to be seen he was not ignorant of the title they give themselves, Lords of the Creation, but like most other potentates to be governed by their Ministers. evening at Anna Poles. when I come home found a young Woman here from New york.
3	Morn: Hannah Nichalson; (the young Woman's Name) and I engaged in looking for lodgeings for her. I was very sensible, in her, of the disadvantages a lone woman, in traveling, or comeing to a strange Place, unavoidably lies under. every man she meets to be looked upon as a wolf in sheep's cloathing, she is hardly to trust the most sanguine appearences least under the guise of disinterestedness, lurk the basest self views! such is man to man, and to his kindred species Woman. afternoon I spent with Mary Armitt & Hannah Foster. evening at Work. I have began to read the Dunciad,[124] for the first time,
4	Morn: out again with Hannah, found Lodgeings. she come recommended by William Hawkshurst of New york to Daddy. & Mamme, she has had rather a learned education, has not bought experience, so but acquainted well in theory with the World, has hardly let that enter deep anough, to guard her against the delusions of it. afternoon at Work with mamme and Caty. finished the first shift.

123. The theory of the Great Chain of Being assumed that all beings could be ranked hierarchically, starting with God and descending to humanity, animals, insects, and plants. Equality was impossible; in every relationship there must be a superior and an inferior.

124. Alexander Pope, *The Dunciad. An heroic Poem. In Three Books*. (1728).

5   Morn: at Work. afternoon Betsey Sandwith hear, drew the roses in my Queen stich Poket book. agreable conversation. evening I finished the 5 Vol: of Pope. to Mamme & Caty.

6   Day. finished the 2d shift. Tommy Lightfoot dined hear, abel James drank tea hear, he was pretty tolerable company. 'tis not his power to be very agreable, yet there is room for him to mend.

7   Morn: John Mifflin deceas'd. and the pretty Sally fishbourn left a Widow; in the most melancholy circumstance, of being with Child. Young says some "surprise us by their Death" we immagined their foundation to be so strong. that our thought direct and imperceptably shuders for ourselves! 'tis the "Midnight Cry."[125] O my Soul pray that thou may be on the Watch. wrote in this book, my place book, and a long letter to Sally Smith. afternoon at Neighbour Warners, Frances and Becky Rawle there, Francis gave betsey Sandwith and I an invitation to go to Lancaster with him in the Spring, which I have a great Curiosity to do.

1 Day   Morn: I read to Caty in Socrates, went to meeting. Grace Fisher and Betsey Morris spoke, my dear Caty Howel under much affliction, her Daughter Anne like to dye, Children those dear young Limbs, how they expand the Mothers heart, and open every sad Capacity of Pain. afternoon at meeting Mordecai Yarnell, a reverend awe o'er spread the Assembly, to hear the awful Importance of Worship to Almighty God! he drank tea with us. evening Caty and I went to meeting. HW: and David Easter spoke.

to Day 2   Morn: finished my double ten stich flower, Nancy Pole hear, afternoon Polly Rhodes and Anna Pole, Anne Howel very ill yet, her distemper relicks[126] of the measels. this morn at a quarter of an hour after Six O'Clock poor Anne died, aged 4 years 5 months and odd days.[127]

3   Morn: I kept house, as my Daddy had never had the measels, which had, and does debar me, from personally sympathiseing with my dear friend, whose poor baby Providence in mercy has taken from the Evil to come, and "as the Buds of Virtue must forever bloom." to the mansions of Eternal Rest.

4   Morn: Work and awful ponderings on Time, standing in eternity, afternoon Peter Worall drank Tea hear, Mamme, Caty and Daddy at 4 O'Clock went to Anne's funeral. I was not well, my poor friend! thy heart is now divided into many shares. Betsey Morris hear, Conversation on Ben: Lay's Life & death, he was a man who chose to live differ-

---

125. Matthew 25:6, "the midnight cry." HCS could have been referring to one of several verses by Young, for whom death was a frequent topic.

126. Relics: lingering complications of an illness.

127. There are three blank lines at this point in the diary manuscript.

ent from the rest of the World, a sort of hermit Life, cheif part of his belief was founded on a good basis, but his passions so strong that they incapacitated him for argument. for if people would not directly join With him, he grew dissatisfied, from this proceeded his aversion to society, a quite wrong manner to convince the World of the goodness of his principles. mankind must be lead rather than drove.[128]

5   Morn: I worked at my scarlet Carnation, Frederick Post dined hear. I have a respect for the man as a good Commonwealth's man. the man who does no hurt to society, is a good Citisen, but the man who for the good of his fellow citisens, will go there errands with his Life as in his hand. this man is worthy the public thanks, and the joy which he must feel on so laudable an action. evening I wrote a few lines to my friend Caty Howel on the death of her child.

6   Morn: at Work, I finished the 4 book of the Dunciad. I think it a most compleat peice of Satire, the best of writers, in the ages in which they have lived, have not been sufficiently Esteemed, people seem as if they could not open there eyes, to work untell they are deprived of it. afternoon Caty and I went to Sammy Noble's, Hannah West there, a pretty woman. we were delighted with the beauty of the prospect, from the hill, of the adjacent valeys, and there little plantations, we went to see Hannah Nicolson, then I went to Becky Rawles spent the evening with her in one of those thoughtful moods which shoud come on us at times, it is yet dubious wether Caty will not lose Sally

7   Morn: run my white yarn stockings, went with Caty to a shop. afternoon finished the third shift. Hannah Nicholson being unwell I carried her something to take, she and I had a good deal of talk, and I see more need of girls to have caution, in the choice of their Company, one fatal hour may undo, or lay the foundation, of all a good Education may have taught: I went thence to Becky's, I found Joshua there, Danny Smith came with Sally Raper & Elisa Barker, from B———n. evening: agreable Conversation.

1 Day   Morn: read in Socrates,[129] at meeting, Will: Brown, Mary Emblen, and BT: spoke, afternoon at meeting, BT:, HW:, and John Pemberton spoke. the latter drank tea with us, Caty & I went to meeting, BT: and DS: spoke. a large company of us come home to gether.

---

128. Benjamin Lay, a former slaveowner, was one of the first abolitionists. At times a hermit, he once kidnapped the son of a slaveowner to show how enslaved people felt. He also went partially barefoot in the winter snow to protest the slaves' lack of clothing; sprayed fellow Quakers with red juice to point out the violence of slavery; wrote an early anti-slavery tract entitled *All Slave-keepers That keep the Innocents in Bondage, Apostates* in 1737, and was disowned by the Quakers the following year. Roger Bruns, ed., *Am I Not a Man and a Brother: The Antislavery Crusade of Revolutionary America, 1688–1788* (New York: Chelsea House, 1977), 46–64.

129. Perhaps Xenophon, *The Memorable Things of Socrates* (1712).

2   Morn: at work, afternoon began the first of 2 shirts for Daddy.

3   Morn: at Work, Went to meeting, BT:, Mor: Yarnel, and HW: spoke. afternoon I went to becky's, Sally howel is very ill with a mortification in her mouth, evening hard at work,

4   Morn: Frederick Post breakfasted hear, Sam Shoemaker come hear and it was an agreable morning, Danny and the Girls set out for B——n, afternoon at Work, evening also,

5   Morn: nine O'Clock I went to Caty Howels, and staid with her till seven in the evening. her poor child is a most melancholy sight. evening I staid at becky's that I mought not see Daddy till next day, mamme's birth day, when she entered her 47 year.

6   Day, I worked hard, finished the first shift, evening at Work,

7   Morn: 8 O'Clock with Caty Howel till 8 in the evening, put the finish to mamme's 4th shift.

1 Day   Morn: at meeting, BT: spoke, afternoon at meeting, James Tasker spoke, and drank tea hear afterward with a large company, he is to go for england to morrow morning, evening Caty and I called at Caty Howels, thence to meeting, James Tasker spoke.

2   Morn: Daddy unwell, afternoon folding cloaths. Anna Pole hear. evening Hannah Shoemaker a little.

3   Morn: Ironing, afternoon betsey Warner come to see me, just recovered from the measels, evening Sam: Shoemaker & Ned Penington hear.

4   Morn: at Caty Howels, afternoon there also, with Polly Sandwith, some wholesome and agreable conversation,

[March 1, 1759]

3 Mo 5   Morn: a hasty quick forward temper, I have to gain the mastery over— Caty & I went to meeting, DS:, HW:, and Sarah Morris spoke. afternoon I went to Neighbour Warners. Polly & Betsey Sandwith, Benja: Sweet, & myself, poor lively man, taken unwell this evening, Caty Smith went to set up at Caty Howels.

[In margin: "the first spring month."]

6   Morn: 7 O'Clock Caty come home and the poor child was relieved from its miserable being, at three o'clock in the morning, being terribly mortified, aged three years three months, I went to Caty's and staid with her till after diner, then being unwell I come home, found Hannah Nicolson hear, to spend the afternoon and take leave for a nother rambling Journey. this night I took to my chamber for the measels. continued there in them till this, the 9th of the month, and the day a week ago that I was taken, poor Han: Miller now Lewes is dead of a violent cholic in 24 hours.———

Figure 5 This tissue paper cutout of a reindeer was preserved in the diary. Whether made by Hannah Callender Sansom herself or one of her children, it reflects her lifelong interest in the arts. Courtesy American Philosophical Society.

1 Day   come down to the Parlour, but went not out. I am now over the 2 distempers[130] which happen but once in one's life, but it no more secure's
me from the Inivitable Dart, than I was before. nothing but the prepa-

130. "2 distempers": smallpox and measles both leave survivors with lifelong immunity.

ration of the Heart, will stand in stead when the point of time, twixt a neverending Eternity and this momentary contingent Life shall arrive.

2   Morn: I rode out with Neighbour James and her children, began a shirt to help Caty. afternoon Polly & Betsey Sandwith, an agreable Conversation, one of the most pleasing things in Company.

to Day 3   Morn: dull wether therefore did not venture out, at Work afternoon, at Work, evening also, and reading a dramatic peice called Socrates.[131]

4   Morn: at Work, afternoon finished a shirt, 4 O'Clock: Caty and I went to see General Forbes funeral, a poor old Batcheler who seemed to be alone in a Croud, no tender ties broken, no one to drop the funeral Tear.

Freedom, restrain'd by reason's force,	*But torn from Virtue's sacred rules,*
Is as the Sun's unvarying course,	*Becomes a Comet gazed by Fools,*
Benignly active, sweetly bright,	*Fore boding cares, and storms, & strife,*
Affording warmth, Affording Light;	*And fraught with all the plauges of Life.*[132]

5   Morn: began the Second Shirt for Caty, mamme thought it not proper for me to go to meeting, afternoon at Work, mamme and Anna Pole went to Sam Noble's child's burying, Caty and I talked agreably to gether. evening at Work.

6   Morn: at Work, Ben: Sweet hear, a good deal recovered. afternoon at work.

7   Morn: finished the 2nd shirt for Caty, afternoon hemed half dozen hankercheifs for Daddy, evening daddy told us of several comical matches, one the young woman that lodged hear Hannah Nicolson, who when she come to take leave of us, said she was going with an old Gentleman as far as Wilmington for to stay awhile, but said to be an elderly man of substance from oyster Bay on long Island, who fell in love with her, and for reasons best known to themselves, chose their marraige should be secret, he come this day 2 weeks [ago] in disguise to town, and next morning by day break, in a chaise and pair, set out for New york with her.

1 Day   Morn: Caty and I went to meeting, HW: and Becky Jones spoke, afternoon reading and contemplation, I hear nor see no one who has got over the measels better than myself, through Mercy. went to meeting. William Rekitts the English friend who was taken by the french, on his Passage hear, and carried into old france, where a french gentleman took him to his house, and used him kindly. with Sally Morris, An-

---

131. Unknown, perhaps the book by Xenophon.
132. Moore, "Fable XIV, The Sparrow and the Dove," in *Fables for the Ladies* (London, 1749), 101.

thony Benezet, and Jos: Morris drank tea hear, I went half an hour to see Polly Howel, Caty Howel & Patience Gray was there: Patience & I went to meeting, Becky Jones, John Hawksworth, and Will: Rekitts spoke.

2   Morn: at Work, began a Shirt for Caty, afternoon folding, evening Sammy Samson hear.

3   Day, Caty and Ironing, evening at Work agreable with mamme

4   Morn: binding my red petecoat, afternoon at Work.

5   Day Caty & I busy in preparations for the meeting, Danny Smith come from Burlington, a pleasent evening.

6   Morn: Busy, afternoon at Caty Howels, talk on Sally Robinson who was almost like to have gone away with an officer, but a timely interposition of Friends, gave as she herself now thinks a lucky turn. Cousins John & Betty Smith in the evening from Burlington. I wrote to Sally Smith.

7   Morn: work and conversation with Caty and Danny. afternoon at Warners in Company with Caty Howel, Betsey Moode, Polly & betsy Sandwith, & Nancy Warner. evening I began the 7 Vol. of the history of England.

1 Day   Morn: at Meeting, Betty Morris, and Mordecai Yarnell spoke, our half Years meeting. a good deal of Company. afternoon at meeting Thomas Ross, James Daniel, and James Thornton spoke, the meeting was favoured with a ray of the Divinity which we profes to be guided by, 'twas plainly told us as ye sow, so shall you reep. if to the flesh Corruption, if to the spirit Eternal Life![133] Joseph Smith, son of my Cousin Sam: Smith, hear. he is come down to go Aprentice to Sam: Shoemaker. evening at meeting Becky Jones, Abraham Griffith, and Ben: Andrews spoke.

2   Morn: at meeting Ann Moore and John Storer spoke. the latter is from England, come with Sammy Emblen, he is a fine minister in Language and Gracefulness of motion. afternoon I drank tea Becky Rawles with Sally Fisher, evening a good deal of Company.

3   Morn: at meeting, Becky Jones, HW:, BT:, and William Rekitts spoke, the latter in a plain manner, but is a sound minister of the Gospel and his demeanour corrisponds, with his doctrines. afternoon at Work. Israel Pembertons Family in much trouble on account of Jos Jordan who is a very bad boy, Josey Pemberton not much better,

God in Externals did not place content.[134]

---

133. Galatians 6:7–8.

4   Morn: at Work, a good deal of Company, afternoon Cousin Betty and
          I went to Neighbour Warners, Ben: Sweet and Henry Drinker there,
          Benjm come home with us, staid the evening, see a picture of Ben: Lay.
          Preserve Brown & Wife lodged hear.
5   Day. Stress of weather gave us the Company of Jos: Noble, John & Betty
          Smith, John Hoskins, and Preserve & Molly Brown, and it pass'd agre-
          ably. I finished the third shirt for Caty.
6   Morn: Jos: Noble, Edward Cathrel, and Johns Smith & Hoskins set for
          Burlington, there has hardly been known as great a fresh[135] as at pre-
          sent in the River Delawar. Patty Noble and Abbey Raper dined hear.
          a letter from Danny Smith, with an account of there being overflowed.
          Abbey Raper Lodged hear.
7   Morn at Work, Agreable Conversation with Cousin Betty & Abbey. af-
          ternoon Anna Pole hear. English Women I take to be of a different
          temparament from most others, and am entirely of Priors mind. no
          method will sooner take with us, than, a degree of Liberty & generous
          Confidence, by generosity we are always over come.

Be to her Virtues very kind
Be to her faults a little Blind,
Then clap your padlock on her mind.
Matthew Priors English Padlock.[136]

[April 1, 1759]

1 Day 4   Morn: Cousin Betty & Abbey set out for Burlington. I went to meeting,
  Mo   Sam: Emblen, Mary Emblen, and John Storer spoke. afternoon at
          meeting, Cousins Lydia & Patty Noble drank Tea with us, I went to
          Neighbour Shoemakers a little, Polly Morris, Caty Smith, & I went to
          meeting, John Storer spoke. there was a Couple of girls of other per-
          suasions at meeting whose behavior made me think of Clarissa Har-
          lowe's saying, "there was both goodsense & good breeding in the old
          saying when at Rome do as they do at Rome." all who go to places of
          worship however should behave with Decency, let them come with de-
          sighn to see & be seen, or to receive Benefitt
2   Morn: at Work on Daddys 2d shirt. afternoon I drank with the Widow
          ball, set an hour with Betty Stretch, 16 weeks yesterday since she kept
          her Bed. a long & tedious Illness! Oh Life we know not what we ask

---

134. "God in externals could not place content," Alexander Pope, "An Essay on Man," Epistle IV, in
The Complete Poetical Works (New York, 1848) 44.

135. Freshet: a sudden surge of water, as from a spring thaw.

136. Prior's poem "An English Padlock" was published in 1707. HCS missed the third line: "Let all
her ways be unconfined." *Poems on Several Occasions by the late Matthew Prior esq.* (London, 1759), 83–85.

when we desire thee: rather ask for Resignation, to the Will of Heaven. evening Polly Rhodes, Anne Pole, Sally Hill, Pollys Pemberton & Jordan with myself spent agreably at Israel Pembertons.

3   Morn: at Shops. Caty & I, we went to meeting BT:, Ann Moor, and Mordecai Yarnell spoke, It was a good meeting to me. I drank tea at Jos: Fox's with Anna Michel and Sally James. Sally Robinson is gone sans seremonie[137] with the officer ——————— Downes. hither too there has been something so infatuating that what ever Girl, has been concerned with them it has proved her ruin.

4   Morn: at Work, afternoon: Nancy Gibson & I spent with Grace Caldwell, Betsey Plumstead is so infatuated with Officer ——————— Williams, I believe she will go with him: evening I spent with Caty Howel.

5   Morn: at meeting Mor: Yarnell, BT:, and DS: spoke. afternoon I spent with, Sally Lloyd who is under an afflicted state of Body, by frequent fallings fitts, but I think she seems in a sweet resigned state of mind. the hours I spent with her, were very Satisfactory.

6   Morn: 8 O'Clock Caty & I set out to walk to Point. it was very agreable, & made more so by the adishon of a new Book, afternoon Johny & Nancy Gibson drank Tea with us. 5 O'Clock we walked home.

7   Morn: finished Daddys second shirt, afternoon drank tea with Caty Howel, Nancy Warner & I took a walk.

1 Day   Morn: wrote in my Place Book. a letter from Sally Smith, Caty & I went to meeting. Sam: Emblen, David Easter, and Grace Fisher spoke. afternoon Caty & I at meeting Mordecai Yarnel spoke. Sam Emblem and Henry Drinker drank tea hear. evening Caty & I went to meeting, Becky Jones, David Easter, and H: Williams spoke.

2   Morn: a fine morning. General Amhurst come to Town, began the first of 2 shirts for Elisa Rue a poor woman. afternoon at Polly Stiles. evening Nancy Warner, Caty and I took a pleasent Walk. the inhabitents of Lancaster are much distressed by the Soldiers.

3   Morn: at Work. went to meeting DS: and John Storer spoke. Henry drinker brought Caty some tokens & hankercheifs to hem & run. I doubt not at all but Caty can by her needle maintain herself with reputation. afternoon, Mamme, Becky Rawles and myself drank Tea With Molly Foulk. evening at Work. great dissentions between our polite Lady R and her Husband, reading in the History of England

4   Morn: Tommy Lightfoot breakfasted hear, the Widow Rodman died Yesterday, of a long Indisposition. afternoon Patty Caldewalder come to see me

---

137. Sans seremonie: Fr. without ceremony, that is, without being married.

5   Morn: engaged in detecting some backbiteing. There is no Conversation so agreeable as that of a man of Integrity, who hears without any Intension to betray, and speaks without any Intension to deceive, ever let me be the Companion of Such. I went to meeting, BT: and HW: spoke. afternoon Becky Rawle & her Daughter Anne, Caty Howel & her Daughter Caty, with myself spent some agreable Hours with Neighbour Warner & Nancy. Evening reading the History of England to mamme & Caty.

6   Morn: finished the 2 Shirts, made a couple of hankercheifs for a poor woman. Mamme & I drank Tea with Betsey Morris, people's Conversation denotes the turn of there minds. thus sometimes it will fall into the Currant Money. evening Caty & I spent a pleasent hour with Nancy Gibson.

7   Morn: Cut out eight Night Caps. gave Caty four, and we made my four. afternoon Caty & I spent with Caty Howel. evening Josey Smith come & told us some news from B——n more havock and destruction of the Sex's fame, by those detested Soldiers.

1 Day   Morn: wrote in my place Book. went to meeting Mary Emblem spoke, Hecter, a Negro man of my Unkle Benjamin Smith's and afterward my Unkle Robert Smith's, who was parted with in the general rack of his fortunes![138] come to see us. afternoon went to meeting John Hawksworth spoke, drank with Han: Mickle. evening at meeting BT: and John Hawksworth spoke. this night there had like to have been a bad fire, Marcus Cool's bakehouse and another house burnt.

2   Morn at work on the 5th of mamme's shifts. Jos: Noble from B——n. read in the History of England. afternoon finished the Shift and read in the history.

3   Morn: at meeting BT:, William Riketts, and DS: spoke. Richard Wells & Rachel Hill were married. the meeting was a decent and composed time, & I believe they took each other in the fear of God. afternoon folding cloaths

4   Day Ironing, drank Tea with Becky Rawle. evening read to Caty.

5   Morn: packed up my cloaths for B——n, noon Bobby Smith came with a Chaise, to carry his Sister, Caty, & I. afternoon I drank tea with Anna Pole and called to see Molly Allison who I think is not like to continue long.

6   Morn: Ten O'Clock Bobby, Caty, & I set out the Jersey road for B——n. found Unkle Daniel under a fitt of the Gout, see myself welcomed amidst my relations and friends, in the place I am so obligated too. the place of my Mothers Nativity. five Sons and a daughter, of Docter

138. Meaning the man was sold because Robert Smith's finances were a wreck.

Richard Smith of Bramham in Yorkshire, come over early to America and setled at Burlington. the eldest Brother Daniel Smith married Mary Murfin, those are my Grand Parents. their children, Daniel Smith born the 2d of the 2d Month 1696. married Mary Hoot, Robert Smith born the 9th of the 8th month 1698. married Elizabeth Bacon. John Smith born the 20th of the 8th month 1700. married Ann Farrels. Joseph Smith born the 7th Month 1702. died the 19th of the 5th month 1713. Benjamin Smith born the 8th of the 10th month 1704. married Sarah Burling. Samuel Smith born the 23rd of the 9th month 1706. died the 19th of the 7th month 1712. Mary Smith born the 3rd of the 8th month 1709. died the 20th of the 5th month 1710. Cathrine Smith born the 22nd of the 12th month 1711.

[In margin: "married William Callender. taken from Daniel Smith's family Bible in 1759. 4th month the 20th day by Hannah Callender."]

7	Morn: at Work, afternoon Edward Cathrel came to see us Sally and I took a walk to see the man plow the Orchard. went to Unkle Roberts found them well. was at Sammy Smiths to see the family
1 Day	Morn: at meeting Abenezer Large and Peter Fern: spoke. dined with John Smith & Wife, Cousin Betty Smith. afternoon at meeting, Benajah Andrews spoke, Betty and Abby Smith drank tea with us, and we had an agreeable conversation, evening Sally Smith daughter of Daniel Smith, Daniel Smith, Betsey Smith, Caty Smith, Children of Robert Smith, and Han: Callender daughter of Catherine Callender, spent in friendship as the children of one father.
2	Morn: turned my Bonnet. afternoon Danny, Sally, & I took walk round the point, and viewed the Soldiers Barracks, which were then empty of their wretched Inhabitents, the Inducements women find to take to their way of Life is past my finding out, drank tea with Abby & Sally Raper, and John Hoskins & Wife.
3	Morn: wrote to Mamme, worked on her shifts, afternoon Betty, Sally, & Abby Smith, Sammy, Danny, & Dicky Smith & I, took a pleasent walk to Sammye's place. it was agreable.
to Day 4	Morn: at work, went with Bobby Smith to see them haul the fish nett, afternoon at Work, had a letter from mamme, Tommy Prior, and Dicky & Dan Smith hear, evening Danny, Sally, & I had some serious conversation, on the Importance of the preceeding days event.
5	Morn: 8 O'Clock I went down to assist the Bride, from thence we went to meeting and Daniel Smith Junr and Sarah Raper were married. Peter Fern spoke. a pleasent day in the eve of which, ten couple of us

young folks walked round the point. 8 O'Clock evening Sally Smith and I took leave and come home.

6   Morn: at Work, 12 O'Clock Cousin Jenny Smith and I went [to] Johsua Rapers to dine, in the afternoon there was an agreable Company of young folks. we played in moderation all that [afternoon] and the evening, Sam: Rodman waited on Sally, and Thomas Rodman on me, we were at home by half after Nine, the Wedding and its diversions was accomplished in a decent manner. we left them to the Happiness I hope they will enjoy

7   Morn: at Work on the shifts, afternoon men Company, evening walking

1 Day   Morn: read in the Accomplished Woman, a new and celebrated Author.[139] at meeting A: Large spoke, dined at Edward Cathrels, went to meeting. a large company of young folks drank tea at Joshua Rapers, then we walked down to the sluice and round into the town by London Bridge.

2   Morn: at Work on the Shifts and reading in Tatitus. afternoon Dicky Smith, Sally and I, took a walk to Rodmans, Anne, Betsey, & Sam: Rodman, Polly Smith, with a relation from long Island made a pleasent Company. we walked home again in the evening with the adission of there company, regaleing ourselves, with the sweet odours that nature at this season of the year exhibits from her universal Garden.

[May 1, 1759]

5 Mo 3   Morn: a beautious morn. Betsey & Caty Smith, Hannah Cathrel; Nancy Decow & I took a walk. this day 500 regulars passed through the town for Philadelphia. one of the officers lodged hear. afternoon Betsey Rodman, Sally Smith & I drank tea with Sally Raper Smith. evening reading in Tacitus, see the comit but it appeared dim.[140]

4   Morn: rose early. the Soldiers set off with musick playing. I went to Unkle Roberts to read and Worked. to the Girls. received a letter from Mamme, Becky Rawle brought a bed of a Son. Betsey, Caty, and I walked to the Church yard and read the tombstones. afternoon drank tea with Eliza Barker, thence we walked to the Sluice, the Company was Edward Cathrel, Tommy Powel, Tommy Prior, Dicky Smith. the two Sally Smiths, Sally Powel, Patty Noble, Han: Cathrel, & Caty Smith and myself.

139. Either Walter Montegu, *The Accomplish'd Woman* (1656), or Jacques Du Bosc, *The Accomplish'd Woman* (1753); neither was a new and celebrated author, however.

140. Halley's comet was predicted to return in 1758; it was first seen in December, but not in North America until April of 1759.

5   Morn: 5 O'Clock Sally and I walked to Eltons. drank dia drink, thence a large company of us walked to Sammy Smiths place, and back to breakfast. went to meeting A: large and Peter Fern spoke. Sally and I spent the afternoon at Sammy Smith's. evening a greable in Company.

6   Morn: Sally and Abby Smith and I took a walk. I went to Edward Cathrels, found Isaac and his wife from philadelphia, my parents well. Sally Smith, Anne Rodman, and I spent the afternoon with Sally Smith. began half dozen hankercheifs for mamme, finished one.

7   Morn: Sally, Abby, & I took a walk, read to Sally in the Accomplished Woman. afternoon Sally & I spent at unkle Roberts. evening reading Tacitus.

1 Day   Morn: wrote to Mamme, at meeting Hannah Smith and Betty Smith spoke. Sally Raper Smith, Patty Noble, Betsey & Caty Smith dined with us. afternoon at meeting the same company drank tea with us with the Addishion of Rich: Smith and Sam: Rodman.

2   Morn: at Work. went to meeting Peter Andrews and Hannah Smith spoke. afternoon 5 O'Clock Sally & I walked to Cousin Caty Wethrill's, evening at Unkle Roberts.

3   Morn: at Work. finished the second hankercheif, and read to Sally in Tacitus. afternoon spent with Cousin Betty Smith. evening reading to Sally.

4   Morn: at Work. finished the third hankercheif. afternoon Sally & I up at Barkers. evening Dan: & Sally Smith, Anne Rodman, Sally Smith, Eliza Barker, Hannah Cathrel, Betsey & Caty Smith, myself, Tom: Prior, Tom: Rodman, and Dick Smith played at Trays ace.[141] a good old Burlington Usage.

5   Morn: see Henry Drinker, all my friends well. finished the fourth hankercheif. went to meeting dined at Joseph Noble's. Bobby Smith, Sally Smith, Hannah Cathrel, Eliza Barker, Sally Smith, & myself, took a ride to John Smiths place, thence to Peter Ferns, an agreable afternoon in pleasent Company.

6   Morn: at Work. finished the fifth hankercheif, afternoon Sally and I spent with Caty Wethrel. evening a large Company of young folks.

7   Morn: at Work. finished the half dozen of hankercheifs. John Murfin a relation of my Grand mothers side, being in town, and offering to wait on us, Sally and I concluded to take a small tour round the Country, accordingly about 3 O'Clock we went out in Company with Dick Smith. just after a pleasent shower of rain, drank tea at Burdentown (a bout nine mile) with Johanna Brooks, went to see Unkle John Sikes, those are relations of my Grand mothers side. walked through the

141. A card game.

town, which is but small. from thence 5 miles to William Murfins, and
lodged

1 Day 6   Morn: Sally and I breakfast with Sarah Murfin, Widow of my grand
Mother Smith's Brother, John Murfin, now an ancient Woman. then
Nancy Murfin agreably enlargeing the Company, we set out for Stoney
Brook meeting, about 12 miles, stoped at James Calerks. a mile & half
from meeting, two young women, his daughters, going with us from
thence to meeting, a most pleasent ride, by the side of Stony brook, for
the most part thro' fine meadow, with the prospect of a fine high Country round. meeting Marget Porter spoke. thence we proceeded a mile
& half to Prince town. dined at —————— Horners. walked round
the Colledge, and the presidents House. good buildings for so young a
country, placed on a well chosen spot of ground, with the command of
the Country round, as far as the ken of Sight. there are several good
buildings in the town, but weather the Colledge Will bring forth more
good than hurt, time must demonstrate. seeing as I thought some traces
of the Monster vice, have made there appearence even in so short a time
as three years. being first day we found them at prayers, therefore did
not go inside the building. it accomadates 100"50 Scollers.[142] thence we
rode ten miles through a pleasent Country interspersed with all the variety that compleat a fine Prospect to Trentown. and drank tea with
Jos: Decows, Molly Derry come to see in testimony of her long acquaintance with my father, and his Country woman. Betsey Bacon
walked round the town with us, we see the barracks. The English
church, and remarked dwellings of several familys that I knew. 6
O'Clock rode 5 miles to William Murfins, and lodged there.

2   Morn: took leave of Aunt, Cousin William and family, rode a mile to
Preserve Browns, there we passed the morning agreably in seeing his
mill and its works attending to the fall of the water, pleasing discourse,
fishing &c till 2 O'Clock, then we set out for Burlington come through
Crosswicks, and pleasently home by Six O'clock, Cousin John Murfin
returned home again, with our thanks, found Unkle well.

3   Morn: at Work, afternoon also, Unkle took a ride, about 4 O'Clock
Sally & I heard a noise in the yard of a horse stumbling, & both run out,
Unkle's horse had flung him, and severely strained the main leaders[143]

---

142. 150 scholars. HCS apparently does not know how to count above 100. Compare the similar difficulty of her contemporary, Annis Boudinot Stockton, who "seems to have known the numbers to one
hundred. Beyond that, she created numbering conglomerations that repeated the original system. So page
118 in the manuscript book, for instance, is numbered by Stockton as '10018.'" Carla J. Mulford, "Political Poetics: Annis Boudinot Stockton and Middle Atlantic Women's Culture," *New Jersey History* 111
(1993): 84–85n19.

143. Muscles.

of his neck, so as to occassion great pain. thus do we meet with Clouds in our most Sanguanery prospects:

4   Morn: rose by half after 4, Unkle still in pain, at Work. afternoon, Rachel Cathrel, Betsey & Caty Smith hear, I have some thoughts of taking a journey to Newyork & flushing, if the work dont appear too great. evening read in Tacitus, the life of his father in Law Agricola,[144] a pretty thing and extreamly fitt for our young Gentlemen of the Army to read and Copy after.

5   Morn: wrote to mamme, went to meeting, Hannah Smith spoke. dined at John Smiths, spent an hour at Unkle Roberts, finished the afternoon with Jenny Burlen who persuades me much to think of going to york. Unkle still poorly.

6   Morn: Caty Smith went to Philadelphia, rest of the Day spent in Work and Discourse, evening Sally Raper Smith & Betsey hear.

7   Day, worked a side of a Pin Cushin, Edward Cathrel hear part of the afternoon, various are peoples thoughts concerning a single life, but if a person must be miserable, they had better be so by themselves.

1 Day   Morn: Nine O'Clock Richard Smith and Anna Pole, come home from P——a, brought me a letter of Permishion from my Parents, to go in Company with Anna to York, and as my Relations hear approve of the Journey I shall prepare to go. Anna Pole, Betsey Rodman & I, went to meeting, H: Smith spoke. afternoon at home geting ready to set out early in the morning. I looked upon myself, in particular under the Care of Jane Burling, who was to follow the next stage day because there would have been other ways[145] too large a company of, us for conveniency. they were Jane Burling, & her Son: Thomas Pryor, Anne & Betsey Rodman, Scaman & Thomas Rodman, Richard Smith Senior, Thomas Powel & his Wife. Anna lodged with me, and we rose

2   Morn: 4 O'Clock dressed ourselves by moonlight, breakfasted with Sally, set out in the Stage Waggon, from Shaws, our more particular Company Rich: Smith Senior and James James, other passingers some Sailors ship wrecked in the King of Prussia, a Humorous old dutch man, an officer of the jersey Blues. some of them found the Stage coach remidy, fell fast a sleep, the military man, and dutch man, one of the Sailors by the last night's debauch, and early riseing, become the Jest of brother Tars, saying 'twas a rough Sea, made the Passingers sick, he believed they must hand the buckit. the Country people were thick along the rode going to the fair at B——n. young Beaus on race horses, the Girls puting on all their airs and graces to Captivate so that it was

144. Cornelius Tacitus, *The Life of Agricola.*
145. Otherwise.

hard to find out which made the deepest Impression on Young fellows minds. Horses or Women. they made me think of Pope.

> *Or with his Hound comes Hollowing from the Stable,*
> *Makes love with nods, and knees beneath the table;*
> *Whose laughs are hearty, tho' his jests are coarse;*
> *And loves you best of all things—but his Horse.*[146]

By Seven O'Clock we arrived at Crosswicks. where we breakfasted at Douglas's. the meeting at Crosswicks is an ancient building but looks well. passed through Allen town, Hannah Rodgers lives there. took another passinger in. Docter Noel. dined in Cramberry at Prigmores. hear we fell in Company with the other Stages, those from Burden town. took the waggon that goes from hear, to Amboy ferry. diversity of objects, and Company filled our minds, with aboundance of Ideas. see the wreck of 2 Stages Occassioned by Crasey drivers and Passingers. crossed the head of the famous South River, whose navigation benefits New York with wood. for the length of two miles see hundreds of trees, torn up by the roots, in a violent storm of Wind that happened about two Years ago, with what fear must the minds of Passingers be filled, at that awful moment. Nature and Miracle and Fate and Chance are thine. We arrived at Amboy ferry by Six o'clock, little fatigued considering the length of the Journey, 50 miles. and our minds absorbed with the prospect of the Oceans, as we could not be content in the House, we walked round the Shore, and was delighted. but weary nature calling for refreshment, we went to the House again, and drank a dish of Tea, with the Gout[147] of Travelers. the house was full of people being the place for both Stages. so many different Kind of folk. all strangers in their manners to us young travelers, which filled our minds with a variety of Ideas. our officer fellow traveler, come to the door to Rich: and asked him where the Ladies were, Rich: brought him into the room to us, and he very civilly bowed, and wishing us well withdrew as also Docter Noel to Amboy. Anna and I looked dilligently to the landlady for clean sheets and pillowcases, and when we had them, notwithstanding [the] drinking & roaring appeared strange to us, it did not keep us awake all night.

3   Morn: 5 O'Clock the people began to stir about the House, them & curiosity roused us, and we went and set at the door, you see the small town of Amboy, Just oposite the ferry. noted the House Governor

---

146. Epistle to Miss Blount on her leaving the town after the Coronation (1715). *The Works of Alexander Pope* vol. VI.

147. Meaning with gusto, to taste, relish.

Belsher lived in. Cornelius Bradford & his Sister, Docter Ogdens Wife and Children breakfasted with us, they were going from york to Philadelphia. and by them I sent my love to my parents. By this the house began to part with some of its inhabitents, and people whom destiny had shown to each other, but now, parted never perhaps to meet again. each moved by different motives. natives of different climes. We see Ships at a great distance out at sea, pursueing the pathless tracts of the mighty Ocean.

> *The Passingers that travel*
> *In the wide Ocean, where no paths are,*
> *Look up, and leave their conduct to a Star.*[148]

Nine O'Clock we took [the] boat, but proceeded no further with our humorous passingers the Sailors, for they had intelligence of a man of War, the Nightingale, being in want of hands. and pressing.[149] One O'Clock they went ashore at amboy, and then brought some ham and cold veal aboard, they very civilly offered us part. this and a generous bottle, inspired them with fresh courage to think of the press Gang. we then set out and went between the Islands. the Shores are pretty diversified with Country Seats, and cultivated lands, we see the post road the Sailors, to spend time, landed first on staten Island, where Rich: and all went a shore, and presently one of the Sailors comes down with wine and a glass, to invite us to drink, we thanked him for his civillity but declined the offer. we hoped they would have staid there, but they all come aboard again, rolling stones in for ammunition, declareing it should be warm work if them then they did [attempt to impress] them, this raised Annas and my fears, but the men were so comical that I told them I believed it took a great deal to break a Sailors heart. very true Mam'e, a merry life and a short one. is there maxim. there was a poor little fellow in the boat, who had run a way from his Parents, about 13 years of age, he said he was the youngest Son of a Merchant in Bristol one ———— Edwards, he had a great notion to go to Sea, and his Parents [were] greatly against it, but consented to let him go on one voyage, in one of there own vessels, under care of the Captain. this insteed of abateing, increased his desire. and they were the more determined that he should not go again. he got what he could privately and took his passage on board a vessel bound for maryland as some time before an elder brother had married and was setled there, with a de-

---

148. From "The Surprisal," a play by Sir Robert Howard. *The Gramatical Works of Sir Robert Howard* (London, 1722), 64.

149. Impressment: the forcible recruitment of sailors into naval service—not an uncommon practice at this time.

sign to find him out. but he soon found the difference of being a Cabbin passinger under the care of the Captain and having no one to take
care of him. when they landed at Charles town the cruel creatures stole
all his cloaths and money from him. he wandered about some time in
quest of his brother but could get no tidings of him, and was reduced
to misery, he hired himself on board a vessel to go to york in hopes to
get home, but when he come there the vessels were all gone for England. he then went on board the privateer king of Prussia, where he
was cast away, and would have perrished but for one of the Sailors
(now in our boat) who touched with his youth and sad relation took
him under his care, and brought him to Philad from thence to York,
and had promised him he would seek a passage for him home, with
many little circumstances besides, my heart yearned and I weept over
him, Anna & I advised him, gave him something, and I doubt not but
he will remember us, as long as he lives. The Sailors landed on York
Island some miles from town, and when we were within Gun shot of
the Nightingale she fired, and some of them come on board of us. but
as there was nobody for them they soon left us. we landed at While hall
stairs about Six o clock and walked up Queen street till we come to
Burlings slip, where we steped into Will: Hawshursts, and found Sally
well, she went with us a little higher up to batemans slip where my
Aunt Sarah Smith And Phebe Pell lives. who were very glad to see us
and made us heartily wellcome. New York struck us at first View, and
we thought it very fine as indeed the outsides of the houses are, being
very fond of Scolloping and painting, it did as the beauteous structure
of the human frame

> *Beauty 'tis true at first may dazel,*
> *The Spectators view, but soon the lovely fathom*
> *glides away or is unheeded if it chance to stay*[150]

the outsides of the Houses too generally, may pass as epitomes of there
masters, they are a gay people, but we found them very polite to
Strangers. Anna and I lodged at my Aunts. who was pleased to see us.

[In margin: "to York, 'tis a very pleasent Sail, and the Porpoises tumbling along
adds to it."]

4   Morn: at our lodgeings, Cousin Phebe keeps shop, and as we set in the
Shop Walter and Thomas Franklin Come and enguired for us, they

---

150. "Beauty 'tis true, / At first may dazzle the spectator's view. / But soon the lovely varnish glides
away. / And grows unheeded, it it chance to stay." "A wish for a wife," in *The Polite Politician,* vol. 1 (London 1751) 148.

were acquainted with Anna in Philadelphia. we went to meeting, they have no public friend, or but one that seldom appears, Jos: delaplain, and a small meeting, afternoon Polly Morris and Polly Burling come to see us and we had an agreable afternoon Joined with a walk down the broad Way, a fine broad street with rows of button wood and locas[151] wood on each side, and for the most part Good houses, the water Carts going about the City was quite new to us, and we hobbled home over the stone paving, having seen anough for that night.

5   Day. we dined with Sally Hawkshurst and in the afternoon Rich Smith and she, went with us to the Milleners, Mrs: Durhams in Wall street, from thence to Allexanders great Shop, in broad street and to see ———
——— Wayman, a country man of ours. this evening I see Thomas & John Burling. Cousin Jenny &c come about Six this evening, and anna pole went to lodge with Polly Burling. I had a letter from Sally Smith.

6   Morn: at our lodgeings, Abby Bound come to see us, afternoon Polly Burling, Polly Morris, Sally Hawks, Anna and Tom: Franklin, Rich: Smith, and I walked up along the north river, then down by the kings docks and the Battery home. evening wrote to mamme, and we concluded to set out to morrow

7   Morn: 5 O'Clock for flushing, Polly Burling, Tommy Pryor, Anna Pole, Tommy Burling, Hallender, and Walter Franklin, it was such a fog that in Crossing the river we were out of sight of land, the ferry on Nassau or long Island is all most a town, and the pleasentess of the road begins from thence, it is pretty thickly settled from thence to Jameca, a little town where we breakfasted at Mashes, it cleared up a fine day and was very agreable traveling, on the window of the tavern I see the names of two Burlington Men: Bowman Hundlock and John Jolly, before we went from there we were met by Polly Morris and Tommy Franklin, Jameca consists of one street adorned with trees, a pretty little town. thence we went to Samuel Bounds fitted our selves for meeting and set out. John Storer and Benja: Andrews spoke. we went to one.   Faringtons by the meeting. I see Ben: Sweet and heard from home, flushing is 14 Miles from York and is a pleasant place, there is a pretty Country seat Just on the brow of the Hill belonging to a gentleman in York. we dined at Sam: Bounds. thence walked along the side of a hill, and recreated ourselves with trays ace in the Orchard. and there we lodged.

1 Day to   Morn: we went to meeting, John Storer and   spoke. full half
day   of the meeting was of other persuasions who made a cantico[152] of

151. Locust trees.
152. Cantico, unknown, perhaps chant, hum from the Italian *cantare, catillare.*

comeing to the great meeting, there was a good many friends from our parts there, James Pemberton, Anthony Beneset, Ester White, Mary Phares, Mary Hinton, several Young women of the name of Tolman from Jersey, and young West the limner, after meeting we were introduced by Anne Rodman to her relations of the same name and received an Invitation to dinner. It is about 4 miles and a half out of flushing and a most beautiful ride, the rode round flushing look like Pleasent Walks, of a two chair wedth, fenced by low walls with trees planted along them, or fine Prims hedge, this rode to Rodman's in particular is pleasent by reason of fine riseing hills which gives a view of the bay and the Country, cloathed at this time in beautiful fields of Grain and pastureing, there was likewise a fine peice of woods so clear from brush underneath and covered with grass that it seemed to invite one to a cool retreat from the noon tide ray. The House is close by yet within a good distance from the Inlet of the Bay, on which it stands. the family then Consisted of the old Gentleman & lady, Cathrine, Caroline, & Penelope, there daugh[ter]s, and John and Thomas, there Sons. and live in a genteel manner. there is a good prospect from the door, of the Bay and big Island. with pretty riseing hills covered with trees. Scaman Rodman, Dicky Smith, and Anne & Betsey Rodman dined there, with a nother of there Unkles. afternoon we all went to Charles Hicks a little further on the same inlet, a Gentleman that married one of the Rodmans. and lives in a very genteel manner. there a shower of rain detained us all night, the evening considering so large a Company, was spent pleasently, I never was of the opinion that numbers increased the pleasures of Conversation. but in the select few dwells the rational pleasure. the Men went in the Neighbourhood to seek lodgeing, Betsey Rodman, Anna Pole, Hallender slept together.

2   Morn: Charles Hicks was a Yorker, he lived with Walton, and from him went to the Savana, Lugan[153] and among the Spainards till he had acquired a fortune, by persuasion he is Church of England but seeing.——
————Rodman, liked her and they married, a reconsciliation of friends followed, and now they jog on, in the good old matrimonial Way. in his person he is tall and maigre, his face is not hansome, but a large Wigg and hat, joined to a blue long skirted coat instantly makes you think of a parson, in his temper there is a fund of humour which diverted me several times, especially in the morning his enquiry after our Dreams, the ensuing night, they had several pretty little Girls. the rest of our Company come, and breakfasted with us. then set out for —
———— Rodmans again. where we staid till meeting time. Hannah

---

153. Perhaps the small town in Northern Spain or one of several similarly named places in the Caribbean.

Bound was there, and Anna put on more youthful airs than was agreable to me, she and I rode in a chair together to meeting.   spoke. then our own company with Richard Smith returned to Sam: Bounds. where we dined. Phebe & Patty Townsend with there brother, was there from oyster bay. afternoon we went to one Judge Hicks and where[154] met there by the Rodmans, Peggy Bound, Hannah Bound, Henry Hadock, and Samy and Abby Bound. Judge Hicks has 4 daughters and a Son. round the Tea table we were five & twenty. his House is situate on the same Inlet; and but at a little distance from Rodmans & Charles Hicks, and another relation just opposite so that there is a good neighborhood, and a most beautiful pleasant Country. Upon an eminence at some distance from the House, our own Company and those from a Neighbours, made five and thirty playing Trays ace. we went home to Sam: Bounds by moonlight. Sammy Bound, Anna Pole, and I in a chair.

3   morn 9 O'clock we parted from Sam: Bounds' family; and Rich: Smith, excepting Sammy Bound and Abby Bound who went with us to Rocky way. it is a beautiful ride, with fine flocks of sheep. we rode till we come to the edge of the plains. where we stoped to dine, and were met by the Rodmans, Tommy Pherson, and   Ridgeaway, we kept tolerably within bounds except laughing at Dicky Smith. afternoon we set out in the following order, over the plains: Tommy Franklin, Caroline. Rodman, John Rodman, Abby Bound, Tommy Rodman, Anne Rodman, Scaman Rodman, Polly Morris, Tommy Prior, Polly Burling, Dicky Smith, Betsey Rodman, Tommy Burling, Anna Pole, Sammy Bound, Caty Rodman, Walter Franklin, and Hallender. Crossed the plains to Hamstead, in some places I observed a bundance of small birds. flocks of sheep and cattle are brought by their owners in the spring, marked and go feed on the plains till fall, when they meet and every one takes his own. Hamsteed is a small villige, where we enquired the road to Rocky way, and found we had come a good deal out of our way, to the divirsion of some of the Company. we then followed direction as we thought but it led us, but, against a fence. we turned and went laughing on, till we got the right. and proceeded down to Rich: Cornwals at the Beach, which is thirty miles from flushing. we enquired the nearest way to it. which was about a mile or too. but going through the Woods, the Chairs one after another, Thomas franklin and Caroline Rodman who were partly the first, and in discourse with the chair behind the other were overset by a stump. which alarmed me much, but they neither received any hurt, Thomas got up, shook himself, and looked as if he had not a word to say. we had not gone a hun-

154. Were.

dred yards further before Dicky Smith, the foremost Chair, makes a full stop which jamed the chairs, back one upon another unavoidably, and threw me upon the forepart of the chair, on my stomach, surprise made it ache badly. but comeing into a feild I told Walter Franklin I would go no further that night and desired him to turn about, to the first hospitable house, when we turned, Tommy Rodman and Anne Rodman did also, and we went to a good looking house a little back on the road which Tommy thought to be a relation of his, one Thomas Cornwal, but the people's name proved to be Rodgers, his relation was there on a visit, half long Island is related, and I am sure I thought this a mighty good time to claim it. there being no public houses nigh. after being there a little I began to come too and could not help revolveing the days adventures. we asked and they very civilly granted us a good dish of tea, which while we drank there come a horse & Chair for the woman Cornwal that some of her relations were come to see her, which we knew to be the rest of our Company. we asked the woman if she could lodge us, she answered without hesitation she could, after tea we rode to the Company. found them kindly received, the women at the table, the men standing round fully employed on divers loaves of bread, cutting for them both, a fine dish of oysters, and they told us they cut a much better figure now than they did at first comeing from the beach. Betsy Rodman, Anna Pole, Hallender, Dicky Smith, Tommy Burling, and Walter Franklin went to Rodgers to lodge. we had a most agreable evening spent with the man & his Wife, giveing him, an account what a company of strolers he had in his house, two from Philadelphia, two from Burlington, two from york. the women never had seen the sea before. I cannot tell the pleasure I felt at seeing the hospitality of the people, a Virtue Inherent by our ancestors, transplanted in our wooden soil, and when I want an incitement to it may I always remember ————————— Rodgers. we had a fine hot supper of fish. and very clean lodgeing.

4

Morn: we breakfasted there, and with thanks bid them farewel. went to see a curious Indian Wigg Wam, made of reads, rought into matts, laid one over the other, so compactly as to keep out the weather. the door was Straw hinges of the same. the fire place in the middle, and an open place in the top, births, round the room for lodgeing, on one of which the old man, father of the family, lay, he had almost lost the use of his limbs last year by hardship at Oswego. the mother was pounding Corn on a stone worn hollow like a morter. milk in a conk shell, the rest of the things agreable to those. they had three Children, and thus lived those ancient tenants of the land. we met the Company at Cornwals and from thence went to the Beach, the fine white sand along it is so hard that rideing makes no impression on it. we rode several miles sometimes in the Waves which seem to meet you, as though they would overwhelm we see some ships out at sea, which looks of a green cast. the hills of Shrewsberry appeared at a vast distance. the rideing is so fine that there is often great Wagers won by racing. and thus we bid adieu to one of the most glorious sights my eyes ever beheld. we rode through a pleasent Country to Jameca. where we dined, so large a company one tavern could not entertain, Anna Pole, Hallender, Thomas Burling, and Walter Franklin dined together, these 4 went to see Polly Sedberry, about a mile before you come to Jameca, she was our old School mate, and we were pleased to see one another, she had a fine little girl in her arms. Children early show there tempers. and one may then form some Judgement, of there future conduct in life. this child seemed to me born with a good humour,—Sedberry is Minister of Jameca, a hansome man, and they seemed to live in Concord, after diner the Company met at Mashes, and were full of mirth, John Rodman Inquiring how I liked the Country, told me there was a place just by called Horsmander's folly[155] or mount look out, built round the body of a large tree to a great higth, assending by winding stairs. on a fine high hill, at the top it is floored, and a table, half a dozen may drink tea on it comfortably. I said I had a great desire to see it, and run from this Crazey Company, we went to a chair & got in, it soon took wind where we were going and they followed. eighteen in number in so small a place, made some of them fearful, the prospect was as far as the ken of sight, we see the beach we had that morning been on, and they look out hear for shiping. in fine it was worth seeing. Anna Pole and Hallender left there names there, in company with abundance more. when we come to the road we parted with all the Company, except those we come from York with: Tommy Franklin, Polly Morris, Tommy Burling, Anna Pole, Tommy Pryor, Polly Burling, Walter Franklin, and Hallender rode to the half way house and drank tea, from thence pleasently to York ferry from whence there is a good view of York, from the South part, and the shiping. divers Country seats on long Island, and above York one Built by a brewer, entirely from the proffits ariseing from [y]east we landed safe about 7 O'Clock, and all our friends well.

[In margin: "there is Beacons placed on a hill to alarm the Country in case of an invasion."]

155. Perhaps a site named for Daniel Horsmanden of Long Island, later chief justice of New York but during HCS's visit recorder and member of the governor's executive council. He was heavily involved in both the Zenger trial of 1735 and the trial of supposed conspirators in the Slave Insurrection of 1741.

5   Morn: at Home, afternoon at John Franklin's, on a visit to his Wife who was Debby Morris of Philadelphia. she has a fine little girl. something in the childs countenance made me, think of my friend Caty Howel, and her Children, Anne especially.

[June 1, 1759]

6   Morn: at Home, writeing to mamme by Rich: Smith, afternoon Polly Burling, Polly Morris, Rich: Smith, Hallander, anna pole, and Tommy franklin walk'd along the north River, the Jersey shore oposite it is very high and rockey. I think the prospects from the north and South rivers, with the prospect from the fort, of the Islands, sandy hook at a distance &c., form a finer view than I ever see before, we met Tommy Pherson and Sammy Franklin and went to the mead House, a sort of liquor made of honey, which is weak and [has] a pleasant taste, there is a row of neat wooden houses a little within the palizadoes,[156] called the mead houses, where it is customary to drink this liquor and eat Cakes.

7   Day: at home. Anna Pole and Polly Burling drank tea with us.

1 Day   Morn: Aunt Sarah Smith, Cousin Jenny Burling, Widow Burling, Polly Burling, Anna Pole, and Hallender went to meeting. William Horn spoke: afternoon at meeting William Horn spoke. drank tea with Polly Burling. Sally Franklin married to an officer.

2   Morn: at home. afternoon at Polly Burlings, we went to John Burlings whose family was very unwell, he has two grown up daughters but for this reason We had not so much of their company as we coud have wished.

3   Morn: Anna and I at shops, wrote to Mamme, went to see Alice Ratsey

4   Morn: at meeting I dined with Thomas Dobson and his Wife. afternoon Polly Burling, Anna Pole, and Hallender spent at Sam: Bounds with his wife Abby Bound.

5   Morn: Anna Pole and Hallender went to Noels the Booksellers. I bought me Seneca's Morals, Thomsons Seasons, Young's Night Thoughts.[157] it used to be our custom often, to walk the streets, and feast our eyes. afternoon we drank tea at home. the evening was spent agreably.

6   Morn: Many pleasent hours I spent with Aunt Sarah, Cousin Jenny, and Phebe Pell, afternoon at Polly Burlings, this is a very good family, and I shall always respect them.   Wright a relation of theirs drank tea with us and kindly Invited us to see her.

---

156. Palisades.

157. Lucius Annaeus Seneca, either the *Moral Essays* or the *Moral Epistles,* various editions. James Thomson, *The Seasons* (1744). Young, *The Complaint* (1743).

[In margin: "x note morning we had a meeting in the family. William Horn, Marget Bound, Sarah Hadock, and Will: Horn, Marget Bound spoke."]

7   Morn: Anna Pole, Hallender, Tommy Pryor, and Tommy Burling, went with a Jew ———————Gomes to the Synagogue, My thoughts were employed on divers parts of the Scriptures relateing to them, they were then called on to Consider, Oh that they were wise,[158] but they were a stif necked people,[159] satisfied with forms and ceremonys, and thus the essential part was rent from them. there moode of worship has nothing solemn in it, nor their behavior neither. I cant say but I shed a tear for them, and secretly prayed, I mought rightly use the blessing, of having my eyes opened, from the Slavery of Tradition. this people were once the chosen people, now the scum of the earth![160] afternoon busy Ironing. wrote to mamme.

1 Day   Morn: at meeting. Anna Pole and Hallender dined with Peggy Dobson. afternoon at meeting went home wiht Sally Forbes.

2   Morn: I spent with Sally Hawks, afternoon Polly Burling, Anna Pole, and Hallender went to William Vanvikes, he has three daughters, Phebe, Hannah, and Eliza, from thence Polly, Anna, Phebe, Hannah, myself and Robinson Hicks took a walk to ——————— Boyard's Country seat, who was so complaisent as to ask us in his garden. the front of the house, faces the great road, about a quarter of a mile distance, a fine walk of locas trees now in full blossom perfumes the air, a beautiful wood off one side, and a Garden for both use and ornament on the other side from which you see the City at a distance. good out houses at the back part. they have no gardens in or about New York that come up to ours of philadelphia

3   Day: most agreably spent in work and Conversation with Polly Burling and Anna Pole, at the Widow burlings, Thomas and Walter Franklin.

4   Morn: at home Cousin Jenny ,Anna Pole, Tommy Pryor, and Hallender dined with Sam: and Abby Bound. afternoon Polly Burling, Anna & I went to Marget Bounds on a visit to Peggy & Hannah. Caty, Pen, and Tommy Rodman come there from long Island. Caty is engaged to Henry Hadock. in the evening being moonlight we walked round the Battery, evening wrote to mamme.

5   Morn: 5 O'Clock Walter Franklin, Anna Pole, Sammy Bound, Polly Burling, Sammy Franklin, Hanna Bound, Henry Hadock, Caty Rod-

---

158. Deuteronomy 32:29.
159. Exodus 32:9; Deuteronomy 9:6.
160. See William Pencak, "Jews and Anti-Semitism in Early Pennsylvania," *PMHB* 126, no. 3 (2002): 365–408.

man, Tommy Franklin, Pen Rodman, Tommy Rodman, Polly Morris, Tommy Pryor, and Hallender set out breakfast at the Glass house in Greenage, a pleasent place about three miles from York, along the north River. from thence took the road to Kingbridge. in view of several fine Country seats, Morrisenea, rode through a fine laural swamp, all in bloom, where we gave our selves the Palm. on many of the riseing Hills the winding little River is seen that goes from York to kingsbridge, and divides the Counties, and the tavern is prettyly situated at the foot of a hill, the little River meandering through a meadow before it. High lands of Woods and Plains, with Cattle graseing, makes a compleat landscape. We were well entertained, and a kind Dutchman that kept the house Would have our names down, and he would send us some Sweetharts. We rode over the New Bridge, which parts York Island, from the ad joining Counties, and a little way round to the old bridge, that we might say we had been through York Island, from hence we rode to hell Gate or Hournshook, and drank tea, the house and appurtenances, with the Water looked so calm, that I was for reveresing the name, but they tell me 'tis not so always, this is the New England channel for small Craft, there is a spot which boils like a pot, continually, and there has been Instances of small boats, perishing. this occasioned its name from a vulgar apprehensian. there was a great deal of Company at the house there is but one road out of York, and those three places we have seen to day, the most frequent rides, of people from the City. we had the South river in view home, so that we had been the length, and almost breadth of York Island, got to Cousin Phebe's just time anough to avoid a shower of rain, which replenished the earth after a warm Day.

6   Morn: wrote to mamme, afternoon Anna Pole and Hallender went to visit Wright, the House is at the corner of Wall street and Queen Street, oposite the Coffee House, and juts into the street a little, the parlour upstairs so that Anna & I feasted our eyes finely.

7   Morn: Polly Burling and Hallender at Work, Anna Pole reading, afternoon Polly Franklin drank tea with us early. then Polly Franklin, Anna Pole, Hallender, Walter Franklin, and Tommy Franklin, walked up the North River, to a fine high hill, set on a bower and drank some Sangree,[161] see the remains of a battery made last War. the Palisadoes as they call them, are stakes drove thick in the earth, at some distance from York, and reach from north to South rivers, there are two Gates. which used to be watched, but tis partly gone to ruin. the space within the palisadoes, is called the feilds, and out side the Commons. in the feilds there is a hansome building, called a Work house but it is for

---

161. Sangree, a punch made of rum, sugar and lemons.

Lunaticks also. a neat building Just finished for a Jail. there is a Colledge[162] began, but it has got into party,[163] and I doubt will make no figure.

1 Day   Morn: at meeting, dined with Aunt, afternoon at meeting, Polly Burling, Anna Pole, Hallender and Walter Franklin went to Phebe Vanvikes, and drank tea, Docter Creguer and Tommy Burling was there

2   Morn: spent with Joshua Delaplain and his Wife. afternoon Anna Pole, Polly Burling, Hallender, Polly Morris, Tommy Pryor, Tommy Burling, Walter Thomas & Samuel Franklin drank tea with Polly Franklin.

3   Morn: at home, afternoon Anna Pole, Polly Burling, Hallender, and Sally Hawks spent together at Polly Burlings. went a little bit to see Phebe Sackit. wrote to mamme.

4   Morn: at meeting, afternoon Cousin Jenny Burling and Hallender went to Visit the Gomes family, Jews some time since from barbados, lived nigh my Grandfathers, and knew all my relations, this was a pleasent 2 hours, in talk about them.

5   Morn: Anna Pole, Hallender, and Walter Franklin, walked down Queen Street to the fort, went into it and took a curious view of it for the last time, 'tis what I must trust to memory and Idea, for I cant describe it. more than that I think it fine, and the prospect from it delightful. we left our names on a large brass Gun at the right wing turning from the Governors house, one of the rooms was open and round it several portraits of the royal family at full length. the bowling green stands at the foot of the fort, and head of the broad Way. Afternoon: Polly Franklin, Polly Morris, Hannah Bound, Polly Burling, Anna Pole, Hallender, and Tommy Burling, spent most agreably at the Widow Burlings. Evening: Polly Burling, Anna Pole, Hallender, Effingham Lawrence, Tommy Franklin, and Tommy Burling spent agreably at the mead house.

6   Morn: Docter Jay visits Cousin Jenny, he and I often passes jokes, afternoon Anna Pole Hallender went to visit Spencer, it was a pleasent Visit, I see one of my early acquaintance a young woman Nancy Gamboe, we had forgot each others persons, but perfectly remembered our intimacy.

7   Morn: Polly Franklin, Polly Burling, Hallender, Walter Franklin, and Tommy Pearsall, went to see the English Churches,[164] the old Church in the broad Way, is a rich Church, tolerably well built, and stands in a beautiful spot, fine large trees before it composes a Walk for the length of a Square, which is the burial ground, the whole look of the

162. King's College, founded 1754, now Columbia University.
163. Political disputes.
164. Anglican churches.

street is pleasent, you would immagine yourself in some of the Citys in England that are much visited by people of Condition, for their health, quite still from business, all the looks of pleasure, not as if the midst of a great City. the New Church or St Georges Chappel, stands in the upper part of the town, in the street. Called after it the new Church street, it is a neat plain building [with] pretty palisadoes and trees planted round it, from the Steeple there is a full view of York, I dont Immagine it stands on above half the Ground of Philadephia, but the houses are very thick, and there may be as many Souls in it. the New Dutch Church is also, a pleasent building, the method, of having a pretty Court and planting trees round their buildings is very pretty. The Exchange is lately built but not well esceuted, it stands at the foot of broad street, close by the South River, and at the head of broad street, is the City hall, which to meet made me think of one of the Gates of London, for there is a resemblance. afternoon Polly Franklin, Tommy Pearsall, Anna Pole, Walter Franklin, Polly Burling, Tommy Burling, Hallender, and Tommy Pryor, rode to Kilbys's place at Greenwick, there is a most beautiful Water View, down the North river to Sandy Hook, several Vessels comeing in, and I believe thirty big and little to be seen, the many little Islands make those rivers beautiful, from thence to Oliver Delancys place Blomandol, which is a hansome house built in good taste of stone whitened. about a mile beyound stoped at a county house, got a good drink of butter milk, and turned toward York cross the hills and plains to the main rode, which for three miles from York is as fine as a Landscape, a good many pretty Country seats, In particular Murreys, a fine brick house, and the whole plantation in good order, we rode close under the finest row of Button Wood I ever see, the Governor James Delancy lives in a good house about a quarter of a mile from York.

1 Day	Morn: at meeting afternoon at home, drank tea at Polly Burlings with Anna Pole, Walter franklin, Tommy Franklin, Sammy franklin, Effy Lawrence, and Tommy Burling. I set an hour with Sally Hawks this day my heart was made glad with the thoughts of returning home to morrow, having staid 2 weeks longer than I at first intended for Cousin Jenny Burling who would not be content to see us go without her, being in an ill state of health,
2	Morn: 5 O'Clock staid at Aunts, till 10 O'Clock, seeing my friends, and parting with them. My aunt perhaps I never may see again, we parted tenderly, and I thank her for her seasonable admonishions, as Anna and I had a good deal of young Company. and young ourselves. I stoped at the Widow Burlings, and she parted with us like a mother! Polly Burling, Sally Hawks, Tommy Burling, Johnny Burling, Walter

franklin, and Tommy franklin, went to white hall Stairs with us, there Cousin Jenny Burling, Caty Lawrence, Anna Pole Hallender, Tommy Pryor, and Sammy Burling, took boat for Wattsons ferry. Tommy Lawrence, Effy Lawrence, Tommy Burling, Watty Franklin, and Tommy franklin Crossed the ferry with us. in three quarters of an hour we went nine miles, the pleasentest sail I ever had both for good wind and fine prospect. nutten Island,

[In margin: "and hear we parted with the Girls, I shall always remember with pleasure the pleasen hours I have spent with them."]

Staten Island, Long Island, divers privateers and other Vessels lying among them, in short, new beauties opening up on me every moment. after diner we set out in the Stage, and the Yorkers returned. we stoped at house intending to Drink tea, but it looked dirty and we did not. stooped upon a hill about the middle of the Island, for a view out to sea, we see a Sheep with 4 Horns, all of them at full growth. looking like for rain we proceeded to the end of Staten Island without stoping. where we staid that night and slept in our cloaths for the bugs were so thick we could not go to bed: but we were merry over our affliction.

To Day   Morn: 6 O'Clock crossed the ferry, breakfasted at the house oposit Am-
3   boy, from thence our own particular Company which was very agreeable: Cousin Jenny burling, Caty Lawrence, Anna Pole, Hallender, Tommy Pryor, and Sammy Burling, set out for Crambery on the stage. Caty Anna and Hannah dubed Tommy our Night,[165] and gave him the title, Night of the four Ladies. we dined at Prigmores, and set again. left Caty Lawrence at Allen town, with her Aunt Montgomery, and got to Crosswicks by 5 O'Clock, where we had a comfortable dish of tea, and concluded to stay all night, the people are cleaver people and we staid with satisfaction

4   Morn: half past 4 O'Clock, we had a most beautiful ride to burlington by 8 O'Clock, we met James and Hannah Kinsey on the road going to breakfast with John Lawrence, all our friends well, Anna and I lit at Unkle Daniels and breakfasted with Sally, Sammy Smith come and set the morning with us, afternoon Anna Pole, Sally Smith, Hallender, Sammy Rodman, and Dan: Smith drank tea together at Unkle's. evening I went to see Unkle Roberts family, and Sally Raper Smith, Betsey and Anna Pole, and Dan: Smith come and suped with us at Unkle Daniels we parted not till 11 O'Clock, giving them an account of the Civilities we met with in our Journey.

165. Knight.

5   Morn: breakfasted and Anna Pole, Hallender, Molly Nuttle, and Sammy Wetherill come to Philadelphia in three hours by water. at the Warf anna & I parted, I come home and had the satisfaction to hear my Parents were well, but at Plantation. I dined with Neighbour Warner, Friend Coleman, Polly and Betsey Sandwith, and Nancy and Betsey Warner. after diner Joshua and Caty Howel rode by for plantation, and were so kind as to go and tell Daddy & mamme I was at home, I went home and from thence to Catys and kissed her child Caty, drank tea with Becky and see the little Stranger William Rawle, and this evening my eyes was once more blessed with the Sight of my Father.

[In margin: "Allison buried this morning. Henry Drinker called in to welcome me home."]

6   Morn: 7 O'Clock Mamme and Caty come home to breakfast well and I again saw myself happy in them. and now O' father of all my Mercies.

> *Blot out my stains, my devious footsteeps guide,*
> *"And lay the uplifted thunder bolt aside."*[166]

Afternoon Caty Howell Hallender went to see Rachel and Anna Pole, Becky Rawle called upon us and we made a short vist to Jenny Groves and Molly Shirly. Charles Norris is married to Polly Parker, a great deal of money on both sides, wether that was the prevailing motive, is known only to the searcher of hearts

7   Morn: closely writing in this book having trusted a great deal to memory, received a letter from Sally, with one that had been sent to me from mamme. Cousin Dick is come back to B——n, from Rhode Island. afternoon closely writeing. evening Caty Smith and Hallender went to Caty Howels, Becky Rawle was there, I gave them the small token of friendship I brought them from York see Abel James and Sam: Shoemaker.

[July 1, 1759]

1 Day   Morn: 5 O'Clock wrote in this Book, Jos: Smith hear,

7 Mo   some things a little disagreable, we must take the rough and the smoth. went to meeting Ben: Trotter, Grace Fisher, and John Pemberton spoke. Grace Fisher dined hear, afternoon at meeting: Mordecai

---

166. The phrases "blot out my stains" and "devious footsteps" appear in a number of contemporary works. HCS has matched them to a single unrelated line, "any lay the uplifted thunderbolt aside," from Joseph Addison's *Cato A tragedy* (Dublin, 1713), 41.

Yarnel and Abel James drank tea hear, spoke to Rachel Wells, evening wrote

2   Morn: writeing. Jerry Elfrith hear. afternoon most agreably spent with Betsey Sandwith in discourse. I was pleased to find her Judgement co-incide with me on reading and books. evening Neighbour Warner.

3   Morn: Anna Pole breakfasted hear, we went and bought Sally Smith & mamme a peice of Persian,[167] I went to meeting. Hannah Smith, Mordecai Yarnel spoke. Han Smith and her Daughter Hannah dined hear. afternoon Caty and I wound thread.

4   Morn: got this book in due course, at Work, afternoon Mamme and I rode to see Mary Lightfoot, she lives at Tommy Lightfoots place, an Innocent old Woman, Henry Drinker brought Caty eight shirts to make.

5   Morn: 5 O'Clock Mamme set for Burlington. went to meeting: B T: Hannah Smith, John Hawksworth, and Joice Beneset spoke, afternoon Caty and I at Work, Daddy drank tea with us. a smart shower of rain after which the token between Heaven and Man, that our next punishment should not be by a deluge, Iris beauteous bow, appeared.[168] Sammy Shoemaker hear, the clouds flew very low, those mists in the mighty Vacuam, coulered, by reflected light from the Sun.

6   Morn: William Rickets, John Smith from Burlington breakfasted hear. Mamme landed at Rodmans. 2 O'Clock Yesterday. wrote in my Place book afternoon Worked on my Pincushin. evening Nancy Warner.

7   Morn: finished the Pincushin, and shall enclose it in a letter to Hallender of Barbados. Daddy went to Plantation, and the intrem[169] of the day passed agreably between Caty and I, Six O'Clock Daddy drank tea with us

1 Day   Morn: at meeting, Will: Brown and becky Jones spoke. afternoon at home, Plymouth Polly Morris, and Ben: Sweet drank tea hear. evening reading.

2   Morn: 5 O'Clock drew out a Pincushin, began a shirt for Caty. afternoon at Work. and spent in an agreable retirement with each other, Daddy drank tea with us. a fine moonlight Night!

3   Morn: Ben: Trotter breakfasted with us, Wrote to Hallender inclosed the Pincushin, by John Hawksworth.[170] Went to meeting, B T and David Easter spoke. afternoon Nancy Warner, Henry Drinker, drank tea hear

---

167. A thin, soft silk fabric used for linings.
168. HCS here mingles the biblical story of the rainbow, Genesis 9:11–13, with classical Greek mythology, where Iris, goddess of the rainbow, serves as a messenger from the gods.
169. Interim.
170. Meaning he acted as courier.

4   Morn: wrote to Sally, by Daddy: at Work. afternoon at Work for Caty
      5 O'Clock went with Debby Morris to a funeral, from thence to see old
      Eliza: Morris and Sally Morris. evening Polly Rhodes and Anna Pole.

5   Morn: Caty and I at some shops from thence to meeting, Dan Stanton,
      Hese: Williams, and Will: Rickits spoke. afternoon John Hawks worth
      hear talk: about my relations in Barbados. Friend Coleman, Neigh-
      bour Warner, Polly Parock, and Hallender drank tea with Neighbour
      Samsom. Polly Cowman deceased!

6   Morn: wrote to Aunt Sarah Smith, Polly Burling, and Sally Hawkshurst
      my York friends to thank them for their Civilities to me. Henry Drinker
      hear talk of his going to England. afternoon Caty Howel and her child
      Caty.

7   Morn: Copied my letters and carried them to Anthony Morris's to be
      sent to York, afternoon at Work. finished a shirt for Caty, and read in
      Night thoughts. evening Henry Drinker.

1 Day Morn: Jos: Smith breakfasted with us, Abel James set an hour with us,
      Caty and I went to meeting, Mary Emblen, Becky Jones, and B T:
      spoke. afternoon we went to meeting, B T: Polly and Betsey Sandwith,
      and Nancy Warner, drank tea with us, evening all went to meeting. B
      T: William Rickitts, and Becky Jones spoke.

2   Morn: 5 O'Clock began a shirt for Caty, 11 O'Clock Daddy come from
      B——n, afternoon Sally Holloway and Polly Stiles, some disagreables
      conserning J: H-s-w, be greatly Cautious, of thy slideing steps, nor at-
      tempt to gain the visibles of the Just man's path, before thou art wor-
      thy. hated and detested is the Hypocrite, both by God and Man. an
      attack made on fort Ligonear,[171] in which one Jones a young man I
      knew fell! Oh my Country thou bleeds in every Vein, but some feel it
      in the nerve most tender, feel it in their friends. evening wrote to
      mamme

3   Morn: at Work went to meeting, Will: Rickitts spoke, Caty Lightfoot
      dined with us, afternoon at Becky Rawle. evening Henry Drinker and
      Sammy Samsom.

4   Morn: James Were from Carolina hear, afternoon at Work, 11 O'Clock
      at Night of the hardest gusts of thunder and lightning I ever knew,
      surely "he is seen in the Storm."[172]

5   Morn: Caty and I went meeting, Mordecai Yarnel spoke. afternoon fin-
      ished the shirt, drank tea with Neighbour Wall. Capt Sterling his down
      at Chester in a forty Gun Ship, the first that ever come so far up our River.
      Caty, Henry Drinker and I took a little round. and called at Warners.

171. Fort Ligonier was fifty miles east of Pittsburgh.
172. Nahum 1:3.

Henry visits Betsey Sandwith.[173] William Rickits went Yesterday for barbados.

6   Morn: James Vereé breakfasted hear, 9 till 10 O'Clock suffered a great deal from my temper. then Daddy & I rode to point-no-point and dined. then drank tea with Neighbour Warner at her place with Becky, Caty, Nancy, Joshua Frances, and Doctor Evans.

7   Morn: at Work, afternoon at Work with Caty. began the 8 Vol of the History of England. wrote to mamme by Josey Smith.

1 Day   Morn: at meeting Mordecai Yarnel spoke, afternoon at meeting. Nancy Warner drank tea with us, evening Nancy Caty & I went to meeting, Ben: Trotter and Dan: Stanton spoke, fashion in some folks needs no excuse.

2   Morn: Anna Pole Breakfasted hear, at Work, and wrote in my Exercise Book. afternoon Anna Pole, Rachel and Becky Moon and I drank tea with Rachel Wells, agreably, looked at some fine Paintings, one the Rakes Progress,[174] which brings him from the gaming table to bedlam!

today 3   Day spent at Plantation with Daddy, finished mammes 6th & 7th Shifts. Josey Smith from B——n, Mamme Well.

4   Morn: at Work, began a shirt for Caty, afternoon at Work, H Drinker set out for York, sent my love to my friends. Neighbour Warner hear. Caty Howel gone to stay a month at Germantown with her sick child

5   Morn: at Work, afternoon at Work Mamme come from Burlington. Neddy Penington and Neighbour Warner hear in the evening.

6   Morn: Copying for Daddy. at Work, afternoon at Work, finished the third holland shirt for Caty. Jos Smith hear in the evening.

7   Morn: at Work. read in the history, afternoon finished the 8 shifts of mamme's. evening Becky Rawle, Polly Sandwith, and Anna Pole.

1 Day   Morn: 6 O'Clock wrote to Sally Smith. went to meeting. afternoon a violent rain Caty and I at home, evening we went to meeting, Sam: Emblem, B T: and Becky Jones spoke

2   Morn: all the family but myself went to plantation. at Work. afternoon at Work. Polly Sandwith. Nancy Warner and I at Neighbour Ashes childs funeral, Billy Isaacs hear

3   Morn: Josey Smith breakfasted with us, at Work, afternoon Mary Armitt: Neighbour Warner and I went to Beaulah Burge child funeral, see Nancy & Sally Mitchel, Polly Rhodes, Betsey and George Roberts, and Isaac Parish. returned from Shrewsberry. wrote to Sally Smith.

173. Widower Henry Drinker, who has been HCS's frequent visitor, especially since her return from New York, has just told her that he has begun courting another. He will marry Elizabeth Sandwith in January 1761.

174. Eight prints by the famed English artist and engraver William Hogarth, first issued in 1735. The series shows the dissolute life in London of the fictional Tom Rakewell.

[August 1, 1759]

8 mo 4   Morn: 8 O'Clock Daddy and I went to Plantation, cheif of the day Ironing, the place looks beautiful. the plat belonging to Daddy is 60 acres
square: 30 of upland, 30 of meadow, which runs along the side of the
river Delawar, half the upland is a fine Woods, the other Orchard and
Gardens, a little house in the midst of the Gardens, interspersed with
fruit trees. the main Garden lies along the meadow, by 3 descents of
Grass steps, you are led to the bottom, in a walk length way of the Garden, on one Side a[175] fine cut hedge incloses from the meadow, the
other, a high Green bank shaded with Spruce, the meadows and river
lying open to the eye, looking to the house, covered with trees, honey
scycle vines on the fences, low hedges to part the flower and kitchen
Garden, a fine barn. Just at the side of the Wood, the trees a small space
round it cleared from brush underneath, the whole a little romantic
rural scene. evening Mamme and Daddy went home.

5   Day Ironing, evening John played on his flute in the Woods

6   Day Daddy and Mamme, come and spent the day with us.

7   Morn: Caty and I set at Work in the barn, Daddy come and dined with
[us], and 3 O'Clock, we set out for town, 6 O'Clock I went with Joshua
Howel to Germantown, found little Caty poorly. Betsey Warner and I
slept together.

1 Day   Morn: Isaac & Patience Howel from town, we went to meeting: Pris-
cilla Davies and Marget Ellis spoke, see the Shoemaker family, Logans,
and Jones kindly invited to there houses, dined at Joshuas afternoon at
meeting: Marget Ellis spoke. afterward at David Deshlers, Isaac & Patience went home, see Molly Foulk, Polly Jones set with me half an
hour, evening very pleasent with Joshua & Caty, Nanny Delaplain.[176]

2   Morn: 5 O'Clock Joshua, betsey Warner and I come home, 11 O'Clock
went to meeting, Mordecai Yarnell and Mary Lightfoot spoke. Samuel
Spencer dined hear, afternoon at Grace Caldwells, who is brought a
bed of a Son John. comeing home stoped at divers of my acquaintance's
doors. Polly Whartons, Patience Grays, and Polly Parish tells me my
pretty Betsey Brooks is on the point of changeing her Condition with
John Hopkins, may every pleasure, blessing, bliss thats worth poss-
esing, fall to there share.

3   Morning: Caty and I at meeting Ellis Hugh, Dan: Stanton, Betty
Stevens, and Becky Jones spoke. William Clothier dined hear, after-

175. In margin, not in HCS's hand: "Plantation or Richmond Seat." Also in margin: "The present Port
Richmond is the same site." GV.

176. In margin, not in HCS's hand: "afterward the home of Elliston Perot, then of Samuel B. Morris
& at present of Elliston P. Morris, Book [written faintly] 1875."

noon spent with Nancy Gibson agreably, evening Betsey Sandwith and Sammy Samsom.

4   Morn: at Work on my pincushin, reading to Caty in Felicia to Charlotte.[177] afternoon reading in the history, Aunt Armitt hear, evening Sammy Samsom suped hear, the discourse of England and his intended voyage.

5   Morn: at meeting B T: and Sally Morris spoke, afternoon, spent with friend Coleman, Mamme, Polly and Betsey Sandwith at Warners, evening at the Sisters cheifly at Beckys admireing her pritty smileing Boy. the Widow Dyer of the lower Counties[178] has paid her debt to Nature,[179] having filled her station in Life, with the odour of a good Character, now abouts the English arms seem to flourish, but War, on the Conquorer or Conquered brings little but oppression and inhumanity, from man to man. the whole World seems in a blaze, as it has been many times since the Creation, War is called one of the almightys lesser punishments, to a rebelious World, he suffers great men to head Armies, this Cyrus, Prussia, men who fear him, and for wise purposes, does he work in Mistery.

6   Morn: read to Caty in Felicia to Charlotte, Sammy Samsom took leave of us, to go for London. afternoon 3 O'Clock some runing visits, Nancy Mitchel, bought Silk intending a purse for Sally Smith, Gracy Caldwell, drank tea with Anna Pole, we went and set an hour with John & Nancy Gibson, she walked with me to market street, some talk on marriage, a great many of my female acquaintance surpass the male in fluency of discourse, and easey delivery.

7   Morn: finished the 8 Vol: Rapins History of England, afternoon began Sally's purse. evening Caty and I an hour at Warners. Henry Drinker, some discourse concerning Romances.

1 Day   Morn: went to meeting Ben: Trotter spoke, Gilly Isaacs dined hear, afternoon Caty and I at meeting B T. and D S. spoke. Ester Hoot drank tea with us, some things in the family very disagreable, but which must have patience and Condesention to over come them.

2   Morn: at Work began the 9 Vol of the history, afternoon Mamme and I spent with Sam: Morris and his Wife. Called to see Joshua and Frances. evening reading to mamme and Caty.

3   Morn: at Work went to meeting D Stanton and John Churchman spoke. afternoon Frances Rawle eat part of a Water Melon with us,

---

177. Mary Collyer, *Felicia to Charlotte: being letters from a young lady in the country, to her friend in town* (1744).

178. Delaware was originally the "lower counties" of Pennsylvania; the two colonies achieved separate governing assemblies in 1701.

179. Died.

Mamme and I drank tea with Sally Lewes, and her mother the Widow Mifflin talk; on new york, set an hour with Sally Pemberton and Polly Richardson, an agreable Walk in there fine Garden. stood a bit with Becky Cooper, returned home and spent the evening agreably with mamme and Caty, read in the history.

4 Morn: Daddy, Mamme and I set out for Point, John and Molly Reynolds and Henry and Molly Groth spent the day very agreably with us. Groth is a man of Singular politeness among us americans having been bred at the Court of England, his Wife is more blunt than one mought expect for his Companion. Mamme and I staid all night

5 Morn: finished and put on, my Irish Stich Carnation Pincushin. afternoon. Daddy, Sammy, Josey, and Sally Samsom, Joseph Morris, and Debby Claypole spent in a most agreable manner with us. Debby Claypole is a Woman of Good breeding, Joined with affabillity, her Company is tempered with that sweetness, which makes some elderly Company vastly pleasing and edifying to me.

6 Morn: Worked at the Purse, Daddy, and John and Mary Armitt dined with us, Aunt and I had an agreable walk in the Wood. those three days in the Country, have been spent with a calm Satisfaction, there Natures Works fill the mind with serinity, and a fund of Ideas, to Instruct. this evening we returned to town.

7 Day. at Work mending. evening Caty and I at Warners.

1 Day Morn: 7 O'Clock wrote to Sally Smith, went to meeting. B T: and Sammy Emblen spoke. went home with Neigh: Warner. Benny Sweet and Sammy Samsom were there who this morning returned from there voyage; the Vessel having sprung a leak 40 Leagues out at Sea. evening at B T: and D S spoke. Sally Smith sent me a fine Basket of Peaches

2 Morn: at Work mending Shirts, afternoon Sammy Samsom eat some Water melon with us. run together Calico for a bed quilt. which is to be quilted by Caty and I.

to day 3 Morn: at Work, went to meeting: Moredcai Yarnel and D S: spoke, half hour at Becky Rawle's. Ann Scofield and Robert Proud dined hear. made two pair of Pokets. evening Sammy Shoemaker.

4 Morn: tis impossible to live in a state of Corruption without feeling the misery Incident to it. Oh man, thou shalt earn thy bread, by the sweet of thy Brow! and in Sorrow shalt thou eat it.[180] worked at the Purse, afternoon at work on the purse.

5 Morn: at Work for Caty, went to meeting: D S:, Will: Brown, and Ann Scofield spoke. afternoon Mamme and I spent with Hannah Mickle,

---

180. Genesis 3:19.

Sam: Mickle, and Will: Callender. 6 O'Clock I walked down town stoped at Polly Parish's who tells me John Hopkins is dead————— O Death thou that often surpases all bold conjecture, and vain hopes of man in bloom of Youth, Prospects opening, warm with cordial Love, and expectation of a blooming Beauty, on the very day appointed to have been with her, the lovely youth bid adieu to all sublunary bliss —————————with constancy of mind exhorting his weeping parents and friends weep for yourselves! for me, you will soon have no need to weep.—————————Poor Betsey Brooks thy Joys nipt in the bud of Prospect, for they looked as tho' heaven might have formed them for each other, as far as "woes well mingled, and well mingled loves." would admit to mortals.

6	Day: Caty and I put the Bed quilt in the frame afternoon betsey Lovett helped, evening read in the history to mamme and Caty
7	Day: Caty and I finshed one third of the quilt. evening read in the history to Daddy mamme and Caty.

1 Day	Morn: at meeting B T: spoke. Josey Smith dined with us, after ward spent an agreable hour with Caty Howel. went to meeting. Mary Night spoke, Robert Proud drank tea with us. evening at meeting Betty Morris, D S: spoke.[181]
2	Day: Quilting, Sam: Leacock sent us a pot of Tamerins. I see Spencer a gentleman of York, news from B————n Thomas Wethril and Patience Clews dead. evening read in the history,
3	Morn: Caty Betsey and I quilting, Nancy Gibson dined with us, and staid till night, ————Spencer drank tea with us. evening Hannah Moor and Rachel Wells. two thirds of the quilt done.
4	Day: Caty and I closely quilting. Daddy and Mamme went to point, staid all night. Henry Drinker hear. read in the history
5	Morn: Caty and I quilting 11 O'Clock Daddy and Mamme come home. Neigh: Warner hear. afternoon 5 O'Clock finished the quilt spent the evening with Caty Howel and Polly Sandwith
6	Morn: Worked at the purse, afternoon spent with Anna Pole, ———— Spencer and Rich: Smith, Jemmy Bringhurst come home with me.

[September 1, 1759]

9 Mo 7	Morn: at Caty Howels worked at my purse, Henry Drinker and Sammy Samsom[182] took leave of our family for England. afternoon worked at the purse. 5 O'Clock Francis Rawle and I set out for Ger-

---

181. Note (in another hand) pasted here into text: "Traytrip- Worcester Dic. An old game at tables or draughts in which success depended upon throwing a tray. Shakspeare and Ben Johnson upon further search suppose it may have been Checkers."

182. An index finger is drawn in the left margin, pointing to Sammy Samsom's name.

mantown, where we arrived through a shocking road by 7 O'Clock. lodged with Nancy Warner.

1 Day	Morn: went to meeting Priscilla Davis spoke, afternoon at meeting.
2	Morn: 6 O'Clock took leave of Becky and Nancy, and come to town with Francis, 10' O Clock Daddy, Mamme, and Caty went to plantation afternoon worked at the purse, the two Sister Hasels come and took one of the houses in second street. evening read the king of prussias memoirs,[183]
3	Day: Worked at the purse, evening reading the same book.
4	Morn: 8 O'Clock Daddy and I rode pleasently to point. found all well, Daddy and Mamme returned in the evening.
5	Day Ironing
6	Morn: Daddy come to see us and went home again, Afternoon Neighbour Shoemaker and Benny. evening read in the history
7	Day: Worked at the purse, a rainy day, 6 O'Clock in the evening a clear skie, adorned with a beauteous rainBow, reflected new beauties upon natures verdant landscape below! Caty and I like the first pair,[184] walked the Garden in delight.

1 Day	Morn: we rose by 5 O'Clock enjoyed the beauties of the morn: while the horse was hetching, and rode home by seven. we went to meeting: Sam: Emblen spoke, Josey Smith dined with us, afternoon Caty and I went to meeting: Moredecai Yarnell and John Pemberton spoke, I went to Caty Howels—she is in much trouble on account of her child, Jos: Howel, Sidney Howel, Sally Evans, Jenny Owen, Polly Rhodes, and Sammy Emblen where there, toward the latter part of the time there was silence, and Sammy spoke, on the instabillity of all worldly Gifts, the grand signature of nature, incribed by heaven is— Failure, or they shall Perish, "but thou O Lord remains for ever." to fix thy peoples affections on things above. Polly, Sammy, and I went to meeting D S: and B T: spoke.
2	Morn: at Work, afternoon drank tea at Anthony Morris's with the old lady, Widow Powel, and Debby and Polly Morris, evening Anna Pole,
3	Morn: at Work, went to meeting: Han: Hulfred and D S: spoke. Martha Barker from B———n dined with us, afternoon with Grace Caldwell. evening Polly Pemberton, Polly Rhodes, Anna Pole, and I walking.
4	Morn: at Work, afternoon Drank tea with Nancy Gibson and the

183. Frederick II, King of Prussia, *Memoirs of Frederick III [sic], King of Prussia, Containing All the Memorable Battles and Transactions of that Great Prince* (1757).

184. Adam and Eve.

Widow Ball, evening at Anna Pole's, those men are encroachers. 'tis hardly possible for Girls to be too careful of there Company. there are so many of the Sex that lead a life of repentance, for the neglect of this Caution.—Tears vainly flow for errors learned too late.

[O. o.
Oaths————Let's hear no more of Oaths.
If they awaken'd Consience in the Breast,
I would demand them of thee. But what do they avail?
Vice betrays them, Virtue frowns at them.
For ous let it suffice to discharge our respective
Obligations.
That's the true Oath; others are good for nought. The Jewish Spy Vol:3 pa: 184][185]

5	Morn: at Work, Anna Pole and I went to meeting to gether. DS: spoke. afterward Anna Pole, Polly Pemberton, and my self bought each of us a blue graset Gound 5" 5" 0"[186] afternoon drank tea with Betsey Fox and Hannah Mickel. called at Catys
6	Morn: Peggy Acre, Caty and I mantua making, afternoon Anna Pole, evening at Becky Rawles, with Neigh: Warner,
7	Morn: wrote to Sally Smith by Martha Barker, Peggy at Work. afternoon four O'Clock mamme was taken with a fitt of the fever and she continued so ill I set up with her. in the night Joshua Howel called for her to go to Caty.[187] but she could not
1 Day	Morn: with mamme, afternoon I went to meeting: Becky Jones and B T: spoke, Josey Smith and Billy Clothier drank tea hear, I went a minuet to see Caty Howel, she has a fine Girl, her name Sally
2	Day: Mamme was very Ill, my good Aunt Mary Armitt and Neigh: Warner.
3	Day: Caty and I pining up beds. Betsey taken very Ill.
4	Day Nurseing the Sick
5	Day: a Friend in time of distress is as a most Salutary Cordial
6	Morn: Sally Smith from B——n, Friends now begin to gether to the Yearly meeting,
7	Morn: Joseph Parker and Son. Daniel and Robert Smith,

185. This passage was written upside down at the bottom of the diary page. HCS was quoting Jean Baptiste de Boyer, Marquise d'Argus, *The Jewish Spy,* a series of essays critical of French society. The author assumed the persona of a Jewish visitor, observing the French through the eyes of a stranger. These essays were published periodically in Holland and later translated from the French and published in the *Gentleman's Magazine* and elsewhere. Collected and published as a multi-volume series in 1739.

186. Grazett, woolen cloth; five pounds, five shillings, and no pence.

187. Caty was in labor.

1 Day	Mamme is now on the mend and my mind and feet begin to have a lit-

1 Day   Mamme is now on the mend and my mind and feet begin to have a lit-
          tle rest. Molly Morris and Betty Williams

to day 2 Day: at home with her, Molly Hoskins and Becky Jones,

3   Day: a good deal of Company.

4   Morn: at home with mamme, afternoon Sally Smith and I went to
          meeting, Jane Ellis and Widow Hinton spoke, Memorials concerning
          Abraham Farrington, Han: Carpenter, and Han: Hill

5   Day: at home, Mary Emblen and Sally Smith dined hear. Anna Pole
          spent the afternoon with us, ~~Peggy Morris~~

6   Morn: Peggy Morris delivered 2 Sons, afternoon Sally Smith, Polly and
          Sally Pemberton and myself went to Sally Loydds funeral, afterward
          Sally Smith and drank tea with Caty Howel.

7   Morn: with mamme, afternoon Sally and I spent [with] Becky Rawle

1 Day   Morn: Sally and I went down town to meeting D S: spoke. Cousin
          Hannah and Josey Smith dined hear. afternoon I met Sally at the same
          meeting: D S: and B T: spoke, Sally and I drank tea with Polly and Sally
          Pemberton.

[October 1, 1759]

10 mo 2   Morn: Daddy Sally and I went to plantation and dined afternoon. Bet-
          sey Sandwith and I went to Becky Rawles funeral, mamme was very
          poorly this evening.

3   Day, mamme was Ill, and continued so 4 and 5 day. that that I began
          to think with dread what might be the event. But Providence. the Doc-
          ter's, and I hope time will produce a recovery.

6   Day: mamme mended as much as I could expect, Sally Smith and some
          good Neighbours and Friends have been great comfort and Satisfac-
          tion to me in this time of distress.

7   Morn: 8 O'Clock Sally set out home with James Smith. afternoon Anna
          Pole,

1 Day   our sick continue mending, Aunt Armitt spent the afternoon with
          mamme, Mordecai Yarnel, John Pemberton, and Marget Wister drank
          tea hear, Molly Strech, Beckey James, and Jones, this evening Nurse
          Johnson came to mamme

2   Morn: with mamme and seting this book to rights. afternoon at Work

3   Morn: went to meeting: D S:, H W:, and Mordecai Yarnel spoke.
          Rachel and Anna Pole dined hear, Caty Lightfoot, evening Wrote to
          Sally Smith.

4   Day at Work, Rebeca Coleman and Sarah Zane hear

5   Day at Work making Jakets for mamme

| 6 | Day at Work, a rainy day agreably spent. |
| 7 | Morn: preserveing Quinces, afternoon Neigh Warner hear. |

1 Day	Morn: at meeting B T: spoke. afternoon Caty and I at meeting. Aunt Armitt drank tea with us, evening Caty and I at meeting: B T: spoke. Mor: Yarnel spoke.
2	Day busy Washing Ester hoot drank tea with us,
3	Morn: at meeting D S:, B T:, Hesz: Williams. Sam: Emblen, and Sarah Morris spoke. George Dylvin and Sarah Hill were married. Sally Morris dined hear, afternoon I hemed her Gause[188] hankercheif,
4	Day Ironing, Mary Decow and Polly Shoot drank tea with us
5	Day Ironing, received a letter from Sally.
6	Morn: Ironing Lydia Noble and Betsey Morris drank tea with us, Betsey and I went to a childs funeral,
7	Morn: at Work, afternoon mamme rode out. eve Caty and I took a Walk, Neddy brooks suped hear.

| 1 Day | Morn: wrote to Sally, went to meeting: Mary Emblen, and Becky Jones spoke, afternoon with mamme. Docter Moor drank tea hear. evening I went to meeting: D S: spoke. |

[Not long ago, sayd a French Writer, this trite frivolous Question was proposed in a cellebrated Company, vis. Which was the greatest Man in the world Caesar, Alexander, Tamerline, Cromwel, & c. One of them made answere Sir Isaac Newton was undoubtedly the greatest Man. His Assertion was just; for if true Greatness consists in haveing received a prodigious Genious from Heaven, and making use of it to enlighten his own and others Understandings, such a Man as Sir Isaac Newton, who is hardly to be met in ten Centuries, is really that Great Man; and those Politicians, those Conquerors, of which there have been some in all ages, are commonly but Illustrous wicked Men.

the Jewish
Spy Vol: 3
pa: 291.][189]

| 2 | Morn: last evening between 7 & 8 O'Clock died Polly Jordan |
| 3 | Morn: at meeting, D S: spoke, 2 O'Clock Nancy, Sally, & Debby Mitchel and myself went Israel Pembertons to the funeral of Polly Jordan, I drank tea with Becky Rawle she is much concerned on account of her children and the small Pox |

---

188. Gauze.
189. HCS also wrote this extract from the *Jewish Spy,* like the earlier one, upside down at the bottom of the diary page. See page 128.

4 Morn at Work, afternoon paid divers visits. drank tea with Caty Howel, and Polly Sandwith. spent the evening hear.

5 Morn: at Work noon Caty Smith went to Burlington. I drank tea with Sally Dylwyn, Becky Moor and Patsey Hill.

6 Morn: Betsey Sandwith and I went to meeting 5 Couples passed: Polly Stiles and Sally Mitchel. Han: Hulfred, and Sally Morris spoke livingly, afternoon at Work, Nanny Emblen

7 Morn: at Work. Daddy went to the funeral of Jane Large at Burlington. afternoon Neigh Warner, Becky Rawle, and I took a walk.

1 Day at Home Betsey was worse, mamme got to the morning meeting having been confined six weeks,

2 Day: I was ill with the cholick. Daddy returned,

3 Morn: Tammy Fox come to learn of me to knot purses. Daddy & mamme rode out, afternoon Nancy and betsey Warner.

4 Morn: at Work, afternoon Becky James, Betsey Sandwith. eveng reading the manners and principles of the times[190]

[November 1, 1759]

11 mo 5 Morn: at Work Daddy & mamme rode out, afternoon Tammy Fox. evening reading

6 Morn: worked at the purse. Sam: & John Smith come from Burlington. afternoon Nancy Warner and I went to Molly Powels funeral, Sally Morris and Sammy Emblen spoke at the Grave.

7 Morn: wrote to Caty Smith. agreable conversation with my Cousins. afternoon worked at Sally Smiths Purse, Josey Smith, brought me from the Library the life of M: Tullias Cicero,[191]

1 Day Morn: at meeting; Robert Jones spoke. some country friends dined with us, afternoon at meeting. drank tea with Betty Morris, she and I went to a funeral from thence to meeting. Marget Ellis, B T:, and R. Jones spoke.

2 Morn: at Work, afternoon Tammy Fox, evening half hour with Becky Rawle

3 Morn: at meeting B T:, M. Yarnel, and D S: spoke, afternoon Mame and I went to old Anthony Morris's. Docter Moor and Wife and Nat: Rigby and Wife were there. how sweet is the odour that rises from the good name of a departed friend, to the survivors. Jos: & Caty Howel, and myself spent the evening in sweet fellowship, at Neigh: Warners with friend Coleman, herself, Polly & Betsey, and Nancy & Betsey.

---

190. John Brown, *An Estimate of the Manners and Principles of the Times* (1758).
191. Conyers Middleton, *The History of the Life of Marcus Tullius Cicero* (1741).

4   Morn: at Work, afternoon Anna Pole and I at Polly Rhodes, an elder
           sister awed by the pertness of a Younger, wroung education. children
           should love and acquease one to the other. little Hetty House, very
           pleaseing to see an early love of books. it has been to me more pleasent
           than company, as agreable as my natural food, in short there is none
           but the lovers of learning, that can be sensible of the satisfaction in en-
           tertaining it.

5   Morn: at meeting B T:, Mary Emblen, and D S: spoke. Polly Stiles was
           married to Masterman: afternoon Nancy Gibson, Sally Stamper, and
           myself at the Widow Ball's. discourse run on the married and single
           states, both eligible when well conducted thro life, History as well as
           our own time furnishes many Instances, of worthy Single Women, one
           occurs: Queen Elizabeth of Glorious memory. evening reading M T.
           Cicero.

6   Morn: at Work, 10 O'Clock mamme and I took a ride up Wisehicken,
           rode as far as Turners, Docter Zacharys place is pretty by nature and
           art, but is the cause of discension amongst Brethren, Peels is pretty by
           art, and will be memorable for four indiscreet Daughters. afternoon
           Mamme and I drank tea with Neigh: Samsom. some talk on keep-
           ing,[192] a wretched instance of it in there next Neigh: a man of credit
           till caught by that bait of Saten, the fear of being shackled for life. given
           himself and family over to Indolent voluptiousness that he cant face a
           person of credit at his own door. see in John Smiths common place
           book pa: 65. reflections on keeping. evening weaveing laces.

7   Morn: at Work making my Winter under coat afternoon and evening
           with Caty Howel

1 Day   Morn: at meeting: H W: and John Pemberton spoke, congratulated
           Polly Masterman. afternoon at meeting: B T: and D S: spoke, Nancy
           Warner drank tea with me from thence to Tommy Says funeral, and
           evening meeting: D S: and Mor: Yarnel spoke,

2   Morn Worked at the purse. afternoon Mamme and I went to Neigh:
           Mase's. Docter Bass and Wife, Betsey Harris, [there]

3   Morn: at Work, afternoon went with mame to Nanny Emblens. From
           thence with Polly Donalson—Gilbert and Jemmy bring hurst, to view
           the State house, and Hospital, we went to the Cells.[193] I see poor John
           Derborah.

4   Morn: at Work. afternoon at Work at Sally's purse

5   Morn: at Work. afternoon at Becky Rawle's, her children are inocu-
           lated for the small pox. evening at home Neigh Samsom and Josey
           Smith,

192. Keeping a mistress.
193. The basement cells at Pennsylvania Hospital housed mentally ill patients.

6   Morn: at Work afternoon Daniel Stanton and John Pemberton hear on a friendly visit, they both spoke in a seaseonable and comfortable manner, give me o lord a grateful heart with sufficient fortitude to follow the dictates of thy Grace and I will follow thee. Hallender.

7   Morn: at Work. Will: Fisher, Sam: Burge, John Reynolds, and Jo: Morris went with Daddy to meet Governor Hambleton. Afternoon with Caty Howel, Governor Hambleton was escorted into town by a number of Citizens.

1 Day   Morn: at meeting Becky Jones spoke, Ben: Sweet dined hear. afternoon at meeting H W: spoke, I drank tea with Polly Masterman, Betty Gardener, Caty Peters, and several men, eve at meeting: B T:, Mor: Yarnel, and D S: spoke.

2   Morn: worked at the purse, Edward Cathrel dined hear, afternoon I went to see Sally Dugdill, her Sister Peggy lays in a very weak condition, I see the Widow Levy also, O Prosperity thou has been the cause of more evil to man kind, than thy hard favoured Sister adversity, poor man altho he brought his fall on himself cannot brook it. want of due submision to the will of heaven hurries some to a dread eternity, robs others of the inestimable Jewel Understanding, evening a large Council.

3   Morn: at meeting: D S: and Sam: Emblen spoke, John Head and Betsey Hastings were married, afternoon Betsey Sandwith, I taught her knoting purses, Docter Hutchins. evening reading in the monthly review, concerning the Assembly.[194]

4   Morn: wrote largely to Sally Smith. afternoon a most agreable one and evening with Polly and Betsey Sandwith, and Nancy Warner. Betsey is a Girl of parts, and a turn of humour extreamly pleasing to me, and when company meets for conversation, without the acrmony of slander, 'tis the pleasure of the human mind

5   Morn: Nancy Murfin & Sally Lovett, afternoon I went with them to Polly Shoots, Betsey Bacon is a good lively girl who will not easily sit down an old maid, that Hydra monster which hurries so many girls into worse fate.

6   Morn: at home. afternoon Nancy Sally and went to Polly browns. 4 O'Clock they set out home,

7   Morn: at Work mending bonets, afternoon Docter Hutchins. evening at Becky Rawle's

---

194. Perhaps the *American Magazine and Monthly Chronicle,* published in Philadelphia in 1757/8, or the British magazine entitled the *Monthly Review.* Right next to this, in the margin, in a different hand: "John Head + Betsey Hastings married."

1 Day   Morn: reckoning cloaths. went to meeting, Caty come from B———n, our friends are all well, afternoon at meeting Thomas ballard spoke, Mor: Yarnel and Owen Jones drank tea with us.

2   Morn: up early and at Work. Afternoon at Work and reading

3   Morn: busy. Aunt Armitt dined hear. Anna Pole drank tea hear

4   Morn: Ironing, Afternoon my esteemed friend Caty Howel, hear

5   Day Caty and I mending Grounds,[195]

6   Morn: Caty and I went to meeting, Docter Evans and Jenny Owen passed. afternoon Caty and I went to Anna Poles. and now 7 O'Clock in the evening I am noteing those trite amusements of mine, as I pass through the busy herd, it often brings me with satisfaction to my home, as the place of more cool reflection,

[December 1, 1759]

12 mo 7   Morn: at Work, afternoon at Becky Rawles, an agreable scene between Francis, Becky, and ~~and~~ the children evening spent with them.

1 Day   Morn: at meeting, Josey Smith dined hear, afternoon at meeting: D S: and Sam: Emblem spoke, evening I read in Dells works[196] to Mamme

2   Morn: began a stocking for myself, a dreadful fire broke out on Society hill, by which many familys were greatly distressed. the wind was very high and it was a melancholy scene. afternoon and evening at Work.

3   Morn: at meeting: B T: and Will: Ricketts spoke: Will: Ricketts and Sally Morris dined hear, Will: returned from St Kitts the other day, being taken on his voyage to Barbados.

4   Morn: kniting. afternoon Caty Smith, Anna Michel, and I at a funeral, D S: spoke, Caty and I drank tea at Joshua Howels, with Sally Fisher, Neig: Warner, and Becky Rawle, we staid till 8 O'Clock agreably, Becky seems relieved of a great burden now her children are happily over the small pox, that unhappy Woman, Betty Shirly's child, is at Catys, her misfortunes were so great as to carry the air of Romance, did not cricumstances evidence the truth, she was the daughter of a Baker in London, her mother died while she was young. a second marriage, ill usage, and the common companion of young minds, impatience of misfortune, drove her, from her fathers house and she took a passage in a vessel going for Jamacai, when they arrived the Capt sold her, for the Passage money, to a gentleman planter of the North side, Monroe (his name). by invidious arts, good and bad usage, as she was intirely in his power, debased her from the dignity of a virtuous servent, to the

---

195. Gowns?
196. William Dell, a seventeenth-century Quaker writer of religious tracts.

wretched state of a kept Miss: she lived in splendor enjoying the Honours of his table, but a slave, without friend or acquaintance, the negro wenches, twice contrived to Poison her, on account of the share she deprived them of, in there masters favour, always desirous of quiting her manner of life, she had one child by him, a girl, this rather made her more uneasey, and at last he consented she should go for england, with the child, upon condition she delivered it to his friend in London to be put to a boarding school, and brought up as his child, betty was to have a sum of money, and set up a little shop. he shiped them at Kingston, but in a few days after, the Vessel was cast away on a desolate Island, and she saved part of her things, some days after, they gave a signal of distress, to a vessel they see, she proved to be one bound for London, betty and the child went on board, intending to pursue the voyage. some time after as they lay a bed one night, the Cabbin boy waked her, and all things were at the last extremity, for the vessil had struck another, and was then sinking, so that they had much a do to save themselves in the long boat, till they got on board the other vessel, Capt Southcol bound for Phila such an adishon to his crew, and beating on the coast brought them to an allowance of provision, in short she an utter stranger to all and no woman but herself, was three weeks in this vessel, and saved no thing but the cloaths they had on in bed. and when they arrived at Phila:d had nothing for herself nor child, till Caty Howel, I, and some others sent cloaths: application was made to the overseers they flung her on the Capt.[197] he looked on her as a wretch born to Ill fortune, and did not care to take her back with him to England nor several other Capts. thus Jos: Howel, as the vessel was consigned to him, coud but look on her with compassion. one day she Informed Caty she was not wretched enough before, but it was confirmed by an adishonal circumstance, she was with child. they boarded her out[198] and some Jamaca men seeing her that were Monroe's Acquaintances, said they knew her, and did not doubt his generousity, in reimburseing Jos: the poor creature lingred her time out, fell into a decay, and layed the remains of an unfortunate person in America, rejoiceing that the end of her pilgrimage was come. thus doth providence deal with some that it may be a Warning to all, Misfortune's are easier brought on, than they are born. the Sexes made for each others aid,

197. Meaning application was made to the Overseers of the Poor for her support, but they responded that the ship's captain should be financially responsible for her care.

198. Apparently Betty Shirley was taken in by William Logan for a time, to the consternation of the family. In a letter dated 4th day at Noon, no month, 1759, William Logan wrote to John Smith, "I recvd thine relat[in]g to the unhappy woman at my house and am sensible in a Great Measure what she is. This I am assured off, she is an Object of Charity & Compassion & as such shall look upon her, and endeavour to get her a passage paid among the Scotch Society that she may get home to her Friends if she has any in England." John Smith Correspondence, HSP.

[then] employ the deceitfulness of there hearts to ruin each other. Monroe has wrote his thanks and desires the child may be sent to england.

5   Morn: at meeting: B T: and D S: spoke. afternoon agreably spent at Warners, Neig: Samsom and Rachel Drinker there. evening I staid till 8 O'Clock and there was 7 knitters of us round the table, I come home and found a person there, a wretched Instance of conjugal unhappiness.

6   Morn: at Work. afternoon Sam:l Samsom and Wife. evening read Cicero.

7   Day. at Work making a bonnet.

1 Day   Morn: at meeting B T: spoke. afternoon at meeting D S: spoke. evening read in the bible to Dady, Mame & Caty.

2   Morn: began the first of half a dozen shirts for Dady. wrote in this book, afternoon steped over to Neig: Walls. evening at Work

to day 3   Morn: Caty & I went to meeting: Will: Ricketts and D S: spoke, Danny and Sally Smith come from B———n with a letter from Sally Smith. John Wilson, son of Cristopher Wilson dined hear, an agreable Young man. 4 O'Clock I went to see Gracy Caldwell's child in the small pox. from thence to Polly Rhodes. Polly Pemberton there, she and I went to Anna Poles.

4   Day. bonnet making. evening agreable with the B———n folks

5   Morn: Caty and I went to meeting: B T:, Sarah Morris, D S:, and Will Ricketts spoke. afternoon Polly & Sally Pemberton, Caty Smith, Hallender, Danny & Dicky Smith, and Josey Jordan, went to see the Lyon whelp we returned to our house and drank tea, with Cousin Jenny Smith & Jos: Morris. Mame and Caty a little ruffled in the evening, in disputes with ones elders there is allways a deference to be observed.

6   Morn: 9 O'Clock Danny Sally and I set out for B———n and had a pleasent Journey and kind reception at Unkle Daniels. even met at Dannys. himself and Wife, Abby Raper, Sally and Betsey Smith, Hallender, and Dicky and Bobby Smith, agreable Conversation

7   Morn: Kniting. afternoon Sally and I at Sammy Smiths, our good Cousin Betty made it very agreable by the account of her Journey to New England.

1 Day   Morn: at meeting. Betty Smith spoke. Anna R-d-n and her young husband there. Cousin Betty & I dined with John Smith, and Sammy & Sally Smith. E^d: Cathrel made the afternoon quite pleasing. Poor Jenny Burlings children were there. even at Unkle Roberts

2   Morn: Kniting. afternoon Betty, Abby & Sally Smith and Hallender drank tea at Dannys. evening Betsey, Sally, & I had a good deal of mirth and conversation.

3   Morn: Kniting. afternoon, Sally Raper & Sally Smith and Hallender at Unkle Roberts. evening Eliza Barker Hathrel, Tommy Pryor, and Billy & Dicky Smith paid us a visit.

4   Morn: Ironing. afternoon at home with Unkle and Sally

5   Morn: wrote to Mamme and Anna Pole, went to meeting: Betty Smith and Petre Fern spoke. dined with Edward Cathrel. afternoon Unkle Dan:ll, Jos: Noble, and Sally & Betsey Smith come there.

6   Morn: Kniting Unkle and I walked to his barracks. afternoon Sally & I spent with Caty Wethrel.

7   Day. agreable at home, had books from the library.

1 Day   Morn: at meeting; Betty Smith & Peter fern spoke. dined at Jos: Nobles. afternoon Sally & Betsey Smith come to us. even at home. Sally read in Judge hale.[199] I had a letter from home.

2   Morn: kniting. afternoon Betsey Smith and other Company

3   Morn: Polly Lightfoot & I at Unkle Roberts, Betsey come and dined with us and staid the rest of the the day. Christmas.

4   Morn: Kniting. afternoon Sally Raper & Sally Smith and Hallender drank tea at Joshua Rapors.

5   Morn: kniting. went to meeting: Petre fern spoke. I dined at Sam: Smiths. Han: & Sally Smith come there in the afternoon. even I wrote to mamme and betsey Sandwith.

6   Morn: Sally, Betsey, Bobby Smith, and I at the pond to slide

7   Morn: wrote to Caty Smith. afternoon the two Sallys & I drank tea together. and made a large parcel of dough nuts.

1 Day   Morn: at meeting. Betty Smith and Petre fern spoke. I dined at home. afternoon Sam: Smith and Sally raper Smith drank tea with us

2   Morn: at Unkle Roberts. betsey come back with me to diner and staid the day,

[January 1, 1760]

1 Mo 3   Morn: finished my stocking, and thus I finished the year, and the events of the next are hid in futurity.

4   Morn: 11 O'Clock Cousin Sam: Smith brought me a letter from my dear Mame, giving me an account that she had been very Ill but was on the recovery, thus had fate while I was at ease like to have given the most dreadful stroke to my earthly happiness. I passed the rest of this day in anciety,

5   Morn: I determined to see her, I left all my friends well, and Danny &

---

199. Sir Matthew Hale, *The Sum of Religion. Written by Judge Hale, Lord Chief Justice of England, and was found in his closet, amongst his other papers after his decease* (1710).

Abby Smith myself set out in the stage, we met with little difficulty at the ferries, and I again see my Parents

ᛒ

[July 14, 1760]

7 Mo 14th Omishion: Till the Seventh Month fourteenth 1760

2   In this interval of Time Daddy sold his house on the bank,[200] in Front street to Thom: Riche, and we removed to Richmond Seat, having apartments, at our good Cousin Sam: Noble's to be at when in town. and from whence we moved this day, up market Street between fourth & fifth streets next door to our land Lord Isaac Greenleaf.

to day 3   Day: very busy moveing.

4   Day: takeing a little rest after great fatigue, Neigh Warner, Sam:l Samsom hear.

5   Morn: sorting drawers, afternoon Nancy Warner, John Jackman, a relation from Barbados, by whom I had an agreable letter from Hallender, and Isaac & Caty Greenleaf suped hear.

6   Morn: at Work, afternoon at Work, evening Anna Pole, Polly Rhodes, and Josiah Huges hear.

7   Morn: Dady & Mame went to Richmond, Caty & I together the day

1 Day   Morn: they returned again, Mame, Caty & I went to the Middle meeting house, afternoon Caty & I at meeting, Tabby Fisher, Betsey Warner, and Sally Lightfoot, drank tea with me. our good friend, and Neighbour Sam: Shoemaker hear evening. at meeting B T: Spoke.

2   Morn: at Work, Capt Mase and Jos: Richardson, afternoon at Work. evening Neighbours Penington, Groth, and Sweet,

3   Morn: at meeting Mor: Yarnel, B T:, and H W: spoke, afternoon at home

4   Morn: at Work. Dady & mame went to Richmond, afternoon Betsey Rodman and Sally Saunders, evening Josey Smith,

5   Morn: wrote to Sally Smith largely, if Hesikiah Williams in a good sermon on third day, had not said, man was the last thing god created, I should have wondered more at the deceiveing of Men but as I presume some of them think us not liable to misery for ever. and so will give us our share in this life. poor E B: set up as a mark for thy Sisters, went to meeting, Sam: Notingham spoke, afternoon Mary Stanley, Cath: Greenleaf, Sam: Samsom Jun, Fran: Rawle, and Robert Proud. Evening Caty & I took a walk a hard gust of thunder and lightning

6   Morn: at meeting With Caty Smith, she carried in her Certificate. af-

200. Of the Delaware River.

ternoon Danny Smith come from B——n, evening Owen Jones Sam: Samsom,

7   Morn: out of errands, afternoon at Work, Dady, Mame, Danny, & Caty, Conversation.

1 Day   Morn: Danny went home. We went to meeting: D S: and H W: spoke. Betsey Rodman, Sally Lightfoot, and Josey Smith dined hear. afternoon at meeting, Polly Pemberton, Anna Pole, Caty Smith, and myself drank tea together. and went to evening meeting, Samuel Notingham made a fine prayer mentioning the royal family. Isaac & Cath: Greenleaf suped hear.

2   Morn: at Work, Polly Sandwith and Betsey Moods, afternoon Widow Harrison, Widow Warner, Lydia Noble, Sally Parish, Nancy Mitchel, and Sukey Shipen, drank tea with us. and an agreable Conversation. Caty and I walked home with Cousin Lydia.

3   Morn: Dady & Mame went to Richmond, Caty & I went to Caty Howels, from thence to meeting, Samuel Notingham, and D S: spoke. afternoon, Caty & I went to Richmond,

4   Morn: busy folding cloaths, afternoon Cousin Samy & Lydia Noble

8 Mos 5   Day: Ironing

[August 1, 1760]

6   Day: folding & Ironing. Sammy Samsom.

7   Morn: Ironing, afternoon gathering flower seeds, & this evening we all returned home. I stept to see Francis Rawle

1 Day   Morn: at meeting Mor: Yarnell spoke, a very rainy day. Tommy Lightfoot drank tea and suped with us.

2   Morn: at meeting: Sarah Morris and Jane Ellis spoke. Han: Cathrell dined hear, I drank tea in Company with Neigh: Warner, Sally Fisher, —————Footman, & Caty Howel. I suped there.

3   Morn: Youths meeting, Caty & I went. D S:, B T:, Polly Pusey, Mar: Ellis, and Sam: Notingham spoke. afternoon Sam: come hear, 5 O'Clock I went to see poor Betty Wiliams, who is sick at Israel Pembertons, Sally Morris, and Peggy Hains. evening Samy Samsom.

4   Morn: worked a Rose in my Irish Stich Screen, Sam: Notingham, Sam: Noble, Lydia Noble, their son Dickey, and Nurse Molly Clothier dined, and spent the afternoon, Betsey Cooper, evening Caty & I went to Neighbour Warners, Henry Drinker come home with us.

5   Morn: worked a leaf. went to meeting D S: spoke, Neddy Brooks dined with us, afternoon grounded,[201] evening at Sammy Nobles. Sammy Samsom come home with me

---

201. Stitched the background for needlework.

6   Morn: Cousin Lydia Noble. Molly Clothier, little Dicky, Caty Smith &
           I spent the day at Richmond. we returned in the evening & as it was
           late lodged at Sam: Nobles.

7   Morn: come home, worked at the grounding. afternoon the same

1 Day   Morn: at meeting D S: spoke, afternoon at meeting Mordeca Yarnel
           spoke, drank tea at Jos: Howel, went to meeting with Becky Rawle,
           Becky Jones and Sarah Morris spoke.

2   Morn: Worked my Yellow flower, Caty Howel eat some water melon
           with Caty Smith & I: afternoon Jenny Jones, and Polly Bryan hear.
           worked my Piony[202] bud.

3   Morn: at meeting, B T: Mary Kirby, and Betty Smith, spoke. afternoon
           Tommy Lightfoot, I worked a bud & leaf. evening Sammy Samsom.

4   Morn: worked a third of the border, afternoon Caty & I set with Molly
           Standley.

5   Morn: Caty & I went to meeting: B T:, John Sleeper, and John Church-
           man spoke. afternoon I went to Rachel Poles and staid all night

6   Morn: returned and worked at my grounding. Nanny Emblen, after-
           noon Abel James hear, drank tea with Caty Greenleaf, evening Sammy
           Samsom.

7   Morn: Daddy & Mame, went to Richmond, I was taken very poorly
           with the fever,

1 Day   so bad Docter Cadwalleder was called.

2   Day, the fever continued, Betsey Warner, Molly Standley hear

3   Day an intermission, Neigh: Warner & Nancy hear

4   Day a clearer intermission and application of my good old Medicine
           the Jesuits Bark.[203] Polly & Betsey Sandwith, Sarah Hundlock, and
           Caty Greenleaf hear

5   Day it lay much in my head. Neigh: Samsom hear, and I was let
           blood.[204]

6   Morn: poorly, but in the afternoon I grounded a little,

7   Morn: I went down stairs. worked my grounding most of the day, even:
           Sammy Samsom.

1 Day   Morn: Mamme Caty & I went to meeting, D S: spoke, Josey Hutchins
           dined with us. afternoon at meeting, Mame and I drank tea withy
           Mary Kirby, James Pemberton, and Ana Thornton at Isaac Zane's.
           evening at Meeting.

---

202. Peony. Probably a peony pattern in needlework.
203. A source of quinine. HCS may have had an attack of malaria.
204. The number "6" was written in the left margin twice—apparently a mistake.

2   Morn: Dady & mame gone to Richmond, at Work at the grounding.
        afternoon Sally Dugdill, evening Sammy Samsom
3   Morn: Caty & I went to meeting, Mary Emblen and John Storer spoke.
        I dined with Becky Rawle, and spent the afternoon with Caty Howel,
        I went a little to see John Jackman.
4   Morn: Neigh: Warner, Nancy & Betsey, and Mame & I went to Rich-
        mond, Peter Reeves, Scaman Rodman, and Will: Lester calld there in
        there way from B——n. about 4 O'Clock we set out for Philadelphia,
        I found my dear Nancy Gibson at home on a visit to me, we went & set
        upstairs in my Chamber, for Conversation, and presently we see a per-
        son ride post hast to Docter Shippen[205] which we took for Casper Wis-
        ter, the Docter mounted, & the person run after as hard as possible, the
        event proved to be, at a game of Billards at the Centre house,[206] the
        room it seems is free for all comers which subjects young men, to no
        distintion of Company. among those that I knew there were Casper,
        Jos: Penock, and Sam: Meredith, with a large company, among the rest
        an unhappy young Broken[207] Officer, they played for hours, till one
        Robert Skull going to the head of the table, made a stroke on which he
        laid a crown, as the stroke was to be nicely made, they gathered round
        the table, the officer at the foot, (he had been a guning before and
        brought his gun, in the room with him) no Sir says he I will show you
        how to make a stroke, and takes up his gun, and shot two bullets from
        it, one of which went into Skull, & Penock standing behind him, but
        whinching a little out of the way, the other went into the Partion. ter-
        ror and amasement seized them for a moment till the officer, turning
        to the [person] next [to him,] pulled a cartridge from his pocket & said
        he should be obliged to them to blow his brains out. Skull said he was
        a dead man, which roused them to seek for help. in the fright no one
        secured the other poor creature, but he never left the room, on being
        asked his reasons for doing as he had, he said he had been tired of his
        life for some time, but coud not kill himself, and so chose that way to
        get rid of it knowing blood would be required for blood. he had never
        seen Skull before, and quite a chance his shooting him more than the
        rest. the sight of the poor creature brought by bound like a Malafacter
        was a great shock to me: some parent's early hope but now, alas, there
        latter grief. Oh wretched man: the pride of broken fortune has been
        the ruin of many.[208]

205. Dr. William Shippen.
206. A tavern of ill-repute, see Peter Thompson, *Rum Punch and Revolution: Taverngoing and Public Life in Eighteenth-Century Philadelphia* (Philadelphia: University of Pennsylvania Press, 1999), 104–5.
207. Broken in rank, demoted or drummed out of his regiment.
208. Charles Biddle wrote the following account, "Sitting one evening at my mother's door with Cap-tain Robert Scull, a cousin of my mother's, one Bruleman went by. He was a genteel looking man. As he

5   Morn: wrote to Sally, Caty & I went to meeting, Sarah Morris John Storer spoke. afternoon Mame & I went to Docter Cadwalleders. even Caty & I went to see Mary Kirby.

6   Morn: at meeting John Storer spoke. Lydia Noble and Anna Pole dined and staid the afternoon. with us. even Sammy Samsom.

7   Morn: at work Grounding, afternoon Skull died! Polly Pemberton and I went to Billy Morris's child's funeral, Sammy Emblen spoke

1 Day   Morn: at meeting: Mary Emblen and John Storer spoke, afternoon at meeting Mordecai Yarnel spoke. Caty & I drank tea at neighbour Warners with Polly Pemberton, Polly and Betsey sandwith, and Nancy Warner and we all went down to the hill meeting where Sammy Emblen and John Storer spoke.

[September 1, 1760]

9 Mo 2   Morn: Grounding, afternoon Caty Smith, myself, and Betsey Lovett went to Richmond. we found the Country very pleasent.

3   Day. we began washing, & carried it on as brisk as we could.

4   Day. Ironing, Sammy Samsom drank tea with us.

5   Day. Daddy & Mame come to see us, and staid with us. all

6   Day. till the noon when we all returned to Philadelphia, I went to Ann Thornton's where my Cousin Sally Lightfoot is put to board. Those poor Girls met with a great loss in there mother, the Amiable Molly Smith, while they were young. from thence to see John Jackman. some pleasent Conversation with him, from thence to Abel Jame's, little Sucky & Henry Drinker Ill of a fever, from thence to Nanny Carlisle and so returned home. a letter from Sally. she has had her trials, hav-

---

walked along he had a cane in his hand, which he kept throwing up, and catching it as it fell. Mr. Scull inquired what strange fellow that was. I told him he was a jeweler, who lived with a Mr. Milne, a few doors from us; that he had been an officer in the army, but was dismissed the servie on suspicion of being concerned with some coiners [counterfeiters]; that he appeared to be an inoffensive man, but was supposed, since his dismissal, to be a little deranged. Mr. Scull expressed himself a good deal concerned for him. A day or two after this, Bruleman went to the Schuylkill with a loaded gun with an intention to shoot himself in the woods, but he said he could not do it. He then determined to shoot some person in order that he might be executed. The first he met after he had made up mind was Dr. Cadwalader, who politely pulled off his hat to him. This saved the Doctor. Another person he met spoke to him in so kind a manner, that he could not shoot him. One other he saw in the woods, but he said there was no person that could be a witness against him. He then went into the billiard room at the Centre Tavern, pulled off his coat and hung it up. Captain Scull was then playing. In passing by where the coat was, he accidentally threw it down; and immediately after, making a good stroke, Bruleman took up his gun and presenting it at Captain Scull, saying at the same time, 'Sir, you have made a good stroke, I will show you a better,' and fired across the table. . . . He was carried to gaol, and soon after tried and executed. He suffered with great fortitude, appearing anxious to leave the world, saying no man should remain in it who had lost his character. Captain Scull was in the prime of life, and had just acquired an independent fortune." Charles Biddle, *The Autobiography of Charles Biddle, vice-President of the Supreme Exeutive Council of Pennsylvania, 1745–1821* (Philadelphia: Claxton, 1883), 387–88.

ing seen the departure of a good mother, and two Worthy and Amiable Sisters, being now the only support and comfort to an aged father!

7 Morn: wrote largely to Sally Smith, and in my place book, afternoon I went to see Grace Caldwell and spent it very agreably with her.

1 Day Morn at meeting: D S: and Eliza Stevens spoke. afternoon at meeting Sam Emblen spoke, Tommy & Sally Lightfoot, and Sammy Samsom drank tea hear. evening at meeting Joice Beneset spoke. after super an alaram of fire

2 Morn: at Work. afternoon Caty Howel & Becky Rawle, Widow Scattergood hear, evening I went home with Caty, and Polly & Betsey Sandwith. we had agreable Conversation, & Joshua come home with me

3 Morn: mending Stockings, afternoon I began to help Caty, about ruffled Shirts. evening Sammy Samsom

4 Day. we worked titely.

5 Morn: worked titely. afternoon to Plymouth & Town, Polly Morris's with Hetty White paid us a visit. it hindred us a little but we got closely to it in the evening.

6 Day we worked closely and about 6 O'Clock finished the three. even I read in Milton.

7 Morn: grounding, afternoon, at Neigh: Greenleafs. evening Caty & I went to Poles. Rich: Smith and James Bringhurst there.

1 Day. Morn: at meeting Ann Crossfeild, a friend from England, spoke, afternoon at meeting, Tommy Lightfoot and Sammy Samsom drank tea hear, even at meeting Ann Crossfeild, and Susanah Hatton, a friend from Ireland, spoke, John Wilson come to see us with Isaac Greenleaf.

to day 2 Morn: put in a blue Calimanco[209] quilt for Betsey Lovet, Caty taken very poorly, wrote to Sally, afternoon did a little at the quilt.

3 Morn: Caty seeming a little better we went to meeting, George Mason, a friend from England, and Ann Crossfeild spoke. after meeting spoke to Eliza Richardson from Rhode Island, went to Caty Howels a little bit, her child is sick. afternoon went to Israel Pembertons, Mary Pemberton, George Mason, Eliza Richardson, and Polly & Sally with myself made up the Company, The friend gave us some wholesome and salutary advice, the Rhode Islander appears to be a modest sober young Woman. after Tea Polly, Eliza, & I went to look at the City, going by Hugh Roberts we in creased our number, with Betsey Roberts, Polly Desher, and Patty Loydd, we walked up Second Street to the Barracks, then down front Street to Neigh: Warners, Polly & Betsey received us Kindly, when rested we proceeded home. I found Caty with a fever.

---

209. Callimanco, a glossy worsted, used both for clothing and upholstery, often highly decorated.

4	Morn: at work and siting with Caty. afternoon Bobby Smith from B——n to see Caty, evening Neigh: Abel James, Nancy Warner, Josey Smith, and Sammy Samsom.
5	Morn: Caty began to take the bark, Bobby returned, I stiched a pair of ristbands for her. afternoon Hetty Kinersley, Han: Jenkins, and Tommy Lightfoot drank tea hear, evening with Caty,
6	Morn: busey & with Caty. afternoon and evening I set with her and worked for her
7	Day. with the Sick. George bad also. I steped to Molly Standleys, see Polly Rhodes

1 Day	Morn: at meeting George Mason spoke, afternoon at meeting Ann Crossfeild spoke, Josey Smith drank tea hear. evening at meeting: Ann Crossfeild, Becky Jones, and D S: spoke. Sammy Samsom suped hear.
2	Morn: quilting, afternoon My dear friend Grace Caldwell, Eliza Richardson & Polly Pemberton spent with me, we spent it in Innocense of Conversation, and that blindness which Gracious Providence has been pleased to afford poor Mortals with regard to the events of futurity! Oh! Time what doth thou not unfold to us; things which we are ready to think is more than we can bear. Polly & Eliza a little before dark went from hear to Polly Rhodes's, soon after they were gone Jos: Howel come in haste & enquired for Israel Pemberton, telling Daddy that Joseph Jordan had stabed Thomas Kirbride in the belly, and he was dead, Israel was rode out, Mary was at Deb: Claypoles, Polly at Rhodes's so that none but Sally was at home, Josey come home very drunk and abusive, she ran after Sally but he flew into the street,[210] which in all provibility saved her life, he went up into his chamber, and the family requested of Tommy, to go and lock him in, but at the door of the chamber, struggling, he stabed him, Tommy run down stairs again & Joe after him, into the Yard, Tommy stoped on one of the grass plats, & says to the young woman maid, Joe has Stabed me, I am a dead man, and fell lifeless instant ly, Joe swagered about, but people from the street secured him, thus in one moment fell the flower of our City, a lad of the most promiseing abilitys! For the State & the Church, by the luckless hand of an abandoned, I had almost said Villain. Daddy says tho' Tommy fell pulseless, yet about half an hour after he strugled and spoke, but died instantly, and when the news rung thro' the house that he was dead, one universal cry of Lamentation seised all, Spectators weept, all but the unhappy father & mother, who seemed robbed of that relief, and the wretched aggressor who was removed to a dungeon now deservedly become the child of Justice,

210. HCS must have meant "*He* ran after Sally but *she* flew into the street."

3   Morn: busy quilting. afternoon Neigh Warner and Polly & Betsey Sandwith, evening Sammy Samsom,

4   Morn: Mame & I went to the funeral of Thomas Kirbride, he was carried from the middle meeting and D S:, Susanna Hatton, a frind from Ireland, Jane Crossfield, Sammy Emblen, and Ann Moore spoke. the whole was solemn and melancholy, and in the intrem, about 11 O'Clock, Caty says they Carried Joe and Bruluman, the officer, to the state house for tryal! Oh wretched companions; both fallen by Evil Communication. afternoon Ben: Sweet, John & Henry Drinker, and I drank tea with Neigh: Greenleafs. even Caty & I took a walk to see the Illuminations for the takeing of Montereal.[211]

5   Morn: Ironing, afternoon at Work,

6   Morn: Mamme went to B——n with Charles, afternoon Betsey Sandwith, Nancy Warner, evening read in Rollins Ancient History[212]

7   Morn: Poorly read a litle in Rollin. Neigh: Shoemaker hear afternoon the same,

1 Day   Morn: 7 O'Clock wrote to Mamme, afternoon Caty Howel, Becky Rawle, and Robert Proud drank tea hear this evening.

2   Morn: doing Pickles, Daddy went to Burlington. afternoon at Rachel Poles, she is very ill, evening Sammy Samsom.

3   Morn: at meeting, dined with Caty Howel, Becky Rawle spent the afternoon with us, evening I returned.

[October 1, 1760]

10 Mo 4   Morn: very busy preserveing Quinces, Barbarys, & afternoon at Becky Coopers, Becky Rawle there. evening at home reading in Rollins Ancient History.

5   Morn: at meeting D S: spoke. Afternoon I went to the Widow Edwards, Betsey Edwards at home, from thence to Neigh: Warners, heard by her from Daddy & Mamme, evening Nancy Mitchel and I went to see Polly & Sally Pemberton, I weept with them there are but little words in such distress can administer comfort theres must come from God alone.

6   Morn: quilting went to see Rachel Pole, afternoon to see Rachel Drinker, eveing Sammy Samsom, Josey Bringhurst, and Josey Smith

7   Morn: quilting, afternoon at Becky Rawle a little drank tea with Caty and in the evening Dady returned from B——n. all well.

---

211. Montreal was the last French stronghold in North America. The taking of the city brought an end to the American phase of the Seven Years War.

212. Charles Rollin, *The Ancient History of the Egyptians, Carthaginians, Assyrians, Babylonians, Medes and Persians, Macedonians, and Grecians. Translated from the French* (1738 and many other editions).

Memorandom Book.

Began, Third Month Twenty Sixth, 1762.

26. I had some Inclination for my own Satisfaction, or some of my Friends if they should think fit in future Time, to leave it for their perusal, or otherways destroy'd and as I had began and continued an account during the Years 1758 and 1759. I chose to reinspect time from this I hope memorable day of my Life.

Morn rose by 7 O'Clock indeavouring to compose my mind, that I might break that awful Silence, in a publick Assembly, with a becoming composure. wrote a note to Jemmy & Anna Bringhurst, by Nancy Cole, Sammy Sansom come here.

9 O'Clock Mame Caty Smith and I went to meeting. we set by Polly Pemberton and Sally Pemberton, John Stevenson, Hannah Harris, Elizabeth Wilkinson were there. Friends from England. the latter spoke, in a mild but convincing manner, to those blessed with affluence, that they walk doubly circumspect. Mary Emblen Benn Trotter spoke. I endeavoured to fortify my mind, by looking on my undertakeing, as a solemn League of Friendship. and in the presence of my Parents and Friends, Samuel Sansom and I stood up. and told them, by Divine permission, and there approbation we intended Marriage, Joseph Thomas & Betsey Edwards, John Levens & Betsy Howell, Sammy Pleasents & Polly Pemberton, Benny Sweet & Polly Howel. passed at the same time. Samuel Sansom & his wife, Neigh Warner and Josey Sansom dined with us. Anna Bringhurst came here in the afternoon and we were looking at 2 peices of my work, one a blue Tafaty stitched bed quilt, drawn by Sally Smith, and worked by Caty & I the other a white peeling wearing quilt drawn by Sally Smith and worked at Unkle Daniel Smiths in Burlington by Betsey Smith & I. evening Jemmy Bringhurst, Anthony & Billy Sykes, Molly Brown Lodged here.

7 Morn at home, Betsey Warner here, Molly Brown, Brialle Newbolds Widow dined here, I went to see cousin Johns children, evening S. Sansom.

Day Morn at meeting John Stevenson, S. Stanton, spoke afternoon at meeting E Wilkinson H. Harris spoke. Josey Smith to tea. evening at meeting, Robert Proud, Ham Foster spoke.

2 Morn at meeting, John Stevenson Robert Croud, Emily, Levens B. Trotter spoke Sam Williams dine here. Sammy Pleasents spent the afternoon with Caty & I. evening Benjamin Sweet sammy Sanso.

3 Morn at meeting Joseph White, Sister Parker, John Stevenson, Susanah Hatton spoke, Polly Howel dined with me, afternoon to see Polly Cadwallader Doctor Hooper there, the day died Elizabeth Lawdale, a woman noted for prudence & resolution. Haddon field is named after her maiden name.

1 Day   Morn: at meeting: Sarah Morris and Ann Moore, spoke, afternoon at meeting Ann Moore, spoke, Debby Mitchel and Samy Samsom drank tea hear. evening at meeting George Mason spoke.

2   Day, bad weather, mending Stokings. Isaac Greenleaf spent part of the evening with Caty & I, reading in the Sixth Vol: of Rollins History.

3   Morn: at Work, afternoon Mary Armitt, evening Isaac Greenleaf.

4   Morn: John Bruleman, the officer, executed! pride fixed by a wrong education produces horrid effects. afternoon Ironing.

5   Morn: Ironing, afternoon George Mason, Sarah Morris, Caty Greenleaf, and Jos: Morris, evening at Work,

6   Morn: at Work for Caty, afternoon at Docter Shippen's. Sukey, Polly Standley & I were the Company, poor Bruleman the conversation, they are Girls of understanding, but difference of education[213] sometime carries narrowness of sentiment with it. I think it appears to me there are not a people in the known World, that in a general way have more enlarged Ideas than the Quakers, inshort the very begining of Quakerisem is benevolence of heart to mankind

7   Morn: wrote to Mame, went to see Neigh: Warner. afternoon at Work for Caty. heard from Mame, even Samy Samson

1 Day   Morn: Edward Cathrel from B———n. went to meeting: George Mason and Eliza: Morris spoke, Josey Smith dined with us, afternoon at meeting George Mason spoke, I went to Rachel Poles and staid till meeting time then went and George Mason, and Susanah Hatton spoke.

2   Morn: at Work, afternoon Samy Samsom,

3   Morn: Worked for Caty. Edward Cathrel dined hear. afternoon Worked for Caty, evening read to her In the Bible,

4   Morn: Worked for Caty, afternoon the same, Tammy Fox hear.

5   Morn: Worked for Caty, afternoon at Becky Rawle, Neigh Warner, Caty Howel, and Beny Sweet there, I spent the evening at Caty Howels with Joshua Francis & Becky,

6   Morn: Worked for Caty, afternoon puting up beds, Mamme, Sally Smith, and Polly Lightfoot come from Burlington. Samy Samsom, hear

7   Morn: preserveing quinces & crabapples, afternoon Sally & I went to Tom: Lightfoots, Daniel Ofleys, and Rachel Poles, and spent the evening at home. Thomas Lightfoot

1 Day   Morn: at Meeting Mary Kirby spoke, Sally Smith, Polly Lightfoot, and John Jackman dined with us, afternoon at meeting Eliza Morris spoke.

213. The Shippens were Presbyterians.

Sally & I went to see the Pembertons, evening at meeting Daniel Stanton and Ben: Trotter spoke,

to Day 2   Morn: worked for Caty, afternoon Mame, Sally Smith, Polly Lightfoot,
and Peggy Emblen, went see Neigh: Warner, we found there, Eliza
Rhodes & Polly Han: Hicks & Caty Howel, evening Caty Sally & I went
to Becky Rawle & spent it with them and their Husbands.

3   Morn: Polly Lightfoot & I went to meeting, D S:, B T:, Becky Jones,
David Easter, and H: Williams spoke, Mary Kirby set out for Chester
this morn, on her way to England, afternoon I met Sally Smith, Polly
& Betsey Sandwith, and Polly & Sally Lightfoot at Caty Howels.
evening we returned and were half a dozen Girls: Sally Smith, Abby
Raper, Hallender, Caty Smith, Polly Lightfoot, and Sally Hoskins,
they lodged with us. and part of the time Betsey & Nelly Moode.

4   Morn: Sally went to Chester, Caty & I out at Shops, afternoon Steped
up to Samy Nobles, to see If Cousin Lydia, and Han: West continued
with their intension of going to Shrewsberry as I talk of going with
them, evening at Work, Samy Sansom.

5   Morn: rose before the Sun & got to quilting, some conversation with
Cousin Johanna Broks, dined hear, Sally returned from chester, fin-
ished the quilt, I walked up to Samy Nobles, and find the events of this
Life Uncertain. called for Sally at the Widow Edwards, come home &
I am makeing some preparations for my Journey to morrow but hold
them at arms length.

6   Morn: Daddy and Caty went with me to Samy Noble's, and from
thence Lydia Noble, Hannah West, Sam: Wethrell and I set out for
Burlington, the wind rose which made it not so pleasent as it would
have been, we baited at Amoses, crossed Hills ferry, and I dined at Unkle Daniel's. one O'Clock then Cousin Lydia, Hannah & I took Bobby
Smith & Paul Saunders for Convoy, we reach Allen Town by evening,
and lodged at Thomas Lowry's who has lately married Ann Murfin,
there was a violent storm of wind in the night I did not know but the
house would have fallen,

7   Morn: we breakfasted and set off, with a great many more who where
going the same rode to meeting, we at 9 miles,[214] and eat oysters with
a large Company, then we went to freehold and baited and the country between freehold and Shrewsberry I think very pleasent, we lodged
that night at Nathan Tiltons. they have several grown up Daughters

1 Day   Morn: after breakfast set out again & reached Shrewsberry put up at
the Tavern till meeting time then went to meeting, through a vast con-
course of people, John Casey, Phillip Dennis, and Heze: Williams

214. The 9 is written over another number, possibly a "4."

spoke, I see a great many People that knew me, we went home with Jos: Parker, and after diner Cousin Lydia, Han:, Bobby, Paul, Billy Parker, & I took a walk to Rich: Worthleys, he & his Wife Molly received us kindly; & come back again to Parkers with us, and we had a meeting: Isaac Andrews and Thomas Wood spoke, Betty Andrews and I lodged together,

2   Morn: Billy Parker and some others with our Company walk down to South River the vast quantitys of oyster shells left along shore for ages by the Indians makes the land very rich & valuable, went to meeting: John Casey, Thomas Wood, and Ben: Trotter spoke, we went home with Richard Curless, his Wife Marget, and Daughters Hannah & Peggy received us kindly, toward evening the Girls & their Brother Timothy with our young men took a walk to Joseph Curless's where there were in all Twenty young folks, I think Tim Curless the most compleat young man I see while I was away, wrote to Daddy this night, and set up so late that I thought sleep had flown from my eyes, there are times of thought which last in ones memory for years

3   Morn: we went to meeting Isaac Andrews, Thomas Wood, and Ben: Trotter spoke, and afterwards Molly Worthly & Caty Tilton went with us to Thomas Whites at Deal, he is a widower but has a daughter Hannah, who was at our House some years ago, after diner we walked down to the Sea, which was calm, but a magnific sight, the Ocean of Waters; Thomas White is a merry old man and we spent the evening agreably.

4   Morn: we walked to the Sea, I cared not how much I looked at it: we see three Vessels off, traversing the Ocean. after diner Molly Worthly, Caty Tilton, & our company set of for Shrewsberry and lodged at Mollys having great plenty of oysters for super. Caty & I sleept together.

5   Morn: we set our faces Homeward parting affectionately with our Friends, Caty Tilton went with us, but Just as we were oposite Jos: Hardels we discovered Paul had left his Saddel bags, and he returned for them about 2 & half miles, this made us very merry but Paul returned before we parted with Caty Tilton, this was good sort of Girl, we parted 7 miles from Shrewsberry, we baited & dined at freehold, meeting there with John Kirkbride and Wife, Isaac Antrem and a young Widower, become so about a month before, and seemmed as if he was pleased he had escaped the Shakles, and with baiting once more we all Joged on to Allen Town, which we did not reach till within Night, and our Company lodged at Thomas Lowrys,

6   Morn: we went to see a fulling mill, and after we had breakfasted set of for Burlington with Isaac Antrem, poor Pauls horse tireing as well as the rider, was the cause of a great deal of diversion. we got safe to Burlington by 2 O'Clock, where I found Sally returned from Philadelphia, and heard of the death of Cousin Rachel Pole,

[November 1, 1760]

11 Mo:s: hear Cousin Lydia Noble & Hannah West left me, as I thought to stay
7   a few days with Sally, but she was taken Sick, and the court Assembly
           and fair meeting I coud not think of leaveing her, Peter Kimble of
           Brunswick, Docter Lewis Jonston of Amboy, and Charles Reed lodged
           there and the 15th of this month[215]   by malice of his foes.
           Abenezer Large died in this Interim, I was taken, after Sally got bet-
           ter, ~~I was taken~~ with a bad cold so that I did not get home for better
           than three weeks, bobby Smith went with me home, I found mame
           very poorly in her Chamber, where I kept her company with my cold,
           Neigh Warner, Sally Morris, Caty Howel, Mary Emblen, Lydia No-
           ble, and Hannah West were to see us, Daddy went to Burlington and
           we hear[216] by the Assembly,

[December 1, 1760]

12 Mo:s: Day, Mame and I seemed better, Anna Pole dined with us, Isaac Green-
2   leaf smoked a pipe with us afterward, Neigh: Walln, Sally Lightfoot
           Sukey Walln, and Betsey Warner hear, note: Betsey Sandwith passed
           last meeting with Henry Drinker,
3   Morn: worked at my purple Carnation, in the Screen. afternoon fin-
           ished the Carnation, Eliza: Coleman, Daddy returned this evening all
           well, worked the Grounding, Sarah Sansom and Rachel Drinker hear.
4   Morn: worked at the Screen, afternoon finished it. Caty Greenleaf
           hear, evening read in the Spectator,[217]
5   Morn: sorting some of my Drawers, worked at my queen stich thread
           Case. afternoon the same. Nanny Emblen hear, evening wrote to Sally
6   Morn: 7 O'Clock Caty Smith went to Burlington, very busey about in
           the family, Bobby Smith dined hear. he says all are well, and returned
           again directly, afternoon went off on an errand or two. made mame a
           pair of Sleave Strings, evening at Work.
7   Morn: wrote to Caty. and gave to Josey Smith to send, at Becky Rawle
           found her poorly. afternoon mending my cloaths, evening reading
           Yoricks Sermons;[218] Sam: Notingham hear.

1 Day   Morn: mame seeming bravely, I went to meeting: Philip Denis and
           D S: spoke, afternoon at meeting: Alex: Seaton, Sam: Notingham, and
           D S : spoke. Wil Smith and Anna Pole, spent part of the evening hear

215. As many as eight or more words of this line were erased.
216. Perhaps four words of this line were erased.
217. Richard Steele and Joseph Addison wrote and published *The Tatler,* 1709–1711, and *The Spectator,* 1711–1712. These essays were republished in many collections and formats and were considered models of style: intimate, rational, moral, and good humored.
218. Laurence Sterne, *The Sermons of Mr. Yorick* (1760).

2   Morn: makeing some alteration in the standing of the furniture on account of Anna Pole, who with Tommy & Nancy, is to Lodge with us.
as they are now bereft of father and mother! afternoon I went down
there. Will: Smith and Billy Govett takeing an Inventory of the goods

3   Morn: Worked at my queen stich, afternoon Anthony Beneset, evening Sam:l Sansom and Isaac Greenleaf.

4   Morn: sowing, afternoon the same, I drank tea with Cath: Greenleaf
and Rueben & Peggy Haines, evening began the first of two shifts for
Christian.

5   Morn: went to meeting: David Easter, Sam: Notingham, and D S: spoke.
afternoon John Reynolds, Tommy Lightfoot, and Billy Smith hear.

6   Morn: with Anna Pole, called at Grace Caldwell, brought Shaftsbury's
Works[219] home with me, Sammy Noble dined hear; afternoon at
Work, evening wrote to Hannah Callender of barbados.

7   Morn: at Work, afternoon went to Caty Howel's, and Becky Rawle

1 Day   Morn: at meeting: D S: and Will: Brown spoke, afternoon at meeting,
drank tea at Neigh: Warners with Henry Drinker and Polly & Betsey
Sandwith. evening we went to meeting: Ben: Trotter, Mary Evans, and
D Stanton spoke

2   Morn: busy. John Jackman dined hear, and Ann Pole & Thomas Pole come
hear to Lodge and board, I went with them to a School [run by] Rebecah
Burchill, from thence to their Sister Anna and as I was returning in the
street I had a brush with Sammy Wethrel on my Unkle Robert Smith's
Account, evening worked at the Shifts. read in Shaftsbury's Works

3   Morn: Worked at the Shifts, Isaac Grenleaf and Billy Smith hear. afternoon Nancy Pole and I at Work, evening finished one of the Shifts.

4   Morn: busey with the children, Billy Smith hear. afternoon at Work,
evening Tommy Lightfoot, read in the Gays Fables.[220]

5   Morn: busy in the Family. makeing Minced Pies. afternoon Hannah
Logan hear, evening Anna Pole come to board and lodge hear. Billy
Smith Lodged hear.

6   Morn: worked at my queen stich thread case, afternoon Mame & I at
Work

7   Day: makeing a cloack for Nancy Pole.

1 Day   Morn: Anna and I went to meeting: Sarah Morris spoke. Israel Morris
dined hear. afternoon Anna and I at home reading, evening we went
to meeting, George Mason, Ann Moor, and Becky Jones spoke

2   Day. very busey the family Wash. Neig: Warner and Nanny Weber hear.

219. Anthony Ashley Cooper, Third Earl of Shaftesbury, *Characteristics of Men, Manners, Opinions, and Times* (1711).

220. John Gay, *Fables*, 1727 and 1738.

3   Day Ironing. evening Jimmy Bringhurst and Billy Govett hear.
4   Day Ironing,
5   Morn at meeting: Mathew Franklin, John Casey, and B T: spoke, af-
        ternoon Nancy Pole and I spent with Hannah Mickle. evening Josey
        Smith and Sammy Samson.
6   Morn: Anna Pole and I went to meeting, Henry Drinker and Betsey
        Sandwith, Israel Morris and Phebe Brown passed. afternoon I spent
        with Caty Howel, evening also, John Howel come home with me
7   Morn: Anna Pole and I out at Shops, afternoon runing Stokings.
        evening Abel James and Cath: Greenleaf hear.

to day 1   Morn: at home a little unwell, with Mamme. afternoon also, Sam:
  Day   Loydd, a promising Youth of Twenty one, was buried. evening read-
        ing in the Bible to Mame and Anna Pole.
2   Morn: worked on my Padua Soy²²¹ long short cloak, afternoon also,
3   Morn: work on the same, John Jackman dined hear, Sam: Notingham
        drank tea hear, evening I displeased my mame unwillingly! ————
        —wrote to Sally Smith.
4   Morn: busy in the family. afternoon Tommy Lightfoot and Betsey Gar-
        rick, evening Jimmy Bringhurst,

[January 1, 1761]

5   Day I finished my Cloak, and staid with mamme as the best service I
        could devout the New year to, towards evening Bobby Smith and Caty
        Smith come home, and now we are altogether in the family again, I
        hope we shall be preserved in Spiritual and Temporal health.

ᴆ

[August 26, 1761]
Journal of my Journey to Bethlehem in 1761.

8 Month   Parents consenting, Anna Pole, Betsey Bringhurst, Hallender, Jemmy
  26ᵗʰ   Bringhurst, and Sammy Sansom, set out for Bethlehem and the Coun-
        try adjacent, intending a Tour of a Week or ten days, in a compleat
        light Waggon designed for a pair of Horses and made by Jemmy
        Bringhurst.
3   Morn: we rode agreably to Germantown 7 miles, dined at Maconets,
        observed the new Colledge a neat building for the Education of youth.
        Noble design to form their ductile minds in all the Laws of Innocense
        and truth. 2 O'Clock we set off, found Chestnut Hill long and difficult,
        Will: Allen has a large Stone House on the top. the Genious of a man is

221. A corded silk fabric.

often seen in his buildings. we met with a complasent Dutch man, a Waggoner. going thro' White March,[222] noted Sam: Morris's large building, by Ambition made desolate. and the back stairs built for his Daughters quite useless because he has no Wife.[223] passed Rowland Evans's and about Six O'Clock rid pleasently down a fine desending lane to the Widow Evans's, Widow of the worthy John Evans, who now lives with her son John Evans. 13 miles. in a little time after Anthony Benezet and Robert Parish arrived from Bethlehem having been so far with the Friendly Indians, Paponon & ᶜ,[224] on their way home. they brought an account that the people were apprehensive [that] the Indians intended to strike a blow soon, which had set them in an alarum. but as they thought we might safely proceed, I wrote to Daddy by them Morn: between 5 & 6 O'Clock rid through a fine Country, thickly inhabited to Trostrum's, 8 Miles, and breakfasted. proceeded thro' very Stony road 10 miles to Insleys, thence 7 miles to Tetters. drank part of a poor dish of Tea yet it refreshed us from a fright we put ourselves in on the road. now we began to see the mountains at a distance. in 5 miles we got to another Public house but a very poor one, proceeded the other 5 to Bethlehem being almost night. you ride a little way along the banks of the Lechia,[225] to a Tavern oposite the Town,[226] hear we began to see the Manners of the People: complasent, mild, and affable. all there buildings and things are designed for use, and are made strong and lasting. we crossed the river, the Brethren's house makeing a pretty Illumination, walked a quarter of a mile to the Inn in Bethlehem. passed by the Stables which were struck with lightening last year. the House is kept by Peter Warbas, during good behaviour, all its profitts go to the Common Stock.[227] Charles Stedman and —————Seaman Just arrived before us from Grayam Park. we had an elegant Super and dilegent waiters. rested well and waked in the.

5

---

222. Whitemarsh. In the margin there is a sketched hand with index finger pointing to this passage.

223. Samuel Morris built this house in the 1740s for his upcoming marriage, reputedly saying at its completion, "Now I have the sty; all I need is the sow," so angering his fiancé, that she broke off the engagement. He never married.

224. Papunhank, a Munsee living at Wyalusing, was an important go-between in treaty negotiations at this time and was willing to criticize both Native peoples and colonists. He had adopted some Quaker principles, but also continued Munsee rituals and beliefs. Merritt, *At the Crossroads,* 84–86. 126–28.

225. Lehigh River.

226. In margin, not in HCS's hand: "The 'Crown Inn,' the first public house of entertainment erected by the Moravians on the Lehigh River." GV. Mr. Vaux may have been particularly interested in annotating this portion of the diary's limited excerpts because John Jordan of the Historical Society of Pennsylvania, Vaux's contemporary, aided him by supplying useful citations. Jordan, for example, alerted Vaux to the presence of a correspondence between HCS and Mary Penry of Bethlehem into the 1780s and likely beyond. Jordan's letter was in the diary's "Bethlehem Journey" pages.

227. "The 'Sun Inn,' which is still [1888] one of the prominent hostelries of Bethlehem. Peter Worbas, its first landlord, was one of the five who escaped when the mission-house at Gnadenhutten, on the Mahoning, was destroyed by Indians in November of 1755." GV.

6   Morn: by one Hundred Cows, a number of them with Bells. a venerable goat and two she goats [were] drove in town by two Sisters. this order was continued morn & even during the time we stayed, and looked very pretty. we breakfasted and set off for Nazereth in Company with C:Stedman.————————Seaman-Jones and two waiting Men. 9 miles, Nazareth is a fine Farm where the Widows and Boys reside. in the Widows meeting room is two peices of painting, the birth and death of our Saviour. we asked for the widow Bromfeild.[228] she come and expressed great satisfaction on seeing us. then we crossed a feild or two to the Boys house. this was built as a habitation for Count Zinzandorf,[229] a large Spacious Stone House. assending by a flight of steps, into a large Hall, used for worship, the minister, our guide, played on the organs. passed thro the childrens eating rooms, long narrow tables with benches, covered with course cloath and wooden trenchers, they were not so clean as all the rest. upstairs are the school rooms. In the 1st room [children] between 3 & 4 years picking cotton, so orderly and still, for any noise they made you mought have been in an empty room. the 2nd room next between 5 & 6 years knitting. the 4th between 7 & 8 years Spyning. the 5th and last employed at their books. peices of their writing fixed on the wall to raise emulation. 14 children in each room. The children's meeting room, a large Hall on the same floor, was adorned with 6 peices of painting of the life of our Saviour, including a representation of him at full length. the third Story is the bed room, containing 1 hundred beds for one person each, two Brethren by turns keep nightly watch with Lamps burning. the great order, decency, decorum and conveniency is hardly to be expressed. we left this pleasent place with due thanks to the minister, going one mile beyond to dine at a tavern.[230] several Indians were at the house, and things carried a solemn aspect in the War. it had been a place of defence, or retreat for the neighborhood, this last rumour had brought a family from 20 miles beyond, and they themselves in much fear. Sympathy is the cheif duty of human life. Compasion is the essence of humanity. after diner 2 miles to Guadendahl[231] lite and went into the meeting room. 2 peices of painting the birth and death of our Saviour, see some women who kindly treated us with peaches, got in the waggon, and at a small distance reached Christian Spring,[232] this is the residence of the

228. "Catherine, daughter of Thomas and Catherine (maiden name Bouroux) Kearney, born in New York, February, 1716, united with the Moravians in 1745. In 1747 she married John Brownfield, formerly secretary to General Oglethorpe. She died in April of 1798, at Bethlehem." GV.

229. Count Nicholas Ludwig von Zinendorf, who founded the Moravian settlement at Bethlehem in 1741.

230. "'The Rose' (from 1752 to 1770), the first house of entertainment on the 'Barony of Nazareth.'" GV.

231. Gnadenthal.

232. Christiansbrunn. "Christian's Spring was named for Christian R., a son of Count Zinzindorf. The

younger single brethren, admired their Water works, milk house, fine large oxen, and went down steps to the spring from whence the place took its name, drank of the Castalian fount, being walled in a sort of room, and very nice, gave it a romantick air, method of makeing and glaseing their pipes, like the dutch, bowles to put wooden stems in. went to the meeting room, a young man played on the organs, till tea time, drank a dish of tea in the Gaurdian's room, opposite the Single breathren's chambers, who pleased and diverted themselves by look-ing at us. returned to bethlehem. at the top of a hill, Just as you enter the town, there is a prospect of the gaps in the mountains at a vast dis-tance and the Length of 40 Miles from each other. those horrid scenes of blood.[233] Oh my suffering Country, how have I felt for thee in those ever memorable years of distress. suped at Warbas's, all together, Anna, Betsey & I left them at the table, Stedman & Seaman are men used to the bottle, and of a very disagreable cast, when warmed by a chearful glass. they made us some mirth, very complasant

7 Day   Morn: rose with Cows, Lovely fine Prospect, writeing, the Bell calling the Sisters to prayers. all the Company breakfasted together, in the large right hand room up one pair of Stairs. Jones and his little son, a promiseing youth, was there. walked into the town, at the foot of the Hill we met Nicolas Garrison who introduced us with form to his wife, Gracy received us with freedom, we had gone to School with each other, a Daughter of Will: Parsons, hear we parted with the men, and had no more to do with them being delivered to the Sisters. Sister Becky Langly come there, we went from hence with them to the meet-ing room. nine Peices of painting [of] the Life of our Saviour, met Sis-ter Miller, a married Sister, and Sister Polly Penry as we had gone to school with the Latter, and knew the history of her unfortunate Life, greatly affected at seeing each other. Walked up the Single Sisters walk, a quarter of a mile Long, adorned with two rows of black cherry trees, to the Monachosee creek, hear Becky Langly and I by free con-versation became acquainted, she was a Lace merchant's Daughter in london, brought up at boarding School genteely, as her agreable per-son, with natural ease grace and affability, were convinceing proofs she had been at court several times, with her mother, but having great cause when young to regrett her loss, preceeded by other misfortunes.

---

diary of the congregation contains a record of the visit of this 'company of Quakers from Philadelphia to view our Settlement," and furthermore, "they were shown the tame trout in the spring, who were fed by hand, and would allow Bro. S. to take them from the water." GV.

233. Colonists who began to settle north of the Endless (or Blue) Mountain, using the Lehigh, Wind, or Water Gaps to cross, faced increasingly violent resistance by Delaware, Susquehannock, and Shawnee bands in 1755/6. Moravian missionaries and Christian Mahickans, Delawares, and Iroquois were attacked and killed at Gnadenhutten in November, 1755. Merritt, *At the Crossroads,* 174–91.

The Father, Becky and a young Sister come to America, and are hear placed as an Assylem from further storms, the good man as a citizen of the world makes his home wheresoere it is his lot. Nancy Langly has not seen so much of the World, as to forsake it with the resolution of a Philosopher. Becky and Polly Penry enjoy a strict friendship; extending our walk along the creek to the Wash house, Dye House, Bleaching yard, Sawmill, & ᶜ· Sister Miller and Betsey Bringhurst going a little before us, Sister Garrison with good humour gave us girls leave, to step cross a feild to a little Island belonging to the Single Brethren, on it is a neat Summer house, with seats of turf, and button wood Trees round it. the Monachosee laves its foot, we brought a little cup from in our pokets from Philadelphia, and hear drank peace & tranquility to each other, from the Hellispont, Polly Penry named it Leanders Stream,[234] in rememberance of those white moments. walked to the oyl mill, fullers Butchers, millers, milk house, parted with the Sisters, went to the Inn highly delighted. found Stedman, Seaman, & Jones Just ready to set off. after diner & Nicolas and Gracy Garrison come to the inn waited on us down to the children's meeting, Leaveing the men with garrison, the meeting held half hour, consisted of singing, playing on the organs, a short sermon in German by a minister, we drank tea with the Sisters in an outer room, they beged to be excused takeing us to their appartments because it was 7th day. in the evening we were at the Love feast. the men and women then meet altogther, the men on one side, and women on the other, going in at different doors, to prevent communication. Brothers waited on the men, and Sisters on the Women. two Persons brought in large baskets with small Loaves of bread, distributeing every one, one, and each person a small cup of Chocolate. returned to the Inn. and lodged.

1 Day   Morn: Ten O'Clock, we girls met Sister Miller, Becky & Polly at the gate leading to the Womens house, went to meeting. the minister spoke in English, his sermon was composed for an ignorent people, no design to open the blind eye or unstop the deef ear. the most Irriconsilable thing I met with, was that persons of good understand[ing], could immagine themselves paying real worship to the deity, in unsubstantial forms, the Minister ——————Hyde is their Limner, who has drawn all the paintings.[235]

---

234. A reference to Christopher Marlowe's pastoral poem, "Hero and Leander."

235. In margin: "Valentine Haidt, a native of Dantzic, in 1714 went to Dresden to study painting, which he continued in the schools at Venice, Rome, and Paris. After uniting with the Moravians in Germany, he executed a series of historical paintings still (1888) extant. In 1754 he was sent to Pennsylvania, where he entered the ministry of his church, and passed his remaining years between the pulpit and the easel. He died at Bethlehem, 18th January, 1780." GV.

PART II

Marriage and Family

Chapter 8

"A New Scene of Life"

Men, Women, and Familial Authority

One of the loveliest objects in the collections of Independence National Historical Park is an elaborate quilt, once bright blue but now faded almost to white. The park itself is a bastion of male politics, celebrating the place where the representatives to the Second Continental Congress declared themselves rebels against British domination in 1775 and 1776, beginning the American Revolution, and where the representatives at the Constitutional Convention in 1787 framed a national government in the name of "the People." But the park also preserves this work of considerable beauty, a contribution not to the new nation but to a pre-Revolutionary wedding trousseau. It was the work of three young women, cousins, who proudly inscribed their collaboration at the top edge: "Drawn by Sarah Smith[,] Stitched by Hannah Callender and Catherine Smith in Testimony of their Friendship[,] 10 mo. 5th [day,] 1761."[1] Friendship referred to their close, almost sisterly relationship, but also to their religious unity as Friends—Quakers. These bonds were about to be tested by Hannah Callender Sansom's upcoming marriage. In five months she would leave the world of un-

---

1. Beulah M. Rhoads, "The History of the Blue Bed-spread," (mss at Independence National Park, Philadelphia, Pennsylvania, 1911); Terri Kettering, "Object Study of the Callender/Smith Quilt," typescript of American Studies term paper, University of Pennsylvania, c. 1979, available at Independence National Park. Unfortunately, this source contains many careless errors, both in its assumptions about the construction of the quilt and in its historical analysis. See Kettering, "'Bear's Paw,' 'Philadelphia Pavement:' Quilts of the Mid-Atlantic Region," *Journal of Regional Cultures* 2 (1982); 130; Karen O'Dowd, "A Trail of History," *Lady's Circle Patchwork Quilts* 84 (November 1992): 30–37; and Patricia J. Keller, *"Of the best Sort but Plain:' Quaker Quilts from the Delaware Valley, 1760–1890* (Chadds Ford, PA: Brandywine River Museum, 1997), passim. Keller was, of course, aware of HCS's diary, but considerations of time and space prevented her from incorporating the diary in her analysis. Her explication of the quilt's construction (30), should be preferred to earlier efforts. Our thanks to Susan Branson for the O'Dowd citation.

married, relatively privileged young Quaker women and enter the world of marriage, shaped largely by her husband. Her female friends would become secondary to her new roles as wife, mistress of the household, and, as everyone expected, mother of many children. Her marriage would bring sons, the pride and joy of fathers, who could carry on the family name and station in life. Daughters could be taught all the social, decorative, and practical skills that their mother had labored to master.

For women, and especially for women of some social standing in the eighteenth century, marriage was a momentous and complex decision. Marriage was, at least in theory, the pinnacle of feminine achievement. It bestowed respectability. Marriage could give young women as much economic security as was feasible at the time. Well-to-do women would acquire a home with servants to command and a career of wifely duties, motherhood, and household management along with a husband whose true character would often only become apparent in the day-to-day trials and tribulations of life. The right husband would bring years of companionship growing into love and mutual respect. A less optimal husband might mean a lifetime of isolation, insults, infidelity, or physical and mental abuse. The home was the husband's castle, and women could only hope to find a kindly keeper. Ann Swett's father "has been letting us know that a husband has a right to correct his wife when she deserves it," but Swett was not entirely convinced, imagining that "the liberties of my sex" might provide an alternative to custom. But according to colonial Pennsylvania law, a wife had few liberties. For example, a wife who murdered her husband was guilty not of murder but of treason, of an attack on the sanctity of the social order, and she would be burnt at the stake. A large popular literature on marriage echoed these themes; in a poem titled "Choice of a Companion," a young woman hopes for a husband who will "kindly govern with a gentle sway."[2] The absolute authority of husbands was just beginning to be questioned when HCS was a young woman.

Marriage was not simply an individual concern. By law and custom, women chose their husbands—at least in so far as they could say yes or no to any man who sought their hand. In practice, various factors limited their choices. Parental success was measured by the advantageous marriages of their children. Daughters, because they required dowries at marriage, were more financially troublesome than sons. Family honor required a substantial dowry be paid, while family solvency demanded parsimony. Fathers negotiated the financial arrangements, taking into account the potential financial rewards of the match, the social standing of the suitor's family, and the suitor's "prospects." The Quaker local meeting added several additional layers of requirements: both the prospective bride and groom must be of the faith, have duly gained the permission of their respective

---

2. Ann Swett to Elizabeth Sandwith, 1752, quoted in Nicole Eustace, "'The Cornerstone of a Copious Work': Love and Power in Eighteenth-Century Courtship," *Journal of Social History* 34, no. 3 (2001): 522; and Martha Cooper Allinson Commonplace Book, c. 1770, Quaker Collection, Haverford College.

families, and have been investigated by a committee as to their "clearness" for marriage (they could not, for example, be engaged to anyone else; they must freely consent to the match). The union must be financially sound, and both must stand before the assembled meeting for worship on three separate Sundays, announcing their intention to marry at two and finally marrying after the third. The marriage certificate would be signed by scores of relatives and friends, signifying the familial and social importance of the nuptials. A wedding party, often very elaborate, and an exhausting round of social visits completed the wedding.

For a young woman, the road to marriage was marked by many potential pitfalls. Would she attract any suitors, and, if she did, would he admire her character or only be infatuated by her person or her fortune? Would he really seek love and marriage, or was he a vile seducer, who would deceive, demand sex, and then flee? Or would he marry only to seize his wife's dowry and waste it on mistresses, drink, gambling, and other dissipations? What if a suitor was found offensive and was refused? Would anyone else ask such a woman to marry, when she might be reputed a tease, or insufferably proud, or flighty? Would her parents, particularly her father, approve of her choice? Would they pass meeting? Would the months of courtship truly indicate the chances for happiness? HCS ruminated on all of these possibilities, and discussed them at length with her friends. The dangers of marriage must have appeared all too real, not in the least abstract. In the first years of the diary HCS lost many young women friends; childbirth was a dangerous aspect of marriage.

As if the path to marriage were not complicated enough, the growing expectation of romantic love during HCS's lifetime made marriage itself all the more difficult. Influenced by novels and a developing emphasis on sensibility, emotion, sexual fulfillment, and romance, couples looked not just for a "yokemate" who would share life's burdens but a soul mate as well, whose love would transform the mundane workings of the household into a labor of love. Love and sensibility promised to undermine patriarchy, although men retained actual financial, political, and social power.[3] True lovers were equals who mutually consulted the wishes of their beloved. An esteemed wife need not fear exploitation or abuse, it was hoped. But how was mutual love to be reconciled with the familial, financial, religious, social, and patriarchal aspects of the marriage process?[4]

HCS was among the first generation of women to grow up reading novels. Sentimental fiction played a formative role in her life, as in the lives of her friends; they read and discussed novels, and the particular themes of most novels, romance and courtship, paralleled their own concerns.[5] When Callender began her

---

3. See Eustace, "Cornerstone," *Journal of Social History,* 517–46.

4. For an important study of the impact of romantic ideals on the marriage relationship, see Anya Jabour, *Marriage in the Early Republic: Elizabeth and William Wirt and the Companionate Ideal* (Baltimore: Johns Hopkins University Press, 1998).

5. The most important work on novels in early America remains Cathy Davidson, *Revolution and the*

diary in 1758, it was intended as a device for self-improvement, a memorandum book on how to manage her time—this function of diary-keeping persisted as long as she wrote. Other purposes soon evolved, and the novelized aspects of the book emerged. During her courtship with Sammy Sansom, she weighed her duty to her "best Friend," as fathers were called in polite circles, with her desire for a loving marriage. Her father promoted the eminently sensible marriage with her wealthy neighbor, but she was less certain. HCS, like other women of her Quaker circle, thought and wrote about what a life without marriage, living single, might be like. In the end, she chose duty to her father over any prospect of love and soon came to regret the choice. Like the heroines in popular novels, Callender had to maneuver between the demands of fathers and of suitors, between social expectation and personal feeling, and between idealism and pragmatism. She especially had to guard her reputation. The outside world was filled with danger, for the scoundrels, vile seducers, fortune-hunters, and hypocrites who haunted the heroines of popular novels were also to be found in real life.

Callender's favorite novel was *Clarissa,* Samuel Richardson's pioneering 1748 exploration of virtue and the emotions. Clarissa was "virtuous, noble, wise, pious," the very model of femininity. Unfortunately the person she thinks "a man of honour" is in fact a "vile rake" who turns her friends against her in order to achieve his base ends. There follows a "series of plots and contrivances, all baffled by her virtue and vigilance." Clarissa is not passive or dependent. The protection of her virtue allows her to exercise intelligence and ingenuity and shows her to be brave and unyielding. This independence of action in the name of a soft and forgiving femininity may have been the primary reason the novel was beloved by so many women: it paradoxically overturned and preserved women's traditional understandings of appropriate femininity. Ultimately Clarissa overawes her tormenter "by virtue only of her innocence"; he, "repenting his usage of so divine a creature, would fain move her to forgive his baseness and make him her husband." She responds by forgiving "the author of her ruin" and becomes "solicitous for nothing so much in this life as to prevent vindictive mischief *to* and *from* the man who has used her so basely.[6] This, concludes the author, "is penitence! This is piety!" Not only does Clarissa triumph over evil, but she transforms an evil man into a good husband as well. It was a novel that asserted women's power to shape not only their own lives but also their husband's lives, a potentially revolutionary rethinking of women's power and influence that left the social and civil inequalities of marriage in place.

This novel and others with similar plots and messages became guides for young women facing an almost impossible juggling act balancing unruly love

---

Word: The Rise of the Novel in America (New York: Oxford University Press, 1986); chapter 6 in particular, "Privileging the *Feme Covet:* The Sociology of Sentimental Fiction," explores the connections between novels and their readers' life experiences.

6. Summary of the plot by Richardson in Samuel Richardson, *Clarissa* (New York: Penguin, 1985), 1206.

against a sober assessment of the pitfalls of life. Duty and resignation were the paths to take. After reading *Clarissa* with her cousin Catherine (Caty) Smith, HCS wrote that "the darkest and most contemptable ignorance is that of not knowing one's self; and that not all we have, and all that we excel in, is the Gift of God."[7] HCS chose duty and a father's wishes over her own (and apparently her mother's) feelings. It was the respectable choice, but it did not bring her the happiness she had been led to expect from marriage. She had yielded too much of her own judgment.

The Marriage of Hannah and Sammy

The exact nature of the marital difficulties of HCS and Sammy are unknown. The surviving diary, intended for the eyes of others, was at crucial moments guarded, oblique, and then occasionally censored by erasure or scissors—a partially legible erasure refers to being "alone" although still newly wed. Contemporaries either did not comment on the Sansom's marriage or were not writing when the marriage took place. Descendants were selective in preserving correspondence and other records. The local meeting approved the marriage of HCS and Sammy Sansom, but their concerns help frame the difficulties that HCS experienced in her marriage. When they first passed meeting on March 26, 1762, Elizabeth Wilkinson preached "in a mild but convinceing manner, to those blessed with affluence, that they walk doubly circumspect." Certainly, this match united a heir and heiress of unusually large expectations. Wealth might well tempt the unwary to forget their salvation. HCS and Sammy passed their second meeting on April 30, with an "excellent Sermon from Mordecai Yarnell, begining with the words of the text, anough, the desiple is not greater than his master nor the servant than his Lord, ending with remember man, thou art made to Fear, Honour and glorify thy Maker."[8] This Quaker minister may have worried that the outgoing, outspoken, and hot-tempered HCS might dominate her diffident master two years her junior. Patriarchy and godliness were to be considered as one. The marriage ceremony itself, on May 25, was more hopeful, less cautionary: "Mordecai Yarnel spoke elegant and emphatical on a happy Life, in all thy getings get understanding."[9] Daniel Stanton prayed most heartyly for us and all mankind." But perhaps there was a subtle message here too, for this chapter of Proverbs also instructs "forsake her not, and she shall preserve thee: love her, and she shall keep thee. Enter not into the path of the wicked, and go not in the way of evil men." And perhaps Sammy already had a reputation for straying. On January 3, 1763, two male Friends paid a religious visit to the newlyweds, advising them "to condescend to each other" and to "fear god, which would consolidate

---

7. HCS, February 7, 1759.
8. See Matthew 10:24.
9. Proverbs 4:7.

SAMUEL SANSOM.
BORN 1738·9. DIED 1824.

Figure 7 Sketch of Hannah Callender's husband, Samuel Sansom, as an elderly man. This was probably drawn by Joseph Sansom. Courtesy American Philosophical Society.

[console for] tryals," both comments portending a stormy marriage. They were also to "beware of the love of the world, to eager pursuit after riches."

This marriage was not a love match, although it was not explicitly a forced union, except by the usual references to a child's duty to respect the wishes of a parent. HCS consented to the proposal and indeed did a fine job of talking herself into the arrangement. After first passing meeting, HCS recorded that "I am now going to enter a new scene of Life, by the almost general example of mankind, it must be looked upon as the most eligible Happiness, and as I hope my expectations are not too Sanguine, look on myself somewhat entitled to a small Share." This notion that marriage in and of itself promised happiness, regardless of the character of the spouse, would have been overly sanguine even by the standards of the time, which stressed amiability, if not love. This justification came in response to "a little uneasiness in the family" on April 5, 1762, which called for "Prudence and Steadiness"—HCS reaffirmed the prudence of this alliance and called for steadiness in following through with her intentions. The doubts were certainly her mother's. While Katherine Callender was present to give her consent as her daughter twice passed meeting in the spring, it was not until September 17, 1762, that HCS felt that she had her mother's full support in marrying Sammy. "I have left my mother, but with her consent, Lord do thou bless it." Her father's approval was never in doubt.

It was the custom for Quaker newlyweds to spend two weeks at the bride's house before removing to their own home.[10] In the case of HCS and Sammy, this "honeymoon" period extended from May 25 to September 14, 1762. Their house was ready for them, but an extended period of adjustment to marriage ensued. That entire summer was an emotional roller coaster for HCS. The diary entry the day after her wedding was "a day of care and fear," hardly a promising beginning, although "some part of the afternoon agreable with Sammy." On June 5 a passage is cut out of the diary, while on June 23, 1762, she and Sammy had an "agreable day except the petulance and pride of my disposition. I write this as my punishment for having given offence where none was intended to me." Rural outings with Sammy and friends produced some happy moments late in the month. July was more tempestuous. "Family divisions are terible and most Irreconsilible," she wrote on July 1. Was her mother again objecting to the marriage, or were she and Sammy fighting? The diary does not say. Three days later she met with her close friends Becky Rawle and Sammy Shoemaker, with whom she found "converse, sweet calmer of the mind." The respite was brief. "There are things happen in a family that require oblivian, . . . require us to pray for direction of temper, and christian Patience, never to desert OURSELVES" reads her comment on July 7. She added three days later that "I must learn Prudence which leads to Silence." She seemed angry and combative during the early summer but blamed herself for her behavior.

In mid-July, she left her parents and Sammy behind to go to Burlington for Yearly Meeting. This was another pleasant interlude, and when Sammy later joined her, they enjoyed several jaunts in the neighborhood. But the following months were miserable, and this time she did not blame herself nor refer vaguely to family troubles. Sammy was the problem. On August 10, she was "much afflicted in my mind." A month later, on September 6, she recorded "evening Disappointments and we must Learn to bear with them. experience of Ages." The "experience of the ages" was the commonplace reference to the double standard, especially as a young wife discovered that the romance of courtship and the vows of fidelity would not survive into the marriage. Sammy was often absent in the evenings after the couple moved into their own house on September 14. Just three days later, HCS spent the "evening Solitary & Serious." Three entries in early October, the third through the sixth, were excised from the diary. She then sought consolation with her parents on the ninth and the twenty-first "at Mames, not very well and very serious." The very next day, after a religious visit by Friends Robert Willis and Joshua Emlen in which they urged more consideration between the two, came her most despairing entry—January 4, 1763. A note in the margin indicated that it was night: "a solitary evening! look only to thine own

10. J. William Frost, *The Quaker Family in Colonial America* (New York: St. Martin's, 1973), 174.

heart for peace, for veryly thou shall meet with tryals, reader, be thou who' thou may." Her prudent marriage had followed the guidelines of Quakerism. It united two families of similar standing in the faith. It was fiscally sound as well, connecting the sole heirs of two considerable mercantile fortunes. It was socially desirable, linking members of an established social circle whose genteel credentials were everywhere visible in their town and country houses, fine furniture, imported prints, literary ambitions, and well-cultivated French. But it failed to consider the companionate traditions of Quaker marriages and failed even more abysmally at capturing those respectable passions promoted in contemporary culture and articulated in novels.

HCS had embarked on her marriage with hopes that it might bring "the most eligible Happiness." She was soon disillusioned. Sammy's unexplained absences and her temper foreclosed a meeting of the minds. One traditional option remained. If friendship was not forthcoming, companionship might evolve through the shared experience of work and commitment. Her parents had been equally active in the meeting, and their religious work was complementary. Her mother had also been an active partner in keeping her husband's books. HCS had for some years assisted her father in various business matters, and she brought personal and real property into the marriage. Therefore, when she finally took up residence with her husband, she wrote, "thus on this day we began the Important affair of House keeping, In which the Woman's care is to make the house agreable to her husband, and be careful of his Interest. there is an old saying: 'a man must ask his Wife if he shall be Rich.'"[11] This was her last-ditch effort to make her marriage meaningful, to make a contribution. It would be a loveless match, she had come to accept that, but surely their mutual interests might be cultivated on the basis of the family economy. It was as forlorn a hope as her aspirations to marital happiness. Sammy's various business activities were separate from the household and increasingly conducted in corporate settings from which women were excluded. His politics in the revolution placed the family at odds with the meeting, and HCS would not become active in the Women's Meeting until the 1790s. In any event, Sammy did not seek her advice or desire her assistance. He was, after all, the master.

The only option for HCS by January 1763 was to retreat into pure domesticity and to seek resignation to her condition. She had made her choice, and she now had to make the best of it. A "solitary evening, not disagrable, a time of relaxation in the mind, 'the Souls dark Cottage batter'd and decay'd / Lets in new Light thro' chinks which time has made."[12] A private, pastoralized existence, personal piety, and the possibility of children: only these remained.

HCS was not, however, inclined to wallow in self-pity. She was too aggressive

---

11. September 14, 1762. Cf. [Daniel Defoe], *The Complete English Tradesman* (1745; repr. Oxford: Talboys, 1841), I:95.

12. January 8, 1763, quoting "Of the Last Verses in the Book," by Edmund Waller (1606–1687).

(and too angry) for that. If Sammy pushed her toward a separate sphere, then she would use it to further distance masculine worlds of work and vice. Parlaville, sometimes the Sansom's primary residence and sometimes their secondary residence, became her suburban retreat. In her "brick mansion, with piazza and back buildings, together with a stone coach and stabling, and a garden to the west and an inclosed lawn to the south," she created a world of her own.[13] It was child-centered, open to those young people who were friends of her children but closed to others. Friends, family, and the occasional business associate came by invitation. No longer could acquaintances simply drop in for chats, tea, or dinner. The rural entertainments of skating, sledding, country walks and drives, the amusements of pet dogs and gardening, and the rational pleasures of serious conversation and decorative sewing dominated. Like her peers in London, she was one of the "eighteenth-century creators of suburbia [who] bequeathed to their successors their positive ideal of a family life in union with nature."[14] And unlike her father's summer estate, Richmond Seat, with its aristocratic name, tenant farmers, and income-producing herds and fields, Parlaville was small, private, and quite deliberately divorced from commercial concerns. The open areas that existed were reforested with mature trees, and while the garden produced raspberries and strawberries, it was largely planted in flowers. It was a feminine space, devoted to intimacy, separate from her husband's primary activities.

The beautiful bedcovering sewn by the three cousins presents an optimistic view of the place of affection and domestic responsibilities in HCS's upcoming nuptials.[15] The eight foot by eight foot quilt has an elaborate blue silk surface stitched with an asymmetrical design of fanciful vines bearing carnations, roses, artichokes, chrysanthemums, and other flowers. In the middle is a medallion depicting an idyllic scene. While the portrayal is nominally pastoral and rural, it shows an urban influence in its three tall townhouses fronted by three graceful and delicate fruit-bearing trees. Each of the three houses has a chimney issuing a puff of smoke, indicative of the warmth and comfort to be found within. The three trees and three houses that fill the circle at its widest point are echoed by three bushes and three large flowers in the pasture in the lower third of the medallion: all testify to the friendship of the three women. Peace, plenty, fruitfulness,

13. Elva Tooker, *Nathan Trotter: Philadelphia Merchant, 1787–1853* (Cambridge, MA: Harvard, 1955), 237n22.

14. Robert Fishman, *Bourgeois Utopias: The Rise and Fall of Suburbia* (New York: Basic Books, 1987), quotation 27.

15. On the significance of women's needlework, see Elaine Hedges, "The Needle or the Pen: The Literary Rediscovery of Women's Textile Work," in *Traditions and Talents of Women,* ed. Florence Howe (Champaign: University of Illinois Press, 1990); Rozsika Parker, *The Subversive Stitch: Embroidery and the Making of the Feminine* (Urbana: University of Illinois Press, 1984); Betty Ring, *Girlhood Embroidery: American Samplers and Pictorial Needlework, 1650–1850* (New York: Knopf, 1993); Susan Burrows Swan, *Plain and Fancy: American Women and Their Needlework, 1700–1850* (New York: Holt, Rinehart, Winston, 1977); and Laurel Thatcher Ulrich, "Pens and Needles: Documents and Artifacts in Women's History," *Uncoverings* 14 (1993), 221–28.

Figure 8 Quilt sewn by Hannah Callender Sansom and her cousins, Sarah and Catherine Smith. Courtesy Independence National Historical Park.

and domesticity are indicated in the very feminine images that dominate the center and bottom half of the medallion. The top half of the medallion is dominated by two large oak branches, symbols of masculinity and strength, that cover and shelter the scene below. Only the branches are shown—the trunks and roots of the two oaks lie outside of this vision. Of the three cousins, HCS would marry first and then Sarah; Catherine would remain unmarried, perhaps she had already chosen that path. Above the two oak branches are two ranges of puffy clouds, possibly an ominous sign, although the puff at the far left may be the sun. If it is the sun, then it shines on the house on the left. Leading from that house is a path that terminates in the pasture, where two cattle lie cozily side by side. The dominant, forward animal is a large bull, with its horns sweeping back from the brow, giving it a stern expression. The recessive animal is smaller, hornless, and wide-eyed. The comfortable, serene domestic world portrayed in this marriage quilt is gendered, and the genders bespeak inequality. Men dominate, shelter, and protect, but their roots are outside this domestic world. Women are delicate, sheltered, and subordinate, even if their activities, like the middle fruited tree, are at the center of this small universe. Peace and plenty, comfort and fruitfulness are predicted in this emblematic drawing, but the oaks and the fruit trees do not intertwine, the cattle barely touch, and there are no courting men and women holding hands, as might be found in other women's pictorial needlework. Romance is conspicuously absent.

On the March 26, 1762, after HCS and Sammy passed meeting for the first time, this quilt and another were displayed in her home for family and friends to see. It was her masterpiece—both the culmination of her apprenticeship in the domestic arts and an omen of her future. It would be emblematic of her goals in the 1760s, but not of her goals for her daughter's marriage in the 1780s. The change in HCS's expectations reflect a contest of values concerning marriage among literate Americans and among Quakers in the second half of the eighteenth century, as expectations of romantic love offered women respect, but also, as most novels warned, presented fortune hunters, seducers, controlling parents, and hypocritical friends with opportunities for the careless woman's disgrace and degradation.

Every year thousands of visitors travel to Independence National Park. Those visitors will not see HCS's quilt, however; it is stored away in a box, brought out only for the occasional researcher. But the images inscribed on the quilt can be seen as an opening cry in women's efforts to achieve a degree of liberty and the pursuit of domestic happiness: love, near equity, and mutual respect between husbands and wives. HCS's marriage failed, on the whole, to achieve those goals, but she was determined that her daughter would find the fulfillment that she did not. There would be a happy ending.

Chapter 4

The Diary: March 1762–November 1772

Memorandom Book
Began, Third Month Twenty Sixth, 1762
(page one)

[March 26, 1762]

26th   I had some Inclination for my own Satisfaction, or some of my Friends, if I should think fit in future Time, to leave it for their perusal, or otherways destroy it and as I had began and continued an account during the Years 1758 and 1759. I chose to retrospect time from this I hope memorable day of my Life.

Day 6   Morn: rose by 7 O'Clock indeavouring to compose my mind, that I might break that awful Silence, in a publick Assembly. with a becomeing composure. wrote a note to Jemmy & Anna Bringhurst, by Nancy Pole, Sammy Sansom come here. 9 O'Clock Mame, Caty Smith, and I went to meeting, we set by Polly Pemberton and Sally Pemberton, John Stevenson, Hannah Harris, and Elizabeth Wilkinson were there. Friends from England. the latter spoke, in a mild but convinceing manner, to those blessed with affluance, that they walk doubly circumspect. Mary Emblen and Ben: Trotter spoke. I endeavoured to fortify my mind, by looking on my undertakeing, as a solemn League of Friendship.[1] and in the presense of my Parents and Friends, Samuel

---

1. The Solemn League and Covenant of 1643 was a forced alliance of convenience between English and Scottish Protestants and a crucial turning point for the Protestant cause during the English Civil War. That HCS describes her marriage in terms of a military/religious alliance, even if one of Friends rather than of Calvinist covenanters, supports what other veiled passages suggest—that this was an arranged marriage and not a love match.

Sansom and I stood up. and told them, by Divine permision, and there approbation, we intended Marriage. Joseph, Thomas & Betsey Edwards, John Lowens & Betsey Elwell, Sammy Pleasents & Polly Pemberton, Benny Sweet & Polly Howel. passed at the same time. Samuel Sansom & his wife, Neigh: Warner and Josey Sansom dined with us. Anna Bringhurst was hear in the afternoon and we were looking at 2 peices of my work, one a blue Tafaty stiched bed quilt, drawn by Sally Smith, and worked by Caty & I. the other a white peling[2] wearing quilt drawn by Sally Smith and worked at Unkle Daniel Smith's in Burlington by Betsey Smith & I. evening Jemmy Bringhurst, Anthony & Billy Sykes, and Molly Brown Lodged hear.[3]

[In margin: "on this day Sammy Sansom entered his Twenty third year——————."]

7	Morn: at home, Betsey Warner hear, Molly Brown. and Brisille Newbold's Widow dined hear, I went to see cousin John's children, evening S: Sansom
1 Day	Morn: at meeting John Stevenson, and D Stanton, spoke. afternoon at meeting E. Wilkinson, and H. Harris spoke, Josey Smith to tea. evening at meeting, Robert Proud, and Han: Foster spoke,
2	Morn: at meeting, John Stevenson, Robert Proud, Phillip Dennis, and B. Trotter spoke. Sam: Williams dined hear. Sammy Pleasents spent the afternoon with Caty & I. evening Benjamin Sweet and Sammy Sansom.
3	Morn: at meeting Joseph White, Peter Barker, John Stevenson, and Susannah Halton spoke, Polly Morris dined with me, afternoon to see Patty Cadwallerder, Peggy Hooper there, this day died Elizabeth Eaustah, a woman noted for prudence & resolution. Haddon feild is called after her maiden name.
4	Morn: Unwell, afternoon better, at Work. evening Ben: Sweet & Samy Sansom.

[April 1, 1762]

5	Morn: at work, afternoon, Peter Worrell, Paty & Hannah Noble, Neigh: Warner & Nancy and Sarah Morris, evening Ben: Sweet & wife, Samy Sansom.

2. Possibly peking, a soft silken fabric.

3. Philadelphia Monthly Meeting Minutes, 26th, 3d mo. 1762, p. 18: "Samuel Sansom junr and Hannah Callender apearrd at this meeting being accompanied from the women's meeting by Mary Armitt & Anna Warner and declared their Intentions of marriage with Each other, their Parents being present expressed their Consent. Richard Blackham and Abel James are appointed to make Enquire respecting the young man's Conversation, and Clearness, to report to next meetin."

6   Day, rainy an agreable working family day.

7   Morn: at work. afternoon Cousin Mary Brown went home, Caty & I waited on her and were caught in the rain. evening finished off my Shifts, to the number of eight.

1 Day   Morn: at meeting Eliza: Wilkinson, Hannah Harris, and John Stevenson spoke. a little uneasiness in the family. Prudence and Steadiness are great preservatives to Harmony. I am now going to enter a new scene of Life, by the almost general example of mankind, it must be looked upon as the most eligible Happiness, and as I hope my expectations are not too Sanguine, look on myself as somewhat entitled to a small Share. afternoon at meeting John Stivenson and Hannah Harris spoke, Caty & I drank tea with Nancy, Debby, Hetty, & Polly Mitchell, and Sally Parish, evening at meeting Eliza Wilkinson, Hannah Harris, John Stevenson, and Dan: Stanton spoke. Thomas Leech was buried this day.

2   Morn: Caty and I out at Shops, spoke to William Vane for my furniture, afternoon Mary Pemberton, Johannah Brooks, and Anna bringhurst hear, evening S:S:

3   Morn: at Work, Mame poorly. afternoon Nanny Emblen hear, I went to see Neighbour Warner, poor Becky Rawle and I took a walk up town for the benefitt of air. she is a mourner having lost a good Husband by an unhappy accident not a twelve month since, at the time it was a melancholy scene, but the good man's hope never forsakes him, which was evidently the case hear, [and it] supported [him] even in death.[4]

4   Ironing, evening Sammy Sansom. Cousin John Smith [is] lately a Widower, separated from a good woman, and he is a worthy man.

5   Day rainy, at Work. evening wrote to Sally Smith.

6   Day. finished the first of my white dimity pokets, the flowers drawn by Sally Smith, and stiched in blue silk.

7   Day. bound a pair of lite coulered sattin shoes for myself. evening S.S.

1 Day   Morn. Caty Smith, Nancy & Tommy Pole, with myself walked to the Pine Street meeting, Eliza Wilkinson, Sarah Morris, and Hannah Harriss spoke. we dined at Jemmy Bringhurst's, Hannah Peak and Richard Smith there. afternoon at meeting, Caty & I drank tea with Polly & Sally Pemberton. evening at meeting, Robert Proud, Hannah Harris, and Eliza Wilkinson spoke.

2   Day. quilting, evening John Drinker and Sammy Sansom.

3   Day, Caty and I put a purple sprig Calico bed quilt in the frame, be-

---

4. Francis Rawle was shot by his own gun while hunting. He lingered a week before his death on June 7, 1761. Crane, Drinker Diary, I:89.

longing to a suit of curtains for myself, Anna Bringhurst drank tea with us, evening Nanny Wishart & Nancy Russel, an invitation to visit Betsey Edwards on Six day, Mame to to be at her marriage on 5 day.

4   Day. Quilting. this afternoon, Caty Smith and I accompanied Cousin John Smith and his Children, James, Sarah, Hannah, & John, to the Waterside, in order to take there departure, and live at Burlington again. Becky Rawle returned home with me for the first time since her husbands death, evening S: Sansom.

5   Day. Quilting, evening, Sally Pemberton & I paid a running visit to Polly Howell, then all three to Polly Pemberton's, thence Polly Howel & I to Hannah Howell's. Dan: Hewes waited on me home

6   Morn: quilting. afternoon Caty & I at the Widow Edwards, a large Company of young folks, we had quite anough of mirth by 10 O'Clock at night, Peter Reeves waited on us home,

7   Day quilting. Robert Proud and Sammy Sanson drank tea with us afterward Caty, Nancy Pole & I took a walk up to Sammy Nobles. Reflections by the way on age and poverty, youth in the road to misery when governed by debauch. at Home Isaac & Caty Greenleaf

1 Day   Morn: at meeting BT:, and Mordecai Yarnell spoke, conversation with Sammy Pleasents, afternoon at meeting. Eliza Morris and Sam: Emblen spoke. Caty and I to see Sally Parish, Nancy & Debby Mitchel there. evening at meeting Susannah Halton spoke.

2   Day, quilting, Polly Pemberton, and Nancy Warner hear, evening Caty and I at Becky Rawle's. Sammy Sansom hear.

3   Morn: quilting, afternoon Becky Rawle hear fitting a black Paduasoy hood for me, evening Sammy Sansom.

4   Morn: finished the quilt, Nanny Webber hear. afternoon Caty & I at Polly & Hannah Rhoades's. Molly Morris, and Anna & Betsey Bringhurst there. Conversation, on the instability of human grandure, and the Just Punishment of the pride in the human heart, from Nebuchadonezer down to this day. the fool hath said in his heart there is no god.[5] makes graven images of the abundant bounty of heaven, which is Idolatry.

5   Morn: Caty and I at shops, I went to becky Rawle's and dined. afternoon Becky & I at Joshua Howels. becky, Caty & I took a walk, evening see fanny Dean, Sammy Sansom hear.

6   Morn: makeing single Hankercheifs. afternoon old Elizabeth Morris & Polly Howel, evening Ann Rakestraw, S:S:

7   finished the Hankercheifs, wrote to Sally Smith. Sukey Shippen hear. afternoon Caty & I at Neigh: Greenleafs, Tommy Harrison there.

---

5. Psalms 14:1 and 53:1.

1 Day morn: at meeting Benajah Andrews and Dan Stanton spoke. afternoon wrote to Sally Callender of barbados, my Unkle Joseph's daughter. went to meeting, Anthony Woodcock spoke, Caty, Nancy, and I went to Judah Foulks. Widow Dickanson, Jemmy, Josey, and anna Bringhurst there. evening at meeting Becky Jones spoke,

2 Morn: Starching & folding, conversation with Tommy Harrison, Sammy Pleasents, and John Scot, afternoon on a visit to Sarah Fisher. evening SS:

3 Day Ironing, Betsey Smith come from Burlington.

4 Day. Betsey & I mantua makeing, my brown Paduasoy, and snuf mantua

5 Day. mantua makeing. Sam: Leacock hear from barbados. afternoon Polly Rhoades hear. the gapeing croud going by multitudes to a Horse race. evening Sammy Sansom.

6 Morn: passed the second ordeal tryal with as much composure as I could, having had an excellent Sermon from Mordecai Yarnell, begining with the words of the text, anough, the desiple is not greater than his master nor the servant than his Lord,[6] ending with remember man, thou art made to Fear, Honour, and Glorify thy Maker. the Company at diner William & Catherine Callender, Samuel & Sarah Sansom, Anna Warner, Isaac Greenleaf, Thomas Lightfoot, Samuel Sansom, Elizabeth & Catherine Smith, and H. afternoon, James and Anna Bringhurst, and Nancy Warner and we young folk spent the evening together,[7]

[May 1, 1762]

5 M^{oth} 7 Morn: went to Becky Rawles. bought me a pearl coulered ducape.[8] Becky, Caty Howel, and I went to see Sammy Sansom's New house. afternoon betsy and I mantua makeing.

1 Day Morn: writeing, went to meeting, Alex: Seaton, Sarah Morris, and Alice Hall spoke. Jane Ellis dined hear. afternon at meeting Ellis Hugh, spoke. Betsey, Caty, Nancy, & I went to George Emblens, Mary and Polly Emblen at home, walked over to the State house to see some orderly Indians. evening at meeting Jane Ellis spoke.

2 Day mantua makeing. Polly Pemberton hear. evening Betsey, Caty, & I at Anna Bringhursts.

6. Matthew 10:24–25.

7. "Samuel Sansom junr & Hannah Callender now appearing, & declaring the Cintinu^a of their Intents of Marriage with each other, & no Cause of Obstruction appearing, the Meeting allows them to Solemnize the same according to the Rules of our Discipline, & appoints Able James and Isaac Greenleafe to attend it, & to see the Certificate be delivered to be recorded." Philadelphia Monthly Meeting Minutes, 1762–64, p. 25.

8. Ducape, a heavy silk fabric.

3   Morn: at meeting, Alice Hall, Ellis Hugh, and Marget Ellis, spoke. afternoon on a visit to Betsey Bringhurst, a melancholy family of old Batchelors and maids. called to see Unkle John Armitt. evening Josey Smith & Sammy Sansom.

4   Morn: Betsey & I began my suit of cloaths, agreable day, SS: hear.

5   Day, we finished the suit, I took a walk with Sally Pemberton to becky Rawle's that she might pin up a hood for Polly Pemberton, from thence we three went to the House my father has purchased in front street, partly opposite where we lived [for] twelve years, and to which we shall move in a few days, caught in the rain comeing home, a very melancholy evening————

6   Day, Betsey and I began two Mantua Gounds[9] for her & Caty. evening SS: hear, brought some Gloves from the Store.

7   Day, we finished the Gounds, at interveaning time, we read two Vol: called the Auction.[10]

1 Day   Morn: went to meeting. Alex Seaton, Joice Beneset, and M: Yarnel spoke, afternoon at meeting, Drank tea with David & Grace Caldwell, Danny Smith come from Burlington this evening,

2   Morn: began to pack up and remove, from Market street to front Street, pretty near our old dwelling in the [river] bank. Nancy Gibson, Sally Stamper, Sally Riche, and Nanny Carlisle hear, and all the family lodged hear this night.

3   Morn: a resting time, afternoon in the family, Neigh: Warner, Tommy Lightfoot hear. evening SS:

4   Day, at Work, Sammy Shoemaker, that most agreable man hear. wrote to Sally Smith. John Reynolds, Jemmy Bringhurst, and Becky Rawle hear, we suped at Beckys.

5   Morn: serious! 10 O'Clock went to meeting, BT:, John Stevenson, and Sarah Morris spoke. Samuel Pleasents was maried to Mary Pemberton, may all happiness attend them. afternoon Neigh Warner. evening Caty & I went to see the old Neighbourhood

6   Morn: at work on my pokets, drank tea with Nanny Carlisle,

to day 7   Day. worked on my poket, an agreable busy day.

1 Day   Morn: Daddy, Mame, Betsey & Caty Smith, Tommy & Nancy Pole, with myself went to the bank meeting,[11] afternoon we girls went to the midle meeting, DS: spoke. I drank tea with Sammy & Polly Pleasents, Israel & Sally Pemberton, Rachel Jory, Sukey Hudson, and Josey &

---

9. Mantua gowns were loose-fitting dresses that were the staples of women's outer attire.

10. Anonymous, *The Auction. A Modern Novel. In Two Volumes* (1760).

11. Bank Street Meeting House.

Abbey Smith. evening set a little with Betsey Roberts and Hetty Deshier. Josey Smith and Sammy Sansom suped hear.

2   Morn. at Work, Isaac Greenleaf. afternoon Anthony Morris, Anna Bringhurst. evening Caty & I at Neigh: Rushes, Sammy Sansom hear.

3   Morn: Ironing, afternoon the same,

4   Day finished stiching my white dimity pokets in blue silk. Caty and I pinning up beds. evening many things disagreable.

[In margin: "a mistake 5 Day]

5   Morn: at Work, Tylpha Fortune brought in her bill of fare, made some alterations in it. drew up a list of friends and acquaintance for Invitation. the bill of fare: 2 rumps of beaf, 2 Gammons, 2 qu^r of Lamb, 2 Calfs heads, Pigeons, Ducks, 2 legs of Veal, breast of Veal, 2 Tongue, Breast of mutton, a pair of calfs feet, Cocanut Almond Orange pudding, Apple Cranberry Goosberry tart with some few decorations of Cookery[12]

Invited Guests, John and Mary Reynolds, Mary Armitt (her husband Sick.) Anna Warner, Sarah Morris, Samuel & Hannah Shoemaker, Samuel & Lydia Noble, Rebecah Rawle, Joshua and Catherine Howel, Samuel and Mary Bell, John and Rachel Drinker, Henry and Elizabeth Drinker, John & Mary Parrock, James and Anna Bringhurst. Peter and Hannah Thomson, Isaac and Catherine Greenleaf. Samuel and Mary Pleseants. Sammy Leacock, Josey Smith, Tommy Lightfoot, Danny Smith. Tommy Fisher, Joshua Creeson, Benny Sweat, My Unkles cant be hear from sickness and hinderance, Sally, Betsey, and Caty Smith, Polly Sandwith, Polly Howel, Polly Rheades, Nancy Mitchel, Nancy Warner. Nancy & Tommy Pole, Josey Samson. afternoon Neighbour Sam: Sansom and his Wife. Caty and I have made new Vallens to Mames blue Camblet bed which she has given to me. John Armitt is departed, since the above, in Peace, rejoiceing for a happy deliverence from extream pain of the Gravel.[13] evening agreable with Daddy, Mame, Betsey, Caty, & Sammy

6   Morn: putting my drawers to rights. wrote to Sally Smith, marked my garter and Sleavestrings. afternoon Caty & Polly Howel called in. Lydia Noble drank tea with us, Mame and she at John Armitts funeral.

7   Morn: Sammy Leacock hear. afternoon dressed Nancy Poles baby.[14] evening very agreable

---

12. "Decorations of cookery": fancy crusts.
13. Kidney stones.
14. A doll exhibiting the latest fashions.

1 Day   Morn: 7 O'Clock Sammy Sansom went to Burlington for Sally Smith. went to meeting Becky Jones spoke. Gracy Peel made her appearance Married to Capt Dowel. afternoon at meeting. drank tea with Friend Coleman, Joshua Howel, Becky Rawle, and Nancy Warner. evening Jemmy & Anna Bringhurst, Sammy Sansom returned without Sally. Unkle Daniel has a relapse of the Gout.

2   Day. very busy in preparations. wrote a note to Nancy Gibson and Gracy Caldwell disireing them to come to the meeting to morrow

3   Day rose by 5 O'Clock reading and meditateing in my Chamber, till 8 OClock, dressed myself, 10 OClock received the company, and went to meeting. Mordecai Yarnel spoke elegant and emphatical on a happy Life, in all thy getings, get understanding.[15] Daniel Stanton prayed most heartyly for us and all mankind. and so excellent a meeting I spoke in a composed frame of mind. Nancy Gibson was at meeting and dined with us. Abby Smith and Sally Pemberton, but not Polly Pleasents. the day was exceeding hot   yet was an agreable day. no Danny, no Sally Smith from Burlington

4   Day, a day of care and fear, some part of the afternoon agreable with Sammy. wrote in this book and to Polly Penry.

5   Day, Mame not very well. Sammy Leacock, Abel James, and Docter Sunmons hear. Benny Sweat & Polly Howel married to day. afternoon Nancy Warner hear.

6   Morn: at work makeing a lawn apron,[16] wrote to Sally Smith, Polly Morris married to blath Jones last third day. afternoon Daddy and Mame Sansom, and Friends Coleman & Warner, about 5 O'Clock I dressed and went with Sammy to see Benny and Polly Sweat, a large company there. home by ten O'Clock. this morn betsey Smith went home.

7   Morn, at Work. Sammy Shoemaker and Neddy Penington brought a mag. with the Picture of queen Charlotte.[17] afternoon at Work.

1 Day   Morn: at meeting Samuel, Sarah, & Joseph Sansom, Richard Smith dined hear. afternoon at meeting Grace Fisher, Ann Moor, and Mary Evans spoke, Cousin Lydia Noble & hannah West drank tea hear. Henry Drinker. 12 months to day since Francis Rawle departed this Life.

6 M°s^th 2   Morn: in the family, steped to Becky Rawle's, afternoon Becky Rawle come with intension to stay, but Company comeing she went away. Molly Harrisson, Eliza Bryant, and Betsey bringhurst. evening Jemmy

15. Proverbs 4:7.

16. Lawn: a sheer linen or cotton fabric.

17. The marriage and coronation of Sophie Charlotte of Mecklenburg-Strelitz and George III had taken place the previous year.

[June 1, 1762]

3   Morn: Mary Emblen hear, went to meeting BT: spoke. Isaac Greenleaf hear, Sally Morris at diner. afternoon Sukey Shippen and Polly Standly. evening Caty, Nancy, and I went to Mamme Sansom's.

4   Morn: at Work, and reading in Pryor. afternoon Hannah Shoemaker, Sally Jones, and Becky & Bettsey Wall, evening Abraham & Nanny Carlisle.

5   Morn: at work, afternoon Nanny Emblen, Molly Mease, and Gracy Caldwell. evening spent at Beckys with all the Family.

6   Morn: at Work, afternoon Hannah & Sally Saunders, Polly Sandwith & Betsey Drinker. the latter & I went to neigh: Warners old house, and viewed the places.[18]

7   Morn: at Work & reading in Steel. afternoon Caty, Sammy, Tommy and I went to Richmond, an agreable ride round Frankford, met Debby & Hetty Mitchel.

1 Day Morn: at meeting BT: spoke, Daddy, Mamme, Caty, Sammy & I dined at Father Sansom's, afternoon at meeting, Mimy Edwards, Nanny Wishart, Betsey Thomas, Molly Foulk, Becky James, Anna Bringhurst, and Nancy Gibson drank tea hear.

2   Morn: at Work. Tommy Lightfoot, afternoon Hannah Morris, Hannah Cadwalleder, Sarah Fisher, Jenny Evans, Caty Howel, Lydia Parker, Nancy Warner, and Becky Warder, evening sick, Nanny Carlisle hear,

3   Morn: took Physick, about Nine O'Clock Sally Smith & Sally Lightfoot come from Burlington. John Stevenson, Mary Emblen, Hannah Logan, and Sarah Morris dined hear. afternoon Betsey Roberts, Becky Carmalt, and Polly & Hetty Deshler drank tea hear.

4   Morn: rose as usual by Six enjoying Sally's company. Tommy Lightfoot dined hear. afternoon Fanny Rush, Polly Jones, Sally Marchal, and Patience Mifflin. evening father Sansom, owen Jones, and Tommy Lightfoot suped hear.

5   Morn: busy in the family. afternoon Susey Jones, Nanny Carlisle, Betsey Fox, Hannah Mickle, Jenny Foulk, and Hessey & Lydia Fisher. evening Neighbour Warner gave us an invitation to Edgely, where Becky, Joshua, & Caty are, but we must conform to business.[19]

6   Morn: Ironing. Bobby Smith from Burlington. afternoon Widow Leech, Widow Ash, Rachel Wells, Sally Dylvin, Patty Hill, Sally Parish, Neigh: Eves, Molly Moor, Nancy & Hetty Mitchel, and Alice Collie.

7   Morn: Ironing. 1 O'Clock, Daddy, Mame, Bobby Smith, Sally Smith,

---

18. Approximately six lines cut out of the end of this diary entry.
19. The business of receiving wedding visits.

Caty, Nancy, & I went to Richmond. 3 O'Clock Bobby & Sally set out for Burlington, an agreable ride round Frankford Home.

1 Day	Morn: at meeting, afternoon at meeting B T: spoke. Sammy Noble and Charles west drank tea hear, a most affectionate Visit from my friends Becky & Caty, Sammy Shoemaker hear.
2	Morn: Ironing, afternoon Mame, Nancy & I at Father Sansoms. went with Benny & Polly Sweat to view the House on the bank in the row with Caty & Becky, that is to to be my residence. they spent the evening wi[20]

3   Morn: dress   M Yarnell.
         spoke Mor   bson her
         two Daughters,   y Wister.
         evening Sammy, Caty, Nancy   hursts.

serious hour, on account of the children. Train up a child in the way he should go.[21]

4	Morn: daddy & Mamme at richmond, Caty & I out on some errands. afternoon Polly & Phebe Shoemaker, Anna Bringhurst. evening agreable with the family.
5	Morn: at Work, went to meeting BT: and Sarah Morris spoke, afternoon at Work, Nancy, Tommy & Hannah the maid went to richmond. evening Sammy Shoemaker, Josey Smith, and Patty James.
6	Morn: 5 O'Clock Sammy, Caty, myself & George went to Richmond an agreable day,
7	Morn: at work wrote to Sally smith. afternoon the Family returned. evening Caty, Sammy & I at Anna Bringhursts.
1 to day Day	Morn: at meeting Becky Jones spoke, Josey Smith dined hear. afternoon at meeting BT: spoke, Rachel Drinker, Polly Rhoades, and Anna Bringhurst drank tea hear. evening Sammy & I spent with Betsey Drinker and Polly Sandwith. poor Neigh: Ritche begins to feel the Follies of high Life, in recollection the painful companion of forced Solitude. fine qualitys abused, gifts of person and nature capable of hapiness, but blind to the Possesion.
2	Morn: at Work, afternoon John Scot, a Virginian hear, Coversation on the difference in the manners and Customs of the Provinces. In Virginia, they are all either rich or poor, so that Education there, cannot be given with that benevolence to mankind, as hear, where all are commonly equal, nature quick in its byas, takes envy at those above us, and

20. Sections of this entry and the next missing because of an entry cut out from the other side of the paper.
21. Proverbs 22:6.

contempt of those beneath, susseptions quite contrary to freedom and publick spirit, evening at Neigh: Warners. letter from Sally

3   Morn: 8 O'Clock, Sammy and I went to Edgely, Becky Rawle and her children, Billy, Ann, & Peggy. Caty Howel and hers, Caty & Anne. an agreable day, except the petulance and pride of my disposition. I write this as my punishment for having given offence where none was intended to me: 4 O'Clock we took a chair and went to Galaways place, situate on the banks of Skylkill, and admits of a delightful variety in Prospect. along this delightful River, you are suited to the most enchanting ~~delights~~ scenes of friendship, the serene composure of Contemplation, or the awful rememberance of things past, present, & to come, having all the ~~beauties~~ Charms of a wide extended Horison, the beauties of nature, and the cultivation of Labour, ~~of Labour~~ afforded to View.

4   Morn: at Work Daddy & Mamme at Richmond. afternoon to see Aunt Armitt, Hannah Logan there. evening Sammy & I at Father Sansoms.

5   Morn: at meeting Stevenson, and BT: spoke, afternoon at Work. Polly Franklin From York, Sally Pemberton hear. agreable evening Sammy Shoemaker, Molly Brown, and Johanna Brooks from Burdentown Lodge hear.

6   Morn: at meeting, Sammy Franklin and Hetty Mitchel, Sam: Bond and Sally Brown, Billy Brown and Becky Jones, passed. BT: and Susannah Hatton spoke. Conversations with Sammy Franklin, ——— ——— Richardson, Anthony Morris, Polly pleasents, Polly Rhoades, and Sally Pemberton. afternoon at Work. 4 O'Clock Caty, Tommy, & I went to Sammy Nobles. he is returned from the treaty at Easton, may heaven avert the revenge of the desperate and uncivilised people, too much provoked, from falling on us,[22] Josey Smith there.

7   Morn: agreable with our Lodgers, afternoon Daddy and Mame went to Richmond, 4 O'Clock John Scott spent some hours with us in a very merry and agreable conversation, evening Caty, Nancy Warner & I at Unkle Fishers.

1 Day   Morn: at meeting, Noon Mary & Johanna went home, at meeting John Stevenson spoke, Abel James, James Bringhurst, and Polly Foulk hear, evening Caty, Nancy, Sammy, & I at meeting Susannah Hatton spoke,

2   Morn: 8 OClock Caty ~~Sammy~~ & I went to Edgely, found Becky, Caty, Peggy, Gregory, Betsey Warner, & Tabby Fisher there, walked agreably down to Skylkill along its banks adorned with Native beauty, in-

---

22. The 1761 Easton Treaty failed to address the grievances of the Delaware and others living on the Susquehanna River. Violence would soon break out, as settlers continued to pour into their country, threatening to kill any who stood in their way.

terspersed by little dwelling houses at the feet of hills covered by trees, that you seem to look for enchantment they appear so suddenly before your eyes, on the entrance you find nothing but mere mortality, a spining wheel, an earthen cup, a broken dish, a calabash and wooden platter: assending a high Hill into the road by Robin Hood dell went to the Widow Frances's place, she was there and behaved kindly, the House stands fine and high, the back front is adorned by a fine prospect, Peter's House, Smiths Octagon, Bayntons House &c and a genteel garden, with serpentine walks and low hedges, at the foot of the garden you desend by sclopes to a Lawn. in the middle stands a summer House, Honey Scykle &c, then you desend by Sclopes to the edge of the hill which Terminates by a fense, for security, being high & almost perpandicular except the craggs of rocks, and shrubs of trees, that diversify the Scene. afternoon, Becky & I, Caty Howel & Smith, and Peggy Gregory & Betsey & Taby, in chairs with Thomas on horse back for our Guide, set out for Germantown by the falls, some mirth on the road, by female fears, Pembertons place, the New Colledge, arrived safe at Maconets, from thence to a Neighbouring house to see some models in Architecture done by an illiterate Shoemaker,[23] intended when put together as a representation of Jerusalem, and all the Actions of our Saviour in the City and adjacent, with other interesting things. I shall mention the houses of most notice and leave those for the ornament of the city nameless, being a large number. as the most accomplished piece, The Temple of Soliman about one yard high, three quarters long, and half deep, noble entrances on both fronts and Sides, all different orders, with their proper embelishments, in the balcony of the First battlement are 4 Priests blowing trumpets, it has a fine Steeple, and is enclosed by three Courts, having twelve gates adorned with Cherubims, Angels, and mosaic. twelve Magnifisent towers at the corners of the Courts, the whole a circumference of yard & half square, a finished model. Solimans House in the Forest built on a high green hill assended by one hundred Steeps, a noble looking pleasure house, it Joins the first battlement of the Temple, by a balcony supported by large columns, King Davids Palace with its towers, Gates, & centinels, Solimans house, the House of Cajafus the High Priest with himself siting Under a Canopy, king Soliman on his Throne, A House where our Saviour & the twelve kept the passover, the rooms may be seen in to and the people sitting at table, the House of Mary Magelen, a Hospital, the High Priests House, The house of Pontious Pilate, the court

---

23. This elaborate, carved wood representation of the buildings, hills, and gardens of Jerusalem and of the life of Jesus was begun by Anthony Sulser and completed by Michael Kraft. It was on display, for a fee of one shilling, at the Sign of the King of Prussia tavern in Germantown. It later was moved to Philadelphia. *Pennsylvania Gazette,* June 2, 1763, and later advertisements.

where our Saviour was called befere Pilate, and Pilate arguing to a multitude for him, then solemnly washing his hands, and delivering him to the people who crown him, mock and abuse him, then lead him thro' the gate of the City and crusify him with the theives! Herods House, the house of Solimans Concubines, Herods banqueting House, with the Ball and John the baptist's head on a Charger, with a view behind into a prison yard [and the] beheading of him, a large Prison with a tower and Peter in it. the Musick House, a magnificent High Tower. our Saviour when tempted on the mount, his deciples overcome by Sleep, the Figure of the Devil appeared the ugliest of forms till our conductress showed us another that exceeded him. I cannot immagine the genious of any other nation so fruitful in pictures of ugliness for the devil as a dutchman, and the dutch mans devil of germantown I shall not forget, a pleasent ride Home by Vanderins Mill, without accident compleated the Tour, except after a good dish of tea with Caty Smith, Peggy Gregory, Mame Sansom and Sammy (who come and staid a half hour), returned to Philadelphia

3   Day. a fine rainy day, and enjoyed by us with book and work, and though for the sight of the Eye, that gader abroad, this day may not take up so much paper yet have adequate share of satisfaction. pleasure dwells in the calm regions of retirement,

4   Morn: between 6 & 7 O'Clock, Sammy Sansom come before Becky & I were up. after breakfast, we walked down to Skylkill,[24] delighted with the plain at the foot of the Hill. Joshua has a convenient fishing boat locked to a tree, this tempted our inclination for a ramble to the other side, Sammy run for the key and oars with a man to help, returned with the key, but no oars or assistant, yet we determined by the calmess of the Stream, (Like the poor disappointed shepherd), to trust a strong rail, for a sculler, Nancy, Sammy, & I without any great matter of female parade, such as fear, Caution, Screek, &c landed safe, borrowed at a Neighbouring house a Sculler and Calabash, laded the water out of the boat made by the rain the day before and he returned for the rest. Becky, Caty, & Betsey got safe over with some interventions of danger and dismay, marched along Shore to the road leading to Peter's. as the day was cool it was pleasent, going by the side of a limpid rill, passed a stone quarry, called at some welch peoples, eat Mulberries, assended a hill, and set down to rest, then went to Will: Peters's house, having some small aquaintance with his wife who was at home with her Daughter Polly. they received us kindly in one wing of the House, after a while we passed thro' a covered Passage to the large hall, well furnished, the top adorned with instruments of musick, coat of arms,

24. The Schuylkill River.

crest, and other ornaments in Stucco, its sides by paintings and Statues in Bronze. from the Front of this hall you have a prospect bounded by the Jerseys, like a blueridge, and the Horison, a broad walk of english Cherre trys[25] leads down to the river, the doors of the hous opening opposite admitt a prospect [of] the length of the garden thro' a broad gravel walk, to a large hansome summer house in a grean, from these Windows down a Wisto[26] terminated by an Obelisk, on the right you enter a Labarynth of hedge and low ceder with spruce, in the middle stands a Statue of Apollo, note: in the garden are the Statues of Dianna, Fame & Mercury, with urns. we left the garden for a wood cut into Visto's, in the midst a chinese temple, for a summer house, one avenue gives a fine prospect of the City, with a Spy glass you discern the houses distinct, Hospital, & another looks to the Oblisk. returned to the house, rested agreably, and departed obliged. returned pleasently to the boat, and behold Scylkill had left her high and dry on land, to our Mortification, Becky, Sammy, & I made an attempt to go over, but it was Ineffectual. the Servants come on the other shore Frightened for our Safty, we bid them to go back and patiently wait our return, at a house we learned it was half a mile to the Ferry, and we walked it cheerful and aggreably, Baynton & Wharton's House at the foot of the Hill, a pretty one adorned with a green and clumps of trees. they have a private ferry, we plassed safely after the method of Scylkill with a boat and rope. winding round the foot of a hill, covered with rocks, shrubs, and earth, we opened on a neat little hut covered with trees, and little conveniencies, Inhabited by an old woman and her Daughter, the Pictures of Goodnature and Hospitality with honest Symplicity, a seat on their bench, with a cordial draught of Water, Introduced conversation, they had heard of the disastrous Death of my friend Fran Rawle, Pity moveing Scene, at thought of the, the heart involentarily becomes susceptable, of that dear regard we owe to Memory, of what providence has once blessed us with, mixed with the secret Joyfull hope that after well doing, he will again restore. this softens all our woes, this supports us thro' the storms of time, chearfully doing each moment as we ought, nay even with satisfaction, remembering the past. may these white moments be recorded, and the walk round Scylkill will never be forgot. Jonathan and Dorothy having got Intelligence of us, brought our chairs, when leaving our good hosts we went to edgely, dined, and Sammy & I look leave for town, on the way a poor wagger[27] Intoxicated with Liquor, degraded the human Species, by the ~~most~~ attrocious crime, of

25. Cherry trees.
26. "Wisto" or Visto, a pathway cut through the woods to frame or focus on a picturesque view.
27. Wagoner, teamster.

drinking over much, and a poor black took care of him. at Home Will: Fisher returned from Bristol, to the Satisfaction of his friend[s] and family, Mordecai Yarnel, Jemmy Bringhurst, and Will: Masters hear. Suckey Shippen, Polly Standly, and Josey Smith hear.

[July 1, 1762]

7 Mos 5 Morn: writeing. went to meeting: Marget Ellis, BT:, and DS: spoke, Sammy Franklin and Hetty Mitchel were married. afternoon my two Mamme's, Neigh: Warner, & I went to Benny Sweats, paid Neighbor: Greenleaf a visit, she was brought a bed with a son, Molly Stretch there, Family divisions are terible and most Irriconsilible, evening Saml & I at Father Sansoms.

6 Morn: at Work and reading to Caty in Pliny, afternoon with Polly Sandwith & Betsey Drinker, evening Caty & I paid an agreable visit to Becky Jones and Hannah Cathrel.

7 Morn: at Work. afternoon Tommy and I went to Jemmy Bringhursts. paid a visit to Nancy Gibson, Mamme Sansom, and Becky Rawle,

1 Day Morn: at meeting Sam: Emblen spoke, Becky harden dined hear, afternoon at Meeting Will: Willson spoke, drank tea with Sammy and his Parents, evening Becky Rawle & Sammy Shoemaker, converse, sweet calmer of the mind.

2 Morn: makeing current Jelly. went with Mamme Sansom to some Stores. afternoon Caty very Sick, better toward evening. Josey Smith hear, my dear Sally has been ill but is now better.

3 Morn: Ironing, Mame Sick, Rachel Pemberton and Betty Service dined hear, afternoon Ironing, evening Debby Mitchel and Polly Richardson hear

4 Morn: Ironing Sam: Leacock hear. there are things that happen in a family that require oblivian, but at the time they give us great uneasiness, require us to pray for direction of temper, and christian Patience. never to desert OURSELVES. afternoon Ironing. a most agreable rain, after along Season of drought, no Subsistance for poor man without the help of the Elements, while in this mortal coil.

5 Morn: sorting the cloaths, at the Joiners,[28] my Parents give me 8 Walnut frame blue damask bottom chairs, ∧[29] Walnut Chest of drawers, two dressing tables, two Sconce Glasses, gilt edge, for the back Chamber. back Parlour, 8 Walnut frame leather bottom chairs, a Walnut

---

28. Furniture makers. See Jay Robert Stiefel, "Philadelphia Cabinetmaking and Commerce, 1718–1753: The Account Book of John Head, Joiner," *APS Library Bulletin* (March 2001), available at www.amphilsoc.org/library/Bulletin/20011/head.htm. Both the Sansoms and Callenders bought furniture from Head.

29. In margin: "∧ bed &c bed sted with walnut feet."

Bookcase, a screen, tea table, 2 Card tables, 2 Sconce glasses. gilt edge. afternoon, to see Hetty Franklin, Betsey Emblen, Pen: Sword, Han: Mood, Polly Richardson, and Polly Haly, there poor Will: West is dead, a fine Genious for a painter of our own country Growth, on his travels.[30]

6   Morn: at Work. Neigh Greenleaf has lost there son. afternoon Caty & I drank tea with Fanny Rush, evening at mother Sansoms.

7   Morn: Caty and I went to our House on the bank, I must learn Prudence which leads to Silence, Paid Polly Franklin a Visit: Conversation with Tommy and Sammy Franklin, Anthony & Israel Morris, Paid Hetty Franklin a visitt, took leave of her, she settles in New York. about twelve O'Clock took leave of my Parents, Sammy, Caty, and I had a pleasent Passage to Burlington, in Charles Gandavin's boat, found Sally Slowly mending of a 2 weeks Ilness. Lodged at Unkle Daniels. was at Unkle Roberts & Dannys.

1 Day   Morn: at meeting Will: Willis spoke, dined at home, paid a visit to Cousin John, went to meeting, several gay Philadelphians spent this day in town: Anthony Morris, Caleb Hughes, Amos Hillburn, and Tommy Mayberry, a disorderly Practice of runing about the Country on first day. Sammy, Betsey Smith, Abby Raper, & Danny Smith & I drank tea with Benjamin Sweat & Wife they live in a delightful Situation, on the banks of the Noble De la War.[31] we Women took a most agreable walk by the River, to the remains of Conroes burnt House, time, or even before that can take effect, Folly, puts an end to grandure and the boasted enjoyments of man: evening agreable at Home. I delight in the calm hour between dusk and daylight, then I enjoy the most free Scope of Conversation or Silence. Betsey Rodman Smith, Abby Smith, and Becky Watson hear.

2   Morn: at home, Edward Cathrel hear, a fine rainy day. afternoon with the 2 familys, Unkle Daniels & Cousin Danils, they live next to each other in great harmony, the latter has 2 children, Benjamin and Joshua. the Queens Company are hear at the Barracks, there cloathing is romantick green with yellow buttons and button holes, green caps dressed with feathers & flowers, in front of the cap is Latin Per Sylvas, for the Woods, the fife and drum make an agreable harmony.

3   Morn: Sammy went to Philadelphia, Rich: Smith breakfasted hear.

---

30. HCS is twice mistaken here. William West was not the artist, but a farmer in Upper Darby. His brother Benjamin West was the artist, born in Chester County, Pennsylvania, in 1738. He travelled abroad from 1760, but contrary to this rumor, lived until 1820. Robert C. Alberts, *Benjamin West: A Biography* (Boston: Houghton Mifflin, 1978).

31. Thomas West, third Lord de la Warr, landed at the mouth of the river that bears his name (Delaware), in 1611.

Sally & I rode out. dined at Dannys, Betsey Rodman Smith spent the afternoon hear. Sally Raper Smith, Betsey Rodman Smith, Rich: Smith Senior, & I took a walk round the Point, Her Majesty's Soldiers exerciseing.

4   Day rainy, agreably spent with the Sallys, Betsey & Caty, went to see some work of Molly Bryants, made with peices of cloath, and in the shadeing chain stich, a woman and child with Lovely loose garments flowing. Joseph & his mistress, the tent bed well executed, a Shock dog[32] lying on a Cushing, well executed, with Squirrel, cherrys, peaches, leaves &c. a rural Scene where a Shepard, Sheep, dog, and cowes come from a bushy place, fine trees, at distance a ceder walk, clouds; a Young fawn. those works resemble paint more than can be thought. letter from daddy.

5   Morn: writeing, took a ride with Sally, walked down town met the Company, returned to Dicky Smiths, tryvial things pass in conversation. went to see Thomas Powels School, he lodges and boards upwards of thirty boys. afternoon, Thomas & Sally Powel, Sammy & Polly Pleasants, Dicky & Betsey Smith. Han: Sansom, Betsey & Caty Smith, Sally Pemberton & Saunders, Polly Richardson. Israel Morris and Clem Bittle. in a couple of light waggons went to see the Hermit, in a wood this side of mount Holly, he is a person thought to have traveled along from Canady or the Misseepy, about ten years ago, living in the woods ever since partly on the charity of the Neighborhood and partly on the fruits of the Earth. he talks no english nor will give no account of himself.[33] went from him to Cousin Johns place, himself, the nurse, and 3 children were there. a pleasent ride home, and [an] agreable evening at Dicky Smiths.

6   Morn: Sally, Danny, & I went a hurcle berrying,[34] see a savage snake but it recovered its hole too soon for us to kill it. afterward she and I worked very agreably at home. afternoon at Unkle Roberts. letter from Sammy.

7   Morn: Sally and I rode out, afternoon at Martha Barkers, and Cousin Sam: Smiths, Sammy & Polly Pleasents, Sally Pemberton, Caty Smith, and I took a pleasent Walk. then to Cousin Johns,

1 Day   Morn: at meeting. dined with Cousin Betty: letter from Sammy, went to meeting. Sally, Betsey, & Caty Smith, Patty Noble, & I drank tea with Becky Scattergood. evening a visit to Betsey Rodman Smith.

---

32. A shaggy dog.

33. Probably Francis Furgler, a German Catholic who died in 1778 after living for twenty-five years as a hermit between Burlington and Mount Holly, New Jersey. John F. Watson, *Annals of Philadelphia, and Pennsylvania, in the Olden Time* (1857; repr. Philadelphia: Stuart, 1899), II:296.

34. Gathering huckleberries.

2   Morn: Sally and I rode out. Dined with Dicky & Betsey Smith. afternoon Sally & I at Unkle Roberts and John Hoskin's, evening agreable at home. letter from Daddy.

3   Morn: at Work. afternoon at Dannys with the Sallys, Betsey, & Caty reading the orations of Demostehenes[35]

to day 4   Morn: unwell, other ways with pleasure, Unkle, the 2 Sallys and the Children. afternoon the Sallys and I at Neigh: Cathrels, Nobles, and Abby Rapers, evening at Sammy Smiths, Sam: Pleasents, Phineas Buckly, and Sally Pemberton from Bristol, wrote to Daddy as they go to Phila: to morrow.

5   Morn: reading, went to meeting Peter Fern spoke, dined at home with Unkle, Caty, & Sally. 2 O'Clock Sammy Sansom come, drank tea at Unkle Roberts, walked to unkle Daniel Meadow, agreable evening at Danny's.

6   Morn: at Work. afternoon Sammy, the 2 Sallys, & I went to Red Hill, Cousin John, his children, Edward Cathrel, Cousin Betty Smith, John & Molly Hoskins, and Tommy Prior, evening suped at home. Becky Scattergood.

7   Morn: Dicky Smith & Sammy on horse back, Sally & I in the chair, set out on the Jersy side, for Trentown.[36] a hot & long road, like to have over set, full of palpitations but relieved by the sight of a Jolly landlady at the patriot sign of Pitt, in burdentown, Joseph Burden drank part of a bowl of Sangre with us. a fine high situation, went no where by reason of the heat. arrived at Trentown by 12 o'clock, Billy Leister gone to York, found Anne & Betsey Smith pretty well, makeing us welcome, Abraham Goodwin an Englishman there. afternoon rain, the time pleasent, lodged there.

1 Day   Morn: Betsey, Sally, Sammy, & I walked about the town. 11 O'Clock we, with Anne Leister & Abraham, went to meeting, Hannah Bickardike spoke. dined at my lodgeing, see Will: Fisher. 4 O'Clock set out on the Pennsylvania side for burlington. Anne and Abraham went to the ferry where we parted. a most delightful ride to Bristol. crossed the ferry, with Sally Denormandy, 2 other Ladies

2   Morn: left burlington, Becky Scattergood & Sally Smith come to Bristol with us, went to Hugh Hartshorns, where Sammy & I parted with them. baited at the Wheat Sheef, Levy there. home by 1 O'Clock, mame dined out, Daddy well. went to work.

3   Morn: at meeting John Stevenson spoke, Joshua Emblen & he dined hear, agreable conversation. afternoon went to look myself a maid, drank tea at Sarah Zanes, went to mame Sansoms found 2 Young

---

35. Thomas Leland, trans., *The Orations of Demosthenes* (1711), or a similar book.
36. Trenton, New Jersey.

women there from the Cape, Sally & Jenny Iszard, went to Neigh Warners.

4   Morn: waited on the Girls at Mame Sansoms, took a Walk to the State House and about the town, the youngest is a sensible Girl who made some pretty remarks, having never seen a city before. at Jemmy Bringhursts: Molly foulks. dined at Father Sansoms, the Girls spent the afternoon with me,

5   Morn: Mame, Tommy, & Nancy went to Edgely. poor Nancy Gibson has lost her child. afternoon Sally Lightfoot hear. Eliza Bryant & I went to Nancy's childs funeral.

6   Morn: Becky Rawle and I went to meeting, John Stevenson and Susanah Hatton spoke. Paul Cripner & Sukey Head passed. Becky & I paid a visit to Sammy Rhoads at his new store. Sally & Jenny Izard dined hear. this day daddy sold the 2 tenements in second street.

7   Morn: at Work, read a Satyr on the times,[37] Tommy Lightfoot hear. Letter from Sally Callender of Barbados. afternoon with mame & Sammy, Sally Pemberton hear.

[August 1, 1762]

8 Mo 1:1
Day

Morn: at meeting Robert Wilson, Mary. Night, and John Pemberton spoke. reading in the bible is agreable and Instructive, afternoon at meeting Mary Knight spoke. Polly Morris, Betsey Warner, Sukey Wall, and Tabby Fisher drank tea with Sammy & I. evening went to meeting John Stevenson spoke on the prodigal son, elegant and well. Susannah Hatton concluded with a good prayer. found Josey Fox & Abel James at home, a lovely moonlight night: contemplation in the Garden.

2   Morn: Mamme poorly, Becky Harden and Betty Service hear, afternoon Starching cloaths.

3   Morn: mame poorly. Ironing, mame Sansom and Neigh: Warner hear.

4   Day: Ironing.

5   Day: Ironing.

6   Morn: putting the cloaths away. Josey Smith brought me a geneological table of the Smith family for one hundred years back. to Docter Rich Smith of Bramham in Yorkshire. married Ann Gates. afternoon Hannah Fox, evening Daddy & mame Sansom and Neigh Warner.

7   Morn: went to Will Vane's about my furniture. Jemmy Bringhurst hear. afternoon our Mothers, Sammy & I took an agreable ride to Frankfort on a visit to Betsey Drinker & Polly Sandwith at Henrys place. evening Caty and bobby come from Burlington. roused in the night by a cry of fire

---

37. Perhaps an earlier edition of Anonymous, *A Satire on the Present Times* (1780).

1 Day   Morn: at meeting, afternoon also, Sammy & I drank tea at Father Sansoms. evening at meeting Becky Jones and Dan: Stanton spoke.

2   Morn: unwell, running stockings, afternoon to see Nancy Gibson, John
Gibson, Josey Stamper, Alex: Lunan, Betsey Chew, and Peggy Oswald
there, paid a visit to Anna Bringhurst, and mame Sansom.

3   Morn: much afflicted in my mind. went to meeting DS:, Sarah Morris,
and Sam: Emblen spoke, Billy Brown & Becky Jones were married.
Grace Fisher dined hear, Bobby Smith went home. afternoon Isaac and
Catherine Greenleaf and Hannah Moor, evening Solitary in Company.

4   Morn: my Mother's and I at the house, called at Neigh Warners, afternoon at Work. Six O'Clock Caty and I went to the funeral of Abel
James child born within the month. evening Caty, Sammy, & I studying French.

5   Morn: Caty & I at Work. afternoon Mame & I to see Nanny Carlisle.
evening Jemmy & Anna Bringhurst. afterwards studying & reading.

6   Morn: at Work. afternoon mame and I visiting at Becky Waln's: had a
letter from Sally Prescod of barbados. evening Nancy Warner, Caty, &
I took a walk,

7   Morn: at Work, afternoon Also

1 Day   Morn: at meeting, afternoon at meeting, Betty Morris spoke. Sammy,
Caty, & I went to Polly Howels, Han: Jones, Han: Howel there.[38]

2   Morn: Neigh Warner, Mame, Betsey & I went in the waggon to Edgely.
Becky in a bad state of Health, a pleasent Day. evening Joshua, Becky,
mame, & I returned. I staid the evening with Becky. Danny Smith hear.

3   Morn: Mame poorly, Danny went home, went beckys a little for she is
unwell, Becky Hardin dined hear, 4 O'Clock mame better. paid a visit
to Becky James, Six o'clock, Patty James and I went to Capt Harrisons
childs funeral. evening with mame.

4   Morn: at Work. 10 O'Clock Will Vane brought my Furniture home to
the House we are to live in, for the Back Parlour and back chamber I
have mentioned the furniture, in the Front Parlour, a large and lesser
dining table, a half, dozen chairs with red leather bottoms, a Clock and
case, Mohogany tea table, low Chair, Hand Irons, shovel & tongs, front
Chamber chest of drawers, [a] pair of tables, Mahagony, half dozen
walnut chairs with dark blue damask bottoms, sconce glass gilt edge,
bed and bedstead, dined with Becky Rawle, afternoon at home with
mame, Sally Lightfoot, evening Sammy & I at Father Sansoms.

[In margin: "a Sconce glass."]

---

38. In the next two entries, HCS's handwriting deteriorates, as if stressed.

5   Morn: at Work, afternoon 4 O'Clock Mame and I packed up my China, a burnt China dish, a half dozen plates, a half dozen burnt china Coffee cups & sausers, a half dozen enameled large cups & sausers, 2 quilted enameled dishes, 2 Large burnt bowls. 2 blue china Dishes, 1 dozen plates, 2 soop plates, 2 small china bowles, 1 delph dish, 8 Wine glasses, 2 decanters, 2 cruets, 2 salts of cut glass, 3 pair of tumblers, a pair of beer glasses. a set of blue & white china for a tea table. (a case of large knives and forks with a half dozen table spoons (given by Sammy)and a case of sweat meat knives and forks.) for the back parlour. Front [parlour] 1 dozen white stone plates, 4 dishes, 6 soop plates—2 oblong, 2 large basons—2 black tea pots, a half dozen blue and white cups and sausers. drank tea with Nancy Warner, Friend Coleman & Joshua. Evening: Tommy Lightfoot hear, goes to burlington to morrow, from thence Sally Smith & he goes to York. wrote to Sally.

6   Morn: busy, a rainy day. the Havana taken with much blood and treasure, of both sides.[39]

to day 7 Morn: at the House, Mame Sansom gave me 2 large burnt china Bowles. Neighbor Warner there, afternoon with mame Sansom, evening at home.

1 Day   Morn: 8 O'Clock Sammy & I went to Edgely, Becky Rawle poorly, from thence Joshua & Caty, Nanny Howel and Betsey Warner, Sammy & I went to fair Hill meeting, Hannah Harrison spoke, the Norris family attend this meeting, many of whom have been the sport of fortune. Josey and Nanny Howel returned to Edgely with us. where we spent the day agreably,

2   Morn: washing silk stockings, mending curtains &c. afternoon visit to Polly & Phebe Shoemaker, they Live in a delightful house and garden,

3   Morn: Caty and I went to shops. Aunt Armitt and Sally Morris dined hear, afternoon with Vane at the House, drank tea with Father & Mother Sansom & Samy. evening at Home reading French.

4   Morn: began a cushin in Irish stich flowers, worked stems & a leaf, Polly Pleasents sick, afternoon Mame, Caty, & I to see Neigh: Rush, Sammy & I paid a visit to Rachel Drinker. Jemmy & Anna B—— suped hear.

5   Morn: at meeting DS spoke, afternoon Rachel Drinker & I went to see Polly Parrock, worked a Yellow flower, we walked to ——————— Thompsons pot house, purchased some ware,[40] went to Rachel's, then Polly and I to Sam: Bells, found Bobby Smith at home, from burlington, Sally gone on her Journey, the rest well

6   Morn: at the House, thence to meeting Mary Emblen, Jane Hoskins,

---

39. British troops captured the city of the Havana from Spain in mid-August 1762.
40. Here "ware" means pottery.

DS: and BT spoke. afterward Nancy Warner and I at John Eliots. chose
a pair of Sconce glasses, Sally Stanton and Benedict Dauce passed, Yesterday was intered Will: Griffits, after haveing known the smiles and
frowns of fortune. afternoon Nancy Warner and I at Betsey Waln's

7   Morn: worked a blue flower, afternoon rainy, worked a Leaf.

1 Day   Morn: at meeting BT spoke, afternoon at meeting Will Brown spoke,
went to mame Sansoms, evening Sammy and I read in the french Testament

2   Day: rainy, running stockings,

3   Day: Ironing.

[September 1, 1762]

4   Day: Ironing, Abel James hear, Just come from the Lancaster treaty

Evil may rule for a time, but right shall bear sway at last.

night 9   Morn: puting cloaths away. afternoon Mame and I at Neigh. Eves,
  Mos 5   Looking at shells. I am not a Virtuoso, yet fond of things Nature's beauties in those little things. evening Sammy, Caty, and I spent with
Jemmy and Anna, admireing the Ruins of Palmyra, well may young
say of past Ages

Half our learning is their Epitaph.[41]

6   Morn: I paid some Visit's to Polly Pleasents, Polly & Nanny Howel, and
Hannah Jones, and some shops, afternoon Sammy and I went to
Francford, Henry Drinkers place, Polly & Betsey, Peggy Parr there.
agreable ride home with Isaac Greenleaf from burlington, Sally &
Eliza are gone to Boston, evening Abel James,

7   Morn Mame & I at the House, from thence to Becky's & Catys, afternoon Becky hear, evening wrote to Sally Callender & Sally Priscod of
Barbados.

1 Day   Morn: Copying, at meeting Mary Evans spoke, Robert Arnoll &
————— Peters dined hear, they are going to barbados so I gave
them my letters, afternoon at meeting Robert Willis spoke. drank tea
with Hannah West and Lydia Noble, evening went to meeting with
Jemmy & Anna, DS: spoke.

2   Morn: at the House. afternoon Mame & I to see Neigh: Jones. evening
Caty and I off on Errands, Daddy very poorly.

41. Young, *The Complaint.* vol. II (1748), 175.

3   Morn: at the House very busy. afternoon on a visit to Sally Fisher. evening Disappointments and we must Learn to bear with them, experience of the Ages

4   Morn: bought Pickles, beans, and Cucumbers. afternoon to see Rachel Drinker, Polly Collins there,

5   Day: Maid Hannah Sick, Caty & I dressed Nancys baby.

6   Morn: family Unwell, Hannah Howel hear. afternoon Becky James hear, I drank tea with Mame Sansom.

7   Morn: at the House Abel James, his Wife, and Patty with my two mames went to burlington in Abels Waggon, afternoon Sammy & I had a pleasent ride Poles place, from thence the 5 mile round, evening with Daddy

1 Day   Morn: at meeting, Samuel and Josey Sansom, Becky Jones and Han: Cathrel dined hear, afternoon at meeting John Pemberton spoke, Samuel & Josey drank tea hear, Caty went to meeting, I had an agreable evening.[42]

2   Morn: Nancy Pole & I ought of [out on] errands, afternoon Joshua, Caty, & Anne Howel, Nancy Warner, Sally Howel, Peggy Rawle, Sammy, & I went to Edgely, Joshua, Sally, & I walked down to Skykill, then over poor Francis's part of the place, the Young Orchard planted by his hand: he even marked ground for a future dwelling: now he is removed to the narrow tomb. may the child be as the father worthy and fulfill all his good purposes.

3   Morn: at the house visit from S:Pleasents. at work for Caty. Neigh: Greenleaf hear, Mame returned with her Company to diner, puting up beds, Anna Bringhurst Sick, letter from Becky Rawle with a return of some papers

4   Morn: we moved, and Betty Wolfe come to live with us. Daddy, Mame, Tommy, Nancy, Caty, and Hannah Wilmington, Daddy & Mame Sansom, Joshua and Caty Howel, and Becky Rawle dined with us. afternoon Neig: Coleman and Warner, and Benny Swett drank tea with us. evening all went home but Caty and Nancy lodged hear. thus on this day we began the Important affair of House keeping, In which the Woman's care is to make the house agreable to her husband, and be careful of his Interest. there is an old saying a man must ask his Wife if he shall be Rich.[43]

---

42. An erasure, possibly "alone."

43. "As a man must ask his wife whether he is to be a rich man or a beggar, so a child must ask his parents whether he is to be a wise man or a fool." There are many versions of this aphorism; one was published much as HCS wrote it in a sermon on the "Duties of the Married State," in *Fifteen Sermons upon Social Duties,* by Patrick Delany (London, 1744), 59.

5	Morn: Caty put up my Calico bed, I went to see Anna, Caty & Nancy dined with us. afternoon Daddy & Mame, and Rich Smith, who has surprised the world by having an Intension to Marry a Girl of no fortune. Hannah Peak. Daddy & Mame Sansom, and Polly Sandwith set with me an hour.
6	Morn: family affairs, steped to Mames, afternoon at Home, Becky & Nancy. evening Sammy & Caty Smith, agreable. finished 9 breadths of Cambrick for Caty since I come home.
7	Morn: in the family, 2 Hours with Anna Bringhurst, afternoon Neigh. Warner. I was an Hour at Mame's, evening Solitary & Serious. I have left my mother, but with her consent, Lord! do thou bless it. When I forget you may I be forgot by those whome most I love.
1 Day	Morn: Sammy and I went to meeting, Mary Evans and Grace Fisher spoke, John and Rachel Drinker, and Henry Clifton dined dined with us, afternoon went to Daddy's, they being poorly, Neigh Warner drank tea there, evening Sammy & I at home
2	Morn: at Work, Washing day. Daddy hear, afternoon 4 O Clock went to see Polly Howel, thence drank tea with Mame Sansom, Will: Spencer come to live with us
3	Morn: Ironing, afternoon Daddy & Mame hear, evening Becky Rawle
4	Morn: at Market, & home preserveing Quinces & makeing tarts, Abraham Goodwin, A young English man dined with us. my poor friend Grace Caldwell has lost her Husband, of a malignant feaver, she Just ready to Ly in, every way an accomplished man. Oh fatal Loss. the City is very sickly. Polly Lyon is dead, a worthy Woman, none shall stay when the dread summons comes. afternoon Caty Smith hear. evening Daddy & Mame Sansom
5	Morn: at Meeting D Stanton and Sarah Morris spoke. afternoon at Mames, eveng: at Mame Sansom's. gave Caty Smith a red Hankercheif. 4 shillings
6	Morn: at Meeting BT: and John Stevenson spoke. Rich: Smith & Anna Peak, Henry Haddock and Hannah Moode. passed. afternoon at Mames, Cousin Betty & betsey Smith come,
7	Morn: busy makeing tarts. Betsey & Caty hear. went off on Errands, afternoon to see Fammy Fox, a fine Young girl who seems to be in a decline, and so the fairest flowers shall fade. Danny, Bobby, & Sally from burlington. Sally Lodges with us.
1 Day	Morn: Betsey & I went to the Market Street meeting, Philip Dennis and John Stevenson spoke. Danny, Bobby, and Betsey dined with us. afternoon betsey & I at the Market Street meeting, Han: Harris and DS: spoke. a very large Assembly. Gideon Wanton of Rhoade Island drank

tea with us. evening went to the bank,[44] an excellent Prayer and Sermon from Susannah Hatton, a Woman of a good delivery, and person. Sally Rigby spoke. Danny, Bobby, Sally, and Betsey suped hear. Sally & Betsey Lodged hear.

2   Morn: John & Sally Baldwin, went to meeting, Ellis Hugh, John Churchman, Robert Comely, and Will: Brown spoke, Gidean Wanton, Joshua & Marcy baldwin, and John & Sally Baldwin dined hear. afterwards half an hour with Becky Rawle who is sick, from thence to the Womens meeting at the bank, Hannah Harris spoke, Lydia & Patty Noble and Betsey Cooper drank tea with me.

3   Morn: rainy, Sally & I went to meeting. Sally Rigby, Susannah Churchman, and Marget Ellis spoke, Joseph & Mary Parker, and Market Curles dined with us, afternoon at meeting, Han: Harris, Susey Hatton, and Eliz: Wilkison spoke, Widow Hopkins & her Daughter drank tea with us. Joshua & John Baldwin and Robert Valentine paid us a seasonable and agreable visit in the evening

4   Morn: made some tarts, went to the Womens meeting held at the bank, and [it was] very Salutary, afternoon Also Jane Hoskins spoke.

5   Morn: Mame, Sally, betsey, Caty & Nancy & I went to meeting, Susan: Churchman, Jane Hoskins, and Han: Harris spoke, Molly Brown and Sally Smith dined with us, afternoon at meeting Susey Hatton spoke, Evening at Mames.

[October 1, 1762]

10 Mos 6   Morn at meeting, which concluded, afternoon Mame, Mary Noble, Gideon Wanton, & my Cousins drank tea hear. the girls, Sammy & I at Beckys the evening

7   Morn: at Market, 9 O'Clock Sally, Betsey, & Danny went home, becky Rawle hear, afternoon John Howel, Becky, & I went [to] Edgely, Joshua & Caty, Joseph Allicock and his Wife [were] there, [had an] agreable walk to Skykill, heard the noise of blowing the rocks up. pleasant ride home, even: Caty Smith.

1 Day   Morn: at meeting BT: and David Easter spoke, Betsey Warner and Caty Smith dined Hear, afternoon at Meeting. Elenor Shotwell one of the meeting representatives from rawvay[45] taken sick and died, buried this afternoon. drank tea at Mames, with Nancy Warner, evening at meeting Han Harris and Eliza Wilkison spoke.[46]

---

44. The Bank Meeting House was on Front Street.
45. Rahway, New Jersey.
46. Three large entries have been cut out here.

5   Morn: at meeting DS:, Mary Emblen:, Sally Morris, Han: Harris, and Eliza: Wilkison spoke, and the poor Friend Alice Hall is dead, in a strange Land————————

6   Morn: mending Stockings. afternoon Nancy Warner and I went to the funeral of Alice Hall, from Isaac Zanes, to the Market [street] meeting house, a large Assembly. Robert Proud, Susey Hatton, and John Stevenson spoke, afterward disently Intered.

7   Morn: at Work, afternoon at Mames, not very well and very serious.

1 Day Morn: at meeting BT: spoke, we dined at mames with Mary Noble. afternoon at meeting Robert Proud spoke, Jemmy & Anna, and Patty James drank tea with us. evening at meeting Eliza Wilkison, Susey Hatton, Robert Proud, and John Stevenson spoke.

2   Morn: doing little or nothing we dined at Mame Sansoms, afternoon she and I paid a visit to Neigh: Harrison, evening at Mames. Caty sick.

3   Morn: at meeting John Stevenson, and Susey Hatton spoke, and to morrow they with Robert Proud take shiping. afternoon at Becky Rawles.

4   Morn: at Market, then at Mammes with Caty, afternoon at Sukey Shippens, Peggy Shippen and Betsey Willing there, evening at home.

5   Morn: Anna Bringhurst hear & Mamme [in the] afternoon Anna and Nanny Wishart & I to see Betsey Thomas, evening Sammy & I at mammes.

6   Day rainy, afternoon Caty Smith & Nancy Warner, evening: betsey Warner, Caty & Nancy lodged hear.

7   Morn: at Work, afternoon at Mames,

1 Day Morn: at meeting we dined at Mames, afternoon at meeting. Caty Smith & I drank tea at Rachel Drinkers, evening: at meeting DS spoke.

2   Morn: washing, afternoon mame hear.

3   Morn: Sick, but well anough to go see Caty Howel, with mame in the afternoon, Caty lodged hear.

4   Morn: better, mame unwell. afternoon Caty hear, Mame better, Caty lodged hear, good parents an inconceiveable blessing.

5   Day: rainy, Betsey Rodman Smith & Abby Smith with Josey Meriot come in a wagan from Burlington, dined hear & staid the afternoon went to see Jenny Evans with becky Rawle

6   Morn: Mame, Neigh: Warner, Becky Jones,& Josey Meriot went up in the Waggon, to B————n on there way to Shrewsberry. afternoon[47]

---

47. Five following entries mostly missing, cut out from previous page.

Caty.
greably
, at meet
evening
ent to

Warner
George
from
ble.

5   Morn: at meeting   acie were married, afternoon at Grace Caldwells, Kitty Miller, & Hervey there. evening agreable with betsey &
Caty Rawle Franceois.

6   Morn: at meeting 9 Couples passed. Come home & wrote to Sally
Smith. afternoon on a visit to Polly Standly, evening Daddy, Henry
Drinker, and Polly Parrock spent agreably with us.

7   Morn: at Market with becky rawle, & shops. gave Caty Smith a silk
Hankercheif [worth] 8/6.[48] afternoon drank tea at beckys, with Pa-
tience & Caty Howel, went a bit to Daddys, suped at Joshuas, with
Sammy & becky, pleasent Conversation.

11 mos

1 Day   Morn: at meeting BT: spoke, Josey Samson dined with us, visit from
John Drinker, at meeting. we went to daddys, Anthony Morris there,
we staid the evening.

[November 1, 1762]

2   Morn: in health, the greatest of temporal blessings. afternoon Becky,
Caty, the 2 girls Anne & Caty Rawle & Howel, with myself went to
Betty Rhoads, Polly & Hannah at home, Peter Reeves & Tommy
Richardson drank tea there. evening: Mame Samson hear.

3   Morn: Ironing, afternoon Anna Bringhurst & I spent with Becky Carmalt. evening Betsey Warner.

4   Morn: at Market, & work. a visit from Caty Howel, afternoon to see
Polly & Hetty Deshler, Tommy Richardson there, evening, Mame
come home, Sammy & I there, Martha Barker also.

5   Morn: at meeting, BT: and M Yarnel spoke, Henry Haddock married.
afternoon, to see Patience Mifflin, evening Joshua & Caty. Becky & Betsey, agreable in Conversation,

6   Day. mame bad with a pain in her face, there most of the day

7   Morn: at Work, afternoon at Mames staid the evening, she was better

48. Eight shillings and sixpence.

1 Day	Morn: at meeting BT: spoke, afternoon at meeting, drank tea at Mames with Becky & Anne Rawle, Sammy & I staid the evening
2	Morn: at Work. afternoon mame Sansoms, evening unwell,
3	Morn: at meeting Betty Morris [and] Mordecai Yarnel spoke, 2 couple married. afternoon Neigh Warner, Aunt Armitt, and Daddy & Mame drank tea with us
4	Morn: 9 OClock Caty come & told me daddy was sick, I went Immediately & found him very ill with a vomiting of blood, but as providence has been pleased to turn it down, we hope he will recover, I staid that night & till 7 day night

1 Day	Morn at meeting BT: and Sally Morris spoke, dined at home, went to daddys, Becky Rawle, there an hour, Tommy Lightfoot, and Jemmy bringhurst. evening Becky James, after supper we returned, leaveing daddy much mended.
2	Morn: at Work, afternoon and evening at Mames,
3	Morn: half hour at Mames very unwell, afternoon there again. evening Also. a hard lesson to flesh and blood [is] to bear affliction and many find it harder to bear prosperity. therefore O Lord preserve me in both:
4	Morn: at Work, afternoon at Mames,
5	Morn: at Mames, afternoon Mame Sansom & I went to Unkle Samuel Bells, John & Rachel Drinker, and Polly Parock there,
6	Morn: at Work, afternoon at Mames. drank tea at home.
7	Morn: at Work, afternoon Becky, Caty & I took a long and agreable walk, drank tea at Mames. Danny Smith from burlington

1 Day	Morn: Danny breakfasted with us, went to meeting, BT: and Grace fisher spoke, after diner Sammy & I went to mames, I staid the meeting time with daddy, Sammy and I drank tea at father Sansoms, & staid the evening.
2	Morn: of errands, to see Grace Caldwell, and Betsey drinker, afternoon on a visit to Neigh Greenleaf, evening Betsey Warner.
3	Morn: at meeting BT: and Mordecai Yarnell spoke, afternoon to see the Widow Edwards, John Cooper there.
4	Morn: busy in the family, afternoon on a visit to Sally Dylvin, agreable
5	Morn: at home rainy, afternoon at Daddys,
6	Morn: at Daddys, Caty fitting a body lining,[49] afternoon Joshua and the 2 Caty Howels, evening Sammy & I at Becky Rawles,
7	Morn: at Market with becky, afternoon at Grace Caldwells and Mame Sansoms, a Melancholy Accident has Lately happened: a woman poisoning her three children in one morning, by an Apothecarys boy mistakeing the medisine and giveing white Arsnick,

49. Body linen, underwear.

1 Day	Morn: at meeting Isaac Andrews spoke, we dined at Daddys, afternoon at meeting, DS: and Isaac Andrews spoke. Caty & I went to Nancy Gillinhams funeral, DS spoke at the Grave.
2	Morn: at Work, afternoon Father & Mother Sansom hear, evening Sammy & I at Benny Sweets to eat pound Cake
3	Morn: at home, went to ~~afternoon~~ meeting, Sarah Morris spoke, afternoon at Beckys, Catys, and Daddys. evening Sammy treated Caty, Betsey Warner, & I with cake

[December 1, 1762]

12 MO 4	Morn: at home, afternoon to See Hannah Smith with Anna Bringhurst.
5	Morn: at Mames very unwell, Daddy & Mame took a ride, afternoon Caty and I went the 5 Mile round, evening Mame Sansom hear
6	Morn: Becky & I went Caty Howels, little Anne has the Small pox, afternoon Becky, & her Anne drank tea with us.
7	Morn: Thomas Guy come to board with us, afternoon Caty Smith hear

1 Day	Morn: at meeting BT: spoke, Josey Smith dined hear, afternoon I spent part with Caty Howel and part with Daddy, Sammy & I went to Peter Thomson childs funeral, spent the evening at Daddys.
2	Morn: Mame come to see me, and we went to Catys, afternoon Mame Sansom & I at Eliza Bryants,
3	Morn: My two Mames, & Becky Rawle hear, I was bleed,[50] Betsey Warner set an hour with me, afternoon my two Mames & father Sansom with Josey. evening Jemmy & Anna Bringhurst.
4	Morn: in the family, afternoon at Caty Howels & Mames,
5	Morn: at Meeting, BT: & Sally Morris spoke excellently, Holiness is in the House of the Lord, therefore be ye holy. afternoon to Visit Polly Pleasents, Robert Proud and our two Sammys drank tea with us, we staid the evening agreably, Doctor Shippen there, so full of his Anatomical schemes, quite tiresome.[51]
6	Morn: at home, afternoon on a visit to Hester & Lydia Fisher. the amiable Neigh: Carney there. Tommy Just gone for England. Evening at Catys
7	Morn: Daddy & I took an airing, afternoon 4 OClock went to Catys. her child a dying and it departed this Life about Six OClock, in the

50. A first sign that HCS is pregnant. According to contemporary medical thought, because a woman stops menstruating during pregnancy, she therefore accumulates excess blood, which has to be removed for health.

51. Dr. William Shippen Jr. had just returned from London with a sizeable collection of anatomical drawings and models, which he wanted to make the basis of a medical school in Philadelphia. He began giving anatomical lectures to the paying public on November 16, 1762. Betsy Copping Corner, *William Shippen, Jr.: Pioneer in American Medical Education* (Philadelphia: American Philosophical Society, 1951), 98–101.

Small pox, the Consolation of a Christian is, in the World ye shall have trouble but in me ye shall have peace.[52]

1 Day	most of it with her, in a melancholy Satisfaction, to read over the lines of our past Life, and remember those that are gone to rest. affords a pleasure which will never fade, but will flourish fresh and green
2	Morn: at home and with Caty, afternoon Mame Sansom, Anna bringhurst, Caty Smith, & I went to the funeral, evening Sammy read to me in book called the death of Abel,[53] Benny Sweet hear.
3	Morn: spent with my father. afternoon Also, evening Becky Rawle & betsey
4	Morn: Ironing, afternoon at Mame Sansoms,
5	Morn: busy, afternoon at Joshua Howels, Sammy also,
6	Morn: at Mames, afternoon Caty & I at the funeral of Will Fishers child
7	Morn: at Market. afternoon at Mames,

1 Day	Morn: at meeting BT: spoke, afternoon at meeting, we drank tea & staid the evening at Mame Sansoms,
2	Morn: at Work, afternoon Polly Parrock & I at Rachel Drinkers. eveng: Sammy & I at mames,
3	Morn: went to meeting, DS spoke, my maid Betsey fell down and hurt herself. my good Neighbours Rawle & Howel, come to her assistance, a good Neighbourhood is the Salt of Life, how good in distress to call thy friend, after diner I sent to Mame & Caty come, evening Betsey Warner also, till bed time, the Girl is mending.
4	Morn: Hung up my Gammons & fliches to smoke, afternoon at beckys
5	Day, rainy at home working on my chair cushin, evening: Betsey Warner,
6	Morn: at Work, afternoon to see Hannah Mickle, evening: wrote to Sally.
7	Morn: the Painter at Work for me, afternoon at home, Nancy Pole hear.

1 Day	Morn: excessive cold, a very moderate season till now, went to meeting BT: spoke, Josey Sansom and Tommy Pole dined with us, afternoon at meeting, Will Brown spoke, Caty Smith and I went to the funeral of Will Fishers 2nd child in the Small pox, drank tea at Mames with Robert Proud & Sammy Sansom, evening we went to meeting, the good Mordecai Yarnel spoke, DS: & BT: also, a lovely moonlight night

---

52. John 16:33.

53. Mary Collyer's *The Death of Abel: A sacred poem, in five books. Attempted from the German of Mr. Gessner,* first published in 1761, was a translation of Solomon Gessner's *Der Tod Abels.*

2   Morn: at Work on the cushin, Caty hear, Daddy & Mame Sansom with Josey, evening Betsey Warner.

3   Morn: Ben: Swett moved into the next house, I went to mames a little. afternoon my Father by the mercy of god walked as far as my house, staid half hour, Anna Bringhurst hear, Sammy Pleasents and Benny Swett drank tea hear, evening Rich: & Hannah Smith, Benny & Polly Swett suped hear,

4   Morn: at home, afternoon at Mames, with Sammy and all the evening, Sammy Shoemaker there.

5   at home

6   Morn: at meeting BT. and William Willis spoke, several passed meeting. afternoon Neigh: Warner and Nancy, evening great trouble with my boy Bill, thus ended the year 1762. with the mixture of this Worlds Joy and trouble, and may my conclusion be

> *This day be bread and peace my lot*
> *All else beneath the Sun*
> *Thou knowest if best bestowed or not*
> *And let thy Will be done.*[54]

[January 1, 1763]

1 Mo 7   Morn: busey in the family, afternoon Becky Rawle and Polly Swett. evening Betsey Warner, I worked at my cushin.

1 Day   Morn: at meeting, went a little to mames, afternoon at meeting. BT: and DS: spoke, Sammy and I drank tea at Father Sansoms, evening at home reading in the bible to the family.

2   Morn: Robert Willis and Joshua Emblen paid us a religious visit, Robert advised us, to condesend to each other, beware of the love of world, to eager pursuit after riches, to attend meetings, and fear god, which would consolidate[55] tryals, and give ease at the last day. afternoon Becky Rawle and I off [on] Errands, drank tea at home with Father Sansom & Jemmy Bringhurst,

3   Morn: at meeting BT:, DS:, and Robert Willis spoke, went to mames, afternoon Mame Sansom and Grace Fisher come to see me, and toward evening we parted with our boy Will: Spencer for he proved very untractable, a solitary evening! look only to thine own heart for peace, for veryly thou shalt meet with trials. reader, be thou who' thou may.

---

54. From Alexander Pope's *The Universal prayer* (London, 1738).
55. Provide consolation for.

[In margin: "night."]

4   Morn at Work. afternoon at home, working on my cushin.

5   Morn: at home busy, Sammy and I dined at Mamys, 4 O'Clock Caty Smith and I drank tea at Caty Howels, spent some hours at Becky Rawles, suped at home with Josey Sansom.

6   Morn: very busy in the family, afternoon very agreable with my old friend Caty Howel at my own house, also little Caty Howel with Anne Rawle,

7   Morn: at Work, afternoon at Becky Rawles, drank tea at home with Anna Bringhurst. a solitary evening, not disagreable, a time of relaxation to the mind, the Souls dark Cottage batter'd and decay'd

Lets in new Light thro' chinks which time has made.[56]

1 Day   Morn: at meeting Eliza: Wilkison and Hannah Harris spoke, dined at home. went to Mames, thence to meeting with her, BT: and Robert Willis spoke. Sammy & I spent the evening with Henry & Betsey Drinker, Betsey Waln and Polly Sandwith there.

2   Morn: made [a] half Gallon of Stouton bitters.[57] afternoon paid a visit to Neigh Swett, Sally Nicolson & Betsey Flower there, evening at home,

3   Morn: at Work, afternoon a visit from Nanny Carlisle, evening: betsey Warner

4   Morn: busy: went to mames a little, afternoon went to Father Sansoms. evening agreable at home with Betsey Warner.

5   Morn at Work. Polly Swett hear, afternoon to see Lydia Parker, Mollys Richardson & Roberts, Betsey Fox, Becky Mifflin, Beulah Burge, Patty Hudson, Betsey Head, Hannah Moor, Rachel Wells, and Peggy Morris, a large Company. Caty Smith and Betsey Warner spent the evening

6   Morn: at Work, afternoon at Mames, Abel James, Henry Drinker, and Charles West there, Sammy and I spent the evening with Becky Rawle, Friend Coleman, & Betsey.

7   Morn: at Work. afternoon Anna Bringhurst & I at Mames, evening Sammy read in Tullys offices.

1 Day   Morn: a great Snow, went to meeting BT:, Becky Jones, and David Easter spoke, Becky Jones and Hannah Cathrel dined with us, after-

56. Edmund Waller, *Poems & c. written upon several occasions, and to several persons* (London, 1722), 259.

57. Staughton's Elixer was a proprietary medicine, patented in 1712, whose main ingredient was alcohol. It was used as a tonic. J. Worth Estes, "Therapeutic Practice in Colonial New England," in *Medicine in Colonial Massachusetts, 1620–1820,* ed. Philip Cash (Boston: Colonial Society of Massachusetts, 1980), 378.

noon at meeting Jonathan Maris gave us a good Sermon. we drank tea at Joshua Howels with him and Isaac Howel, evening the men went to meeting, Caty and I had an agreable hour or two. tho' on melancholy Subjects: true Joy has its Source from Serious things.

2   Morn: Ironing. afternoon Polly Swett and I went to see Sarah Fisher, evening at Work, Caty Smith hear,

3   Morn: went to meeting Jonathan Maris and BT: spoke, a visit from Israel Pemberton and Polly Pleasents, she and I concluded to meet in the afternoon at Rachel Wells, Sally Dylvin and Patty Hill there.

4   Morn: at Work, afternoon, Sarah Decow: Fanny Rush, Polly Sandwith, and Henry and Betsey Drinker made us an agreable visit.

5   Morn: Went to meeting with Caty Smith, Robert Willis and Hannah Harris spoke, Neddy Thomas and Sally Holoway were married. afternoon Sammy, Caty Smith, and I went to Richmond in a Slay.

6   Morn: at Work, afternoon I went to see Sally Parish, Friend Mitchel and Debby there. evening at home agreable with Sammy & Betsey.

7   Morn: at Work, a visit from my dear Mame, afterward Robert Proud. afternoon Father and Mother Sansom, Benny and Polly Swett. evening Becky Rawle and Caty Smith.

1 Day   Morn: at meeting BT:, Becky Jones, and Grace Fisher spoke, afternoon at meeting, we went to Daddys, Rich: & Sally Wister, and Becky Rawle there, evening Caty Smith and I went to meeting, Eliza Wilkison, Hannah Harris, and Robert Willis spoke,

2   Morn: made myself a flanen[58] Jaket. afternoon Nancy Warner, Hannah Howel, Father Sansom, & Josey hear,

3   Morn: at home worked a Scarlet flower in my cushin. afternoon Caty Smith

4   Morn: at Work wrote to Sally, afternoon Benny & Polly Swett, Sammy & I took a ride within the new Slay that they have purchased between them

5   Morn: at Mames, afternoon the same Company Joined by Joshua & Caty, little Caty, Becky & Anne Rawle, and Nancy Pole, went to Richmond, [on] the Frankford road, the open Country covered by the sleted snow glittering in the Sun, gave an agreable prospect. the frigid winter is not without its beauties. evening: Betsey Warner.

6   Morn: at Work, Anna Bringhurst dined hear, and at three O'Clock she and I went to Mames, Neigh: Warner, Sarah Decow, and Fanny Rush there.

7   Morn: in the family, afternoon and evening at Polly Swetts, H: Howell there

58. Perhaps flannel, a soft, napped fabric.

1 Day   Morn: at meeting BT: spoke, afternoon at meeting Sammy & I went to Mames, staid the evening, Henry Drinker there.

2   Morn: at some shops. afternoon Cousin Lydia Noble, Han: West, and Mame hear, evening Polly Parrock, we went to Mame Sansoms.

[February 1, 1763]

2 Mo 3   Morn: made me a Night Gound. afternoon Caty Smith, Nancy Warner, Becky Jones and I at Sammy Shoemakers child's funeral, a young Woman followed by her husband & 2 children entered the grave yard at the same time, Benny and Polly Swett and Sally Pemberton drank tea with me, and staid the evening, also Caty Smith & Josey Samson.

4   Morn: at Work, afternoon at Father Sansoms, evening Betsey Warner hear. people vary from themselves sometimes.

5   Morn: worked two yellow flowers in my Cushin. afternoon Joshua & Caty, Grace Dowel, Hannah North, and Peggy Gadis come to see me, evening Betsey

6   Morn: at Mames, an hour, and at home busy. afternoon Sammy & I at Mame's

7   Morn: at Work, afternoon Benny, Sammy, Caty Smith, Betsey Warner, Josey Sansom, Billy Rawle, and I went to Richmond in the Slay.

1 Day   Morn: at meeting Eliza: Wilkison and Hannah Harris spoke, afternoon at meeting Thomas Carlton, Becky Jones, and Betty Morris spoke, we drank tea at Mames with Anthony's Benezet & Morris, Caty & I went to see Betsey Drinker. they have Inoculated their child. Sammy & I at Neigh: Sweets,

2   Morn: Ironing, afternoon Sammy & I drank tea at Becky Rawle's & staid the evening,

3   Morn: at meeting Hannah Harris, Eliza Wilkison, and James Thornton spoke, afternoon on a visit to Hannah Morris, evening Josey Smith with news from Burlington

4   Morn: at Market, wrote to Sally Smith, afternoon working at home,

5   Morn: went to meeting Robert Willis, Eliza Wilkison, and Hannah Harris spoke afternoon Isaac Greenleaf and his Wife, evening Joshua & Caty, Becky and Betsey, the time slipt so agreably we parted not till 11 O'Clock,

6   Morn: at Work paid a visit at Mames, John Reynold there, afternoon at Hannah Saunders, an agreable Woman, who by the order of her household and their behaviour of made me think of that elegant Chapeter, "who can praise a virtuous Woman, her price is far above rubies, her husband is Honoured by her, and her family rejoices in her."[59]

59. See Proverbs 31:10–11, 28. HCS has altered and strengthened these verses. "Who can find a vir-

7   Morn: at Work, afternoon Grace Caldwell and I went to Neigh: Mases, as we sat Chating and working innocently, come a letter with an account of the Murder of William Read, Husband to her neice Betsey Chambers, by some ruffians who broke in his store at the Havana, murdered him and his partner boyd, —————— this news quite changed our Hearts and looks, we felt for his Wife, his Mother, and in our several connections of Friendship, Oh death thy surprises are greivous to bear, thou wounds poor Mankind most affectingly, robs us of our budding hopes, and our expected Joys. yea nothing can console for thy breaches in the Human weal, but Immortality, the glorious theme of Angels & of men. this evening come to town Sally, Betsey, & Bobby Smith, Sammy & I staid at Daddys to sup with them, and they Lodged there.

1 Day   Morn: at Meeting Robert Willis spoke, Sally, Betsey, & Bobby dined with us. Becky Rawle & Caty smith come hear afterward, 3 O'Clock Sammy, myself & the Smiths went to Daddys, and we staid with him, and Mame till dusk when we went to Becky Rawles, in company with Caty Howel, this day was buried Evan Morgan a worthy Citizen.

2   Morn: went to mames about 9 O'Clock, Bobby & [the] Girls took leave of my father who is in a bad state of health, at the warfe, we were Joined by Becky & Caty we parted with our friends, and returned to my House where we had an agreable half hour. afternoon I went to see Betsey Bringhurst,

3   Morn: at meeting James Gillinham and Phebe Holloway were married. BT:, Mor: Yarnell, and Robert Willis spoke, afternoon to see Betsey Fox.

4   Morn: worked a leaf and Crimson tulip, afternoon Neigh: Warner, Becky Rawle, and I went to Mame Sansoms.

5   Morn: Caty Smith and I went to meeting, Anthony Woodcock and Sarah Morris spoke. there was two marriages at meeting, Peter Barker and Betsey Grisley was one, afternoon at Mames, Neigh Warner and Nanny Emblen there, had a letter from Sally, Caty & I went to Betsey Drinkers, the child quite well, we suped at Daddys.

6   Morn: worked a Carnation and blue flower, afternoon at Mame Sansoms who gave me all the baby Cloaths she had left, evening at home very agreable with Polly Rhoades and Betsey Warner.

7   Morn: at Work, afternoon at Mames, Caty Smith makeing me a wrap. went to the funeral of a poor Neighbour, mame gave me all the baby things She had left, so I shall not need to make [but] little, as all we can enjoy is but conveniency, the rest is Vanity,

tuous woman? For her price is far above rubies. The heart of her husband doth safely trust in her. . . . Her children arise up, and call her blessed; her husband also, and he praiseth her."

1 Day   Morn: at meeting BT: spoke, afternoon at meeting, Sammy & I drank tea and staid the evening at Joshua Howels, in agreable converse.

2   Day. washing, afternoon acceptable visit from Neigh Warner, she staid in the evening to hear Betsey Translate.

3   Morn: Ironing. 12 OClock Sammy went to Burlington, Mame come hear till 3 OClock, when I paid a visit to Docter Caldwaleders family. evening Becky Rawle and Caty Smith, the latter lodged with me

4   Morn: at Work, afternoon Nancy Warner & Peggy Rawle, Sammy returned in the evening, all well. Sally sent me a silk worme.[60]

5   Morn: ripped my blue grazet Gound, Caty has finished my Calico & makes this. afternoon at Mames, Molly Stretch, Caty Greenleaf, and Neigh Warner, three sociable agreable Women, there. evening at home worked at my Cushin.

6   Day, cold and Snow. this doubles the pleasure of a good fire side, and ought to enhance the thankfulness of the Rich. afternoon Polly Swett, Betsey Flower, Sally Nicolson, and Betsey Warner hear,

7   Morn: quite alive by the beauties of a clear morn, the whole face of nature cloathed in Virgin white. afternoon Billy Rawle, Sammy, & I at Daddys. evening at Becky Rawle's, Sammy & I paid a short agreable visit to Becky Jones.

1 Day   Morn: at meeting BT: spoke, afternoon at meeting Robert Willis spoke, we drank tea and staid the evening at mame Sansoms,

2   Day, dull weather but we enjoyed ourselves at home, worked on my grazet gound, evening Sally Nicolson and Betsey Warner Parle' Franceois[61]

[March 1, 1763]

3 MOs 3   Morn: Aunt Armitt made me a visitt, rest of the morn I was with Daddy, afternoon Father & Mother Sansom with Josey, & Mary Emblen were hear, evening Daddy sent for us being seized with a relapse, I staid all night O Death thou destroyer of this mortal Coil, how ceaseless are thy depradations on our Joys. and yet the good man praying for support is enabled to endure thee!

4   Morn: breakfasted at home, went back till diner time, dined at home, there in the afternoon with Mame Sansom & Neigh: Warner, Sammy & I suped there. my maid Betsey set up with daddy.

5   Morn: at Daddys, dined at home, afternoon Will: Fisher his Wife and Taby, with Benny Swett drank tea hear, evening Sammy & I at Daddys.

6   Morn: went to Daddys worked on my Cushin, dined at home, after-

---

60. Silkworms were cultivated, unsuccessfully, in the colonies in hopes of establishing a silk industry. Silk production, like other textile work, was considered a feminine occupation.

61. *Parlons francais:* We speak French.

noon went there again, Sammy & I drank tea there, evening at home, Abraham Goodwin come from Trentown for a docter to poor Anne Leister who is like to leave this World, on the birth of a Son who is dead, he lodged hear, I wrote to Sally by him,

7   Morn: Abraham set off with the docter, went to Daddys, dined at home. afternoon Sammy & I there again, received a letter from Sally dated last night, with the information of Anne's Death, they are were to bring her this morn to Burlington that to morrow her dust may be Desently intered with that of her family, 7 of which grown to mans estate, since my memory, have been deposited [in the grave], Father, Mother, 2 Sons, & 3 daughters. all within the course of 10 years.

1 Day   Morn: 8 OClock Peter Reeve, James Logan, Israel Morris, and Samuel Sansom went to Burlington, to the funeral, I went to meeting, from thence to Daddys. dined there with Tommy & Sally Lightfoot, then come home locked up the house, and returned again, staid with daddy & mame, till evening when my maid and I returned. Nancy Warner spent the evening and lodged with me,

2   Morn: finished my Cushin, the river De la War by a sudden thaw is clear of Ice, and 27 vessels have arrived this morn, Father Sansom and Benny Swett hear. afternoon I went to Daddys, 3 O'Clock Sammy returned from Burlington. spent the evening at home very agreably, worked a bunch of stalks in my second Cushin.

3   Day, very rainy, worked a yallow flower and part of a leaf, afternoon my friends Becky & Caty hear,

4   Morn: my maid set up with Daddy & he is much better. I went there & finished my leaf and began a pin cushing, after diner Sammy went to Darby, and I to mames, worked at my baby things, note George hung up my Gammons.

5   Morn: wrote to Sally, went to Mames, dined at home, afternoon there, Caty tried on my grazet gound, I drank tea at Mame Sansoms, with Sally Fisher & Polly Sweet,

6   Morn: at Daddys, Neigh: Warner there, stiched a boys cap, afternoon there again, drank tea at home with Sammy, evening: Betsey Warner.

7   Morn: finished the Pincushin, afternoon at mames begun another pincushin, for mame Sansom, evening at home. Betsey sat up with daddy

1 Day   Morn: went to meeting Eliza Stevens and Becky Jones spoke, the latter Elegantly on Religion, if any man hath Christ he hath Life, but if he hath not Christ he hath not Life. Sally Lightfoot dined with us, then we went to my dear father's, who is very low and weak in body

2   Morn: bad weather, worked on the shirt of my black gound which I [am] new doing, afternoon at daddys,

3   Morn: worked on the gown, my Neigh: Polly Sweet passed an agreable hour or two with Sammy & I. he read to us, a very rainy morn. afternoon at Daddys, worked on the baby things

4   Morn: at Work on the pincushin, afternoon at Daddys. 5 OClock I went Joshua Howels, drank tea with Sammy, Becky Rawle, & them, evening we Women went to Beckys, Neigh Warner poorly, all suped there,

5   Day, not only Daddy but mame very poorly, I was with them all day, evening Danny & Sally Smith come from Burlington, to my great Satisfaction, Josey Smith there,

6   Morn: Ironing, afternoon at Daddys, we suped there, and [he] seemed very poorly. the latter days of man, cannot be sweeten'd by any thing but the divine grace.

7   Morn: at mames running a pair of Stockings, afternoon there again, with Sammy, & we staid the evening

1 Day   Morn: 9 O'Clock I went there to daddys and was bled, we Sammy come to me before meeting, Sally and he went to meeting, we dined there agreably as the circumstances of this melancholy house would admitt, in life thou meetest with affliction. yet in Death the Goodman is consoled.

2   Morn: family affairs, 10 O'Clock went to daddys, Sally come and dined with us, then we went back again, Sammy come to tea, Sally come and suped with us on oysters.

3   Morn: at Work, finished mame Sansoms pincushin, afternoon at Mames, Sally Smith, Becky Rawle, Sammy & I drank tea at Joshua Howels,

4   Morn: mending my black Russel peticoat, afternoon Sammy & I at Daddys.

5   Morn: busy in the family, afternoon at Daddys, worked a leaf

6   Morn: went to Thomas Mauls, 14 miles to Accompany the corps of Content Nicolson to her Son Benny Sweets, a very rainy day and the company very wett, Father & Mother Sansom with Josey drank tea hear, evening at Neigh: Sweets,

7   Morn: made some tarts, Hannah Howel dined hear, Sammy & I drank tea at Mames, with Cousin John & Betty Smith and Edward Cathrel

1 Day   Morn: Sally Smith hear, we went to meeting BT: & one I knew not spoke. James Farrow, Becky Jones, and Hannah Cathrel dined with us, Edward Cathrel, and father Sansom, hear, I spent the afternoon with Daddy & Mame, after meeting Content was buried, evening Caty Smith & I went to meeting Widow Hopkins, Jemmy Rigby, Becky Jones, and Betty Smith spoke

2   Morn: daddy seems better, went to meeting Isaac Andrews, Jemmy
           Rigby, Han: Harris, Betty Wilkison, and Joseph White spoke, Mary
           Emblen dined with me, and we went [to] Will: Fishers were, where the
           English friends two sociable agreable women [were,] we drank tea at
           Daddys with Nanny Weber, and suped there with Cousin Betty & Sally
           Smith,

3   Day, they dined with us, afternoon Mame Sansom & Caty Wethrel, and
           I worked my blue flower

4   Morn: went to Daddys. Edward Cathrel, John Hoskins, John Betty, &
           Sally Smith set out for Burlington, this day Caty Smith made up for
           me a baby Pincushin worked by my mother in the year 28,

5   Morn: washing, busy in the family, afternoon Mary Noble, Abby
           Raper, and Polly Pleasents hear, worked a leaf,

[April 1, 1763]

4 MOs 6   Morn: Ironing, afternoon at Daddys, he seems better, Anna Bringhurst
           delivered of a Son, Bobby Smith from B———n wrote largely to Sally.
           Josey & Bobby Smith, suped hear

7   Morn: mending Shirts, at daddys. afternoon Joshua & Caty hear,

1 Day   Morn: at meeting BT: spoke, after diner Sammy & I went to Daddys,
           we drank tea there, evening at home reading alternately in the Bible to
           our small family

2   Morn: poorly went to Daddys, afternoon Mame Sansom & I went to
           see Polly Sweet, Patty Powel, and Sally Nicolson & Maul there.

3   Morn: at Daddys, afternoon my worthy friend Sally Morris spent with
           me, evening Sammy & I at Daddys, worked a small yellow flower,

4   Morn: went see Anna Bringhurst and her son John, found them
           bravely, afternoon Becky Rawle and Abby & Caty Smith. Hannah
           Jones steped in.

5   Morn: Sammy, Caty, & I went to Richmond, Joseph Fox paid us a visit,
           the [plantation] begins to recover its verdure, we dined with mame,
           and I staid till evening

6   Morn: at Work on the Cushin, afternoon at Daddys, Caty Smith had a
           violent pain in her head,

7   Morn: at Mames, they seem tolerable, afternoon Sally Nicolson, mame
           Sansom, & I in her Garden, then we paid a visit to Molly Harrison and
           hers. she has a most amiable daughter growing up. a good and dutiful
           child, may be called the finest flower in nature, Father & Mother, with
           Josey, and Benny Swett drank tea with me, John Drinker suped with us.

1 Day   Morn: at meeting BT: & Grace fisher spoke, Rachel   Dined
           with us. I spent the afternoon with Daddy & Mame.

2   Morn: a letter from Sally, Dicky Smith has a Son called Scamon, afternoon at Daddys, they being poorly, worked a Yellow flower.

3   Day: our wash, Polly Jones brought a bed with a Son.

4   Day: washed my Counter pain and suit of curtains,

5   Day: washed the seiling of my front Chamber.[62] paid a visit to Neighbours Swett, Rawle, and Howel, drank tea at Daddys. but poorly, evening, Mame Sansom

6   Morn: at Work, went to Mame Sansoms, afternoon Neig: Warner, Sammy & I, Taby Fisher, Betsey Warner, and Nancy Pole went to Richmond in Joshua's waggon, had a very agreable afternoon, tho' some part in the sadly pleasing rememberance of a good man, for we called at Warners place where poor Francis fatally hurt himself, more for the loss and grief of his family than himself, who there by entered an early Immortality! evening at daddys.

7   Morn: at Work, went to Neigh Sweet, afternoon at Daddys, drank tea at Caty Howels, with Friend Coleman, and Patience & Nanny Howel.

1 Day   Morn: went to meeting BT: and DS: spoke, Father & Mother Sansom with Josey dined with us, then we walked in their Garden with Polly Harrison, afternoon at Daddys, Mordecai Yarnel John Pemberton, and Molly Stretch there,

2   Morn: at Work on my cushin. afternoon at daddys, but drank tea at mame Sansoms, for she is poorly,

3   Morn: at Mame Sansoms, Aunt Betty Smith from Burlington dined with us, She and I went to Daddys,

4   Morn: rainy, worked at my cushin, afternoon at Mame Sansom with Patty Johnson, evening, a visit from Betsey Roberts, Polly & Hetty Deshler, and Becky Carmalt, we walked over [to] the House,

5   Morn: at mame Sansom's. afternoon. Aunt Betty went home, I was at Mames folding cloaths, evening at Caty Howels

6   Morn: Sammy & I went to Richmond, afternoon at Mame Sansoms.

7   Morn: began to ground my Cushin. Afternoon Becky Rawle and her children, Bill first clad in mans Attire.[63] How pleasing to his father would this day have been, may the growing Virtues of the Son make him still dearer to us, for he is now a little charmer.

1 Day   Morn: at meeting Robert Willis spoke, Sally Lighfoot dined with us. I was at Daddys afternoon and evening,

---

62. Pregnant women were not supposed to lift their arms over their heads on the theory that the umbilical cord would wrap around the neck of the fetus and cause a stillbirth. She is either being reckless or she means that she supervised a servant while the ceiling was being cleaned.

63. Boys and girls were dressed alike, in gowns, until the boys were five or six. They were then "breeched" and dressed like men in pants, shirt, and jacket.

2   Morn: at Work. My maid at Mames, washing my baby linen, afternoon at mames

3   Morn: our wash, Hannah Harris and Eliza Wilkison are at meeting this morn, tis thought they will take shiping to Morrow, in the Vessel goes Will: Allen and his Daughters. afternoon at Daddys, Sally Smith, Unkle Roberts daughter, come from burlington

4   Morn: Becky Rawle and Caty & Sally Smith come and pinned up my beds, and placed the things in the drawers, afternoon a Visit from Hetty Franklin, Nancy and Debby Mitchel, Polly Rhoads, the latter sets out for Virginia to morrow with Sammy & Polly Pleasants and David Potts.

5   Morn: busy, afternoon 4 OClock went to Daddys, found him worse than Usual, thus art thou chequered O' Life, evening my Neigh: Benny, Polly, and Sally Maul, I had a most beautiful crop of double Hyacynths from Richmond, the Labour of my poor Fathers Hands!

6   Day: at Mames, Daddy very Ill,

7   Day: at Daddys, who is very Ill, but patiently waiting for the Conclusion of tedious Winter,

[May 1, 1763]

1 Day   Morn: Half past Eight O'Clock, died my Father William Callender! in the Sixtyeth Year of his Age, ie 59 the 7 of last November, he had a quiet passage from time to Eternity, in the Presence of his Afflicted Widow, Daughter, & Son. his Friends Sarah Sansom, Ann Warner, and my good Cousins Caty & Sally. He filled many Stations in Life with Reputation, and was my father whom I loved, whose memory will be ever Sacred: His latter years, where more particularly cloathed with Mortality, being in a bad state of Health for some years.

2   Day. my dear father desired to Lye quietly with my Ancestors in the Grave Yard at Burlington, and at 2 O'Clock as my friends thought it not safe for me to go, I took an everlasting leave of my poor fathers Body: he was Accompanyed in the boat by Mame, Ann Warner, Mary Armitt, Sarah Zane, Betty Morris, Caty Howel, Polly Sweet, Father Sansom, Will Fisher, Sam: Noble, Joshua Howel, Abraham Carlisle, Abel James, and Tommy Lightfoot, they had a good passage, received with afflicted love at Unkle Daniel Smiths,

3   Day morn: 5 OClock Sammy Sansom went to Burlington, my small family & I come to my poor fathers house, at 10 O'Clock the Corps was carried to meeting, accompanied by numbers, upwards of 50 reputable Citizens from Philadelphia besides the Adjacent Country. Betty Smith and Betty Morris spoke, partly on the same subject: He that believeth and is Baptized shall be Saved. he was carried to the Grave by Israel Pemberton, Abel James, Tommy Prior, and John Hoskins, Sammy

Sansom returned at Night, with many more, Joshua, Caty, Becky, and Benny Sweet were hear.

⟨⟩

[This supplemental material about William Callender's death was preserved in the diary written on the back of a letter to John Smith. Also included was the obituary. HCS or a later descendant may have tucked them into the pages at this place.]

⟨⟩

Persons who came from Philadelphia to Attend the funeral of Willam Callender who was Buried at Burlington the 3^d. of the 5 mo 1763—————

Anthony Morris
John Reynell
Doc.^r Moore
Reese Meredith
W.^m. Fisher
Israel Pemberton
Thos Lightfoot
Samuel Noble
Samuel Sansom
Abel James   &
Samuel Shoemaker
Edw.d Pennington
Capt. Dowell
Jos: Redman
Judah Foulke
Jam^s. Bringhurst
Joseph Warner
John Parrock
Henry Drinker
Benjamin Swett
Abraham Carlisle
Thomas Wharton jun^r   &
Charles West
Joseph Smith
Joseph Morris
Isaac Greenleaf
Thomas Shoemaker
Peter Barker

Samuel Robins
Cadwalader Evans
Rob.^rt Hopkins
James Kimsey
Joseph Fox
Edan Haddock
Thos Clifford
William Parr
Israel Cathrall
James Dikindry

Elizabeth Morris
Mary Armit
Ann Warner
Kath: Greenleaf
Kath: Howell
Mary Swett
Sarah Zane
Mary Sandwith
Sarah Drinker
Mary Foulke
Mary Haddock

⟨⟩

To cousin   Phila^d 4 m° 13th 1761
John Smith

John Ross Tells me you have Agreed for his place in Chesnut Street and that Thou art Like to be our Neighbour Again very Soon, I cannot Say I am Sorry for it nor that I am Glad of it in Regard to Poor Burlington. however I Think Thou hast Given money Enough for it and I hope it will make thee a Pleasant Seat. I Think it will be best to Advertise Poles Lot in Burlington for a public Sale that we may Get Rid of it for the Advantage of the Children and Shall I Leave the Manner of Advertising it to thy self & Edward whether in the public paper or Printed or writen only to be Set up in Burlington &c. this matter will Require Expedition and Shall Depend on your Care————— we Through Mercy are pritty well and with much Love to Self, Wife, &^c and all Friends—————am thy To cousin

                                         Wm Callender^64

⚬

On the first Instant departed this Life William Callender in the 60th: Year of his Age. During his Illness which was long & lingering he was patient beyond Expectation, earnestly desiring to be resigned to the divine Disposal either in Life or Death. He was a Man remarkably affable in his Disposition [and] agreeable in his Coversation: firm in his Opinion Respecting Matters of Religion yet charitable to all of different Societys. He serv'd several Years in the House of Assembly, & was justly reputed an upright Member who had the true Interests of his Country at Heart. His Family now regret the Loss of a loving Husband, an affectionate Father & kind Master: and his intimate Acquaintance will sensibly know that a former good and sociable Friend is now no more.

                                         Philad:^a May 3. 1763—^65

[Return to diary]

⚬

4   Morn: my family & I removed to Daddys! afternoon 3 O'Clock Mame
           returned with Mary Armitt, Ann Warner, Molly Foulk, Patty Noble,
           Tommy Lightfoot, and Sammy Noble.
5   Day: at Mames, a Melancholy one, Mame Sansom and Neigh: Warner
           there.
6   Day: as the former, may our afflictions work together for good, may
           they be sanctified unto us, my scene of life is now changed, former con-
           nections, alass, it has pleased god to dissolve on Earth, Just at the In-

64. In the hand of George Vaux: "My great-great grandfather. Father of my great grandmother Hannah Sansom and husband of Katharine Callender." The envelope for this letter is addressed to "John Smith Jnr. Burlington" and written on the side is "4 mo 13. 1761. W Callender."
65. In the hand of George Vaux: "Written by Samuel Sansom Son-in law of W. Callender."

trem when I may be like to feel the pangs of a Parent! Rotation shall not cease till man arrives at home.

7 Day: as the Past, they are not as blanks, but ever to be remembered as the feasts of Affliction. there being Joy even in Sorrow, let each day work out its own Salvation[66] and we land at last with those who are gone before.

1 Day Morn: the Aniversary of a week, Oh time quick in thy Elapse, momentary in thy duration. I went to mames, dined at home, Solitary afternoon with Sammy, Father Sansom, and Molly Foulk. Jemmy and Anna Bringhurst hear,

2 Day: Washing: Benny Sweet & Sally Nicolson drank tea with us,

3 Day: in the married State, you shall know trouble if you have been strangers to it before. Thus, O child of man, place not thy affections on things below,[67] he that maketh unto himself a Downy bed may find there in disappointment. reconsile thy self to mortality. bear the lot of thy humanity with becomeing Patience. this day twelve months, my Parents moved so near there old dwelling! but now one is removed to a more lasting final home, without duration, even to Illimitable space with Joy beyond conception there to reep the benefitt of a well spent Life. Neigh Warner & Nancy suped with us.

4 Morn: a cloud which sat upon mine Understanding removed in part, for all things will I bless thee Oh my Heavenly Father. support me even as thou hast done, in all future tryals. went to Mames. drank tea at home, Josey Smith suped with us.

5 Morn: Melancholy, my mame Poorly, afternoon Sammy & I went to Richmond, come home laden with flowers. Jemmy & Anna Bringhurst, with the child John, paid us visit.

6 Day. Aunt Betty and Danny come from Burlington, afternoon Sammy & I at Mames, Aunt Armitt, Lydia Noble, and Patty there. Danny & Josey Smith suped with us.

7 Morn: Danny breakfasted with us. Mame, Aunt Danny & Sammy went to Richmond. this day I experienced a short lived Joy, afternoon Sammy not well.

1 Day Day at home, several hear at different parts of the day. a couple of hours at mames,

2[68]. afternoon Becky Rawle, John Smith, and Benny Sweet. evening Mame Sansom and John Drinker.

66. Philippians 2:12.
67. From Colossians 3:4.
68. Line and a half erased: "Morn: the Keav?"

3   Morn: worked at my Cushin, Solitary: afternoon at Mames, Neigh: Warner and Nancy, Old Anthony Morris with his Mother Eliza: Morris, Sally and Debby Morris were there, 4 O'Clock Nancy Gibson come to see me

4   Morn: at Work, Sammy & I at Mames, afternoon Joshua, Caty, & little Caty Howel, evening Sammy and I spent together.

5   Morn: Mame Sansom and Becky Rawle, my 2 mothers and mine walked to Richmond, afternoon Betsey Warner and Sally Lightfoot hear,

6   Morn: at Mames. afternoon Benny & Polly Sweet, Sally Maul, and Caty Smiths. an evening of deep thought, Lord enable me to support all things as they come.

7   Morn: at Mames, afternoon my poor dear Mother & Caty come hear.

1 Day   at home, Sammy with me [the] cheif part [of the time,] we read in Watts.

2   Morn: washing, afternoon Rachel Drinker hear, evening at Mames Sansoms

3   Morn: Ironing, visit from Mame, Joshua, Caty, Becky, & Aunt Fisher set out for York and flushing, afternoon Mame Sansom, Aunt Bell, Nancy Mitchel, & Caty.

4   Morn: very poorly, afternoon better. My 2 Mothers and Neigh: Warner hear, mame and Caty Lodged hear.

5   Morn: at Work on my cushin. afternoon Nancy Warner and Caty Smith.

6   Morn: at Work on my cushin. Mame Sansom hear, afternoon Neigh Warner and the children, Anna Bringhurst, and Nurse Peggy Gregory, who is to Nurse me.

7   Morn: at Work, afternoon Mame and Tommy Lightfoot hear.

1 Day   at Home, Billy Rawle drank tea with us, the dear little representative of his Father, evening Daddy & Mame Sansom, and Caty Smith.

2   Morn: I went to Mames, afternoon Nancy Warner, Caty Smith, and Polly Lighfoot. evening sober thought creept in upon my Soul, the Stars were wittness of my Solitary scene, I gave a loose to grief as one placed in State of probation. Poor woman let thy Happiness take its rise in Resignation. for thou will never wittness it otherways. note I finished my cushin, Jemmy Mears went for Barbados.

3   Morn: began a pincushin for mame, afternoon finished it. Caty Smith hear,

[June 1, 1763]

6 Mos 4   Morn: unwell,[69] began a needle book back, mame hear, afternoon mame hear.

᷂

[January 1, 1768][70]

mos 6   Morn: as I seem now in a good state of health I have a mind to continue this Memorandum a nother year, since the day mentioned above, it has pleased god to bless me with three children, William, Sarah, and Joseph, my daughter, if she lives, it may be will look in this with some pleasure, as I hope to be a humble Instrument in fixing her mind to the path of Virtue. one generation presseth the steps of another, yet a little while and a perseverance in Virtue shall fitt us for the company of angels and glorified Spirits, My dear Mother lives at Burlington with Unkle Daniel Smith, my servants Eliza Montgomery, Polly shingleton, and George Shoft. afternoon: Nurse dined hear and the child Josey, he is ten months old,[71] Molly Hoskins hear, borrowed 2 Vol: of Clarissa, books that shoud be read by all young women, for the excellent precepts that are interspersed about them.

evening at Mame Sansoms, John Drinker there,

7   Morn: cut out 8 Lawn caps, afternoon my Son Billy and I took a long walk beyond the Barracks, viewed the Soldiery, drank tea with Polly Parrock, even: at mame's

1 Day   Morn: at meeting, Dan: Stanton gave us a good Sermon, Ben: Trotter spoke, heard from my mother, afternoon reading in Young

---

69. That is, she has begun to go into labor.

70. James or Jemmy Pemberton (1723–1809) will be a source of scandal and heartbreak in the coming year. In the late 1760s he was a widower, but with a reputation as a ladies man. In 1760, his brother was so concerned about his behavior that he wrote a letter to John Smith asking for assistance. James, he wrote, "was gone with some young Women into the Countrey . . . tell him thy mind Respectg the Dangerous Consequence that may attend his behavior at all times to Young Women that they may not form any Just occasion to Expect he has Intentions of Marriage when he really had none" (William Logan to John Smith, 1 mo., 23, 1760, John Smith Correspondence, HSP). In a letter dated Philada, 5 mo. 11 1767, Jemmy wrote John Smith concerning his intention to marry HCS's cousin, Sally Smith, daughter of John's brother Daniel, "Loving Kinsman, my early departure from Burlingtron the morning of my last return, prevented my seeing thee, or I should have taken an opportunity *inter nos* (as Elias terms it)[Latin for "between us."] to have given thee some account of the circumstance of the affair which has been depending with Sally, . . . on my part, I hope on all occasions to demonstrate by word & conduct a just esteem for her merit, the principal cause wch has preduced this determination being the effect of the most tender sensibility of affection & duty must ever speak in her praise. . . . I confide in thy prudence in respt to what I have now mentioned concerning myself" (John Smith Correspondence, HSP). The language reflects a rather lukewarm courtship.

71. HCS's infant son lives at the house of his wetnurse, a common practice.

The smothest course of nature has its Pains;
And truest friends, thro' error wound our rest.[72]

drank tea at mame Sansoms, John and Rachel Drinker there, evening Samy reading

2　　Morn: bound a pair of black cotton velvet shoes for myself, afternoon Neigh Footman and I went to Rachel Drinkers, Polly Parrock and Hannah Thompson there, evening at Mame Sansoms,

3　　Morn: at meeting BT:, DS:, and John Hunt spoke, went to see Josey, afternoon at Mame Sansoms, Daddy [Sansom] is very poorly,

4　　Morn: finished my third cap, afternoon Neigh: Footman and I spent agreably with Neigh: Carney. she is a fine woman possessed of true female Complacency, which Joined to an agreable person must always have charms to a bystander, evening at Daddys.

5　　Day Ironing, afternoon Polly Parrock hear, evening at Mame's and to see my son who is a dear fine boy

6　　Morn: mending, Neigh Warner hear, discourse on circumstances very disagreable concerning Jemmy[73]　　afternoon visit to Han: Smith, she and I stept into Sally Rhoades she lays in with a girl. even: at Mames, Docter Evans there,

7　　Morn: at Work Neigh Scattergood hear, afternoon at Caty Howels, and evening also in agreable conversation, the food of the mind. received a letter from[74]　　Smith confirming the report of Jemmy[75]　　's Courtship to Sally Smith being finished.

[In margin: "clogs heal taped."]

1 Day　　Morn: at meeting BT:, Hezekiah Williams, and Sally Morris spoke, afternoon My Son to see me, evening very agreable reading,

2　　Morn: at Work, Sammy Pleasents, who says the report is a mistake, After diner I went down to Patty James Just come from Burlington, and as she cannot say of a certainty, I have consented to go with Sammy Pleasents to John Pemberton's where the candid treatment I met with has partly reconciled me to Jemmy Pemberton,

3　　Morn: at meeting Betty Morris and John Hunt spoke, Mary and Nancy Pemberton made me a visit, afternoon Sally Parish and Nancy Mitchel very agreable. evening I went to Joice Benezet's who confirming me in my Sentiments of the affair. I come home and wrote my mind to Sally Smith,

---

72. Young, *The Complaint* (1749), 14.
73. Erased word: "Pt," meaning "Pemberton."
74. Erased word ending in "y" possibly "Sukey."
75. Erased word: "Pbt," meaning "Pemberton."

4   Morn: Sammy Sansom went to Burlington with my letter, Sammy Pleasents hear, afternoon Becky and Sally Shoemaker hear, evening at Mames

5   Morn: read a novel called Henrietta,[76] afternoon at Work, Sammy returned. things carry so intricate a face, one cannot fathom them, if Jemmy Pemberton has made dupes of us, H Loydd has made a greater of him.[77]

6   Morn: Cut out 7 Shirts for my Son Joe, afternoon Neigh Kearney and I drank tea with Neigh: Riche, Bob: Feild and his Wife there. evening at Joshua Howels, Sammy Shoemaker there, an agreable man, that my friend becky Rawle has chosen for a partner,

7   Morn: finished the 3rd shirt, afternoon and evening at Mame's, Rich: Blackham there, finished my 4th Shirt and Cap.

1 Day Morn: at meeting, BT: and DS: spoke, afternoon at meeting BT: spoke, drank Tea at Joice Benezets, talk concerning Jemmy Pemberton, evening reading

2   Morn: John Pemberton hear, I went to see my Nurse and child, noon John Pemberton hear, going to send a messenger with a letter from Jemmy to Sally. Neigh: Warner, Anna Bringhurst, and I at Sally Rhoades, the rest of the company were the Wives of the three Docters: Cadwalader, Bond, and Redman, Judy M'Call, Polly Lewes, Sukey Wharton, Polly Donalson, and Franky Griffits, evening at Work,

3   Morn: at Work, stept [to] Caty Howels. Poor Nurse Peggy Gregory there, deprived of her reason, well may Massinisa[78] say

> all deaths all tortures in one pang combin'd
> Are gentle to the tempest of the mind.[79]

Sally Lightfoot dined hear, Lancelot Cooper, a Bristol Gentleman, brought a letter hear, that was inclosed to him from George Watson of Bristol to Jemmy Dinwoody who was apprentice to Sammy Sansom, and left us last November. Neighbour Warner & I drank tea with Becky Waln who Lys in with her tenth child. evening at Mame Sansoms.

76. Charlotte Ramsay Lennox, *Henrietta. A Novel* (1758).

77. Probably Hannah Lloyd, the mother of Jemmy Pemberton's first wife. The same day, John Pemberton wrote to John Smith, "I am sorry for the Infatuation & Stupid blindness of my Poor Brother in being directed by the most mischievous woman I know." John Smith Correspondence (nineteenth-century transcriptions), Historical Society of Pennsylvania, 262.

78. Masinissa, King of Numidia, ally of the Romans against Carthage.

79. James Thomson, *The Tragedy of Sophonisba* (London, 1730), 14. In this play, the character Masinissa recites those lines.

[In margin: "pair of shoes heal taped."]

4	Morn: John Pemberton hear. I wrote to Sally, went to Joice Benezets, inshort this is a dull day to me, noon Sammy Pleasents hear, I have Copied Watsons letter because I think it contains good advise to young persons
5	Morn: at Work, afternoon Polly Pleasents and I spent with Becky Shoemaker, evening reading
6	Morn: at Work; John Pemberton hear, afternoon Polly Hunt an agreable woman. evening Sam:[l] Pleasents
7	Morn: at Work: 11 OClock took a round to visit the Sick, after dinner Sammy Pleasents come hear and informed me [that] Isarel, James & John Pemberton were gone up to Solicit Sally Smith. Caty Howel & I drank tea with Becky Jones and Hannah Cathrel, Polly Coates there, evening at mame Sansoms.
1 Day	Morn: Meditation I went to meeting Heze: Williams spoke,[80] Nurse Harrison (who nursed me with Josey) and Nancy Pole drank tea hear,————————[81]
2	Ironing, Meloncholy passed this day. I drank tea att Mame Sansoms, had a note from John Pemberton on their return from Burlington.
3	Morn: my mind returning to a Composure, John Pemberton hear, Sally has consented [that] the match shall come on again, we went to meeting Mary Emblen spoke, Israel Holowal & Polly Webb were married, Israel Pemberton, Sam: Pleasents, Becky Shoemaker, and Nelly Footman hear, afternoon Neigh: Carney, Nelly Footman and I spent with Neigh: Harrison, Polly Harrison is an agreable Girl: Religious disputes too often sour conversation, evening at Mames.

[In margin: "pair of Sally shoes soaled."]

4	Morn: at Work. Lancelot Cooper hear, finished my 5th cap & shirt, afternoon Neigh: Horner, and Anna Bringhurst spent with me, evening at Mames.
5	Day: made my Sally a bonnet, Joe and his Nurse hear, John Drinker drank tea with us, a sensible good sort of man. evening finshed [the] 6th shirt
6	Day: my maid Eliza & I began to make 4 bonnets, John Pemberton hear, Jemmy spoke for a marriage Certificate at meeting to day, and

---

80. A line and a half erased.
81. Three quarters of this line erased. Possible section of line: "I would explain."

they are to pass Burlington meeting on 2 day, Neigh: Carney & I drank tea with mame Sansom. evening running visit's to J Drinkers, Neigh: Warners, and Jos: Howels,

7   Day work on the bonnets, wrote to mame, Neigh: Scattergood hear.

1 Day   Morn: went to meeting, Joe & his nurse nurse dined hear, afternoon at meeting William Brown and John Hunt spoke, Lydia & Hannah Noble drank tea with me, evening at meeting Betty & Sally Morris spoke,

[February 1, 1768]

[2]Mo 2   Morn: finished the Bonnets, 11 O'Clock went to Quarterly meeting John Hunt and DS: spoke, after the meetings parted, John Hunt and Dan: Stanton to accompany him come into our meeting, when John spoke in a Salutary and agreable manner on the Beauty of Bretheren liveing in Unity, whence all the christian Virtues flow, if yea[82] love me yea will love one another, neither Slandering nor evil surmiseing, but watching for good. afternoon I drank tea with the Widow Edwards, Hannah Tongue & Nanny Wisher there. even: at Mames

3   Morn: Becky Shoemaker & I went to meeting, John Hunt and DS: spoke. I drank tea with Sukey Smith, evening a letter from mame, informing Jemmy & Sally passed the monthly meeting yesterday, the day 9 months they were to have passed last year, evening at Mame Sansoms,

4   Morn: altered my brown russel coat, afternoon very agreable at home, with Henry & Betsey Drinker and Polly Sandwith, evening at Mamme Sansoms,

[In margin: "pair of shoes for George."]

5   Morn: Starching cloathes, afternoon at Caty Howels, finished the 6th Cap & Shirt,

6   Morn Ironing, afternoon Caty Howel & I drank tea with Nelly Footman met with a book entitled memoirs of the Ladys of Great Brittain,[83] but in fact a Jumble of religion and romance, a shame to its Author, and hurt to mankind. pertinent was the speach of a noble Earl to Lord Bolinbroke upon his writeings "do not take away from us, my lord, what we have got, unless you give us something in the room of it"

7   Morn: at Work, afternoon at Mame Sansoms, John & Rachel Drinker there, Charles West, discourse on the frequent [financial] failures of men in our society, observed with concern, evening Sammy & I went

---

82. "Ye" is a poetic form of thee, thou, or you.

83. Thomas Amory, *Memoirs of Several Ladies of Great Britain. Interspersed with Literary Reflections* (1755).

to John Drinkers, a book talked of intitled the Fool of Quality,[84] a valuable tract, and very fit for young minds.

1 Day	Morn: at Meeting, Nurse and the child dined with us, servants went to meeting & the rest of the day and evening with my children, very agreably,
2	Morn: at Work, afternoon Neigh Carney and I at Neigh Gilberts, evening at Work. finished the Caps and Shirts.

[In margin: "George a pair of shoes mended."]

3	Morn: at Meeting Daniel Stanton gave us an excelent Sermon on the Benefit of meeting together, for religious Worship, and the Power of recollection, when separated from the Hurries of Life, then think yea for yourselves and for your children. Israel & John Pemberton hear, afternoon Caty Smith & Polly Lightfoot from Burlington, my maid & [I] began 2 frocks for Joe, finished one,
4	Morn: Caty & I at shops, short visites to mame Sansom, Neigh Warner, and Shoemaker & Howel.
5	Day: Caty & I at shops, short Visit to Joice Benezet and Polly Pleasents, evening Sammy & Polly Pleasents, Sally Lightfoot, Caty Smith, and ourselves speant a most agreably in friendly Converse, Susey Wright mentioned, an extraordinary Genious, the Author of Anna bullens Letter: to King: Henry 8th in verse
6	Day at Shops, Caty & I drank tea with Mame Sansom, evening we suped at Neigh Warners in Company with Israel & Polly Holoway,
7	Day we bought Sally a dark Sattin gown, with all the numerous &c belonging to Matrimony, Taby Fisher & we drank tea with Polly Holoway,
1 Day	Morn: Caty & Polly set out for Burlington, I went to meeting H: Williams spoke. noon:

By condescension, as thy glory great,
Enshrin'd in man! of human hearts, if pure,
Divine inhabitent! the tie divine
Of heaven with distant earth! by whom I trust,
If not inspired, unsensur'd this address
To thee, to them, to whom? Mysterious power
Reveal'd, yet unreveal'd! darkness in light.

Number in unity! our joy! our dread!
The triple bolt that lays all wrong in ruin!

---

84. Henry Brooke, *The Fool of Quality; or, the History of Henry Earl of Moreland* (1766–69).

That animates all Bright, the triple Sun!
Sun of the Soul, her never setting Sun!

Triune, unutterable, unconconceiv'd,
Absconding, yet demonstrable, Great God!
Young's Night thoughts page: 229[85]

	4 O'Clock paid a visit to Betsey Head she lays in, the Company were Becky Sattergood, Molly Warder, Lydia Parker, ———————— Tucknis, & myself, evening Sammy read in young
2	Day, ripped up my brown Paduasoy & blue ducape, Polly Sweet hear, Rachel Drinker & I drank tea at Mame Sansoms, John Drinker has a pretty poetic vein. Letter from Danny, the Girls got up safe.
3	Morn: runing visits to Joice Benezet & Hannah Pemberton, Sam: Pleasents hear. discourse on many disagreable circumstances in the family. Nurse brought Joe home and is to leave him hear, afternoon at three OClock Betsey Drinker & I went to the funeral of Young Charles Brogden, a poor young man fallen a wreck to the folly of his Parents; Letters arrived from Bristol to our unthinking Jem Dinwoody,
4	Morn: bordered a cap for Joe, afternoon Neigh.ˢ Gilbert & Montgomery[86] drank tea with me, chatty agreable women
5	Morn: runing visit to Joice Benzet & Polly Peasents, afternoon my son Joe and I drank tea with mame Sansom. evening made Joe a pair of stockings.
6	Day at Work
7	Day at Work, Neigh: Warner hear, I wrote to Caty Smith,
1 Day	at Home all day, reading and tending Joe, Daddy & Mame drank tea hear
2	Morn: Mantua makeing, with a young woman I hired, one Polly Dolby,

[In margin: "billys shoes mended."]

3	Day: the same, evening Mame Sansom and Neigh Carney,
4	Day: we finished having new done up my blue ducape, brown paduasoy, part of my blue grazet, turned a gown for Polly, made a frock for Sally, evening Becky Shoemaker, read Langhorns, Effusions of Fancy and friendship

85. Young, *The Complaint*. It is unclear which edition HCS referenced, although one London edition of 1749 has this passage on page 230.

86. Probably the mother of HCS's servant Eliza Montgomery.

5   Morn: began 2 frocks for Joe, afternoon went to see Grace Allison, met
           with Sukey Perviance there, an agreable afternoon, evening at Work,
6   Day at Work, evening at Caty Howels, Sammy & Becky Shoemaker.

[In margin: "Polly a pair of shoes."]

7   Day finished the frocks, drank tea with Caty Howel, Nancy Warner
           there,

1 Day   Morn: at home, reading in Miltons Poems. Comus page:201[87]

*Is this the confidence
You gave me, Brother? Answer, Yes, and
    keep it still,
Lean on it safely; not a period
Shall be unsaid for me: against the threats
Of malice or of Sorcery, or that power
Which erring men call chance, this I hold
    firm,
Virtue may be assail'd, but never hurt,
Surprised by unjust force but not enthrall'd;
Yea even that which mischeif ment most
    harm*

*Shall in the happy tryal prove most Glory:
But evil on itself shall back recoil,
And mix no more with goodness, when at
    last
Gatherd like scum, and setled to itself,
It shall be in eternal restless change
Self fed, and self consumed! if this fail,
The piller'd firmament is rottenness
And Earth's base built on stubble.*

           afternoon at meeting George Dylvin spoke, drank tea with mame San-
           som, evening at meeting Sally Morris and Dan: Stanton spoke.
2   Day made myself a bonnet out of the tail of my Paduasoy suit, the sec-
           ond I have made of it.

[March 1, 1768]

3 Mos 3   Morn: at Work, afternoon Betty & Hannah Rhoades drank tea with
           me. discourse on this mysterious affair of JP whom I have not seen yet.

[In margin: "billy a pair of shoes."]

4   Morn: altered my white pelong quilt, afternoon Mame Sansom & I
           at Neigh Warners, Nancy Warner, Taby Fisher, & I went to Rachel
           Drinker's to see the Funeral Prosession of Thomas Lawrence's Widow,
           evening Letters from Sally & Caty,
5   Morn: Caty Howel delivered of a Son, named Edward, at Meeting
           William Hunt a friend from Carolina spoke, afternoon on a visit to

87. John Milton, *Comus* (1634). It is unclear from HCS's pagination which edition she referenced.

Sally Marshall. began a queen stitch thread case, evening Sammy & I
at Sam: Pleasents, discourse on the family differences, which run so
high it looks likely to me we shall be separated from JP

6   Morn: at Work, afternoon on a visit to Becky Carmalt, Anna Bring-
       hurst, Hetty Deshler, and Nancy Pole there, evening at Becky Jones's

7   Morn at Work, lengthend a lawn apron for it is now the custom to wear
       the cloaths long. afternoon Daddy & Mame hear, evening at Caty How-
       els

1 Day Morn: at meeting, afternoon at home, John & Rachel Drinker drank
       tea. with, Peggy Gadis hear, John staid the evening with Sammy.

2   Morn: starching, afternoon Jemmy & Anna Bringhurst, and Becky
       Scattergood

3   Morn: busy in my family, Sally Lighfoot dined hear, afternoon Neigh:
       Warner and Sammy & Becky Shoemaker, evening John Pemberton
       called hear from Burlington. Jemmy & Sally are to be married this day
       2 weeks,

4   Morn: mending Stockings, afternoon Jemmy & Anna Bringhurst, &
       myself took a walk to the House of Employment, we follow our
       mother country who is Justly renowned for her Charitys of every
       kind.[88]

5   Day: Ironing, Josey Smith drank tea with us, he brought me a letter
       from Sally

6   Morn: visiting the Sick, afternoon at Daddy Sansom's

7   Morn: at Polly Pleasents, spoke to Molly Newport as a cook for Sally
       Smith. afternoon at the funeral of Docter Evans Wife Jenny, a sensible
       good sort of woman. drank tea with Anthony and Joice Benezet

1 Day Morn: at meeting Becky Jones and Hezikiah Williams spoke, after-
       noon at home writeing, John Sleeper and Isral Pemberton drank tea
       with us, that family excepting the offender himself, have behaved with
       so much kindness and respect to our family that I shall always esteem
       them. evening at meeting John Hunt spoke.

2   Morn: ristbanded 2 shirts, afternoon Molly Footman and I spent with
       Friend Coleman, Neigh: Warner and the Girls

3   Morn: at meeting, John Hunt spoke, afternoon Polly Pleasents & I at
       John Pembertons

---

88. The House of Employment opened on October 16, 1767. It was supported by tax dollars but run
by a private corporation that hoped to be financially self-sufficient by requiring able-bodied paupers to
support themselves. "Although based on an English model, the contributorship system signaled a bold, in-
novative attempt to support greater Philadelphia's poor at a reasonable cost. But the new system mal-
functioned almost from the start." John K. Alexander, *Render Them Submissive: Responses to Poverty in
Philadelphia, 1760–1800* (Amherst: University of Massachusetts Press, 1980), 90.

[In margin: "Shoemakers account paid."]

4	Morn: fitting Molly Newport off to burlington. Lancelot Cooper took leave of us, for Bristol in old england, cut 3 pair of stockings for the children, out of their fathers old ones, afternoon at Mame Sansoms,
5	Day: busy in the family, evening Jemmy Pemberton sent us a written notice of the wedding on third day next,
6	Day Ironing, Sammy & Polly Pleasents drank tea hear, Neigh Carney & John Pemberton hear, Jemmy has invited Caty & Sally but none else to the weding,
7	Day setting my house in order for a voyage to burlington,

1 Day   Morn: Myself and son Billy, with Polly Shingleton set off in the Stage boat, where we met with a kind reception. and on third day James Pemberton & Sarah Smith Were married, I continued at Burlington till the 4 of April when Sammy Sansom, Jemmy Pemberton, my son & I returned to Philadelphia in Jemmy's Carriage. (Billy Dylvin and Sally Smith passed the burlington meeting that day)

[April 5, 1768]

5 4 Mo   Morn: put Billy & Sally to school to Betty Greanway, Sammy Pleasents
  5th 3   hear, afternoon at Mame Sansoms She is poorly, evening Sammy & I spent at Joshua Howels, in company with Neigh Warner very agreably.

4   Morn: busy in the family, my maid returned from burlington, afternoon at home 3 O Clock stept to John Pembertons, Israel & Jemmy, Han: Logan & Sam: Pleasents there

5   Day: washing, busy in the family, Anthony Benezet drank tea hear.

6   Morn: Ironing: afternoon at Mame Sansoms, Rich: Blackham & his wife there. evening Polly Pleasents hear, we had a serious conversation.

7   Morn: at Work, afternoon my Sally & I went to see Polly Parrock,

1 Day   Morn: at meeting, afternoon Rachel Drinker and Neigh: Gilbert hear, evening I spent with Joice Benezet,

2   Morn Ironing, afternoon on a visit to Neigh: Hunt, the company Molly Foulk ————— Douffel, ————— Simms ————— & Young. Polly Parrock spent the evening with us.

[In margin: "Eliza & Polly's shoes mended."]

3   Morn: at meeting Sally Morris and Becky Jones spoke, afternoon Widow Mifflin, Sally Lewis, & Mame Sansom hear, evening visiting the distressed

| 4 | Morn: at Work. afternoon Richard & Betsey Waln drank tea with us. evening read the tragedy of Sir Walter Raleigh,[89] |
| 5 | Morn: Sammy Sansom unwell, he was bled, Neigh: Carney spent the afternoon with us very agreably. |

[In margin: "Josey a pair of shoes."]

| 6 | Morn: in the sorrows of mine own heart! Sammy Allison from burlington, he is a relation I esteem much, afternoon the greatest unhappiness of many proceeds from triffles, in themselves hardly worth a moments thought! |
| 7 | Morn: Sammy Allinson went home, afternoon I drank tea with H: Pemberton |

| 1 Day | Morn: Sammy Pleasents & Sammy Sansom went to Burlington. myself to meeting, afternoon at meeting John Hunt spoke, Caty Howel and Betsey Warner drank tea with me, evening at meeting John Hunt spoke |
| 2 | Morn: at Work, 11 O'Clock Sammy & his friend returned, and this evening James & Sarah Pemberton are to come home, afternoon at home, |

[In margin: "Sally a pair of shoes, & shoe mended."]

| 3 | Morn: I went to Polly Pleasents, from thence Joice Benezet & I went to Jemmy's. the company there was Sally Pemberton, Mame, Sally Smith, H Loydd, P Pleasents, S Rhoades, and Nancy Pemberton, afternoon Neigh Warner & I went to the funeral of Myme Edwards, a woman who left an amiable Character behind her! thence I went with Sally Lightfoot to see her Aunt Pemberton, Han: Moor and Sally Logan there, Sally Lightfoot lodged with us. |

[In margin: "Billy a pair of shoes & pair mended."]

| 4 | Morn: at Work, Sally Smith dined with us, and we drank tea at mame Sansoms, I went with her in the evening to Jemmy Pembertons, |
| 5 | Morn: Ironing, afternoon Sally Smith & I went to Han: Morris's, thence to Benjamin Sweets, evening Sally Pemberton come hear, she and I walked to her house, thence I went into John Pembertons & H: Catherel returned with me |

---

89. George Sewell, *The Tragedy of Sir Walter Raleigh. As It is Acted at the Theatre in Lincoln-Inn-Fields* (1719).

6   Morn: cut out 6 shirts for billy, afternoon a visit to Neigh: Carney &
            mame Sansom
7   Morn: at Work, an English Gentleman of the name Hyde dined with
            us, afternoon Neighbour Footman

1 Day   Morn: at meeting, afternoon at home, J: Drinker and Steven Collins
            drank tea with us, evening Neigh: Gilbert & I at Neigh: Carneys.
2   Morn: Mame & Sally Smith come and breakfasted with me, Mame & I
            went to mame Sansoms but dined at home, afternoon at Becky Shoe-
            makers, Polly Holloway, Nancy Warner, and Han: Shoemaker there,
            evening a chat with Polly Pleasents,
3   Morn: Mame very poorly I was with her at JP, afternoon Neigh: Saun-
            ders & her daughter Sally, and Sukey Hartshorn, evening Sally Smith
            and I at J Pembertons

[In margin: "Billys shoes soaled & healtaped."]

4   Morn: with mame, she is brave again, Sally Smith dined hear, we drank
            tea with Caty Howel, thence we went to Becky Shoemakers, Sally
            Pemberton come to us, we all suped at Sally Pembertons
5   Morn: at home. afternoon at Neigh Warners, with Sally Smith.
6   Morn: at Work, afternoon Sally Smith, Han: Clifford, & I at Josey
            Fox's, thence Sally & I went to JP's: [and] Sally P went with us to Rich:
            Smiths,
7   Morn: Danny Smith from B——n, afternoon Danny & Sally, George
            & Nancy Dylvin set out for B——n, thus Sally P—— has parted with
            one of her friends—and may it Please God to turn the heart of JP to
            the Just mans path

[May 1, 1768]

1 Day   Morn: at meeting Sally Morris spoke, afternoon at meeting a stranger
            spoke. Henry Drinker drank tea with us, evening at Han: Pemberton,
2   Morn: quarterly meeting I attended at the School house 4th street, John
            Hunt, Sally Morris, and Joice Benezet spoke, Mame, Becky Shoe-
            maker, & I come home together, mame dined with me, in the After-
            noon paid a visit to Sally Pemberton, the company was Betty Norris,
            Molly Norris, Han: Harrison, Neigh: Carney, Becky Shoemaker, Caty
            Howel, and Rache Drinker, mame lodged hear that night,
3   Morn: at meeting Mordeca Yarnal Sally Morris spoke, rest of the day
            at home as we are white washing the Kitchen,

[In margin: "Polly & George a pair of shoes Sally soaled."]

4	Day. Billy taken with a fever and soar mouth, Sally Pemberton hear
5	Day. with the poor boy
6	Day. he was a little on the mending hand, Caty Howel hear,
7	Day. Sally a little unwell—much as billy is handled,[90] at noon Cousin James & Sally with mame went to Burlington. Neigh Footman hear.

1 Day	at home Nurseing. read in Pamela,[91] Neigh Foulk hear
2	Day Nurseing. Josey Smith hear from Burlington, evening Caty Howel

[In margin: "Josey a pair of shoes."]

3	Morn: wrote to mame. rest of the day with the children: billy took a ride with his Granny, evening wrote to Caty Smith
4	Day. at home, children better evening stept to Caty Howels,
5	Morn Sammy, Sally & myself took an airing, afternoon Caty Howel & I at Becky Shoemakers, Benny Shoemaker is a sober well incleined youth, I have never felt a greater pleasure than at the sight of a young person, who seemed determined to go thro the world with credit, to his God, his Country, and his family something so solidly noble, in a good heart, it must encompass every beholder with an enchanting view of a happy hearafter!
6	Day. Sally took Physick. Neigh Warner drank tea hear, even: red in Sir Charles[92]
7	Morn: Polly Pleasents Abby Smith hear, afternoon Jemmy Pemberton and Billy Dylvin hear, Just going to set out for B——n. Billy is to be married on 5 day

1 Day	Morn: Sammy Pleasents & Sammy Sansom went to Abbington, I to meeting. Sally Lightfoot dined with me, afternoon we went to meeting, thence to mame's
2	Morn: at Work. Sally Pemberton come hear, they returned last night, afternoon Polly Parrock spent with me, and evening
3	Day Eliza & I put a quilt in the frame, for herself, evening stept to Becky Shoemakers, thence Betsey Warner and I took a walk
4	Day quilting
5	Morn: went to meeting: John Hunt spoke, finally Brethren no other foundation can any man lay save that which is all ready laid—add to your faith Virtue, Temperance, Brotherly kindness, and Charity. af-

90. That is, she and Billy have the same symptoms.
91. Samuel Richardson, *Pamela: or, Virtue Rewarded* (1742).
92. Samuel Richardson, *Sir Charles Grandison* (1754).

ternoon I met Sally Pemberton at Joice Benezets, evening at home very serious,

6   Day at home busy in my family the cares of life are also its comforts. what a dull scene woud it be if spent in Idleness!

7   Day Ironing, this day John Hunt sets off for England with Billy Logans 2 sons

1 Day   Morn: at meeting. afternoon at home. Sammy Pleasents drank tea with me, some serious converse, Men will not Sanctify affliction, but return to Indolence and Luke warmness than which no state is more displeasing in the Eye of Heaven, thou art neither one thing nor the other,

2   Day, cleaning the House, prepareing for white washing, drank tea at mame

3   Day, busy in the family white washing the first & second story, Sally Pem: hear

4   Morn: at Work, afternoon visit to Neigh: Footman, English Gentleman named Barron, they are a volitile People, evening Jemmy & Anna Bringhurst

5   Morn: at Work, afternoon finished the second of Billys shirts

6   Day. the fair began, and 'tis next to impossible for people who have young familys to keep from the noise of it. notwithstanding the wise man saith how many things are there hear which I dont want, Sally Pemberton Caty Howel & I drank tea with Neigh Warner,

7   Day. fair also, Israel Pemberton Sally Rhoades, & I in company with our Husbands drank tea, with Sammy & Polly Pleasents. even: at Sally Pembertons, H: Logan there

1 Day   Morn: at meeting, afternoon at meeting D Stanton spoke on the benefit of keeping our children from seeing of Evil, early impressions sometimes are erased, yet I believe an early care has saved souls from Perdition, Recollection has caught them, they have been snatched as brands from the fire! drank tea with Betsey Drinker, evening John & Rachel Drinker spent with us. a beautiful evening, the Lamp of Heaven shone Delightfully, spread its mild glorys o'er our lower World!

2   Morn: at Work, afternoon Neigh Warner, Caty Howel, Sally Pemberton, & I drank tea with Becky Scattergood, note I took my Sally with me & thou behaved prettily, my little dear, If this comes to thy hands, know thou hast had a Mothers early hope that thy feet might be stayed in the paths, of Virtue, and thy latter days, crowned with the blessing of the Highest, the humble partner of some worthy man.

[June 1, 1768]

3   Morn: Richard Vaux son of Docter Vaux of London come hear on tryal
         as an apprentice, Edward Penington has the care of him, Grace Fisher
         hear, aafternoon at home, evening wrote to Caty Smith

6 Mo 4   Day, at Work Josey Smith from B——n he is makeing a proposal to
         Sally Norris, evening agreable chat with J Howel S Shoemaker & their
         Spouses

5   Morn: Josey Smith hear, my son William cloathed in mans apparel on
         this day he enters his 5ᵗʰ Year! God grant his mind may be cloathed
         with innocency during Life!

Not too much Wealth nor Wit come n'er thee
Too much of either may undo thee[93]

         afternoon Daddy & Mame Sansom drank tea with us, Sally Pemberton
         hear

6   Day at Work,

7   Day Ironing, the Kings birth day, 30 years of age, Captain Hay's House
         hansomly illuminated, by small lamps,

1 Day   Morn: at meeting Becky Jones spoke, an English Gentleman named
         Baron dined with us, afternoon with the children, drank tea at mamme
         Sansoms,

2   Morn: at Work, afternoon Sally Pemberton & I at Mame Sansoms,

3   Morn: reding & blacking my chimneys, afternoon at Rachel Drinkers,
         quilting in company with Han: Elfrith, evening had some very serious
         moments,

4   Morn: finished 3ᵈ shirt for my son, Benny Sweet dined hear, afternoon
         at home

5   Morn: busy, afternoon Neigh Carney agreable Conversation

6   Morn: Lined a hat for Sally. afternoon at Polly Parrocks, toward
         evening Rachel Drinker. she & I took a walk, the City is most surpri-
         seingly inlarged since my memory,

7   Morn: altered my bonnet, drank tea with mamme Sansom. Sammy &
         I took a ride round Frankford, I set down many happy hours in the
         early part of my life passed there about, they live in memory!

1 Day   Morn: Billy & Sally went with us to meeting. now must we be engaged
         to form the Young Idea, with an early bent to good, favour us all gra-

---

93. Richard Corbet, "to his son Vincent Corbet," in *The Sixth Part of Miscellany Poems,* by John Dry-
den (London, 1727), 310.

cious power with Success, let them return to thee, as bread cast on the waters after many Days. afternoon at meeting Robert Willis spoke, Sally Pemberton, Becky Fisher, and Hannah Fox drank tea hear, letter from Caty Smith,

2   Morn: at Work, afternoon at Becky Shoemakers in company with Neigh Waln & Sukey, Neigh Warner & Betsey, and Sally Pemberton,

3   Morn: went to meeting Isaac Andrews, Martha Harris spoke, afternoon at home,

4   Morn: wrote to Caty, afternoon at Mame Sansoms, but drank tea at home

5   Morn: Ironing, afternoon my friend Caty Howel spent with us,

6   Day Polly Dolby & I mantua making, Polly Sweet from B——n. my unkle very poorly, Sally it seems is gone up.

7   Day finished mantua makeing,

1 Day   Morn: at meeting, afternoon at home, drank tea at mame Sansoms, with John & Rachel Drinker, Molly Foulk, we had an agreable walk in mames garden

to day 2   Morn: at Work, afternoon on a Visit to Fanny Rush, took a walk to Sammy Nobles

3   Morn: a letter from Caty Smith, went to meeting: George Dylvin, Daniel Stanton, and Eliza: Stevens spoke, afternoon Sammy & I took a ride to John Gibson's place, some hours very agreably with him and his Wife,

4   Morn: finished the 4th shirt, afternoon Rachel Drinker & I on a visit to Sally Fisher

5   Morn: at meeting D Stanton spoke, Polly Sweet dined hear with us, Betsey & Polly Flower Joined us in the afternoon, evening Sammy Allinson

6   Morn: at Work, afternoon on a visit to Peggy Glentworth, company Debby Penock and Betty Kemble, evening John & Rachel Drinker suped with us, and to morrow afternoon John & Rachel and Sammy & I are to set off for Chester, Concord & the Valley,

[July 4, 1768]

7 Mo 2   Returned on 2 day week following, having had a very agreable Tour, taking the Yellow Springs in our way, evening Polly Parrock hear,

3   Morn: at meeting Sally Morris spoke, afternoon finished billys 5 Shirt, Drank tea at Mame Sansom's. Rachel & Betsey Drinker there, evening at Neigh Carney's

> *"and yet believe me good as well as Ill*
> *Man is at best a contradiction still.*[94]

4   Morn: cut out some baby linen for Cousin Hannah Millhouse, wrote a letter of thanks to her for our kind treatment when there, on our late Journey, rest of the day at Work, there must be a degree of happiness when the mind is easey at home.

[In margin: "Billy a pair of Shoes."]

5   Morn: at meeting D S spoke, afternoon Neigh Warner and I spent with J Benezet. evening Caty & Joshua Howel.

[In margin: "Billy a pair of shoes."]

6   Morn: worked on the caps, afternoon Becky Shoemaker & I spent together, evening Nancy Warner and I took a walk, to view the Improvements of our City, it may be called a "City set upon a Hill" as the Good Docter Young says of our mother Country

> *A Land which from her seems to push the rest,*
> *A Land within herself compleatly blest.*[95]

7   Morn: finished Billys 6 Shirts, afternoon at home. Israel Pemberton hear,

[In margin: "billys shoes mended."]

1 Day   Morn: my Spouse, Billy, Sally, & self at meeting, Sally Morris spoke, excellently on the passage of Elisha strikeing the waters with the mantle of Eligah which had proved effectual, but for want of faith Elisha was obliged to call, "where is the Lord God of Eligah."[96] see ye not unless we seek, we shall not find.[97] afternoon at home, Sammy & Polly Pleasents hear. I love there company.

2   Day at Work spent agreably in my family. evening reading in Belisarious[98]

94. Alexander Pope, *Of the characters of women* (London, 1735), 14. The line is "woman's at best a contradiction still."

95. Although these lines could not be traced to Edward Young, they are quoted in *The Letters of Pliny the Younger* (London, 1752).

96. 2 Kings 2:14.

97. Proverbs 1:28.

98. William Philips, *Belisarius. A Tragedy* (1758), or Jean Francois Marmontel, *Belisarius* (1767).

to day 3	Morn: at meeting Theophilous Shove and D Stanton spoke, afternoon Mamme Sansom and I spent with Neigh Carney, many things which attend mankind [are] worse than Death,
4	Day Ironing
5	Day made my Son William a pair of breeches.
6	Morn: Sally Pemberton & Bobby Smith come hear from B———n Unkle poorly. afternoon at home. Daddy Sansom, Polly Harrison, and Peggy Gaddis hear,
7	Morn: mending Stockings, afternoon at Mame Sansom's

1 Day	Morn: 5 O'Clock Sammy Sansom, my dear little Sal and I set out for Burlington, 11 O'Clock arrived. found all well but Unkle & he better, afternoon at meeting[:] Samuel Notingham and George Dylvin spoke. Aunt Betty Smith and Sarah Decow drank tea with us at unkles.
2	Morn: put Sally to school. Sammy Went to Burdentown, afternoon Mame & I went Cousin Betty Smith's, found there John & Dicky Smith, Friend Worrel & Wife, and Sally Dylvin, even: Sammy returned
3	Day Sammy returned, Mame Caty & I at Danny Smiths
4	Day, Caty & I at Sammy Allinson, a very a greable walk round the point
5	Morn: at meeting, afternoon Caty Sally & I at Aunt Betty's
6	Day, spent at home with Mame & Unkle, till 5 O'Clock when Mame, Cousin Jenny, & I went to the Governors,[99] the company we found there Docter De Normandy, Mrs Tredway, Mis Hopkison, Mis Wright, and Lord Rosell a Strange Gentleman, Mrs Franklin is an affable woman, but my highest Pleasure, was in the pictures whole length of our Gracious King and Queen,
7	Morn: Sammy Sansom & my son Billy come up, afternoon Caty & I drank tea at R. Smith evening agreable walk

1 Day	Morn: at meeting Samuel Notingham spoke, we dined at unkles, afternoon at meeting, Sammy, Caty, and Tommy Guy & his Wife drank tea at Neigh Sweets
2	Morn: 6 O'Clock took leave of Mame, Unkle & the family. Sammy, the 2 children, and myself set out for Philadelphia, arrived about 11 O'Clock, to a pleasing home, afternoon at Mame Sansom's. 5 O'Clock Caty Smith & Sally Lightfoot arrived from Burlington, evening I went with Caty to Sally Pembertons where Caty Lodges
3	Morn: Caty Sally & I went to meeting, Sam: Notingham spoke finely on the subject bear & forbear, afternoon at home evening Caty & I at Neigh Warners
4	Morn: Nancy & Betsey Warner Caty & I went to Edgely. Joshua Howel

99. The royal governor of New Jersey was William Franklin, the son of Benjamin Franklin.

has a fine Iregular Garden there, walked down to Shoolkill, after diner we were Joined by Sammy, Benny & Becky Shoemaker, Sammy Sansom, and Sally Pemberton, walked to the Sumer House, in view of Skylkill when Benny Played on the flute.

[In margin: "Josey a pair of shoes."]

5   Morn: at meeting Sam: Notingham gave us an excellent Sermon, Lord thou knowest all things, thou knowest I love thee, drank tea with mame Sansom. 5 O'Clock, myself, Nancy & Betsey Warner, Sukey Waln, Taby Fisher, and Caty Smith, went to see a fine Peice of Wax work large as the Life. King Herod in a chair of state, when the Damsel danced before him so much to his satisfaction that he promises what she shall ask even to the one half of his kingdom, (he must have been in doatage), she instructed by her mother, Herods Brother's Widow whom he married, the Good man John the Baptist having freely told him of his Wicked life, the woman entertains a hatred for him and She thro her daughter asks for John the Baptist's head in a charger. He councels with his councellors two of whom are represented, much to the life. the one expressive of astonishment, silent Wonder the other, astonishment & Greif, a Musicianer & little Negro boy, 7 Persons, the Damsel is too unconcerned for nature considering what she has in her hand[100]

6   Morn: at meeting, afternoon at home, finshed the 4 Caps

7   Morn: at Work, afternoon also, evening an agreable walk with Caty

1 Day   Morn: at meeting, George Mason spoke, afternoon at meeting Sam: Notingham spoke, Nancy Pole drank tea with me, enjoyed myself an Hour alone

[August 1, 1768]

8 Mo 2 Morn: at Work. cut out 2 Jakets and 2 pair of trowsers for my son Billy, 11 OClock Becky Watson & I went to quarterly meeting, she & Caty Smith dined with me, then we went to Sally Pembertons, Company there Nancy & Betsey Warner, Anna Bringhurst, Nancy Pole, and Eliza Barker,

3   Morn: at the Youths meeting: D Stanton, Martha Harris, Sally Morris, and Sam: Notingham spoke, afternoon Hannah Pemberton, Caty Smith, & I spent with Nancy Pemberton, a sensible agreable woman,

---

100. Rachel Lovell Wells and her sister, Patience Lovell Wright, were sculptors in wax who toured with their work after both were widowed in 1769. Wells specialized in Biblical subjects, while Wright preferred contemporary portraits. The Women's Project of New Jersey, *Past and Promise: Lives of New Jersey Women* (Syracuse: Syracuse University Press, 1997), 38–39, 41–44.

4   Morn: at Work. afternoon Caty & I at Mame Sansom.

5   Morn: at meeting Sam: Notingham spoke, afternoon Nancy Pember-
         ton & I at Jemmy Pemberton's

6   Day at Work. Caty hear a pleasent family day,

7   Morn: at Work, afternoon Sammy Sansom & I took a ride to Jemmy
         Pemberton's place, company there he & his Wife, Sam: Notingham &
         his Wife, H Lloydd, and Betsey Bringhurst, the scene filled me with
         reflection, as it had belonged to a man whose memory is a blessing to
         his Country, a man who filled his station with honour, not one foot of
         his possesions remain to his children. so mutable are human possisions,
         flatter not thyself Oh writer or reader that thy Lands shall desend in
         thine own line, I am a witness as well as they of the changes a short
         space of time may bring about, but let us look for a home unchange-
         able, the grand desighn for which the sons of Adam Inherit this Globe:

1 Day   Morn: Caty Smith & I walked to the Hill meeting: Sam: Notingham
         spoke, Let your moderation appear before all men, circumscribe it not
         to eating, drinking, & wearing, but let all you posses & the tempers of
         your mind be to the Glory of the Highest. Betty Morris prayed, after-
         noon Neigh Carney & I at meeting: Sam: Notingham spoke, drank tea
         at Mame Sansom's [with] John & Rachel Drinker. even: at meeting,

2   Morn: at Work. wrote to Mame & Cousin Han: Millhouse, afternoon
         Caty Smith & I at Neigh Warners, evening Caty & I at home, in seri-
         ous converse the food of the Soul, when face answers face as in a glass

3   Morn: Ironing, afternoon Caty & I at Henry Drinkers. evening at home

4   Morn: Billy cut himself badly. Watts I think says somewhere "how
         many veins and arteries hang to a Lovers heart."[101] 10 O'Clock Benny
         & Sally Shoemaker, Nancy & Betsey Warner, and Caty Smith and I
         went to spend the day with Becky Shoemaker, at Skylkill, The house
         stands almost on the edge of the Hill with the River in the vale, as you
         ride up the lane the House which is surround by a fine woods, cleared,
         under the branches you see the Hills and vales, cots and inclosures, on
         the other side, when you arrive an agreable surprise to see the river,
         from the Parlour windows you see up Skylkill to Docter Smiths place
         & Redman's with the highlands beyond. afternoon Joshua & Caty and
         Sammy Sansom Joined us, we walked to the River. Benny played on
         the flute,

5   Morn: at Work. afternoon Caty & I at Rachel Drinkers, evening we
         took a walk thro' our increaseing City————

6   Day at home

---

101. Isaac Watts, *Horae Lyricae* (London, 1700), 231. "Strange is the Power, O' Love! What numerous
Veins, / And Arteries and Arms, and Hands, and Eyes, / Are link'd and fasten'd to a Lover's Heart."

7   Morn: Caty Smith & Dicky Vaux went to burlington, rest of the day at Work even: stept to see Neigh Gilbert,

1 Day   Morn: Sammy, myself, and the children went to meeting, afternoon at home. Daddy & Mame Sansom Neigh Carney hear,

2   Morn: Dicky returned. my mamme very poorly, rest of the day at home,

3   Day Ironing. evening stept to see rachel drinkers child sick of the flux

4   Morn: wrote to caty Smith, Eliza Montgomery went in the country for a week. afternoon Neigh Carney with her son, and Sammy, myself, & the children went to Egely, Peggy Gadis there

5   Morn: unwell, afternoon Molly Foulk and Daddy Sansom hear

6   Morn: at Work, afternoon at home unwell, H Drinker drank tea with us

7   Morn: at Work, afternoon Sammy, myself, and the children took an airing to Henry Drinkers place, at Francford. when we returned Sammy Shaw was there with a letter from Sammy Allison on Betsey's account who lies very Ill, it was then too late to set off but next Morn:

1 Day   Morn: 5 O'Clock Docter Evans & Sammy set out, I staid at home the day with my children, evening 9 O'Clock Docter Evans returned bringing word he thought Betsey coud not live over the night—if the lot of all men was not, to die[102] Death would be held sacred, I went to bed with a troubled mind

2   Morn: 5 O'Clock Sammy Shaw went home, 10 O'Clock Neigh Warner come and set with me till 12. Sammy come home and Poor Betsey is no more, or rather the gloomy gulph is passed and she lives forever more; his mother Elizabeth Allinson died 3 hours after her, aged 70 Years. Betsey was about 31 Years, niped in the bloom of every pleasing Expectation! afternoon Daddy & mame hear,

3   Morn: 6 O'Clock Sammy & I set out for burlington, on the road met a funeral, thus is the Almighty calling home his Immortal spirits at all times throughout the world, we dined at Unkle Daniels with my dear Mame and Jemmy & Sally Pemberton. thence Mame & I went to Sammy Allisons, when we all accompanied the Corps to there Interment, in the quiet inclosure of the grave, whence follows to the spirit the treasure "which moth shall not corrupt nor theif break thro' and steal."[103] when we returned to the house we sat and weept under the hand of the almighty, be ye in some degree
           Comforted, seeing the mistress of this house went not with out mourners,

---

102. Erased: "the."
103. Matthew 6:19–20.

> *Man is Responsible for ills received;*
> *Compell'd to refuge in the right for Peace.*
> *Those we call wretched are a chosen band,*
> *Amid my list of blessings infinite,*
> *Stand this the foremost, "that my heart has bled."*[104]

4   Morn: at Unkle Roberts & Sam: Allinsons, afternoon 3 O Clock
     Sammy & I returned to Philadelphia,

[In margin: "George Polly Billy Sally Josey all shoes billys soaled, my shoes heal
taped."]

𝕯

[November 1, 1769]

4 day of   I left off this Memorandum, I see at a time of my Life, not to be for-
the   gotten, when my mind was chastened by Affliction, the wise man's
Week   school from whence he profiteth

> *Daughters! we leave our Names our Heirs*
> *The rest old Time and waining Moons have swept away;*
> *Or left beneath the Spheres. Watts. Poems. Sacred to Virtue*[105]

     in this Intrym of time I have Lost the Company of my Mother Sansom,
I hope but for a Season, as I have full aspirance her Innofensive Life
and Conversation, will place her in the blest abodes, where after many
Tryals I hope to Join Her, and those whom I Love, gone before!
     Morn: Ironing, afternoon agreably at Work, Evening also, my family
at present are its beloved Master, my little dear Billy, Sally, Josey and
the last come Kitty, who is with her Nurse Wood, Dicky Vaux, Eliza
Montgomery, Mary Shingleton, and G: Shofts

5   Morn: at meeting: Mary Cox, from mary Land, Susannah Lightfoot,
from Yoke land,[106] Sammy Emblen, and Dan: Stanton spoke, John
Moreton & Ester Deshler were married. afternoon: drank tea with
Nancy Pemberton, The Company her Mame (Friend Thomas,) John
Pemberton, John Dickinson, (the Pensylvania Farmer),[107] and Sammy
Pleasents and Wife, in the evening I went home with them, they sent

---

104. Young, *The Complaint* (1748), 197.

105. Watts, *Horae Lyricae,* 166. HCS has elaborated, "Thus, Blackbourn, we should leave our Names
our Heirs, / Old Time and waning Moons sweep all the rest away."

106. Uwchlan township.

107. John Dickinson, *Letters from a Farmer in Pennsylvania* (Philadelphia, 1768), a protest against the
Townsend duties.

for Sammy Sansom and we spent a very agreable 2 or 3 hours, some performanses of Hy[G]riffitts[108] were read, see my Silver Covered book,

6   Morn: writeing: Visit to Neigh: Carney, afternoon at Work, enjoying a rainy day,

7   Morn: mending Stockings, afternoon Sammy Allinson from burlington, letter from mame

1 Day   Morn: Sammy, Billy, Sally, & I at meeting, Betty Morgan spoke and prayed, afternoon at meeting Becky Jones spoke, Love not the world, for if yea love, the world, the love of the father is not in you, Daddy Sansom, Rich: Blackham, and Nancy Pole drank tea with us. evening Sammy Allinson returned from Newtown in company with our worthy friend Rachel Wilson, a friend from kendall in Old England, one of the greatest Ministers the World can boast, preaching the words of Eternal Life and truly proveing, as her text was this evening, John, unto the 7 Churches, he that hath an ear let him hear, what the spirit saith, for he speaks as surely now as ever he did to the 7 Churches in Asia![109] thou greatly favour'd land, of whom it is not yet said "Let Ephraim alone for he has Join'd himself to Idols"[110] bow in the day of mercy that your Candlestick may not be removed from out of its place, nor the Call of God be hid from your Eyes:[111]

2   Morn: Sammy Allinson went home, being quarterly meeting. I went to a large congregation at the market street meeting, George Mason, Sammy Emblen, and Rachel Wilson spoke, her text. man cannot serve two masters, either he will hate the one and love the other, or love the one and hate the other'[112] therefore arouse thou that sleepest least thou sleep, the sleep of death: when the meetings separated, the women had a solemn and composed meeting, concluding with a prayer by Sarah Hopkins, for herself and I belive a majority of the Assembly, for our respected friend R Wilson on her passage. afternoon. my Neighbour Wicoff and his Wife drank tea with us, Mame, Polly Sweet, & Sally Maul come from burlington,

3   Morn: Neigh: Carney, mame, & I went to meeting George Mason and Rachel Wilson Preached and prayed, standing up afterward and affectionately biding us fare well and after this meeting I saw her face no

108. Manuscript literature circulated like print literature in the colonies. Hannah Griffitts was a talented and prolific author whose work survives largely in letters and commonplace books of the period. See the introductions in Blecki and Wulf, *Milcah Martha Moore's Book*.

109. Revelation 1:4–11.

110. Hosea 4:17.

111. Revelation 2:5.

112. Matthew 6:24.

more, she was a comely and majestick woman and her affability gained more if posible than her doctrines, she told us since she come among us she had desired "to seek nothing but Christ, and him Crusified" my message was Love and nothing have I for you but Love, and it has flowed over your Land as a mighty stream! the Lord looketh for fruits, and I hope I shall return in Peace. afternoon at home kniting, Mame was at Joshua Fishers

4   Morn: Mame &^c went home, George & Sally Dylvin with them, afternoon at home

5   Day, engaged on my poor Eliza's account, she has suffered herself to be deceived by a young man of family,[113] who has used her cruelly, but I have opened the affair to his mother, and I believe the young man, wont pitch on my house in his next exploit. all the misery falls on the woman, and yet daily are they trusting in man

6   Morn: Ironing afternoon at Work, evening Rich: Wall spent with us.

7   Day, this is the day on which my dear Sally finishes her 5 year, and may I ever have as much reason to love her as I have now, as she showes the dawnings of a Sweet disposition. and my dear little Caty is also 7 months this day.

[In margin: "Sallys birth."]

1 Day   Morn: Sammy & myself Billy and Sally went to meeting, John Hunt and David Eaustah spoke, Daddy Sansom dined with us, afternoon Caty and her Nurse with Whom I have agreed to make enquiry of her Sister in the Jerseys to take Eliza for some months. the girl seems more composed to her fate. evening betsey Warner. Sammy read us a sermon from fordyce,[114] let your speech be season'd with salt.[115]

2   Morn: at Work, Becky Shoemaker hear. talk on Elizas affair as her husband is Mayor of the City, the Laws have been so careful of the rights of men, that a woman who is not robed of all which shoud adorn a woman is excluded from any benefitt, for very often the sufferers are far the fitest Inhabitents for this world or the next, oh my daughters remember the delusions of men. especially if you shoud have any share of Beauty. afternoon a brides visit to Hetty Moreton, the Company her Mame, Sally Lewis, Polly Shoemaker, and Caty Deshler, evening at Work, and half hour Mrs: White and moor Firman hear. if a son of mine commits such a fault may I be enabled to talk of it knowing the characters with more generosity than I think she does.

113. That is, of a good or reputable family. Eliza was probably the daughter of neighbor Montgomery (see entry of February 17, 1768).

114. James Fordyce, *Sermons to Young Women* (1765). Mary Wollstonecraft devotes a section of *A Vindication of the Rights of Women* (1792) to the inanities of Fordyce's advice to women.

115. Colossians 4:6.

3   Morn: at meeting Deborah Hudson and Samuel Emblen spoke, afternoon Neigh Howell, Becky Shoemaker, & I paid a visit to Peggy Gadis, a Lady there in much distress concerning the Illness of a child, there are ten thousand Ills in Life, which a happy death does avoid:

4   Morn: busy in the family, Eliza's poor mother hear, afternoon Sammy & I drank tea with unkle Bell and Polly Parrock, at Alice M'Calls. evening reading

5   Morn: at meeting, Mary Emblen, Elizabeth Stevens, and Daniel Stanton spoke, Evans and Barbary Crookshanks were married, afternoon, settled with my washer woman and drank tea at John Drinkers, where we spent the evening, and on a particular relation of the death of Robert Parish's child, by an accident, my husband reallised it, to himself, that he fainted away, so short and uncertain is the tenor of breath, held in our narrow Nostrills!

6   Morn: Ironing, afternoon Rachel Drinker and I went to see Becky James, her husband abel James is gone to England in the Vesel with friend Wilson, Betsey Waln there, this day twelve month my Mother Sansom departed this Life, for a happy Immortality.

7   Morn: wrote to my mame, afternoon engaged with my children, not so well in my mind as I should be, let me guard more the door of my own heart

1 Day   Morn: Sally & I went to market streat meeting: Danil Stanton and Joice Benezet spoke. afternoon Sally and I walked down to see Caty and her Nurse, thence to market street meeting, Sally Morris spoke, Daddy Sansom and John Drinker hear, evening Polly and I went to meeting: Danil Stanton and Martha Harris spoke.

2   Morn: our folks schouring,[116] afternoon at work, my mind in some degree composed again

3   Morn: at meeting Danil Stanton, John Hunt, Sammy Emblen, and John Eliot spoke, afternoon John & Rachel Drinker, Samuel Bryan and his wife, with Daddy Sansom drank tea with us, they are the persons with whom daddy Sansom lodges.

4   Morn: an agreable visit from Neigh: Warner, setled with my washer [woman], afternoon drank tea with Nanny Wisher, the company Betsey Thomas and John Cooper, Nanny's mother Lays intirely bedriden by age, J C waited on me home, and spent the evening with us, also Jemmy and Anna Bringhurst,

5   Morn: Ironing. afternoon Polly Holloway and Nancy Warner hear. evening Sammy and Polly Pleasents and we enjoyed the true pleasures of Conversation

---

116. That is, scouring, meaning the servants are housecleaning.

6   Morn: monthly meeting, Mary Emblen, Danil Stanton, and John Eliot
         spoke, after the meetings parted John Hunt Rachel Jory,[117] Abram
         Dawes & Marcy Grey passed the 2 time. I paid my Years Collection 12
         L[118] which I have paid ever since my Marriage yearly, signed Betsey
         Hopkin's removal sertificate for Mary Land.[119] afternoon Polly Plea-
         sents, Sally Rhoades, and Neigh Carney and I paid a Lying in visit to
         Neigh: Hopkinson, the custom of paying Vails[120] to Nurses[121] begins
         to drop. evening wrote to Dicky Vaux's Sister Sukey Vaux
7   Morn: mending Stockings, afternoon ditto. Sammy Allinson came from
         burlington with a letter from mame, evening a sea fareing Young man
         from London, who knew Sammy's Relations came, they that go down
         to the great Waters see the wonders of the Almighty in the deeps.[122]

1 Day   Morn: Sammy, Billy, Sally, Polly, and I went to meeting, Mary Emblen
         and John Hunt spoke, Hezikiah Williams read an extract of the Dis-
         appline and the London Epistle,[123] afternoon at meeting William
         Brown spoke, Sally and I drank tea with Becky Jones and hannah
         Cathrel, evening at meeting Sally Morris and Samuel Notingham
         spoke, note S Allinson went home after diner.
2   Morn: Fair, which sets the childrens heads crazey, little Becky Gilbert
         was with Sally all day, afternoon Neigh: Gilbert and his Wife drank
         tea with us, evening kniting Stockings for Sammy, read Voltairs l'In-
         genu[124]
3   Morn: went to meeting: Danil Stanton, Mordecai Yarnell, and Sammy
         Emblen spoke. John Hunt and Rachel Jory were married, John appeard
         in public testimony the words of the prophet 'Hitherto the Lord hath
         helped us.'[125] afternoon. William Fisher and wife drank tea with us,
         Nurse brought little Caty, and Peggy Rawle and Rachel Shoemaker
         come to play with Sally, evening the honest Sailor come & spent with us.
4   Morn: a walk with Polly Pleasents, wrote to mame, afternoon Rachel
         Drinker and I went to the Funeral of Polly Steel, widow of Henry
         Steel, Danil Stanton spoke at the Grave, Sammy & I drank tea at
         J Drinkers, cousin John Baldwin there
5   Morn: kniting, afternoon Neigh Carney. an agreable evening kniting

117. Erased: "&"
118. Twelve pounds.
119. As an older married woman, HCS is being given positions of responsibility within the women's
monthly meetings for business.
120. Money given as a gift.
121. Post-partum women.
122. Psalms 107:23–24.
123. The London Yearly Meeting sent annual reports to the Philadelphia Yearly Meeting.
124. Voltaire, *L'Ingenu: Histoire veritable, tiree des manuscripts du P. Quesnel* (1767).
125. 1 Samuel 7:12.

[December 1, 1769]

12 month	Morn: knitting. afternoon Nanny Wisher & I paid a visit to Neigh
6	Sewel, the company Polly Hunt, Han: & Betsey Sewel, pretty Girls, & Dicky Smith.
7	Morn: bought and put together Ingredients for Daffys Elixer,[126] rest of the day mending

1 Day Morn: Sammy, Billy, and I went to meeting, John Hunt spoke, afternoon I went to the market Street meeting, thence to see my dear little Caty, evening at meeting D Stanton preached and prayed to the honour of his Master, a good man

2 Morn: Eliza and I makeing up bedticks,[127] afternoon Sammy and I drank tea at Joshua Howels, the company his good wife, my early friend, and John & Sally Howel. we staid the evening, Sammy & Becky Shoemaker enlarged our company and spent it pleasently, except feeling for the misfortune of others by relation.

3 Morn: paid a visit to the Childrens school, went to meeting John Hunt, Martha Harris, and Sally Morris spoke, Grace Fisher dined with me, afternoon Neigh Carney, Sally Fisher, and I went on a visit to Joshua Fishers family, a large Company there, see some beautiful little east india fish p[128] kept alive in water by changeing the water, my birth day, in which I enter my 33 year, the larger half of my Life

[In margin: "my birth day."]

4 Morn: Ironing, afternoon Neigh Foulk drank tea with us, evening kniting,

5 Morn: at Work, afternoon at Neigh Warners, the Company Nancy & Betsey, Sammy Sansom come and we spent the evening there, Unkle & Aunt Fisher.

6 Morn at Work, afternoon SS: and I drank tea with Neigh Blackham. the Good Thomas Say there, who is general Gaurdian and Before that the overseerer at the House of Employ &c for the City. evening a lovely moonlight night took a walk.

7 Morn: Amy Matlock come to town, who is to take care of my poor maid Eliza. the day employed in seteing her out, and about 3 O Clock afternoon she weeping left me

1 Day Morn: Sammy, Billy, Sally, & I went to meeting, afternoon at meeting Sammy Emblen and Becky Jones spoke, Daddy drank tea hear, evening at meeting D Stanton and S Emblen spoke

126. A decoction of senna used for stomach complaints.
127. Covers for pillows or mattresses.
128. A small ink spot covers most of this word.

2   Morn: busy, setled with my washerwoman, afternoon at Work, evening John & Rachel Drinker spent with us, they are people who love peace, and to this a blessing was always annexed: they shall Inherit Peace, let my communion be with such.

3   Morn: Ironing, afternoon Neigh Carney and I drank tea with Neigh Clifford, the company Betsey & Anne Clifford and Amy Horner, evening at home working. Sammy Reading, the source of Joy must always be at home.

4   Morn: mending. afternoon at Work,

[In margin: "Shoemakers account setled Billy & Sallys shoes mended."]

5   Morn: at meeting Danil Stanton and Sally Morris spoke, afternoon at home,

6   Morn: Ironing, afternoon also, Sammy Allinson came, received letters from Mame & Caty

7   Morn, wrote to Mame, Caty, & my poor Maid Eliza, as nurse returned then, with my dear little kitty, afternoon Sammy Allinson went home,

1 Day   Morn: Sammy, Billy, Sally, Polly, and I went to meeting, John Hunt spoke, afternoon some uneasiness for want of curbing my temper, I have not learnt yet that another persons being in the wrong will not excuse me from bringing myself there also: my little Sally and I drank tea with Betsey Drinker, and Polly Sandwith, we staid the evening. Giles Night, a friend from abbington, and Sammy Sansom suped there, very agreable

2   Morn: Ironing, afternoon, at Work, evening also, closed the day in duty,

3   Morn: at meeting Dan: Stanton, Sammy Emblen, and John Hunt spoke, afternoon Nurse and my dear little Kitty, evening Nancy Warner,

4   Morn: mending afternoon, Neigh Wicoff and I spent with Neigh Carney, evening a letter From Mame, Sally Pemberton very poorly so I went down there, Sally Grean there.

[In margin: "Sallys shoe mended."]

5   Morn: at work, Dicky Vaux went to burlington, wrote to mame, 11 O Clock went see S: Pemberton, she is better, Han: Pemberton, Han: Loydd, and Polly Pleasents there. Polly Pleasents and I called in to Sally Rhoades, Nancy Pemberton there. afternoon at Work, evening also, with my maid Polly Shingleton.

[In margin: "a pair of shoes soaled for me."]

6   Morn: at Work, afternoon at Drinkers, and Sammy and I staid the evening, very pleasent

7   Morn: mending Stockings, afternoon stept to see Sally Pemberton, H Smith and H Pemberton there

1 Day   Morn: Sammy, Billy, and I went to meeting, John Hunt and Deborah Hudson, spoke. afternoon a visit to Neigh Foulk, Molly Harrison there, Sally and I went to meeting, John Hunt and Sammy Emblen spoke, Sammy and I drank tea at home, evening Polly & I went to meeting, Sally Morris visit Dan: Stanton spoke.

2   Morn: busy in the family, afternoon at home Nanny Carlisle hear, evening with Nurse

3   Morn: Ironing, afternoon Sally and I at Cousin Lydia Nobles,

4   Morn: at Work, afternoon Han: Smith and I drank tea with Sally Rhoades. toward evening our company encreased, and myself with the following suped with them, Israel Pemberton, Josey & Nancy Pemberton, Josey & Dicky Smith, Betsey Warner and Sammy Rhoades.

5   Morn: at Work, afternoon Rachel Drinker, Neigh Gilbert, and Nancy Guy, Drank tea with me. evening at Work.

6   Morn: monthly meeting, Mordecai Yarnel spoke, Sammy Emblen and Sally Mott passed.

[In margin: "billys shoes soaled & healtoped, Toby a pair of shoes, Sally shoes soaled, George a pair of shoe and soaled, Polly shoes soaled, Billy a pair of shoes."]

[February 11, 1770]

1 Day   Morn: In this Interval of time, my 2 Youngest children were Inoculated for the Small Pox, Josey had it very finely, but my Poor little Caty fell a sacrifice to the cruel disease! on the 1 of the 2 Month, carried with her to the grave this Label, the counter part of which, viz—

> *Is Resignation's lesson hard*
> *Examin we shall find*
> *That Duty gives up little less*
> *Than anguish of the mind.*[129]

---

129. Young, *Resignation in Two Parts* (London, 1762), 21.

The buds of Virtue must forever Bloom. Catherine Sansom
was born April the 13: 1769, Departed this Life Febuary the 1: 1770.
buryed Febu: 3: Philadelphia. afternoon at meeting. Sammy Emblen
spoke, Rich: Waln and Neigh Horner and his wife drank tea with us,
evening reading in the Oydisse[130]

[In margin: "my shoes healtaped."]

2	Morn: at work, afternoon also, this day Josey enters his fourth Year
3	Morn: Ironing, afternoon also, Josey began to go to School again, for which I am thankful!
4	Day at Work, a pleasent day to me as I began to reconcile myself to my state!
5	Morn: at meeting Samuel Isbourn, Hes: Williams, George Dylvin, Dan: Stanton, Mary Emblen, and Eliza Stevens spoke. afternoon at the Interment of Margery McCMutry, one I was acquainted with when a girl
6	Morn at Work, afternoon Joshua & Caty Howel and Neigh Gilbert spent with us.
7	Day. a day of tryal, we must pity the follies and help to alliveate the Miserys of Life. the Circumstance of the unhappy Eliza has often given me pain.
1 Day	Morn: Sammy, Billy, Sally, & I at meeting, Nurse Wood & her daughter dined with us, afternoon at meeting Lydia Noble and Hannah West drank tea with us.
2	at home busy in the family, some grating things on Eliza's account,
3	Morn: Ironing, afternoon at Rachel Drinkers
4	Morn: finished 6 neckcloath's for Daddy, afternoon Neigh Harrison, Footman, Smith, Gadis, & Betsey Warner drank tea with me,
5	Morn: at meeting William Horn, Dan: Stanton, and Joice Benezet spoke, afternoon, on a visit to my old friend Becky Shoemaker who Lyes in with her first son Edward, the company Sidney, Patience, & Caty Howel, Neigh Carney, Sally Fisher, Becky James. Molly Foulk, Anna Bringhurst, Betsey Waln, Johanna Haselhurst, and Neigh Lega
6	Morn: received letters from Mame, and Sammy Allinson. Answered them, R Smith hear. afternoon spent a couple of hours with Betsey Drinker & Polly Sandwith, Docter Redman
7	Morn: some disagreable things. afternoon I went see Eliza who goes on second day to live with Jenny Shippen. evening at Work.

130. Homer, *The Odyssey;* various editions available.

1 Day   Morn: at home, afternoon at meeting, Polly Parrock drank tea with us. evening reading in Young, Each moment has its Sickle—

—Each Moment plays
His little Weapon in the narrower Sphere
Of sweet Domestic comfort, and cuts down
The fairest bloom of Bliss.[131]

2   Morn: at Work, afternoon paid a Lying-in visit to Polly Hunt, see a picture of Betsey West and her baby,[132] evening at work.

3   Morn: Ironing, went to meeting Betty Morris and John Hunt spoke, afternoon at the funeral of Sally Jones,

4   Morn: mending stockings, afternoon Nancy Hopkinson hear, evening at John Drinkers, Steven Collins and John Glover there.

[March 1, 1770]

3 Mo 5   Morn: at meeting Sally Morris and Danil Stanton spoke. afternoon SS. and I drank tea at Richard Waln's. evening SS had the Company of Rich: Waln, Steven Collins, John Glover & John Bosley, the 2 latter Englishmen.

6   Morn: at Work, finished the first of Mame's shifts, S:S and I drank tea and spent the evening with our Neigh: Carney

[In margin: "Polly a pair of shoes."]

7   Morn: mending stockings, afternoon and evening John and Rachel drinker spent with us.

[In margin: "Chimneys Swept."]

1 Day   Morn: Sammy, Billy, Sally, & I at meeting. David Eaustah and John Hunt spoke. Afternoon at meeting Deborah Hudson, John Foreman, and John Hunt spoke,

2   Morn: at Work, SS went to Burlington, John Watson dined with us. afternoon at Caty Howels, Nanny Howel there.

[In margin: "to day Josey a pair of shoes, Billy a pair of shoes & shoes mended."]

---

131. Young, *The Complaint* (1749), 11. The final line HCS quotes should be "The fairest bloom of sublunary Bliss."

132. HCS probably saw an imported print of Benjamin West's painting, "Mrs. [Elizabeth Shewell] West and Son Raphael" (1768).

Today 3	Morn: Eliza Montgomery come hear to stay some weaks, I went to meeting Danil Stanton, Sammy Emblen, John Foreman, and John Hunt spoke, afternoon on a visit to Sally Pemberton, Billy Logan, Robert Proud, Owen Jones, and Peter Loydd there,
4	Morn: at Work, afternoon Rachel Drinker & I on a visit to Sally Bryan, evening S S returned
5	Morn: at meeting Mary Emblen, John Hunt, and Danil Stanton spoke, Charles Pemberton and Ester House were married, afternoon Rachel Drinker and I paid a Lying-in visit to Hannah Morris, Peggy Morris there
6	Day at Work, Sammy Allinson from Burlington
7	Day at Work, Sammy returned again
1 Day	at home of a bad cold, evening Betsey Warner spent with us.
2	Morn: at Work, afternoon on a Visit to Sarah Fisher. her two Girls at home, her husband a Jocose man, evening Sammy & I spent at Neigh Warner's with her and the Girls.
3	Morn: at meeting Danil Stanton, Sammy Emblen, Deborah Hudson, George Dylvin, and John Foreman spoke. John Feild and Eliza: Wilson were married, afternoon & evening Sammy & I spent at John Drinkers, Polly Parrock [there],
4	Day: wash, and Just at one O'Clock on the ninth day of her Lying-in my Neigh Wicoff was struck with the Palsey, a great shock to me and many more,
5	Day with her
6	Morn: Ironing, afternoon at Neigh Wicoffs & Sally Pembertons,
7	Day Ironing, this night I sat up with my Neighbour
1 Day	Morn: took a nap, afternoon at meeting Sammy Emblen spoke, evening at S Pembertons
2	Morn: at Neigh Wicoffs, afternoon Hannah Ashton and Sally Nicolson hear on a visit,
3	Morn: with my Neighbour again, afternoon also, and this night Neigh Carney, Gilbert and myself sat up with her expecting it to be the last! but contrary to expectation she lived till
4	Day night,[133] yeilding up her Soul in the prime of life, and bloom of every expectation, in the 19 year of her age,

Not Friends alone such Obsequies deplore
They make Mankind the Mourner; carry Sighs
Far as the fatal fame can wing her way;

133. HCS meant daylight.

And turn the gayest thought of gayest age,
Down their right channel, thro' the Vale of Death[134]

5	Day at home excepting the time I was in at my Neighbours
6	Day the same paying the last sad office of a friend
7	Day noon Mame & Sammy Allinson come, 4 O'Clock Altha Wicoffs remains were interred in the burying ground of St Peters Church on the Hill

1 Day	began our spring meeting, Sammy Emblen, Ann Scofeild, Robert Valantine, and George Dylvin spoke, Bobby Smith from Burlington. afternoon at meeting Thomas Carlton spoke, evening Billy and I took a walk to see Eliza, who has left her place thro' distress of mind,
2	Morn: at meeting John Woolman, George Dylvin, and Deborah Hudson spoke, Afternoon at Work, Caty Wetherel hear. evening Mama & I suped at Joshua Howels
3	Morn: at meeting George Dylvin and Ann Moor spoke, Afternoon engaged in a melancholy office, moveing a distressed person to the [Pennsylvania] Hospital, evening Benny & Polly Sweet spent with Mame and us.
4	Morn: washing, busy in my family, afternoon spent an Hour with Polly Parrock

[In margin: "George & Sally a pair of shoes."]

5	Morn: Mame, Sally Pemberton, & Bobby Smith went to B——n. afternoon at Work. evening a visit to my poor solitary Neighbour Wicoff
6	Day. Ironing. evening Sammy & I spent very agreably with Han: Smith, her Husband gone to Boston, Mrs: Day there.
7	Morn: mending Stockings, afternoon Rachel Drinker, myself, and our children took a walk,

[April 1, 1770]

4 Mo 1 Day	Morn: Sammy, Billy, Sally, and I at meeting, afternoon Sally and I at the market street meeting, on account of the funeral of Sally Stretch, a worthy Young woman, Betty Morris, Sammy Emblen, and Danil Stanton spoke. a solid meeting
2	Morn: at Work, afternoon our Neighbours Carney & Hopkinson with their Spouses drank tea with us. Carneys staid the evening with us,
3	Morn: at meeting, afternoon at home, this night an attempt was made to break open the house but by the hand of Providence they were dis-

11 Month 4 1772

1 Day 4 Billy recovering for the measels, Sammy gone to Burlington to the Funeral of Cousin Betty Smith, ____ to characterise whom needs no more, than to say, she lived the Christian Life, and died the patient Death; over which the Grave has no Victory, Morn: Posey and I at meeting Sam: Hopkins Hez Williams spoke

1 Day 11 at home with Billy who is on the recovery

1 Day 17 Morn: Sammy Billy Posey & I at meeting, H Williams Sam: Hopkins David Caustah spoke, noon Billy Sansom returned to his Master Thomas Powel of Burlington, our man George Shoft went with him; wrote to mamie

1 Day 24 Morn: Sammy Posey and I at meeting Hez Williams spoke; Tommy Lightfoot dined with us, afternoon at meeting Becky Jones spoke; Daddy at tea

Eleventh month first 1784

2 Day 1 after an omission of 12 years, in which more of anxiety has passed than I wish to recollect and our dwelling place changed from Philadelphia to Barlaville, about 2 miles & half from the City, on the banks of Schuilkill _____ a pleasant habitation. at present I am at Burlington, where I have been for between five and six weeks, with my aged mother Catherine Callender who is in a declining way. say O my soul what period of life is unmixed with bitters. at our first offset we weep the remnant of our days is full of pains, which nothing but hope and trust in futurity can alleviate. in the evening my sons William & Samuel arrived from Barlaville

3 day my mother lives with Daniel & Sarah Smith our kind relations, and now I shall also mention that in the ninth month, 87 mother and I met with the afflicting loss of Catherine Smith, she was the companion of my early years, and by her friendly acts to us, who loved to serve her friends, gained much peace to herself, and great benefit to all around her, verily those things follow after her, to the abodes of bliss, they were not done in self sufficiency, but meekness, they beam a glory round her head I have got Sophy Lane to nurse mother, and am preparing things to return home for a few days, our cousin Polly Smith the Daughter of D.S. very kind to mother

4 Day in the morning, Billy Sammy & I set off home, with a sorrowful heart on account of my poor mothers health, it began to rain before we crossed the ferry, and continued so all the way, yet thro' mercy I seem to have received no cold, my family glad to see me it consists of, mon enfans, Sally, Sammy, Betsey Mecom, John Mcevers, Jenny a negro, very busy in my family, making ready to return to mother, son Joseph sent up 80 trees, to plant at our pleasant Barlaville

5 day morn pleasant at work, with Sally, Clement Richards, a sensible french man, passed the day with us, he relieved our good dog Gunner, from the miserable prospect of choaking by piercing an abcess in his throat, which discharged abundantly, evening from the weather and a wearisomness, more impatient than I ought to have been

6 day a pleasant day at work, Evening Posey lodged at home; mother something better

7 Day Morn mon enfans, Sammy Betsey Mecom & I went to meeting, I dined at John Thomas afternoon at meeting, on our return found Clement Richards Sam: Fisher there, heard of the death of a young woman, to her own sorrow, I hope she is removed from trouble

who married against her friends consent

Figure 9 Hannah Callender Sansom put aside her diary during times of stress. Here she stops writing during the American Revolution and picks up her diary again only a year after the end of the war. Courtesy American Philosophical Society.

covered by my wakeing before they had got in and rouseing the family by the Bell,

4   Day Ironing, and many people come to see their attemps

5   Morn: at Work, took a walk to Eliza, afternoon Nancy & Betsey
Warner, Taby Fisher & I on a visit to Polly Holloway, see Miss Hamil-
ton a person of family in distress by being a daugter, cruel england that
can disinherit thy younger branches, nay thy kindness is cruelty. bring
them up in grandure, then toss them on a rude world, or a dependant
Station[135]

[In margin: "Billy & Sallys shoes mended."]

6   Morn: at Work, stept to see Betsey Howel who is sick. afternoon Nancy
Hopkinson & I paid a visit to Patty Wicoff, the Sister of my Neighbour

7   Morn: mending Stockings, afternoon Sammy, Sally, & I took a ride
round frankford

1 Day   Morn: at home afternoon with my friend Caty Howel, 5 O Clock
Rachel Drinker & I at the funeral of Richard Parker's child, evening
read a pretty performance of a Youth 17 Years of age called The day of
Judgement,[136] O Gilvie's

> *—Oh may it never depart,*
> *But warm each thought and burn within my heart*
> *Woo this young breast to seek some fairer clime*
> *And rase the soul with pleasures all sublime.*

> *Then, at that hour, when swifter than the shade*
> *Time, life and youth, and pomp, and beauty fade,*
> *Ten thousand blissful scenes shall charm the mind*
> *More sweet than life, than beauty more refined;*[137]

2   Morn: at work went to see a poor sick person, afternoon Rachel
Drinker, Hannah Thompson, Polly Parrock, & I on a visit to Sally
Bonne, a widow woman who has brought up six children with repu-
tation! evening at Becky Shoemakers.

135. Under the laws of primogeniture and entail, the eldest son would inherit the entire estate of his
father. The care of the younger siblings was often dependent on the heir's good will. In particular, a woman
would need her eldest brother to grant a dowry in order to marry. Pennsylvania only granted a double
share to the eldest male; otherwise brothers and sisters shared the inheritance equally if there was no will
to the contrary. The colonies were by implication also being placed in a dependent station.

136. John Ogilvie, *The Day of Judgment A poem in two books* (1759). Ogilvie was certainly young, but
not seventeen when the poem was first published.

137. Ogilvie, *The Day of Judgment*, 36.

[In margin: "Sally began Schooling to Mrs: Wood the kniting Mistress."]

3	Morn: at meeting Sammy Emblen and Danil Stanton spoke, Tommy & Peggy Dobson from York dined with us, afternoon I devoted to Peggy and we paid running visits to Sammy Shoemaker, Sally Penington, Widow Shoemaker, & Widow Strettle.
4	Morn: writeing & work, afternoon Friend Saunders & her daughter Sally & Sukey Hartshorn, Nancy Pole, evening reading,
5	Morn: wash, busy in the family, afternoon at Work,
6	Morn: Ironing, afternoon Nancy Hopkinson and Rachel Drinker hear, I spent the evening with Rachel
7	Morn: Sammy Allison from B———n, Mame well, Sammy dined with us, drank tea & lodged with [us,] a pleasent day

1 Day	Morn: Sammy, Billy, Sally, & I at meeting, Hezekiah Williams and Deborah Hudson spoke, afternoon at meeting Betty Morris spoke, John Pemberton drank tea with us. evening at Caty Howels my friend Becky Shoemaker there,
2	Morn: at Work afternoon also
3	Morn: Nurse Doudle's daughter, died and left her mother in great Affliction. afternoon at Work, evening at Sally Pemberton's
4	Day bonnet makeing. 4 O Clock went to the funeral of Nurse's daugter
5	Morn: at meeting George Dylvin and Sammy Emblen spoke, afternoon at Neigh: Carney's, the afflictions of the Righteous are Sanctified,
6	Morn: at Work, afternoon Nanny Carlisle
7	Day Ironing

1 Day	Morn Sammy, Billy, Sally, and I at meeting, John Pemberton spoke, afternoon at home. Josey not well, my Neigh: Ashton have lost their baby Just in the same stage of the small pox with my dear little Caty.

Look round my soul on every scene below,
What millions rise distinguish'd by their woe!
See Widows, Orphans, mothers infants slain,
A feeble harmless weeping fainting train!
What crouds, extinct by an untimely doom,

Are torn from life in youth's deludeing bloom!
A throng of mourners sighing by their side,
the Hoary sire perhaps and virgin bride,
The friend whose eyes with gushing streams o'erflow
The mother peirc'd with agoniseing woe.

Tho' all her sons, the victims of thy pow'r
Her sons, that fall by millions in an hour
Yet know, should all thy terrors stand display'd,
'Tis but the meaner soul that shrinks with dread:
That solemn scene the supliant captive mourns;
That scene, intrepid Virtue, views and scorns.[138]

evening at Cousin Hannah Smiths, Polly & Nancy Hoffman and Betsey Bringhurst there.

[In margin: "Billy & Joseys shoes mended."]

2   Morn: scowering, busy in the family, afternoon 5 O Clock Neigh Gilbert & I at the funeral of Ashton's child, took a walk among the tombs.

[In margin: "chimneys sweept."]

3   Morn: washing, went to meeting, John Foreman and Mordecai Yarnel spoke, afternoon Sally & I at Neigh: Warner's, evening Nancy Warner & I took a walk, and suped at our House
4   Morn: at Work, afternoon Nurse Doudle hear
5   Day Ironing
6   Day. Nurse Doudle hear bonnet makeing
7   Morn: mending stockings, afternoon Sally, Josey, & I took a walk and drank tea with Polly Compton, the daughter of my fathers friend Edward Cathrel.

[In margin: "Josey a pair of shoes."]

1 Day   Morn: Sammy, Billy, Sally, & I went to meeting, S Emblen spoke, afternoon Tommy Lightfoot from Virginia—an unfortunate man. Sally & I went to market street meeting, S Emblen and D Stanton spoke, we drank tea with Han: Smith, Nancy   Polly and Nancy Hofman, thence paid a visit to Sally Pemberton, so night brought us home and the day wound up with serious pleasure.
2   Morn: Began 7 Shirts for Daddy Sansom, Nurse to help me, afternoon my friends Joshua & Caty Howel, Becky Shoemaker, and the children, Peggy Rawle, Rachel Shoemaker, and Betsey Howel,

138. Ogilvie, *The Day of Judgment*. The first two stanzas can be found on page 20; HCS skipped to page 30 for the third stanza she copied.

[May 1, 1770]

5 Mo 3   Morn: Nurse & I took a walk partly over our flourishing City, ten O'-Clock at meeting John Hunt, Sarah Morris, and Danil Stanton spoke. afternoon on a visit to Becky & Sukey Waln, 5 O'Clock Caty Howel and I on a visit to Sally Rhoades, She lays in with Betsey, Polly Pleasents and Hetty Pemberton there. Sammy Rhoades waited on us home, he is possesed with a fund of agreable railery.

4   Morn: finished one shirt, afternoon drank tea with Sally Pemberton, evening S Allinson from Burlington, Daddy Sansom hear.

5   Day bonnet makeing, evening John & Rachel Drinker suped with us, S Allinson

6   Day. washing, finshed mame's half dozen of shifts, afternoon at Work,

7   Morn: Ironing. 12 O'Clock, SS, Rachel Drinker, her Sons Henry & Joseph, my Josey, Sally, & self set out for Burlington, after a pleasent ride drank tea at Sammy Allinson's with him & my dear Mother, where we lodged.

[In margin: "Billy a pair of shoes."]

1 Day   Morn: at meeting George Dylvin spoke, we dined at Sammy's with mame, afternoon we spent with Unkle, Aunt, Katy, Sally, & Polly Lightfoot, [we] suped at our lodgeings,

2   Morn: monthly meeting, H: Clifford and Neigh Carney, come from their place Rocky Point to B—n, we went to meeting together, John Sleeper spoke. Josey Smith & Polly Burling passed the 2^{d} time and are to be married on 5 day. Neigh Carney dined with me at Danny Smith's, we returned to SA, took a pleasent walk in his Garden, and parted. SS & I went to Edward Cathrel's, thence to Benny Sweets, Thornhill Stevenson, his Wife and daughters there, after there departure, Polly Sweet, Sally Maul, Rachel Drinker, SS, & I took a pleasent walk down to Conro's, snufing in the delightful exalations of the Spring, on our return met George Dylvin who accompanied us to BS's where in a degree of the silence of all flesh——————the divinity blessed us with a ray of his presence, George Dylvin spoke

3   Morn, Rachel, Mame, & I together. we dined at Danny Smith's, thence Sammy Allinson & Mame, Rachel Drinker & Betty Johnson, Danny & Sally Smith, SS & I went to SAs place, thence to Tommy Wetherel's and drank tea, evening SS & I paid a runing visit to George & Abby Bound, they set out for New york on 2 day, a new scene to her having never seen New york, Cousin Jenny & Caty Smith go with her, I see Polly Burling [who] feels all the axixous uneasiness of her situation!

4   Morn: at Unkle Roberts helping Caty quilt, after diner we set out on

our return home, arrived safely & pleasently, Whitefield arrived from england[139]

5   Day bonnet makeing, Nourse Doudle went to her lodgeings

6   Morn: mending stockings, afternoon Neigh Carney and I at Neigh Gilberts

7   Morn: runing stockings, wrote to mame, afternoon at Work, Isaac Wicoff hear,

1 Day   Morn: Sammy, Sally, & I at meeting, John Hunt spoke. afternoon Sally & I at the market street meeting, drank tea with John & Hannah Pemberton, Josey Bringhurst and Tommy Lightfoot there, the latter waited on us home, and suped with us, his misfortunes require Compasion, JP is his faithful friend.

2   Morn: washing, afternoon on a visit to Sally Rhoades, the company Lydia Parker and Betsey Waln, Shew[140] makes great part of peoples allowed happiness

3   Morn: Ironing, afternoon Peggy Parr and her daughters Polly & Nancy. made the first of 3 aprons for mame,

4   Morn: began a shirt, afternoon drank tea with Sally Pemberton, company Jemmy, Han: Moor, and Sally Green, a view in [a] telescope, thought of Newton's mighty soul!

5   Morn: at meeting Danil Stanton spoke, afternoon Polly Parrock, 6 O'Clock, Neigh: Carney and we went to hear Whitefeild preach, if I did not think my own persuasion right before, he has helped to fix my feet in the right, he is loud, ludicrous and inconsistant. the Wind of doctrine indeed

6   Day. at Work finished the shirt. 4 O'Clock drank a dish of tea with Hannah Smith, Widow M'Call there, called on Sally Pemberton. Dicky [Vaux]'s Mama has sent me a Genteel present, [a] milk pale and Ladle [from Engand] which I design for thee my dear Sally

7   Morn: mending Stockings. afternoon Sammy Billy and I took a ride to Rich: Waln's place. his wife, Robert Waln & Wife, and Jacob Shoemaker & Wife were the company

1 Day   Morn: Sammy, Billy, and I at meeting, John Hunt, Deborah Hudson, and Becky Jones spoke, afternoon at meeting, John & Rachel Drinker drank tea with us. evening Rachel and I at meeting, Sammy Emblen spoke, afterward we took a walk with Lydia Gilpin to Joshua Fishers

---

139. Rev. George Whitefield, evangelical preacher associated with the Methodist movement, who attracted huge crowds wherever he spoke. This was his second trip to the colonies. HCS had critiqued him earlier in the diary too.

140. Show, ostentation.

2   Morn: finshed mame's aprons, Tommy Lightfoot dined with us, afternoon at Work

3   Morn: at meeting John Hunt, David Eaustah, and Sammy Emblen spoke. Parson Whitefeild and Stringer there, afternoon Rachel Drinker & I went to see Polly Parrock, Sally Bonell, and Parson Joe Mather there, evening we were silly anough to go hear Whitefeild again, for the last time I believe with me.

4   Day Nurse Doudle and I Ironing

5   Day whitewashing,

[June 1, 1770]

6   Day washing, evening Nancy Warner & I took a walk

7   Day mending stockings

1 Day   Morn: Sammy, Billy, Sally, & I at meeting, Hezekiah Williams spoke. afternoon Mary Emblen spoke. Sammy & I drank tea at Henry Drinkers, talked of a Journey to Lancaster at distance, we called at Sammy Shoemakers

2   Morn: at Work, took a walk to the fair bought Sally an undressed baby [doll], afternoon Rachel Drinker, and Sammy & I took a ride to look at some land of Skylkill which John & he have bought between them, a pleasent situation, evening Sammy & I spent at Neigh Warners, the girls at home.

3   Morn: Sally & I at meeting, Sammy Emblen spoke, afternoon at home, Neigh Hopkinson, Lydia Johnston, and Han: Drinker hear,

4   Morn: began a Jaket for Dicky Vaux, afternoon James & Anna Bringhurst, and Sammy and I took a pleasent ride with Tommy Clifford and his wife to there Garden.

5   Day titely at work, finished the Jaket

6   Day, washing, busy in the family, Polly Harrison hear an agreable girl.

7   Day mending stokings

1 Day   Morn: Sammy, Billy, Sally, and I at meeting, fternoon John Drinker hear. S Sansom and I drank tea at Joshua Howels, with his two brothers and their Wifes and Neigh Warner,

2   Morn: Polly Kite come, a mantua maker, and we set closely to work. passed a pleasent day

3   Day, the same evening wrote to mame by Dicky Vaux

4   Morn: we finished the third gound, I took an airing with Patty Wicoff and she spent the afternoon with me, her sister's early death is a continual momenta to me!

5   Day titely at Work, finished Dickys Jakets. evening letters from mame & Caty,

6   Day Nurse and I Ironing. afternoon Neigh Foulk & I on a visit to Aunt Fisher, H Clifford there.[141]

7   Morn: mending stockings, afternoon drank tea at Neigh Hopkinsons, Joseph Burden there

1 Day   Morn: Sammy, Billy, Sally, & I at meeting, John Pemberton spoke, afternoon at home the children, Dicky, & I drank tea together,

2   Morn: Eliza Montgomery come to sew a week for me, we began Jakets for Sammy & Billy

3   Morn: at meeting Sarah Morris spoke, afternoon Caty Howel and I on a visit to Anna Bringhurst, called in at Sally Rhoades & Sally Pemberton's

4   Day at Work

5   Day Eliza & I Ironing. Dicky went to the Capes with his Cousin Ames Strettle

6   Morn: at Work, afternoon Caty Howel and I on a visit to Neigh Footman, Sally Fisher and Sally footman there

7   Morn: at Work, afternoon Sally Pemberton hear, our Neigh Montgomery is dead in a foreign land, young, and left an opulant fortune!

[In margin: "Polly a pair of shoes, Georges soaled."]

1 Day   Morn: Sammy, Billy, Sally, & I at meeting, John Hunt spoke, afternoon at meeting. evening Sammy & I at John Drinkers,

2   Morn: at Work. my man George whitewashing, afternoon John Baldwin

3   Morn: at meeting, afternoon on a visit to Neigh Milner. evening to see Unkle Bell,

4   Day at Work, evening Joshua Baldwin

5   Morn: at Work. afternoon Caty Howel and I on a visit to Neigh Carney, Betty Loyd there

6   Morn: at Work. afternoon Neigh Carney, Molly Foulk, and I on a visit to Neigh Ashton

7   Day mending stockings. Sammy Allinson from burlington, my friend and the friend of my family

1 Day   Morn: Sammy went home, wrote to mame, afternoon at meeting. Daddy Sansom at tea

2   Morn: engaged in behalf of Negro Toby, my fathers freedman, afternoon at Work

141. Written at the top of a sketch inserted in the diary, of a royal family attired in clothes reminiscent of the era of Henry VIII: "This drawing is probably very ancient—perhaps more than one hundred years old. 4/12 1861. GV."

3   Morn: at meeting John Pemberton and Becky Jones spoke. afternoon
       Sammy & I at Rachel Drinkers, rented a house of theirs in the Neigh-
       bourhood for toby, but the neighbours objections set it aside,[142]
       evening Peter Wicoff spent with us,

4   Morn: finished 2 shirts [I] began this week for Josey, evening they got
       a place,

5   Morn: at Work, afternoon Neigh Carney and I on a visit to Neigh Har-
       rison & Polly, Polly Peters, Billy White, and Sammy Sansom there.
       evening I took a walk down to Rich: Smiths, Hannah Lys in with a
       daugter,

6   Day home busy at Work. evening 4 O'Clock at the funeral of our wor-
       thy friend Danil Stanton, the corps was carried to the market street
       meeting, Isaac Andrews and George Dylvin spoke, thence it was
       solemnly attended by a vast concoure of People to the grave.

       Behold the perfect man and mark the upright for his end shall be peace![143]

7   Morn, Ironing, afternoon most of my family went a walking.

[July 1, 1770]

1 Day Morn: at meeting Becky Jones spoke, afternoon at meeting,

2   Morn: at Work, afternoon at the funeral of Mrs. Lega a barbadian
       woman universaly esteemed by all who knew her,

3   Morn 8 O Clock at the funeral of age and infirmity in the person of
       Sarah, Sermon from Joshua Howels, called at Rachel Drinkers.[144]

🖎

[January 2, 1772]

1 Day Morn: Sammy, Sally, & I went to meeting, Samuel Hopkins and Hez
       Williams spoke, afternoon at meeting, thence to the funeral of Peggy
       Parr—a woman of a quiet Life

1 Day: 12 Morn: Sammy, Sally, Billy, and I at meeting, Sam: Hopkins spoke.
       afternoon at meeting, Daddy Sansom, Sammy, Dicky Vaux and I
       drank tea together, evening my dear little Joe & I read in the book of
       Books[145]

---

142. Freedom for African Americans in the North did not mean full equality. Segregation in hous-
ing, education, burials, and other aspects of life was enforced by custom if not by law. See Gary B. Nash,
Forging Freedom: The Formation of Philadelphia's Black Community, 1720–1840 (Cambridge, MA: Harvard
University Press, 1988).

143. Abiah Darby, *Useful Instruction for children, by way of question and answer* (London, 1763), 17.

144. About five blank lines follow.

145. The Bible.

1 Day: 19 at Burlington, Sammy Sansom, Mame, Sally, & I at meeting, Cousin
         Sam: Smith read the last years Epistle from the yearly meeting in Lon-
         don, and James Smith, son of the worthy John Smith, made his ap-
         pearance after Marriage with Ester Hewlings, we dined at Daniel
         Smiths, remained there the evening and the agreable Adishion of Caty
         & Sally Smith

1 Day   at home with a bad cold, Daddy Sansom and John Drinker at tea

[February 3, 1772]

M D

1 Day: at home, having been Ill the last week, John Glover, a young english
 2:3:   man, & Caleb Baldwin dined hear, Daddy Sansom, Benny Sweet, and
         Dicky Vaux at tea

1 Day: 9 afternoon at meeting Sarah Hopkins, and Becky Jones spoke, the
         Widow Sarah West was buried: a woman of a good life and conversa-
         tion arrived to a series of years. It is appointed unto all men once to die,
         the time when, and manner how, mercifuly hid from human eyes

3 Day 11 Morn: at meeting Sarah Morris, Sammy Emblen, John Eliot, and Betty
         Morris spoke, afterward I bought of David Hall Watts's Lyric poems
         for thee my Sally, afternoon a visit to Hannah Ashton, Nancy Gibson
         there, in the evening a visit to Becky Jones & Hannah Cathrel

1 Day 16 Morn: Sammy, Billy, Sally, & I at meeting, Sammy Hopkins and He-
         zekiah Williams spoke, afternoon at meeting Sammy Emblen and
         Samuel Delaplain spoke, Rich: & Betsey Waln, Daddy Sansom, and
         Dicky Vaux drank tea with us, evening Betsey & I at meeting, Sammy
         Emblen and Sarah Morris spoke

3 Day 18 Morn: at meeting Sammy Hopkins, Sammy Emblen, Sally Morris, and
         Martha Harris spoke, afternoon on a Visit to Jenny Foulk, Betsey
         Waln, Sukey Jones, and Caleb Foulk there

5 Day 20 Morn at meeting, Joesph Oxley, a friend from England, Mordecai
         Yarnel, Sarah Morris, and Betty Morris spoke, George Roberts & Tamy
         Fox were married, Bobby & Sally Smith in town from Burlington. Let-
         ter from Mame

1 Day 23 afternoon Sally & I at meeting. Daddy Sansom and Dicky Vaux at
         tea

3 Day 25 Morn: at meeting Sally Morris and John Pemberton spoke

6 Day 28 Morn at meeting Becky Jones, Sarah Morris, Thomas Carrington,
         Joseph Oxley, Samuel Neal (a friend from Ireland), and Betty Morris
         spoke. Tommy Fisher, Sally Logan, James Creson, Sally Hooten,
         Caleb Creson, and Annabella Elliot passed, it was a meeting signally
         favoured

[March 1, 1772]

1 Day: 1   Morn: at meeting Samuel Hopkins, Grace Fisher, [and] Hezekiah Williams spoke. afternoon at meeting John Hunt spoke, drank tea with Rich: & Betsey Waln. in the evening we went to meeting: Samuel Emblen, Joseph Oxley, [and] Sarah Morris spoke, the two latter take their departure on the Morrow for England

3 Day 3   Morn: at meeting Betty Morris, Becky Jones, and Sam: Hopkins spoke, afternoon on a visit to Neigh Horner

1 Day 8   Morn: Sammy, Sally, & I at meeting, Sam: Hopkins spoke, afternoon at meeting Betty Morris, Sam: Emblen, and Mary Emblen spoke, the ancient and honourable Widow Hannah Carpenter was intered, worth makes honour in the estimation of the Noble followers, of him whom the world was not worthy of., evening at meeting Samuel Neal spoke. he was the Husband of the deceased Worthy, Mary Peasely

3 Day 10   Morn: at meeting Betty Morris and George Dylvin spoke, afternoon Visit from Neigh Stiles

1 Day 15   Morn: Sammy, Billy, & I at meeting, Becky Jones and Hezekiah Williams spoke. afternoon at meeting Samuel Neal spoke, Sally & I went to the funeral of Mary Pollard, a woman of an orderly life. evening at meeting Samuel Neal and Sam: Emblen spoke.

3 Day 17   Morn: at meeting Mary Emblen, Hugh Howel, Samuel Neal, Samuel Emblen, and William Brown spoke. Thomas Fisher and Sarah Logan entered the bans of Matrimony, afternoon employed for the poor, a work, my Sally, which we all ought to have a hand in

1 Day 22   Morn Sammy, Billy, and I at meeting, John Foreman, Ben: Sweet, Joseph Saunders, Thomas Ross, Joseph Istburn, [and] Sam: Neal spoke. afternoon Josey & I at meeting Ben: Sweet, Thomas Carrington, Thomas Carlton, and ——Brown spoke. evening at meeting Polly Sweet, James Saunder, Philip Dennis, and Robert Valentine spoke.

2 Day 23   Morn: at meeting Sam Hopkins, Marcy Redman, and Philip Dennis

3 Day 24   Morn: at meeting George Mason, James Willet, and James Lee spoke. afternoon at Neigh Warner, evening Sammy Allinson, Danny Smith, Sammy, and I spent at Joshua Howels

5 Day 26   Morn: at meeting Mary Emblen, Sam: Hopkins, William Jones, John Churchman, and George Mason spoke, afternoon Visit from John & Rachel Drinker, evening S Sansom at the first meeting with the overseers of the poor, being one for the ensueing year.[146]

---

146. The Overseers of the Poor were the officials who determined who was worthy of receiving aid and how much assistance each approved applicant needed. They could relieve some at their homes, while others were sent to the House of Employment; poor children were frequently sold to farmers' families.

1 Day 29   Morn: Sammy, Billy, Sally, and I at meeting, Sammy Hopkins spoke. afternoon Josey & I at meeting, George Mason spoke, Jemmy Vaux & Daddy at tea, evening billy and I at meeting, Patience Brayton a New England friend, and Sam Neal spoke.

3 Day 31   Morn: at meeting Sam: Neal, Grace Fisher, and Sam: Hopkins spoke. afternoon Ironing. evening John & Rachel Drinker, on fourth day morn, William Sansom went to school with Thomas Powel at Burlington, our man George Shoft with him

[April 5, 1772]

1 Day 5   Morn: Sammy, Sally, Josey, and I at meeting, Sam: Hopkins and Becky Jones spoke. James Vaux dined with us, afternoon at Meeting Timomy Davis (a friend from New England,) and Patience Brayton spoke, Sally and I attended the funeral of Charles Brogden, evening at meeting Timothy Davis and Sam Neal spoke,

3 Day 7   Morn: at meeting Joice Benezet and Susannah Lightfoot spoke, in the afternoon a meeting was held at Market Street, for the interment of an ancient Friend Hugh Evans, of worthy memory, Timothy Davis, George Mason, and John Hunt spoke. James Vaux drank tea with us.

1 Day 12   Morn: Sammy, Sally, Josey, & I at meeting, Hezikiah Williams spoke. afternoon at meeting Timothy Davis spoke, Daddy drank tea with us. evening at meeting Patience Brayton, and that excellent Minister Timothy Davis who handles the word of God aright

3 Day 14   Morn: at Meeting David Eaustah, Sam: Hopkins, Sam: Neal, Eliza Stevens, and Sam: Emblen spoke, a letter from my son billy, Cousin Sally Smith in town

1 Day 19   Morn: Sammy & I at meeting, afternoon at meeting Becky Jones, and David Eaustah spoke. Daddy, and Dicky Vaux at tea. evening: I wrote to billy.

6 Day 24   Morn: at Meeting, Sam Hopkins, John Hunt, and Sam: Emblen spoke, Docter Watson, Fanny Hilbourn, George Dilhorn, Polly Betterton, Edward Pole, and Polly Warner passed, sighned the Widow Sarah Logan's certificate for her return to England. Death having early[147] annuled her marriage Vow. spent the afternoon with Nanny Wishart

1 Day 26   Morn: Sammy, Sally, Josey, & I at meeting, Sam: Hopkins, Mary Emblen, and Becky Jones spoke, afternoon at meeting Sam: Emblen spoke, Daddy, Nancy Pole, and Dicky Vaux at tea, evening wrote to Sukey Vaux & Billy Sansom

---

147. Word or phrase inked out here.

3 Day 28 Morn: Caty Smith from Burlington. we went to meeting, Sam: Emblen, John Hunt, and John Permberton

[May 3, 1772]

M D

1 Day 3 3 Morn: Sammy, Sally, and I at meeting, John Foreman, Sam: Hopkins, Becky Jones, and Hez: Williams spoke, afternoon at meeting James Thornton and Patience Brayton spoke, Steven & Polly Collins John & Rachel Drinker, and Daddy Sansom at tea, evening at meeting Patience Brayton and George Dylvin spoke

2 Day 4 Morn: at meeting Sam: Sitburn, Thomas Ross, and James Thornton spoke. afternoon at home Neigh Ashton and James Vaux at tea

3 Day 5 Morn: at meeting Patience Brayton and George Dylvin spoke, Nancy Brooks dined and spent the afternoon with me.

1 Day 10 Morn: at meeting Sam: Hopkins, David Eaustah, John Eliot, and Hez Williams spoke. Nancy Brooks dined with us. afternoon at meeting Mark Reeves spoke, Caleb Baldwin, Henry Drinker, Jemmy & Dicky Vaux, and Daddy Sansom at tea. evening at meeting John Hunt and Mark Reeves spoke,

5 Day 16 Morn: Sally and I at meeting in Burlington, Betty Smith and Ann Hume spoke, we dined at Danny Smith's and in the afternoon, Sally & Sally Smith, Betsey & Caty Smith, Betsey Barker, Becky Godly, Polly Sweet, Sally Maul, Isaac Allen, and Dicky Smith took a pleasent walk

1 Day
18[148] Morn: Mame, Sally, and Sammy Allinson at meeting, George Dylvin, and Benny and Polly Sweet spoke, we dined with mame & cousin S Allinson afternoon at meeting George Dylvin spoke. we drank tea at Unkle Robert Smith's

1 Day 24 Morn: at meeting ———————— Everet spoke, afternoon at home, evening at Meeting

1 Day 31 Morn: Sammy, Sally, Josey, and I at meeting, Sammy Hopkins and Heze Williams spoke, afternoon at home, Daddy and Jemmy Vaux at tea

[June 2, 1772]

M D

3 Day 6 2 Morn: Caty Howel & I went to meeting, John Pemberton spoke. to day Josey was drest in man's Gard,[149] his little heart was delighted.

---

148. Some of HCS's dates are confused in this section.
149. Garb, clothes.

1 Day 7   Morn: Sammy, Sally, Josey, & I at meeting, Sam: Hopkins spoke, afternoon at meeting, Daddy, Jemmy, & Dicky Vaux drank tea with us, evening at meeting Benjamin Sweet and Sam: Neal spoke.

3 Day 9   Morn: at meeting Eliza Stevens, Becky Jones, and John Hunt spoke, afternoon Nancy Guy & I quilting.

1 Day 13   Morn Sally, Josey, and I at meeting, Mary Emblen, John Elliot, and Hez Williams spoke, afternoon Sally Fisher, Becky Shoemaker, & I on a visit to Sally Rhoades. SS at burlington

3 Day 15   Morn: at meeting Thomas Carlton, Samuel Neal, and John Foreman spoke. Thomas Lightfoot and Benjamin Parvin dined with me. 4 O'Clock on a visit to Han: Saunders & her daughters.

1 Day 21   Morn: Sammy, Josey, Sally, & I at meeting, Sam: Hopkins and Hez: Williams spoke. afternoon at meeting. Daddy & Tommy Lightfoot at tea.

1 Day 29   Morn: Sammy, Josey, Sally, & I at meeting, Sam: Hopkins and Hez Williams spoke. afternoon at meeting, Daddy at tea. evening at meeting William Brown, Joice Benezet, and Sam: Hopkins spoke.

3 Day 30   Morn: at meeting David Eaustah, Betty Morris, and Sam: Neal spoke

[July 5, 1772]

M D

1 Day 7:   5 Morn: Sammy, Sally, Josey, & I at meeting, Hez: Williams and Becky Jones spoke, afternoon at meeting John Hunt spoke, drank tea at Will: Fishers, his Wife and daughters, evening at meeting John Hunt and Sam: Neal spoke.

1 Day 12   Morn: Dicky Vaux, Josey Sansom, & myself went to Burlington, afternoon Mame, Sammy Allinson, and we went to meeting, Betty Smith spoke

5 Day 16   Morn: at meeting Betty Smith and Polly Sweett spoke, Caty Smith, Billy Sansom, & I dined at Danny Smith's

1 Day 19   Morn at meeting Betty Smith and George Dylvin spoke. dined at Joseph Nobles, Molly & Betsey Wetherel there. afternoon at meeting Betty Smith spoke, Mame, Caty Wetherel, Nanny Carlisle, & I at tea with cousin Betty Smith

[August 27, 1772]

5 Day 27   Morn: at meeting Betty Smith spoke, afternoon at John Hoskins. evening a pleasant Walk

1 Day 29   Morn: at meeting Betty Smith spoke. afternoon at meeting Betty Smith and George Dylvin spoke. tea at Unkle Robert Smiths

3 Day 31   Morn: at meeting in Philadelphia John Hunt spoke,

[September 1772][150]

Mo D

1 Day 9:   2 Morn: Sammy, Sally, Josey, and I at meeting, Sam: Hopkins and Hez: Williams spoke, Caleb & Sammy Baldwin dined with us. afternoon at meeting Samuel Neal spoke, Han:, Betsey, & Sally Clifford, Polly Pleasents, Nancy Warner, and Daddy Sansom at tea.

2 Day 3   Morn: at meeting. Betty Morris, Samuel Neal, Joice Benezet, and Susey Lightfoot spoke, afternoon Visit to Richard & Hannah Smith.

3 Day 4   Morn: at meeting Thomas Carrington, Joice Benezet, and Sam: Neal spoke. Cousin Sammy Allinson from burlington in the afternoon. I went with him to his Aunt Scattergoods.

5 Day 6   Morn: at meeting Betty Morris, John Hunt, and Sam: Neal spoke, it is said Sam: Neal will take shiping, for Ireland on 7 day, he has been a worthy minister of the gospel to us, may he return with sheaves in his bosom,[151]

1 Day 9   Morn: Sammy, Sally, Josey, & I at meeting, Sam: Hopkins and Hez: Williams spoke. Danny & Caty Smith from B——n dined with us, afternoon at meeting Benjamin Sweet and Sam: Neal spoke, Caty Smith and I drank tea at Neigh Warners, thence to meeting where Samuel Neal appeard in Testimony and prayer

3 Day 11   Morn: Caty Smith and I at meeting, Eliza Stevens and Grace Fisher spoke.

1 Day 16   Morn: Sally and I at meeting Sam: Hopkins spoke[: "]thou, even thou shalt discontinue, and thine heritage and all that thou hast."[152] Hez Williams spoke. afternoon at home 5 O Clock drank tea with Betsey Waln, and Becky Shoemaker, Sukey Waln there.

1 Day 23   Morn: Sally, Josey, & I at meeting, John Foreman and Hez Williams spoke. afternoon at home, Aunt Fisher drank tea with me, we went to meeting

1 Day 30   Morn: Josey, Sally, & I at meeting, Sammy Hopkins spoke, afternoon at meeting, Daddy Sansom at tea, visit to Neigh: Horner,

---

150. HCS's dates for this and the next few months do not correspond to the numbered days of the week according to the calendar for 1772.

151. That is, Neal has had a goodly harvest of saved souls.

152. Jeremiah 17:4.

[October 1772]

M D

3 Day 10: 1   Morn: at meeting John Elliot and John Pemberton spoke. afternoon Visit: to Jemmy Pemberton and the girls, H Lloyd there. wrote to mame.

1 Day 5   Morn: Sammy, Josey, Sally, & I at meeting, Becky Jones spoke. afternoon at meeting, Daddy and John Thompson at tea.

1 Day 12   Josey Ill of the measels that required my attention

1 Day 20   Sally Ill of the Measels

[November 1772]

1 Day 4   Billy sickning for the measels, Sammy gone to Burlington to the Funeral of Cousin Betty Smith,   to charactarise whom needs no more, than to say, she lived the Christians Life, and died the patient Death, over which the Grave has no Victory,
Morn: Josey and I at meeting, Sam: Hopkins and Hez Williams spoke

1 Day 11   at home with Billy who is on the recovery.

1 Day 17   Morn: Sammy, Billy, Josey, & I at meeting, H Williams, Sam: Hopkins, and David Eaustah spoke, noon Billy Sansom returned to his Master Thomas Powel of Burlington, our man George Shoft went with him, wrote to mame.

1 Day 24   Morn: Sammy, Josey, and I at meeting, Hez Williams spoke. Tommy Lightfoot dined with us, afternoon at meeting Becky Jones spoke, Daddy at tea.

Interlude

Hannah Callender Sansom and a Revolutionary World

Hannah Callender Sansom did not record her reactions to the American Revolution, either at the time or, except for a very few hints, in retrospect. We can recreate a few incidents through the diary of her old schoolmate and friend, Elizabeth Sandwith Drinker, and a few other sources, including a single surviving letter written by her husband. But the close friendship of HCS and Elizabeth Drinker had faded over time. As married women with young children in the 1760s and 1770s, Drinker and HCS saw much less of each other than they had when they were single. For many years prior to the Revolution they socialized only two or three times a year. Their families' different assessments of the Revolution no doubt helped to divide the old friends. Henry Drinker was a close ally of James Pemberton, "who seems to have been at or near the center of Quaker opposition to the Revolutionary movement"; James was HCS's nemesis during her cousin Sally's broken engagement and was the person to whom Samuel Sansom would address a letter of protest on the eve of the Revolution in 1774.[1] The relationship of the two families illuminates the fraught position of Quakers during the war and after, but also the ongoing connections within their community.

Most Quakers, especially the wealthy Quakers whose papers have been preserved, were officially and publicly neutral in the war—and privately pro-British. Their pacifist beliefs meant an aversion to violence, a violence that most regarded as the regrettable result of an American unwillingness to compromise. In addition, most Quaker merchants had strong commercial, religious, and per-

---

1. On Pemberton and Drinker as political allies, see Richard Bauman, *For the Reputation of Truth: Politics, Religion, and Conflict among the Pennsylvania Quakers, 1750–1800* (Baltimore: Johns Hopkins University Press, 1971), 153.

sonal ties to their peers and extended families in England. There were also for-
mal institutional ties: the Philadelphia meeting was under the authority of the
London meeting. So religion, kinship, and economic interests joined pacifist
principles to keep prominent Philadelphia Quakers from supporting revolution.
Early in the war, however, Sammy had struggled to stake out a contrary position.
He argued for a middle ground, a moderate support of the American protests.
He favored the "Proceedings of the People" over the position of the crown and
found the "Hand of Providence" in revolutionary activity, particularly in the possibility of an end to the slave trade. This last point was of importance to both HCS
and Sammy. Their ties of friendship with the Benezet family brought them into
the circle of radical abolitionists.

⟡

Samuel Sansom to James Pemberton[2]
Much Esteemed Friend.—
As the Diffidence of my Nature is such as effectually to prevent me from
speaking my Sentiments in Public, I hope the Freedom I now take of communi-
cating some of them in this Manner, will be receiv'd with a kindness of Disposition equal to that which I believe will actuate the Writer in making the following
Remarks.————
The uncommon Difficulty in the Minds of several Friends in acceding to the
Propriety of the Propos'd Meeting, I think was very observable by their Expressions, and many I doubt not who did not speak, were very desirous that Friends
might be easy without having such an Appointment, of this Number I can truly
say I was one, however as the Meeting is now appointed, I sincerely wish that Wisdom & Prudence may attend it, and that no just Occasion of Offence may arise in
Consequence of it.————
If by the Meeting it is only intended to advise those who profess with us to
avoid being nominated to Services inconsistent with our Profession, and in general to attend to our Principles in these Times of public Commotion, I shall rejoice if the end is answer'd, but if any Thing should be done by way of Testimony
against the general Proceedings of the People I shall dread the Consequences, and
think it in some Degre Duty to declare my Belief, that Providence will over-rule
the Measures of the People for Good, that therefore it will be well for Friends to
endeaver to trust to him, and not suffer their Zeal to carry them beyond the
Bounds of true Knowledge.
Let them consider that the Abolition of the Slave Trade will be a great
Work:————if that only, or if that in some Degree, should be the happy
Consequence of our present Difficulties, who is there among us who can say that
the Hand of Providence in not in these Things?————

2. Pemberton Papers, Historical Society of Pennsylvania.

the Zeal of Friends for the support of our Testimony has been great, many Pieces of Advice & Caution have been written, printed, & dispers'd among the society on various Occasions: The Yearly Meeting Epistle (which I much approve of) will be spread abroad, and will effectually invalidate any Imputation that Friends have joined as a People in the late general Measures, what then have we to do but be quiet? we are not forced to be active in these Measures, I pray that none may officiously & unnecessarily attempt to counteract them, all Things I hope will work together for Good, and that happy Union of Harmony may succeed our present Difficulties.————————

Thus my Friend I have freely imparted some of my Sentiments, and not in the least doubting our united Wish for the general Welfare. I remain with much Respect

thy truly *affectionate* Friend

Sam:l Sansom.————————

5:th [day] 11ᵗʰ [month] 1774.————————"

That the political position of the Sansoms remained at odds with the Society is suggested by the following entry in the diary of Sarah Logan Fisher, from June 1777, that obliquely refers to the outsider status of HCS and her daughter. "To Coz James Pembertons place, to see Hannah & Sally & could not avoid looking upon some that were present, with a degree of pity & sympathy, that I cannot express—"[3] The Sansoms' moderate stance persisted throughout the war. For example, officers were billeted in private houses during the American occupation of the city after June 1778. A Lieutenant Leroy, a Frenchman fighting on the American side, was peremptorily turned away from the Drinkers' house on Henry Drinker's orders, but Leroy and his servant soon found a welcome at Sammy Sansom's. The Sansoms reported that he "behaves well."[4] No doubt HCS and Sammy's love of all things French as well as their politics helped smooth the relationship between officer and host.

Despite these differences of opinion, the Sansoms stayed in fellowship with the meeting. They did not join the Free Friends, a splinter group whose members took up arms on the American side. On September 2, 1777, when Henry Drinker was among twenty-one prominent wealthy Quakers arrested by the revolutionary government on suspicion of aiding the British, the Quaker community, including the Sansoms, pulled together. A large number of friends began regular visits to support Elizabeth, who had a sick child as well as an imprisoned, and soon to be exiled, husband. They helped Drinker with her household responsibilities and helped formulate an appeal for the release of the political prisoners.

3 Diary of Sarah Logan Fisher, III: 17, HSP.
4. Crane, Drinker Diary, I:383.

HCS and Sammy Sansom were among those friends, although their presence may have been especially awkward, since Sammy had not been among those arrested. At first, HCS and Sammy alternated visits, each stopping by several times a week during the first month of the crisis. But HCS was a regular visitor only during the first month. The later visits, for tea, coffee, or supper, were taken by Sammy alone, both before and after the former prisoners returned home on April 30, 1778. HCS quickly reverted to only very occasional visits, which Elizabeth Drinker, who did not go out much, rarely returned. However, HCS later singled out what she considered false arrests of Quakers as the greatest injustice of the war,[5] even while she and her husband were admirers of George Washington and Benjamin Franklin.

In the last years of the war, Billy Sansom, age eighteen by 1781, played an increasingly important role in the Drinkers' lives. He ran errands, delivering letters and hauling hay, and he stayed at the Drinkers' house whenever Henry Drinker was out of town. On one occasion, Billy very nearly got into serious trouble. On December 22, 1781, two sheriff's deputies came with a writ and searched the Drinker house for contraband goods. Henry Drinker came home and ordered the men out of the house, while Billy stood behind him and said something that so offended the head deputy that he pulled out his pistols, offering one to Billy for a shootout. Fortunately Billy did not accept the proffered pistol, and the tense situation defused.[6] Billy Sansom was apprenticed to Henry Drinker in January 1782, to learn the mercantile business.

5. See HCS's diary entries of May 13, 1785; July 27, 1785; and September 15, 1788.
6. Crane, Drinker Diary, I:394.

PART III

Sensibility

Chapter 5

"This man seems formed for Domestic Happiness"

The Marriage of Sally and Elliston

Most of Hannah Callender Sansom's considerable intelligence, energy, and temper were focused inward to self, house, and children. Hers was a less public existence than her mother's, but not less powerful, especially when it came to the future of her beloved daughter. Her moral position as mother and her control over the household allowed her to challenge her husband, her friends, and religious authority in general.

On March 3, 1785, HCS casually noted the visit of "a stranger Gentleman named Perott." He quickly became a regular visitor, and HCS would come to associate his visits with moonlight walks: by the middle of April, romance was in the air. Within three months, by May 31, he announced his intentions to HCS: "Elliston Perot a man of Character, and uncommon openness of disposition, fond of and ardently seeking a lasting acquaintance with our family————.” This application was not to be taken lightly, particularly because Perot was not a Quaker. By the late eighteenth century, both the migration of overseas Quakers into Philadelphia and the conversion of local residents to Quakerism had largely ceased. The city's Quakers were an increasingly insular group, intermarried, conformist, and mistrustful of outsiders. Many had been disowned for causes large and small in the previous generation. Others, particularly the poor, who had difficulty maintaining the elaborate requirements of the faith concerning marriage, had left more or less voluntarily. For some time, wealthy Quaker men had been finding the Anglican faith more attractive. The loss of members only intensified Quaker mistrust of outsiders. The dense networks of kinship, the commonalties of similar upbringings, and the sense of moral superiority in what was perceived to be a hostile society produced a tribal orientation. In addition, those interconnected kinship networks were accompanied by equally dense, and mutually profitable, business networks. Strangers seeking entrance, especially men, might be suspected of avarice.[1]

Thus the delicate nature of Sally and Elliston's courtship was immediately apparent. "Ellison Perot spoke to me on a very serious occasion, his manner was so artless and sincere, that I wished he had been born within the pale of our church," HCS fretted, but she immediately seized on a possible path to Perot's conversion. She began constructing a theological argument for his admission: "does not this [reluctance to admit new members] show a narrow mind, are not all men born of one universal parent, 'if thou doest well shalt thou not be accepted,'" she wrote on June 9.[2] Three days later she acquired an ally in her twenty-one-year-old eldest son. "Will: Sansom talk on many serious things, E P having generously disclosed his mind to him—" And she was prepared to offend her friends "what my friends may think of it I cannot tell, the children of our society are the children of the public, marriage is a solemn act and confirms our happiness in this life, or by a series of afflictions that must be our own bosom companions, fits us for a nother world, where sorrow shall cease"[3] During these important early stages of the courtship, HCS, Sally, and William kept the intentions of "EP" a secret from Sammy, producing some awkward moments, as on June 23, "afternoon, restraint [concerning] Ellison Perot, mon epouse for reasons of state having not been let into the secret occasions." The courtship progressed for nearly two months before Sammy was informed. He was not inclined to be encouraging and "mentioned [Perot's] errand to Sally and I, as a thing of difficulty, that the path in which our society are to walk is narrow anough for this world, without laying our selves under unnecessary causes of trouble and mortification." Sally and HCS leapt to Elliston's defense, protesting that "the young man from the first always declared a steady resolution to be come one of the Society."[4] Sammy continued to present obstacles. On August 4, HCS "had an oppertunity with my husband, he acts cautiously, I hope the event will be better than he may expect at present." On August 8, she persisted in pressuring her husband, bringing William into the sessions for support and adding a bitter and sarcastic theological critique: "mon epouse and William had some discourse conserning Elliston, I cannot find he has much other objection but religious oppinions. I dont remember the nick name of quaker is mention, in the scripture, but Abel tells his Brother all who offer meekly shall be accepted."[5] Tensions mounted, both within the family and between HCS and her friends.

1. Tolles, *Meeting House and Counting House;* Gough, "Economic Elite"; Davidoff and Hall, *Family Fortunes;* Marietta, *The Reformation of American Quakerism;* Levy, *Quakers and the American Family;* and Doerflinger, *A Vigorous Spirit of Enterprise.*

2. God speaking to Cain, Gen. 4:7, "If thou doest well, shalt thou not be accepted? And if thou doest not well, sin lieth at the door: and unto thee shall be his desire, and thou shalt rule over him [his brother Abel].

3. HCS, June 19, 1785.

4. HCS, July 29, 1785.

5. It is God speaking, not Abel. See note 2.

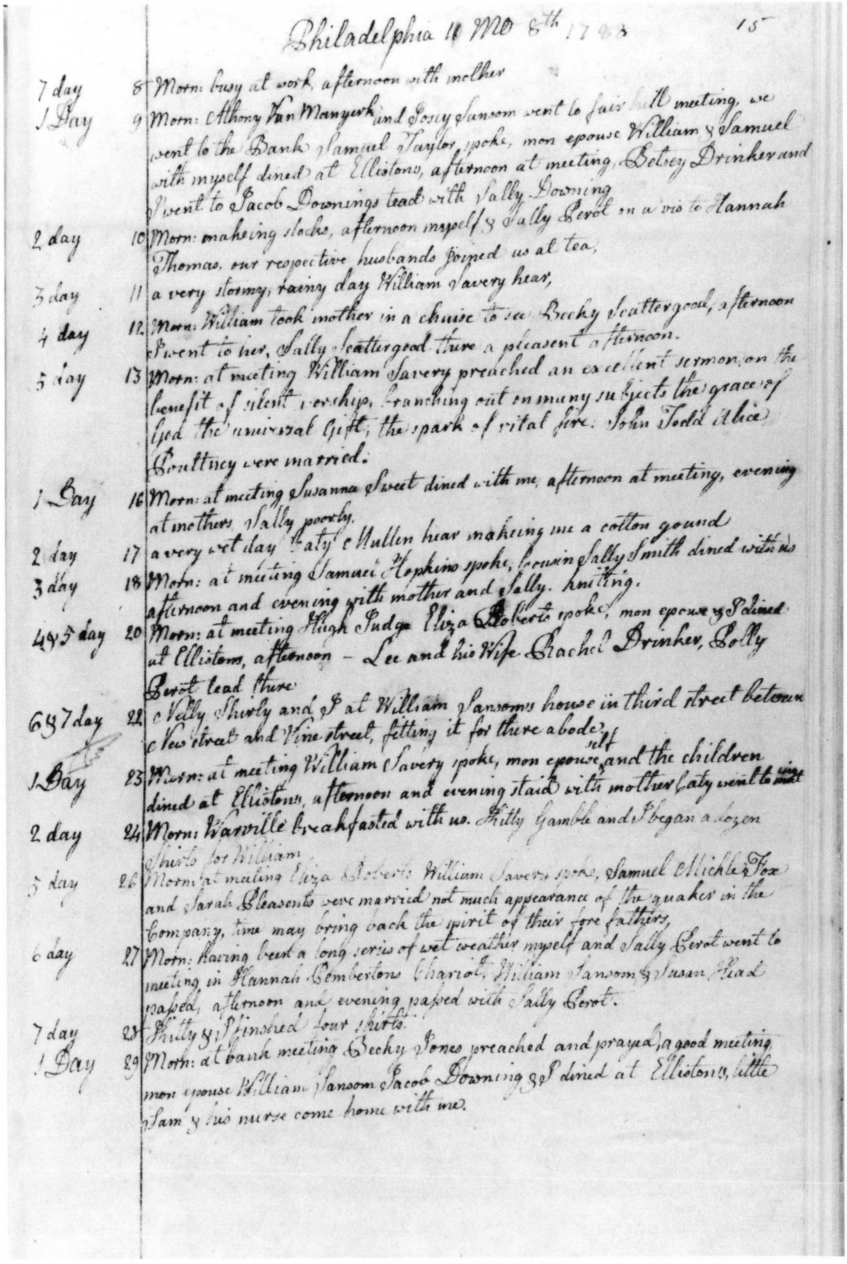

7 day   8 Morn: busy at work, afternoon with mother

1 Day   9 Morn: Anthony Van Manyerk and Joseph Sansom went to fair hill meeting, we
            went to the Bank, Samuel Taylor spoke, mon epouse William & Samuel
            with myself dined at Ellistons, afternoon at meeting, Betsey Drinker and
            I went to Jacob Downings tead with Sally Downing

2 day   10 Morn: makeing stocks, afternoon myself & Sally Perot on a vis to Hannah
            Thomas, our respective husbands joined us at tea;

3 day   11 a very stormy, rainy day William Savery hear,

4 day   12 Morn: William took mother in a chaise to see Becky Scattergood, afternoon
            I went to her, Sally Scattergood there a pleasent afternoon.

5 day   13 Morn: at meeting William Savery preached an excellent sermon, on the
            benefit of silent worship, branching out on many subjects the grace of
            God the universal Gift, the spark of vital fire. John Todd Alice
            Coultney were married.

1 Day   16 Morn: at meeting Susanna Sweet dined with me, afternoon at meeting, evening
            at mothers Sally poorly.

2 day   17 a very wet day Caty Mullen hear makeing me a cotton gound

3 day   18 Morn: at meeting Samuel Hopkins spoke, Cousin Sally Smith dined with us
            afternoon and evening with mother and Sally, knitting.

4 & 5 day 20 Morn: at meeting Hugh Judge Eliza Roberts spoke, mon epouse & I dined
            at Ellistons, afternoon — Lee and his Wife Rachel Drinker, Polly
            Perot tead there

6 & 7 day 22 Nelly Shirly and I at William Sansoms house in third street between
            New street and Vine street, fitting it for there abode,

1 Day   23 Morn: at meeting William Savery spoke, mon epouse and the children
            dined at Ellistons, afternoon and evening staid with mother Caty went home

2 day   24 Morn: Warville breakfasted with us. Kitty Gamble and I began a dozen
            shirts for William

5 day   26 Morn: at meeting Eliza Roberts William Savery spoke, Samuel Michler Fox
            and Sarah Pleasents were married not much appearance of the quaker in the
            Company, time may bring back the spirit of their fore fathers,

6 day   27 Morn: haveing been a long series of wet weather myself and Sally Perot went to
            meeting in Hannah Pembertons Chariot, William Sansom & Susan Head
            passed, afternoon and evening passed with Sally Perot.

7 day   28 Kitty & I finished four shirts

1 Day   29 Morn: at bank meeting Becky Jones preached and prayed, a good meeting
            mon epouse William Sansom Jacob Downing & I dined at Ellistons, little
            Sam & his nurse come home with me.

Figure 10 In pencil, a pointed finger points to an entry about William Sansom's upcoming
marriage on the last page of the diary. Courtesy American Philosophical Society.

By late September, HCS felt beleaguered and began to waver in her lifelong commitment to the absolute truth of the Quaker vision, alternately blaming herself and the rigidity of the meeting's response to Perot. She feared that her daughter, if forced by circumstances, might choose love over faith or even love over marriage: "I love my friends and am fully convinced my profession is the true christian profession as any of them can be, but alas! I have not lived up to it not withstanding my judgement is convinced! and I most fervently pray my child may never depart from the religion of the Gospel, and that the follys of youth may not lay a foundation for a repentance."[6] By October, HCS aligned herself even more closely to her daughter, refusing to submit to the "serious" warnings of weighty friends: "I cannot yet blame my child for her conduct, and I hope I never shall have reason in the event, to do so, . . . she and I mourned together, that he had not been born within the pale of nominal Quakerism, or Birth right, for as to the true birth right as [Nicholas Waln] told us on a first day night, handed to us from Adam, to Noah, [and] we are told, by the Son, are prepared by the Father for all those who believe in him."[7] Quaker theology was adopted to HCS's cause and used against the pronouncements of respected women elders. While she was obviously torn, her loyalties were familial, as she argued in defense of her daughter's emotional interests.

HCS's control over the household allowed her to continue to encourage and support the young people's courtship while her husband remained doubtful and her women friends adamantly opposed it. On November 9, it was "very wet, [Elliston] staid all night with us. which gave him great pleasure." This was a major change in their relationship; afterwards Perot frequently stayed with the family. A few days later HCS was in Burlington to garner additional support for her daughter's cause: "I related all our concern with Elliston Perot to [Mother] and have the satisfaction to see she is easey with our proceeding." Only a week later Elliston Perot came in person to Burlington, and "my mother received him kindly."[8] Now all three generations of Callender/Sansom women were in agreement on the suitability of this match, even if the Quaker meeting was not convinced. After a few months, Elliston began to introduce his relatives to the Sansoms, starting with his sister-in-law and moving several days later to his brothers. After another month, the two families were socializing over dinner.[9]

In the meantime, the Philadelphia meeting proved more intractable than the two families. Elliston had applied to become a member, but his application's approval was by no means assured. On April 6, 1786, HCS noted that "EP and I had an interesting and satisfactory conversation, he must have a good heart, My friends delay his application, but I am not able to change my opinion of him from the first, Candour and Ingenuity are his characteristics." At this point the prepar-

6. HCS, September 23, 1785.
7. HCS, October 25, 1785.
8. HCS, November 13, 20, 1785.
9. HCS, May 1, 5, July 4, 1786.

ative meeting, an intermediate committee between the local and the Philadelphia meetings, had jurisdiction. Something untoward occurred just after this comment on the dilatory handling of Perot's application, for two entries, April 21 and 22, 1786, were cut out of the diary, and no notations were made for the next three days. Only on July 28 was the application forwarded to the Philadelphia Monthly Meeting, which could only agree to wait yet another month to consider the issue, after conferring with Elliston himself. The interview was satisfactory, so the meeting gave its unenthusiastic endorsement of his acceptance into the meeting. The committee first passed on his economic and social condition, that is, "considering how he is circumstanced," for he was wealthy, soon to be allied to a family in good standing, and approved of by a weighty elder, Katherine Callender. Then the committee approved of his character and profession of faith, "a person of sober Conduct, measurably convinced of the principle of Truth as held by Friends."[10] Finally, even Sammy was convinced: "Elliston stayed with us, spoke in his manly way to mon epouse sueing for our child, this fall, and so it is, he has over come ever one's difficultys by a most engageing perseverance, and true love for our child. I desire nothing more in this life, than that she may by a prudent conduct retain his affections."[11] Sarah Sansom and Elliston Perot were married on January 9, 1787.

Revolutionary Crosscurrents

If HCS's diary reads like an eighteenth-century novel, with its female (HCS and Sally Sansom) and male (Elliston Perot) protagonists, an antagonist (Sammy), and a plot centering on the tumults of romantic love, it is in no small part due to its author's aesthetic and literary sensibilities. HCS loved books. She loved to read them, and she loved to talk about them. She described herself, her husband, her children, and her friends and kin in literary terms. This tendency accelerated over the course of the diary.

In HCS's novelistic diary, some of the subplots received the most explicit language, the most heated expressions of opinion; they were allowed to stand in for her own experiences. Rather than fully develop the narrative explanation for her marital unhappiness, HCS shrouded her relationship with Sammy in implication and innuendo. The reader is left with no doubt about the state of their marriage but with plenty of questions about what transpired to have placed it on such rocky ground from the start. The courtship of Sally and Elliston, by contrast, is fully and joyfully detailed. Here, we are to understand, was the kind of love on which a marriage could be built.

10. Philadelphia Monthly Meeting Records, 1782–1789 (microfilm of mss, Swarthmore College), 274, 277.
11. HCS, July 31, 1786.

In between these two nuptials, the souring of other relationships allowed HCS ample scope to define the limits and expectations of romance. The courtship and marriage of Sarah Smith and Jemmy Pemberton and the pregnancy of the unwed Eliza Montgomery had provided potent examples showing that two extremes threatened the achievement of respectable domesticity and the companionate ideal: illicit passion could degrade virtuous women, while crude self-interest placed money above affection. Smith and Pemberton had seemed perfectly matched. He was the widowed scion of a prosperous and powerful family; she the daughter of the devout and well-connected Burlington Smiths. Sarah terminated their engagement after Jemmy Pemberton defered their appearance at the Quaker meeting because his first wife's mother was threatening financial consequences should he remarry. Ultimately Sarah reconsidered, but Jemmy appeared to be a mere fortune-monger. Even after the marriage his character remained suspicious to HCS.

An even more serious affair had been that of young Eliza, HCS's servant and the daughter of a friend. Eliza had become pregnant by a "young man of family, who has used her cruelly." This seduction and abandonment allowed HCS to give full vent to her frustrations at women's limited capacity for negotiating the dangers of heterosexual relationships. While the legal privileges of gender and class protected the crimes of the young man, the innocent and essentially virtuous Eliza was left with the permanent loss of her reputation. Her chances for marriage and the respectability and economic support that a husband could bring were negligible. For HCS, weaned on Richardson's heroines, this was too much. In a case such as Eliza's, she noted, "All the misery falls on the woman and yet daily are they trusting in man." As she complained to a friend, "The Laws have been so careful of the rights of men that a woman who is not robbed of all that should adorn a woman is excluded from any benefit, for very often these sufferers are far the fittest Inhabitents for this world or the next." And HCS did not confine her remarks about the affair to her intimates; indeed, she took up Eliza's case with the mother of the "young man" in question. She "opened the affair to his mother" with such heated depiction of the dire consequences for Eliza that she felt sure he "wont pitch on my house in his next exploit."[12]

The larger context for the romantic struggles of the diary, from HCS's own marriage to the courtship troubles she recounts between her cousin Sarah Smith and James Pemberton to the triumph of Sally and Elliston's union, is the late-eighteenth-century revolution of sensibility. While historians who cite "Revolutionary America" intend to reference the political revolution that divided Great Britain and her North American colonies and inaugurated the United States, that revolution plays little role in HCS's diary. Although early portions of the diary include brief observations on the diplomatic efforts of the Friendly Association to broker a nonviolent conclusion to conflicts between Pennsylvanians and Indi-

---

12. HCS, November 9, 12, 13, 1768.

ans, because HCS served as her father's secretary during his involvement with this group, politics was principally a subject of passing commentary or a source for shorthand characterization of local figures. The diary is then silent from November 1772 until November 1, 1784. As if to catch the reader up on the events of her life "after an omission of 12 years," HCS began her new phase of writing noting only that those were years in which "more of anxiety has passed than I wish to recolect." The real story belongs to the principal figures in her life, rather than to war or national politics. Thus she tells the reader that her family has moved their residence from Philadelphia to Parleville; that she is writing from the Burlington bedside of her sick mother, who has needed her care for more than five weeks; and that her dear cousin Catherine Smith died the previous fall. The diary then commences its usual pace and storyline, following the Sansom family and their friends and kin.

The revolution in sensibility affected how HCS experienced and articulated her world and her life. Historians and literary scholars have performed an archaeology of sensibility, demonstrating that in the late eighteenth century, emotions themselves—love, anger, grief, and joy—may not have changed but emotional expression became a preeminent mode of communication. Sensibility was prized as the quality essential to understanding others and making oneself understood. Unconstrained, untempered sensibility was unreasonable; without the possession of some sensibility, reason alone could not qualify one for membership in society. Sensibility allowed one to appreciate refinement in all things: nature, the arts, and domestic life.[13]

Within the revolution of sensibility, the discourse of companionate marriage contrasted the loving, voluntary union with that of monetary or political interest. An almanac aphorism of 1772 reconciled these two very different marital practices: "the marriage of love is pleasant, the marriage of interest easy, and a marriage where both meet, happy."[14] Over the course of the eighteenth century, the practice of contracting marriage alliances for economic enhancement was increasingly derided as antique and autocratic; affection and choice were the requisite ingredients for marital harmony. Companionship moderated the traditional power valences in marriage. Patriarchy was replaced with mutual concern, at least ideally. Husbands considered their wives' opinions, while wives obeyed their husbands' wishes not out of obligation but out of respect.

But Quakers traveled a peculiar cultural crosscurrent. Long depicted as

---

13. The literature on sensibility is expansive; a critical early secondary work on the subject is G. J. Barker-Benfield, *The Culture of Sensibility: Sex and Society in Eighteenth-Century Britain* (Chicago: University of Chicago Press, 1992). See Nicole Eustace, *Passion is the Gale: Emotion, Power and the Coming of the American Revolution* (Chapel Hill: University of North Carolina Press, 2008) on emotion; and most recently on the contours of sensibility in the American context Sarah Knott, *Sensibility and the American Revolution* (Chapel Hill: University of North Carolina Press, 2009.)

14. Timothy Trueman, *The Burlington Alamanack . . . for 1772* (Burlington, NJ, 1771), n.p. (entries for October).

holding views of marriage consonant with or even prescient of the new companionate marital ideal, Quakers have even been portrayed as the model for nineteenth-century domesticity.[15] While their emphasis on mutual regard, gender equality, and the centrality of the child may have earned Quakers this reputation among historians of the family, the reformation movement in mid—eighteenth century Quakerism also tugged Quakers back toward a much more rigid and narrow set of marriage practices. The renewed insistence on conformity resulted in a curious retreat into arranged marriages, late marriages, and higher rates of spinsterhood, even as non-Quakers were embracing their new ideals of marriage. As Quakers faced an ever shrinking pool of eligible marriage partners, anxieties ran high.

HCS's diary provides ample evidence of the clash between the ideals of companionate marriage and the new rigidity in Quaker marriage disciplines. It was obvious in HCS's own marriage decision. And this tension is particularly plain in the events surrounding Sally and Elliston's marriage. Yet if the crosscurrents are apparent, if at times the cultural waters seemed treacherous, HCS also evinced confidence in the power of sensibility. Like the heroines in her beloved novels, HCS triumphed because of, not in spite of, her increasingly successful ability to assess the world and the lives of her family and herself through the lens of sensibility; to feel, to persuade, and to know by feeling—that was her goal. This was how she might have known the right moment to conclude her story. By 1788, occupied with her first grandchild and surrounded by family, she could report a happy ending.

15. See particularly Barry Levy, *Quakers and the American Family: British Settlement in the Delaware Valley* (New York: Oxford University Press, 1988).

Chapter 6

The Diary: November 1784–October 1788

[November 1, 1784]

Mo D

2 Day   after an omision of 12 years, in which more of anxiety has passed than
  11: 1   I wish to recolect and our dwelling place changed from Philadelphia,
           to Parlaville,[1] about 2 miles & half from the City, on the banks of Schuil-
           kill[2]   a pleasent habitation. at present I am at Burlington, where I
           have been for between five and Six weeks, with my aged mother
           Catherine Callender, who is in a declineing way. say O my Soul what
           period of life is unmixed with bitters. at our first offset we weep! the
           remnant of our days is full of pains, which nothing but hope, and trust
           in futurity can alleviate. in the evening my Sons William & Samuel ar-
           rived from Parlaville

3 day 2   my mother lives with Daniel & Sarah Smith our kind relations, and
           now I shall also mention that in the ninth month, 1783, mother and I
           met with the afflicting loss of Catherine Smith, she was the compan-
           ion of my early years, and by her friendly acts, to us, who loved to serve
           her friends, gained much peace to herself, and great benefit to all
           around her! verily those things follow after her, to the abodes of bliss!
           they were not done in self sufficiency, but meekness, they beam a glory
           round her tiara. I have got Sophy Lane to nurse mother, and am pre-
           pareing things to return home for a few days, our cousin Polly Smith
           the Daughter of DS, very kind to mother.

1. Parlaville, French for "by the city."
2. A line and a half were erased here and covered by a long line.

4 Day 3   in the morning, Billy, Sammy, & I set of[f] home, with a sorrowfull heart on account of my poor mother's health, it began to rain before we crossed the ferry, and continued so all the way; yet thro' mercy I seem to have received no cold, my family glad to see me. it consists of, mon epous,[3] Sally, Sammy, Betsey Mecom, John Mac evers, Jenny a negro,

5 day 4   very busy in my family, making ready to return to mother, son Joseph sent up 20 Trees, to plant at our pleasent Parlaville

6 day 5   morn: pleasent at Work, with Sally, Clement Richards, a sensible french man, passed the day with us, he relieved our good dog Gunner, from the miserable prospect of choaking by peirceing an abcess in his throat, which discharged abundantly, evening from the weather and a wearisomness, more impatient than I ought to have been,

7 day 6   a pleasent day at work, evening Josey lodged at home, mother something better.

1 Day 7   Morn: mon epouse, Sammy, Betsey Mecom, & I went to meeting, I dined at John Thomas's. afternoon at meeting, on our return found Clement Richard & Sam: Fisher there, heard of the death of a young woman, +[4] to her own sorrow, I hope she is removed from trouble!

2 day 8   agreable day at work, afternoon mon epouse, Sally, and I walked over to Robert Morris's seat, from whence a most delightfull view of Schuilkill, John Penn Junior's retreat, rather a morass, but mankind has offended him.

3 day 9   at work. a letter from Ashfeild Hunt, a gentleman who has as much occasion to differ with the world, yet bears it with fortitude, supporting the younger branches of his family to the utmost of his power,

4 day 10   busey at work, mon epouse brought us inteligence from the City of many deaths! poor Jos: Fauset in the Hospital! a man of as comely a figure, as most men, but by bad company and want of a due reverence of himself, come to an untimely end.

5 day 11   as usual at work. this day Sally has quited miss in her teens,[5] and high time for her mother to think seriously, with two children of full age. the acquaintance of my youth Martha Noble is gone! our age was near alike. thus thy foundations should be shaken for time is uncertainty!

6&7 day   Clement Richard dined with us, afternoon Polly & Sukey Drinker,
12 & 13   and Betsey Hough[, we had] an agreable walk, 13 at work, a rainy day.

---

3. Mon epous, French for "my spouse"; henceforth in the diary "Sammy" refers to HCS's youngest son.

4. In margin: "who married against her friends consent+"

5. "Miss in Her Teens; or, the Medley of Lovers," was a 1747 farce by David Garrick. The main character, Miss Biddy Bellair, is a flighty and flirtatious young woman with three suitors. It was one of the first plays performed in Philadelphia, presented by David Hallem's Company in a warehouse in 1768. It was enormously popular and inspired a dance tune, a poem, and a series of prints.

1 Day 14 this day my son William and I set out for Burlington, on our arrival found mother better than I left her.

2 day 15 Billy returned with a small addition to our family, a little boy bound to us named William Moor,

3 day 16 with my dear mother, my sincere prayer is that Providence may sweeten her last moments! bought two flannen sheets, one for each of us.

4 & 5 day 17&18 breakfasted with Aunt Betty, 18 afternoon, Mary Hoskins hear.

6 day 19 wrote to my son William by John Hoskins Ju[nior]: the boat returned like to have overset

7 day 20 letters for William & Joseph, Cousin Sam: Noble struck with the Palsey.

1 Day 21 at home with mother. a questian from Butty's Journal, What will make a feirce man meak, what a drunken man sober, and not only so, but an earthly minded man heavenly. Addison's evidences of christianity undeniable,[6] what remains then but a conformity to the precepts of christ. mother so bad this night I sat up with her.

2 day 22 wrote to Billy & Josey, mother mended again this day

3 day 23 took a little excursion in the morning Dolly Lovett keeps a little school, things look so clean and happy round her, I Hope her last days, will be her best. as by repeated follies the world had frowned severely on her.

4 day 24 letters from William & Joseph. wrote a peice for Sally

5 day 25 mothers fever returned with a lax,[7] I set up with her,

6 day 26 she had an easey day, for which I am thankful, there is a strong contest between the remains of a constitution, unhurt by intemperance, and [the] sharpness of disease.

7 day 27 rose by moonlight, the face of heaven looked beautiful, Daniel & Sally, Peter Worrell, Eliza Barker & Will Savery set out for Crosswicks quarterly meeting, Sally & Peter returned at night.

1 Day 28 mother much better, this day, letters from Billy, Josey, & Sally, wrote to them in the evening, Polly Watson and Hetty Smith hear.

2 day 29 Morn: 7 O'Clock Nancy Dylvin, Polly Smith, & John Cox set of[f] for Crosswicks, a most delightfull day, mother better.

3 day 30 mother mending, Rachel Smith daughter of Rich: & Han: Smith, to see us, an orphan child, with large possesions! evening they returned from Crosswicks.

6. Joseph Addison, *Evidences of Christianity Undeniable, with Additional Discourses* (1745, and earlier editions).

7. Diarrhea.

[December 1, 1784]

4 day 12   Mo 1 agreed with a young woman named Anne Chambers to tend mother, and discharged Sophy Lane, a visit to Ann Hame, a sensible woman who has passed a variety of scenes in Life! proveing as the wise man says much vanity and vexation of spirit[8]

5 day 2   heard from home. Sam: Rhoades deceased, Cousin William Smith says mother is declineing gently away! yet may continue the winter.

6 day 3   Morn: I took leave of my dear mother, and the small body of relations, small to the number I have seen there, Andrew Craig & I took boat for Philadelphia, landed at three O'Clock, Thomas Wharton's funeral was Just passing along, Josey took me home.

7 day 4   an agreable day at work

1 Day 5   Morn: mon epouse, myself, Betsey mecom, & Sammy went to meeting, Han: Cathrel and Will: Savery spoke. dined with my good old friend Ann Warner, Rebecca Shoemaker, Peggy Rawle, Nancy Warner; and Sam: Shoemaker Ju^r there, afternoon at meeting Sam: Smith spoke. this evening Ann Page was intered. a well disposed woman.

2 Day 6   Clement Richard spent with us, afternoon Thomas Howard and his Sisters Betsey and Alice

3 day 7   myself, Sally, & Sammy at meeting, Eliza Roberts, Sarah Harrison, David Estaugh[, and] Will: Savery spoke. dined at Han: Thomas's, visit to Rachel Drinker, left Sally & Josey returned with me

4 day 8   Morn: he returned, busy looking after my maid Jenny cleaning chambers, Billy Sansom he returned soon finding me too busy to talk with him.

5 day 9   Sammy & I went to meeting Eliza Roberts, Dan: Lofly, and Sam: Smith spoke, myself, Sally, and Sammy dined at Mary Armitts, after diner MA went with us on a visit to Sarah Rhoades, who has lost an affectionate husband, Thomas Franklin (Molly Pemberton (Charles's child) Molly & Betsey Rhoades. Sally and Josey Sansom & I spent the evening with Rebecca Shoemaker & Peggy Rawle, Sally, & I lodged at John Drinkers.

6 day 10   Morn: breakfasted at Abra: Mitchell's. mon epouse come and took Sally & I home. Joseph Francis dined with us, he is planning and regulateing our garden.

7 day 11   busey at work, Josey lodged hear.

1 Day 12   Morn: mon epouse, myself, Betsey Mecom, & Sammy went to meeting, Peter Thomas, and Sam: Smith spoke. dined at Will: Fishers, Sarah Fisher & I went to meeting, Robert Willis spoke. a visit to the Widow

---

8. Ecclesiastes 1:14.

Eliza: Rhoades & Han: Rhoades, Thom: Franklin, Thom: Paschal, Polly Davis, and Betsey Nickson there. T Paschal accompanied me to Abra: Mitchels where I lodged

2 day 13 Morn: went to Han: Thomas's, she was delivered yesterday of a son called Arthur, Lydia Johson there, mon epouse come for me, and we dined at home, Joseph Francis still at my garden

3 day 14 busey at work, John Pemberton, a young virginian, hear,

4 day 15 Betsey Mecom makeing myself & Sally gounds of Tabinet.[9]

5 day 16 at work, Clement Richard hear, our Cousin Joshua Smith lodged hear and put up our stove, a preparation for the winter, which has held off yet.

6 day 17 some disagreable occasions for patience, I have not a sufficient share, afternoon Will: Sykes, his Sister Polly, & child Sammy with Billy Sansom hear

7 day 18 at work mending stockings,

1 Day 19 myself & Sally at home, an agreable day, wrote to mother. Josey dined with us, Will: & he board at Abraham Mitchells, a well disposed family, Sally & Josey went to Dan: William's, fine moonlight night, returned nine O'Clock.

2 day 20 Morn: Josey went to town, Sally & I tayloring, the first snow to cover the ground

3 day 21 myself, Sally, & Sammy went to meeting, Betsey Roberts spoke. I dined at John Heads. afternoon at H Thomas's who is very ill, but has a tender mother to care for her, heard from my mother she is very poorly yet evening we returned.

4 day 22   or I shall not get to the right[10]

5&6 day 23&24 Sally & I busey at work, 24 the same with satisfaction of mind.

7 day 25 we finished a coat for Sammy & one for Billy, Moor, mon epouse, & Sammy scating[11] on Schuilkill, Josey lodged hear

1 Day 26 Mon epouse, Betsey, & Sammy went to town, Josey and I took an agreable walk over the hills, afternoon Will: Sansom and John Head at tea. H Thomas very poorly again, evening Josey read to the family, heard of mothers being much better.

2 day 27 Morn: Josey returned to town, Sally & I began to turn a coat for Josey, mon epouse and Sammy went a scateing

3 day 28 Mon epouse and I went to monthly meeting, Will Savery and David Estaugh spoke. dined at Ann Warner's with Joshua Howel, his wife, &

---

9. A mixed weave poplin.
10. Most of this line was erased and is illegible but could concern Sally.
11. Skating.

son, Molly England, H Cathrel, and Ann & Han: Jesop, a friend from Virginia. Hugh David & Sarah Greenleaf married, returned home, a pleasent ride.

4 day 29 at work.

5 day 30 morn: mon epouse, Sally, Sammy, & John Macevers, went beyond Landsdown or Penns place on Schuilkill, afternoon mon epouse and Sammy went to Joshua Howells

6 day 31 eight O'Clock morn: myself, Sally, & Sammy went to the monthly meeting, held in fourth street, Thomas Scattergood spoke, we dined at John Drinker's. after some errands we returned home about dusk, the day as mild as spring, Young mentions it a pretty simily for Age

Mistake fair days in Winter for the Spring. young[12]

[January 1, 1785]

7 day 1 Mo 1 busey at work, Josey come in the evening.

1 day 2 A sleaty bad day, that no one went to Town but mon epouse, writeing all day.

2 day 3 Morn: Josey returned, afternoon William hear.

3 day 4 Sally and I busy at work.

4 day 5 the same, those days do not leave the mind unoccupied because the hands are employed

5 day 6 in the afternoon, Will: Sansom, Will: Parker and his Sisters Sally & Lydia, Sukey Head, and Sally Williams come in a Slay,

6 day 7 in the afternoon, Will: Sansom, John Head, Polly Drinker, & Betsey Hough come in a slay. the men returned.

7 day 8 Morn: mon epouse, Polly, Betsey, & Sally Sansom went to town, mon epouse returned with Josey Sansom and Anthony, Joseph, & Thomas, sons of Thomas Morris to dine,

1 Day 9 mon epouse, Josey, and Sammy & Betsey Mecom went to meeting, I had a pleasent day at home, Sammy brought me at noon no small addition to it, [news that] my mother walked from her room to the Parlour, last sixth day, evening wrote to her.

2 day 10 day at work

3 day 11 Morn: mon epouse and I went to meeting, Will: Savery spoke excellently on the mystery of Godliness. dined at John Drinkers with Rachel & Polly Drinker, Thomas Wister ,& Sally Sansom. visit to Han: Thomas, bought me a carpet 12 yards, £3

4 day 12 at work

---

12. Young, *The Complaint* (1749), 66. "We take fair days in Winter, for the Spring."

5 day 13 Morn: at work, afternnon William and Sally come home,

6 day 14 Morn: Will: returned, afternoon Thomas Wister, Daniel & Sally Williams, mon epouse & self, Sally Sansom, and our man John with a small
sled, went on the Ice three miles up Schuilkill, on the Ice, got home by
dusk, they lodged hear.

7 day 15 Morn: they went home, Clement Richard dined with us, Thomas
Howard hear, Josey Sansom come home,

1 Day 16 Morn: mon epouse, self, and Sammy went to market street meeting,
Benja: Gibbs, Sally Dickinson, and Betsey Roberts spoke, went home
with the latter, and dined at Hugh Roberts's with him & his Wife, Rich:
& Nancy Vaux, and Molly Warder, afternoon at meeting, a most fer-
vent and well adapted supplication on behalf of the youth, and that a
people might always remain in this place for the Lord and his Truth.
by Sarah Dickinson & Eliza Roberts

2 day 17 Morn: a large wash busy in the family. Josey returned home, Anthony,
Joseph, & Thomas Morris dined hear, mon epouse, Sammy, John, &
they on a scateing match, Danil Willams Senior and Josey Sansom hear

3 day 18 Morn: Josey and his father went to town.

4 day 19 Morn: William come for Sally and they set of[f] for Burlington, afternoon mon epouse & I went to Joshua Howells, his wife Betsey, & Neddy
Howell, and Sam: Fisher there, we come home by moonlight, I have
passed many disagreable scenes in life! have they wrought nothing
I must confess, and amend.[13]

5 day 20 at work!——

6 day 21 Day a great thaw, Schuilkill broke up, Soliloquy, my son Samuel; read
that beautifull Poem, the Deserted Village[14] to me, we were both in the
feeling state of mind, this is not always in our power. that I had some
hours happy refflection. discard the stormy passions and prise the
blessing! the sky had cleared and the sun went down in its gayest glory.

7 day 22 day busy at work, got the pump mended, Joshua & Neddy Howell hear.
Sammy went to town

1 Day 23 Morn: Josey Sansom breakfasted hear, mon epouse and Betsey Mecom
went to meeting, Josey, my self, Jenny, & Moor took a pleasent walk
round the hills, appetite to diner. afternoon reading & writeing, Josey
went home, Sammy returned

5 day 27 Morn: very cold. myself & Sammy went to meeting, Eliza Roberts,
Samuel Willson, & Thomas Scattered [Scattergood] spoke. dined at
Abraham Mitchel's bought 13 3/4 p[er] y[ard] & quarter yards black rus-

---

13. Half a line erased, a line drawn over it.
14. Oliver Goldsmith, "The Deserted Village" (1770).

sel for quilts for Sally and I. paid a visit to Sarah Fisher, who comeing from her son James weding had a fall and broke her arm, thus all things meet with there alloy. Sammy and I rode pleasently home, and I had a comfortable evening, truly feeling happiness is equally distributed to the minds of all who will seek it.

6 day 28   Morn: makeing a jaket for Sammy. afternoon mon epouse & I on a visit to Neighbour Williams. himself, Debby, & Sally, with their dear little companion, Maria, the child of their unfortunate Brother, the mother now dead! brings a reconsiliation to the family, the child I believe will cement the fathers forgiveness.

7 day 29   a snowy day, finished Sammy's Jaket

1 Day 30   Morn: half past seven, Josey arrived to breakfast, as I was feeding my chickens, he looked the picture of health, walking over the Hills, nine O'Clock mon epouse, Betsey Mecom, & Sam: set off for meeting, the chaise broke at the end of the lane, and they continued on foot, got to morning meeting, Joseph and I had an agreable day in chat and books, five O'Clock he went home, our folks returned some what weary, evening mon epouse and the family reading

2 day 2   Morn: at work, afternoon Rumford & Cephas Daws, Schuilkill frose
Mo 1   again

[February 1, 1785]

3 day 2   Day. a compleat snowy time, toward evening changeing to rainy sleet, that in the

4 day 3   morning, many of our young trees were broke and others hardly able to support the weight of congealed snow on the limbs, but, this admits of a beautifull winter prospect, glittering against the sun, and my eyes are at this moment enchanted, with the delightfull prospects before me, of distant hill and dale, the trees all silvered to a distant view. Mon epouse, Sammy, John Macevers, and Jenny gone in the Slay round to Kensington.

6 day 5   Morn: mon epouse and Sammy went to town and returned with John & Rachel Drinker, and Polly Howell Drinker and her son Henry, we passed the day agreably. Cousin John presented me with a Narrative of the Captivity of Ben: Gilbert,[15] and his family, fifteen in number, for upwards of two years.

7 day 6   Morn: at work. afternoon Sally Parish & her son Josey, Han: Mitchel, Henry & Polly Howell Drinker, and Josey, Billy, & Polly Drinker. a fine slideing match.

---

15. William Walton, *A Narrative of the Captivity and Sufferings of Benjamin Gilbert and His Family, who were surprised by the Indians, and taken from their farms, on the frontiers of Pennsylvania, in the spring, 1780* (1784).

1 Day 7   Morn: Josey come from Town, where Billy arrived last night, having
             left Sally at Cousin Molly Sykes's. my mother quite recover'd. mon
             epouse, and Sammy & Betsey Mecom went to meeting. evening they
             returned and with them Olen Gamble and Caty Mullen,

2 day 8   Morn: being quarterly meeting we all went to town, at meeting John
             Foreman, Marget Porter, Hannah Cathrell, and James Thornton spoke.
             mon epouse & I dined at Samuel Pleasents, the company his Wife, Sally
             Pleasents, John & Robert Pleasents, Joseph Potts, and John Kirbride,
             evening mon epouse & I returned. some melancholy events, yet the lat-
             ter part of the evening seemed to brighten.

3 day 9   Morn: myself and Sammy and Betsey Mecom went to meeting, John
             Foreman, Thomas Scattergood, John Simson, William Savery, and
             Marget Porter spoke. I dined at Thomas Clifford's the company him-
             self & Wife, Anne Giles, Peggy Guest, Tammy Clifford, and Thomas
             Smith, after diner an agreable discourse between Myers Fisher and a
             Gentleman called the Philospher who is entirely blind, ever since he
             was six months old, yet from the care of his parents, his great strength
             of memory, and natural abilitys is a man of great learning, he is a scot
             by birth, and has come to America to exhibit lectures on Philosophical
             subjects in Public. evening Billy Sansom went home with us.

4 day 10   Morn: mon epouse & Billy went to town, passed the day at work.

7 day 13   afternoon Josey come home, some well wrote political peices, my coun-
             try miss[es] there old leaders[16]

1 Day 14 Mon epouse and Sammy & Betsey Mecom went to town, evening on
             their return brought me inteligence, of the decease of Mary Chovet, an
             elderly woman, but the remains of a woman with [the] finest and
             [most] engageing presense I have ever seen, thus moulders into dust all
             human perfections, nothing but the pure etherial spark will remain,
             and as it has been cherished so shall its future illuminations be!

2 day 15   Morn: myself and Josey went to town, a lighting at Docter Chovets, I
             staid the day with the Docter and Sukey Abbington, four O'Clock in
             the evening Mary Chovet was buried! lodged with Rachel Drinker, it
             is strongly woven in our Nature's that a decency may attend our inter-
             ment, some sacred tears be shed!

3 day 16   Morn: at meeting Will: Savery and Thomas Scattergood spoke, dined
             at Benjamin Horners. himself & Wife, Henry Clifton, Thomas John-
             son, and Polly, Sally, & Amy Horner, afternoon a visit to Sally Waln,
             the Wife of Nicolas Waln who is at present in Engand on a religious
             visit. Sammy come for me, and I returned home.

---

16. HCS may be thinking of the loss of Quaker control of the Assembly, when her father and others
resigned their seats in protest over the wars of the 1750s.

4 day 17   Morn: at work. afternoon Sammy and I paid a visit to our Neighbour Crouch

5 day 18   Morn: reading a poem Called Lousia a pathetic peice by Anna Seward.[17] afternoon Hannah Walker, an unfortunate Orphan!

7 day 19   Josey come and we had an agreable evening.

1 Day 20   Morn: mon epouse, myself, and Betsey Mecom went to meeting. Thomas Scattergood, David Eaustah, and Samuel Smith spoke. dined at Neighbour Warners. Nancy Warner and Molly England there, afternoon at meeting. got home tolerably considering it rained, evening but poorly in health.

2 day 21   Morn: mon epouse and Josey went to town. afternoon Will: Sansom.

3 day 22   Morn: mon epouse and I went to town, to monthly meeting. Thomas Scattergood. dined at Neighbour Warners with Becky Shoemaker, Hannah Cathrell, Benjamin Sweet, Joshua, Caty, & Betsey Howell, and Nancy Warner, some agreable anecdotes from Becky Jones. spent an Hour with Sukey & Anne Head.

4 day 23   Morn a visit from Debby Williams. mon epouse & Sammy scateing.

7 day 26   this day Sally returned from burlington, with her Brothers, left Mother in a state of mind contented with her lot, what can go beyond this, support, the Ills of this life in full assurance of a better! Billy returned in the evening

1 Day 27   Morn: mon epouse, Sammy, and Betsey Mecom went to meeting, Sally, Josey and I spent the day agreably with books, Josey ardently searching after the knowledge of short hand.

2 day 28   Morn: Josey returned, Sally & I turning a Coat for mon epouse & one for Sammy

[March 1, 1785]

3 day 3   month 1 Morn: at work, afternoon John Head and Josey Sansom, the latter staid all night

5 day 3   a visit of ceremony to Sally from Sally Fisher, Sally Pemberton, and a stranger Gentlemen named Perott, (S Fisher is engaged to Abijah Dawes,) the roads were very bad, the Horses wild, that the poor girls had a severe fright

7 day 5   finished Sammy's coat. evening Josey Sansom brought inteligence of the death of Joseph Read one of the prime actors in the scene of fifty nine,[18]

17. Anna Seward, *Louisa* (1784), a verse novel.

18. Joseph Reed would only have been eighteen in 1759, but he was a prominent radical during the Revolution and in 1779 was president of Pennsylvania. He was a general in the Continental Army and member of the Continental Congress. His wife, Esther deBerdt Reed, organized the first women's politi-

1 Day 6   Morn: mon epouse, myself, and Betsey Mecom went to town, Thomas Scattergood, Hannah Cathrell, and Hezekiah Williams spoke, dined with Caleb and Annabella Creson, a sensible happy couple, afternoon at meeting Sarah Dickinson spoke

2 day 7   Josey went home, Sally and I at work.

6 day 11   a letter from Josey Sansom, encloseing one from George Le Roy, finished the coat for mon epouse and a Jaket for Sammy, mon epouse and Sally went to town, in the evening he returned

7 day 12   Morn: Jenny & I cleaning house; afternoon Thomas Chalkley James, and Josey Sansom, Tommy is a mild pretty lad, the unfortunate Father, striveing to raise a lasting and permanent foundation of earthly goods, to his offspring, has put it in the power of fortune, that fickle Goddess in the heathen mythology, who is pictured all ways deceiveing her voteries, he has robed them of what they had!————————

1 Day 13   Morn: mon epouse went to meeting, a snowy rainy day. afternoon a little clear, Tommy and Josey went home

2 day 14   mending men's cloaths,

7 day 19   Morn: mon epouse and John Macevers went to town in a Slay, Josey and Sally returned with them

1 Day 20   Morn: mon epouse and Betsey Mecom went town, the children and I spent an agreable day at home reading and writeing, evening Josey & Sally: one reading and the other translateing the french Testament.

2 Day 21   Morn Josey went home, John Macevers left us to put himself apprentice to a Carpenter. Sally and I turning a coat for Billy.

3 day 22   Morn: mon epouse went to town, afternoon John Head and Jemmy Olden, inteligence of the death of Thomas Potts[, he was] well last night at Docter Moyes lectures on natural Philosophy and dead at noon to day! he lived at Potts grove five & thirty miles from Philadelphia

4 day 23   a very cold day. my mind has been with T Potts's family, received the inteligence perhaps in the dead of the night! now on the melancholy Journey.————————

Oh Death how keen are thy surprises, make ye ready.

5 day 24   Morn: mon epouse and I went to meeting, John Foreman spoke, dined at John Drinkers with mon epouse, Tommy Wister, and Josey and Polly Drinker, afternoon at home William Sykes.

cal society, raising money for the troops in 1780. The family therefore stood for many things anathema to HCS and the Quakers. Later entries in the diary indicate the anger HCS felt at the arrests of Quakers during the war. It is curious that HCS conflates the events of the Revolution in 1778-79 with the factional disputes of the Friendly Association in 1759.

6 day 25   Morn: mon epouse went to town, afternoon William Sansom, lodged hear.

7 day 26   mon epouse and Josey Sansom come home, Billy returned

1 Day 27   Morn: mon epouse and Betsey Mecom went to town, the children and I had an agreable day, Josey brought us Wesley's Compendium of Natural Philosophy,[19] an entertaining book, fit for young minds. wrote to my mother,

2 day 28   Morn: myself, Sally, Josey, & Sammy went to town, meeting Jacob Linley spoke. dined with Joshua & Caty Howel at Johns Hopkins, with divers [others]. Sammy and I had a pleasent ride home.

3 day 29   Morn: mon epouse & I went to town, meeting James Thornton, Mary Cox, and Jacob Linley spoke, mon epouse & I dined at Neigh: Warners with Becky Shoemaker, Molly England, & Nancy Warner, afternoon Mary Cox come there and we spent an instructive and agreable two hours. mon epouse & I returned rain come on and

4 day 30   a violent storm. however he who will not strive to live, thro' the storm, will not be found worthy of the Calm!

5 day 31   afternoon William and Sally in company with Samuel Rowland Fisher, evening wound up disagreably!

[April 1, 1785]

6 day
fourth
month 1   Morn mon epouse and I took a ride, afternoon Sally and I at work calm and serene, the evening wound up pleasently, thus shall life be chequered, our own wills frequently constitute our unhappiness.

7 day 2   a deep snow, this has a winter like march

1 Day 3   Morn: mon epouse and Betsey Mecom went to meeting. afternoon Josey Sansom,

2 day 4   Morn: Josey went home, and we had a New servant, a hired Negro man named Benjamin, Joseph Francis called to look at my Garden.

3 day 5   Mon epouse went to town, William Sansom returned with him

4 day 6   afternoon Debby, Sally, & Maria Williams hear,

5 day 7   afternoon John Head, Betsey Hough, and James Olden hear, Betsey staid all night, agrable conversation in the evening.

1 Day 9   Morn 7 O'Clock Josey Sansom arrived from town, Mon epouse, myself, and Sammy and Betsey went to meeting, Eliza Roberts spoke. Dined at John Drinkers with Cousin Rachel, Polly, & Josey, afternoon at meeting Friend Say, Hannah Cathrell, Samuel Smith, and

---

19. John Wesley, *A Survey of the Wisdom of God in Creation; or, a compendium of natural philosophy* (1770).

Hezikiah Williams spoke, Jemmy Olden and Betsey Hough went home

2 day 10 Morn: Josey Sansom went home, we planted our peas, afternoon Mon epouse & Sally went to town,

3 day 11 Morn: Sammy and I went to meeting, William Savery and David Eaustah spoke, ———— Elfrith and Rachel Cathrel were married. afternoon gardening, the primative occupation of man, <u>designed</u> by the almighty for a happy life!

4 day 12 Morn: Sammy and I took a ride, brought home variety of Trees, flowers, and plants, worked so hard that I had the blessing to know and consider the value of the goods bestowed upon us, and

5 day 13 Morn: rose blythly to sow my seeds, and may the great Husband Man, favor the Earth with vegitation, mon epouse went to town. Sally & he returned to dine, afternoon John & Abigal Parish, John Olden, John Head, and William Sansom.

6 day 14 Morn: Richard Waln, Thomas Wister, and Polly Waln spent the day with us.

7 day 15 Morn: Clement Richard, afternoon myself, Sally & Sammy went to Daniel Williams, the company Abjah and Sally Dawes, Sally Gilpin, and Ellison Perott. come home by moonlight, Perott waited on us home, Josey Sansom hear

1 Day 16 Morn[:] mon epouse, Betsey Mecom, Josey & Sammy went to meeting, Josey and Sammy returned to dine, afternoon Neddy Howell and Abram Carlisle, hear. the boys all went to Joshua Howells.

2 day 17 Sally and Sammy went to town, I was very busy in the garden. Clement Richards hear, I hope for the last time, proveing him[self] to be a very dubious Character.

[In margin: "paid Debby Mitchel three dollars"]

5 day 20 Morn: mon epouse and Sammy went to town, Sally and they come home to diner, afternoon Charles Starton and William Sansom

6 day 21 Morn: mon epouse and I set out on a Jaunt Six miles up Schuilkill to Anthony Levering's, an honest family moveing on in the still path of life, we spent a pleasant day, got some young trees, had a most agreable ride home,

7 day 22 Morn: busy gardening, afternoon Edith Newbold, Thomas & Alice Howard, Harry Haynes, Beulah Biddle, Polly Attmore, and William & Joseph Sansom.

1 Day 23 Morn: mon epouse, myself, and Sammy & Betsey Mecom went to meeting. Thomas Scattergood, Hannah Cathrell, Sam: Smith, and Hez:

Williams spoke, dined at John Clifford's with himself and Wife, afternoon at meeting Sam: Smith spoke, returned home, John Head and William Sansom there, this day Edith Hoze come to live with me.

2 day 24 Morn: Buckridge Syms and Neddy Brooks, rest of the day very busy in the garden. mon epouse and Sammy went nine miles up Schuilkill for white pine trees.

3 day 25 Morn: mon epouse and I went to town, Thomas Scattergood spoke, being monthly meeting. Abraham Russel and Polly Shoemaker, and George Dylhorn & Polly Brooks passed. dined at Ann Warners with Joshua and Caty, Neddy and Betsey Howell, Hannah Cathrell, Molly England, and Nancy Warner, drank tea at John Head's,

4 day 26 made Moor a Coat, evening Tommy James and Josey Sansom,

5 day 27 Morn: an accidental visit from a young Stranger, an Hibernian. afternoon Charles Starton, Allison Perott, Rumford Daws, two Strangers, and William Sansom

6 day 28 Morn: Josey Sansom brought me two Tuby Rose roots that John Parish brought from Barbados, all the day very busy in my garden,

7 day 29 Morn: mon epouse took Betsey Mecom to town, who is gone to live with her mother at Raway, evening Josey Sansom,

[May 1, 1785]

1 Day 5   Morn[:] mon epouse myself and Sammy went to town, market street
Mo. 1   meeting, Eliza Roberts, Sarah Harrison, and Arthur Howell spoke, dined at Docter Chovet's with Sukey Abbington, thence to Rebecca Shoemaker's, the company Benny, & Betsey Shoemaker, Rachel Carpenter, Peggy Rawle, and John Clifford,

2 day 2 Morn: quarterly meeting, Sally, Josey, and I went to town, a most agreable walk, and good meeting. James Thornton, Marget Porter, and Hannah Cathrell spoke, dined at Thomas Hough's with Betsey Hough and Sally Sansom, afternoon at meeting the memorial of our good friend Anthony Benezet was read, the memory of the Just is as a sweet perfume, to the mind. evening myself & Sally at John Thomas's, lodged at Abram Mitchel['s]

3 day 3 Morn: we breakfasted at Friend Mitchel's with Joseph & Polly Potts, ten O Clock went to meeting, Thomas Scattergood, Samuel Smith, Peter Thomas, and Marget Porter spoke, dined at John Drinkers with the family, William brought me home, and mon epouse went to town, Josey and Sally come together,

4 day 4 Morn: very rainy. Josey went to town, mon epouse returned and brought me a letter from Dan: Smith, importing mother is worse than useual,

5 day 5 Morn: William and I crossed the Delawar, at the Arch Street ferry, the Birmingham just come up, a fine view of the shiping along shore, a

pleasant ride to burlington, found mother much mended, and the good family well,

6 day 6   Morn: Billy returned, placed myself to work, passed the time happily, Ann Hume paid us a visit, an english woman who has had a varied scene in life.

7 day 7   Morn: Anne Chambers went into the country, visit from Mary Barker, John & Mary Hoskins.

1 Day 8   spent the day at home with my mother, visit from Docy Craig and Polly Hoskins,

2 day 9   Morn: visit from Lydia Hosking, Grace Beaucannon, and Hannah Smith Cox

3 day 10   afternoon Mary Hoskins, Sarah Smith, Mary Watson, & I went to Robert Grubs about two miles from town, formerly Sam: Allinson's—where I have passed many happy hours, with those who are now, free from anxiety, and glance an eye of pity on our toils! Perhaps, my beloved Betsey Allinson, Sally Pemberton, and Caty Smith, dear companions!

5 day 12   dined with Aunt Elizabeth Smith, Relick of my good Unkle Robert Smith, and her children Robert and Sarah, Burlington wears a different face, with my relations, from twenty years past, yet blessed be Providence, they are favored with food convenient for them, I trust in body and mind. afternoon we adjourned to Daniel Smiths, my mother is much mended since I come, Rachel Hoskins and Nancy Dylvin there.

6 day 13   Morn: visit to Nancy Odell, she and her family, being shortly to remove, to her Husband Jonathan Odell, at Nova Scotia, he having thro' [a] variety of incidents been termed a Refugee![20] — 9 O Clock took leave of my Burlington dear friends. Myself and Polly Smith took passage in Jacob Myres boat, with many more, not disagreable Companions, who when we arrived at the warf in Philadelphia, parted never perhaps to meet again in this Life! Polly and I dined at friend Mitchel's, I left her at Josey Richardson's and William brought me home in a chair, four O'Clock Polly Drinker, Polly & Amy Horner, Allison Perott, and Josey Sansom walked hear, Billy & Allison returned,

7 day 14   Morn: Sally poorly, Josey and the girls took an agreable walk, afternoon Allison come, mon epouse, Josey, Sammy, and I attended them to Hambleton's Bush hill [estate,] walked over that good house, viewed the fine stucco work, and delightful prospects round, when we parted they went to town well pleased with the excursion.

---

20. Term for British collaborators during the American Revolution in New Jersey. Jonathan Odell was an Anglican cleric and poet associated with Loyalist governor William Franklin who had to flee to England during the war. He had just been rewarded by being named provincial secretary to New Brunswick. Cynthia Dubin Edelberg, *Jonathan Odell, Loyalist Poet of the American Revolution* (Durham, NC: Duke University Press, 1987).

1 Day 15　Morn eight O Clock William and John Jackman arrived, a relation from Barbados, mon epouse, John Jackman, Josey, Sammy, and I went to meeting at fair Hill which has been discontinued till now ever since the ravage of the war! Will: Savery gave us an excellent sermon, I come unto you not with enticeing words of mans wisdom[21]　　　　James Creson and Richard Humphrys spoke, Caleb Creson, his wife, and son dined with us, afternoon William Savery, Jesse Waln, John Jackman, and Josey Sansom

2 day 16　Morn: mon epouse and Josey went to town, returned to dine with Benny and Polly Smith, afternoon Philip and Molly Benezet, Betsey Dowers, and Will Sansom,

3 day 17　Morn Billy went home, planted my Carolina beens, afternoon mon epouse & I went to the funeral of Mary Garigues. Will: Savery and Eliza Roberts spoke at the Grave. Josey Sansom went home with us, Allison Perott there.

4 day 18　rainy day Josey went home, agreable at work, a half hours tribute to some of my departed friends, whom I have not quite as yet intered! afternoon Will: Sansom set out for Virginia

5 day 19　busy in my Garden, Neddy Brooks hear

6 day 20　Morn: went to town, Rachel Drinker returned with me to dine, afternoon Josey Drinker, John Jackman, and Josey Sansom, a Baloon was raised from Bush hill,[22]

7 day 21　Morn: mon epouse and Rachel Drinker went to town, afternoon Sam:¹ Shaw,

1 Day 22　Morn: 6 o clock Josey Sansom, mon epouse, Josey, Sally, and Polly Smith, went to town, Olin Gamble, Caty Mullen, and Josey Sansom returned to dine, afternoon a pleasent walk, evening reading to the family,

[In margin: "paid Debby Mitchel 3 dollars"]

4 day 25　Morn: very busy in the garden, afternoon mon epouse and I went to see Buckridge Symms, there seat wants nothing but water to compleat an elegant scene,

5 day 26　Morn: garden, afternoon Daniel Williams, John Head, Polly Smith, and Sally Sansom,

6 day 27　Morn: garden, afternoon Neddy Brooks, John Biddle, John Jackman, and Josey Sansom,

---

21. I Corinthians 2:4.
22. There had been an unsuccessful ascension the year before. This one is not mentioned in the general histories of the city.

7 day 29   Morn: at work afternoon Debby and Sally Williams, John and Hannah Thomas, and Benny Smith, Polly and he went to town this evening intending for burlington tomorrow

1 Day 29   Morn: mon epouse, Sammy, & I went to meeting, at market street. Richard Humphrys and Eliza Roberts spoke, dined at Isaac Parish's, afternoon at Bank, Drank tea at Henry Drinkers with his wife Polly Sandwith and Billy, Sally, & Nancy Drinker,

2 day 30   Morn: Benjamin Shoemaker,

3 day 31   Morn: 7 O Clock Caty Mullen and Josey Sansom, afternoon Abjah and Sally Dawes. Elliston Perot a man of Character, and uncommon openness of disposition, fond of and ardently seeking a lasting acquaintance with our family————————

[June 1, 1785]

4 day 1   Morn: at work, afternoon Olin Gamble, Sukey and Josey Head, Henry Drinker,

5 day 2   Morn: half past four o'clock Caty Mullen and Sammy and I went to town, breakfasted at friend Mitchels, went to meeting, Rich: Humphrys, David Eaustah, and Eliza Roberts spoke. dined at Mitchells, went to meeting, Rich: Humphrys, David Eaustah, and Eliza Roberts spoke. dined at Thomas Cliffords with his wife, John, Anne, and Tamy Clifford, and Anne Giles, paid a visit to Caty Hopkins, and one to Rachel Drinker, John Head brought me home to tea. where I found Henry and Elizabeth Drinker, Becky and Sally Scattergood, and Benny and Polly Garrigues,

6 day 3   Morn: at work, afternoon Debby Foulk, Polly Drinker, and Elliston Perot. the young folk enjoyed themselves,

1 Day 5   Morn: mon epouse, Josey, Sammy, and myself went to fair hill meeting, Sarah Dickinson   spoke, James Pemberton Mary Pleasents, Anthony Joseph & Thomas Morris and Molly Mitchel dined hear, we had an agreable afternoon,

3 day 7   Morn: John Macevers come home sick, John Lancaster dined with us, wrote to mame,

5 day 9   Morn: Ellison Perot spoke to me on a very serious occasion, his manner was so artless and sincere, that I wished he had been born within the pale of our church, but does not this show a narrow mind, are not all men born of one universal parent, "if thou doest well shalt thou not be accepted,"[23] afternoon Will: Sansom returned from Virginia, likes Pennsylvania best.

23. 2 Cor. 5:9 and following.

6 day 10   Morn Billy went to town, afternoon myself, Sally, and Sammy at Neighbour Williams. Neddy, Debby, and Sally at Home, Jonathan Mifflin there,

7 day 11   at work, evening Josey Sansom,

1 Day 12   Morn: mon epouse, Josey, and Sammy went to meeting, afternoon Will: Sansom talk on many serious things, EP having generously disclosed his mind to him—

2 day 13   afternoon Sally, Sammy, and I went to see Friend Gibson's Family, with whom John Jackman is, and a Widow Thornhill, a pleasent situation near Schuilkill, speant an agreable afternoon, this evening had a new Servant Jo: Canue

3 day 14   Morn: parted with negro benjamin, Sammy and I went to town. at meeting Robert Valentine and Thomas Scattergood spoke. dined at Friend Warners with Hannah Cathrell, Molly England, and Nancy Warner, visit to Cousin Rachel, and Neigh Horner, tea at home, with Betsey Hough, Jemmy Olden, John Jackman, and Caty Mullen

4 day 15   Morn: busy afternoon, Debby and Sally Williams,

6 day 17   Morn: Sammy & Caty Mullen went to town, evening mon epouse, Sally, & I took a pleasent walk, Josey Sansom hear,

1 Day 19   Morn: 5 O'Clock Josey Sansom set off to Burlington, with Will: Moor who is returned to his Grand mother, mon epouse, Sally, Sammy, and Edith went to meeting, eleven O'Clock Elliston Perot, I have never seen a man that looks as though I could have trusted my child with to more satisfaction, what my friends may think of it I cannot tell, the children of our society are the children of the public, marriage is a solemn act and confirms our happiness in this life, or by a series of afflictions that must be our own bosom companions, fits us for a nother world, where sorrow shall cease——————— four O'Clock he went [to] town, evening mon epouse, Rachel Drinker, & Sammy returned

2 day 20   Morn 7 O Clock breakfasted, then Cousin Rachel, Sammy & I with mon epouse on horse back, crossed Brittains bridge, to John Penns elegant Villa, passed a Couple of delightfull hours, mounted our chaise and rode a long the Schuilkill to Peters place the highest and finist situation I know, its gardens and walks are in the King William taste,[24] but are very pleasent, We had a very polite reception from Rich: Peters, his Wife, and mother, took to our chaise and by his direction, thro a pleasent rode to Riters ferry, crossed and continued our route along Schuilkill, to the falls tavern where we had a fine diner of fish, see two rafts pass thro' the falls, four O'Clock we took the chaise and went to

24. King William reigned 1689–1702, so the garden is quite old-fashioned.

our good friend Joshua Howells, Caty and Betsey were in town with her daughter Caty Hopkins who was Lying in. passed some agreable hours, returned home, Cousin John Drinker arrived from town, John Macevers went home,

3 day 21　Morn: Thomas Wister breakfasted with us then we all went to town, monthly meeting, a Stranger and Eliza Roberts spoke, dined at Friend Warners with Sarah Harrison, Molly England, Hannah Cathrel, Caty Howell, Nancy Warner, and Sarah Sansom, afternoon Sally and I at James Stuarts, his Wife, a Capt Riche & Wife, and Docter spence, we had a delightful ride home by moon light,

4 day 22　Morn: John and Hannah Thomas with Arthur, Madame Reynear and her son. she is a singular instance of the power religion holds over temporals, having those lines truly verified. For in misfortunes this advantage lies / they make us humble and they make us wise,

5 day 23　Morn: John Thomas, Will Sansom, Hannah, and they whent home together, afternoon, restraint, [with] Ellison Perot, [since] mon epouse for reasons of state having not been let into the secret occasions

1 Day 26　Morn: mon epouse, Sammy, and I went to meeting Thomas Scattergood and Will Savery spoke, mon epouse & I dined at Caleb Creson's, in a very genteel and pleasent manner, afternoon at meeting, mon epouse & I drank tea with Docter Chovet, and Sukey Abington, a pleasent ride home,

2 day 27　Morn: Josey Sansom went home, afternoon Sally, Sammy, & I went to Friend Gibson['s],

3 day 28　Morn: Sammy and I went to meeting, Thomas Scattergood and Marget Shoemaker spoke, dined at home, afternoon John Head, Will: Sansom, and Ben: Smith,

4 day 29　Morn: busy, afternoon Polly Drinker, Ellison Perot, and Sally Sansom & they went to take a ride, Rumford Dawes drank tea with us.

5 day 30　Morn: Ironing, had the first feast of our Raspberrys,

[July 1, 1785]

6 day 7　Morn: busy, afternoon Sally and I went to Neigh: Mc Dowels, and
Mo 1　Rumford Dawes, his Wife & Daughter, Patty Whitelock, Sukey Head, and Will Sansom, come to see us, teaed with mon epouse,

7 day 2　this day James Johnson made the steps to our front door, Josey Sansom hear,

1 Day 3　Morn: mon epouse, Sally, Josey, and Sammy went to Fair Hill meeting, Henry Drinker & his daughter Molly, and Rebecca Scattergood and her grandson Joseph dined with us. spent an agreable afternoon, Josey Sansom went to town, to the funeral of Joseph Morris,

2 day 4   this day three years we come to live at Parlaville, and James Johnson
           finised the steps to our front door, Friend Gibson, John Jackman, and
           Eliza Hunt at tea,

3 day 5   Morn: Sammy and I went to meeting, Sam:[1] Smith and Will: Savery, a
           friend from Tortolow,[25] spoke, dined at Home, Benjamin and Betsey
           Shoemaker, with their son Benjamin, Rebecca Shoemaker, Ellison
           Perot, and mon epouse went to town with them in the evening, Josey
           lodged hear, note I paid John Macevers £3-

4 day 6   Morn: Josey went home, mon epouse painted the steps,

5 day 7   Morn: Sammy and I went to meeting, dined at friend Mitchel's, after-
           noon Isaac & Sally Parish with three children, and Debby Mitchel &
           Myself rode to our house and passed some agreable hours, enlivened
           with a pleasent walk,

6 day 8   Morn: Ironing, afternoon. Belle and Nancy Marchall, Will: Sansom.

7 day 9   Morn: busy afternoon, a pleasent walk, Josey Sansom hear,

1 Day 10   Morn: Sally, Sammy, and I went to town, at market street meeting,
           Eliza Roberts prayed in a solemn manner, she is a sensible woman, and
           her words fitly spoken, dined with Hannah Pemberton, her Husband
           John Pemberton being in Ireland on a visit to friends, John Zane and
           John Pleasents there, afternoon at meeting Sam: Hopkins and James
           Creson spoke, paid a visit to Hannah Morris, Widow of Joseph Mor-
           ris, the company Sam: and Mary Smith, Dan: Lofly, Abby Griffiths,
           Sally Waln, Tommy Benny, the two Pattys and Phebe Morris, and
           George Mifflin

2 day 11   Morn: busy afternoon John Head and William Sansom. a grand and
           awful Gust, we have as fine a display of the Heavens, as any place I
           know,

3 day 12   Morn: mon epouse & I went to meeting, William Savery gave us an ex-
           cellent discourse founded in the words of Truth and Life! dined at
           Friend Mitchells, with Hannah, Debby, and my two Sons, afternoon,
           a visit to Molly Courtney and Friend Stuart where Docter Spence the
           dentest cleaned my teeth and drew two stumps, cost 2 dollers

4 day 13   Morn: Sukey Head and Anne Dawson, afternoon Will: Sykes, John
           Head, James Olden, and Betsey Hough, Sally and they took a walk.

5 day 14   Morn: Betsey Hough, Sally and I spent pleasently, afternoon James
           Olden and John Head come, and took the Girls to Harrogate springs,
           Inteligence by Billy Sansom [that] George Mifflin died very suddenly
           this morn [at] ten O Clock, he was well in health on first day last, when
           we were in company,   the young men returned to town

---

25. Tortola, in what is today the British Virgin Islands.

6 day 15 Morn: very agreable, Debby, Sally, and Maria Williams hear, afternoon a fine Gust, and one of the finest rain bow's I ever see.

7 day 16 Morn: at work, afternoon Thomas & Mary Hough, and Rebecca Scattergood & her grandson, Betsey Hough went home with her parents, Josey Sansom come home

1 Day 17 Morn: Mon epouse, Sally, Josey, and Sammy went to meeting, this morn: 8 O Clock is to be intered Docter Samuel Preston Moor, he was an aged man, but, this man I also see at meeting this day [a] week [ago], well in health, he was taken ill fifth day morn: Remember thy end, and let enmity, cease; (remember) corruption and death, and abide in the commandments. Remember the commandments, and bear no malice to thy Neighbour, (remember) the covenant of the highest, and wink at Ignorance.[26]

2 day 18 Morn: Jane washed the parlour, my chamber, & entry, afternoon Peter & Hannah Thompson, Lydia and Sally Parker, Will: Sykes and son, and Elliston Perot, Sally having staid in town all night, brought the intelegence of Will: Norton's decease. he was well the morning before at the Docter's funeral, and [was] intered himself this evening! the Brevity of Human life, he has left a good Character behind him, an insense breathing perfume.

3 day 19 Morn: mon epouse and I went to meeting, William Savery and Eliza Roberts, spoke. also a Widow Lilly a Friendly woman from St A Croix, the only person on the Island professing our principles, dined at home, afternoon Sally Pleasents, Sally Gilpin, and Debby Foulk

5 day 21 Morn: 7 O Clock Polly Drinker, Debby Foulk, and Josey Bringhurst breakfasted with us, then went to Harrow gate, 10 O Clock Neddy Howell, then Henry, John, Rachel, and Polly Drinker, they staid the day with us, and in the afternoon we had a most agreable walk, for near a mile along side a pleasent run, through a wood.

6 day 22 Morn: at work, afternoon Edward Penington, Rumford Dawes, and Will Sansom

7 day 23 Josey from town. note on the 20th Elliston Perot, Sally William, and S Sansom went to Friend Looselys,

1 Day 24 Morn: mon epouse, Sammy, and I went to meeting, David Eaustah, Sam: Smith, and Hannah Cathrel spoke. we dined at Will: Sykes's with Polly & Tommy Sykes, Rachel Wharton, and Nancy McCoulough, I paid a visit to Anne Clifford. she is very poorly. we had a pleasent ride home, Elliston Perot and Will Sansom there

2 day 25 morn: Madame Reynear and her son, afternoon mon epouse and I

26. Luke 1:71, Acts 17:30.

went to Friend Gibson's, his Wife has got a Daughter, the Widow Thornhill is a fine old woman, on our return found Will: Sykes, Neigh: M^ac Douell, Wife & Daughter,

3 day 26   Morn: mon epouse and I went to monthly meeting, Eliza: Drinker and Sarah Harrison, spoke, dined at Friend Warners, Jos & Caty, Molly England, Hannah Cathrel, and Nancy Warner there, this day dead Phebe Morris, daughter of Samuel Morris, she was also one of the company the last first day two weeks! being likely for rain drank tea at home, with Elliston Perot,

4 day 27   Morn: Peter Miller hear, one of those men who have been called before a Court and tried for their Lives, without commiting a crime, in the turbulent times past,[27] afternoon: Neighbour Bass and Betsey, Debby & Sally Williams, they brought our Neighbour Holker, he is a foreigner raised to consequence in America, by what is passed, a man of disipation, a great talker, because he cannot bear reflection: such are not the men one should wish to improve an acquaintance with.

5 day 28   Morn: busy, afternoon William Sykes & son, Isaac Barnes, John Head, and Will: Sansom

6 day 29   Monthly meeting mon epouse went, this day died Rebecca Jones, wife of Esra Jones, a young woman with her first child. Afternoon Elliston Perot [was here], mon epouse, mentioned his errand to Sally and I, as a thing of difficulty, that the path in which our society are to walk is narrow anough for this world, without laying our selves under unnecessary causes of trouble and mortification, but the young man from the first has always declared a steady resolution to be come one of the Society.

7 day 30   Morn: Ironing afternoon Molly Mitchel, an elderly good sort of woman, John Jackman, and Will: Sykes come and Sally Sansom and Debby and Sally Williams went with him to Harrow gate, Josey Sansom hear,

1 Day 31   Morn: Sally, mon epouse, Sammy, & I went to meeting, market street, James Creson, a stranger, and Debby Cracson spoke, we dined at John Drinkers afternoon at meeting James Creson and Richard Humphrys spoke. drank tea at Rumford Dawes, Cephas Dawes, Joshua Gilpin, and Patty Whitelock there Elliston Perot there, Sally staid in town, Billy Sansom sets of[f] for New York, to morrow morning,

---

27. Peter Miller, a Philadelphia scrivener, was among the men attainted with high treason by the Supreme Executive Council of Pennsylvania. *Pennsylvania Packet,* May 23, 1778, p. 1. A warrant for his arrest was issued the following year.

[August 1, 1785]

2 day 8   Morn: Molly and I at work, our poor Polly Shingleton, having married
MO 1   about a twelve month ago, died some days since, of twins, her life
        passed in a degree of Innocency, that I hope her death was happy. James
        Johnston began to finish the Schuilkill Parlour.

3 day 2   Morn: Sammy and I went to youth's meeting Eliza Roberts, Robert
        Valentine, Marget Porter, Daniel Lofly, and Eliza Drinker spoke. Sally
        and I dined at Friend Mitchels, Elliston Perot come there and we had
        a serious conversation. all we can do for our children in the great event
        of marriage, is to Judge from the then most promising appearances, de-
        sire a blessing on our hopes! then leave the event to the Father of all. I
        would not blindly follow Passion, yet where the man appears of an
        Amiable disposition, yet a manly mind, in some degree fit to bear up
        under the cross accidents that will happen in Life, I must prefer it to a
        match of entire discretion, and affection to follow after, Thousands of
        women may, and do make themselves reasonably happy in the latter
        case, yet where an appearance of enjoying the finer feelings of the Soul,
        does chance to offer! Oh my friends who may see this, forgive a Mother
        if she errs in Judgement. ——————I drank tea with my good friend
        Warner, Benny and Betsey Shoemaker, and Nancy Warner, evening
        Will: Sykes waited on us, Sally and I returned home.
        "Stevens, Molly Harrison, Polly Foulk"[28]   had an oppertu-
        nity with my Husband, he acts cautiously, I hope the event will be bet-
        ter than he may expect at present,

7 day 6   Morn: mon epouse and Sammy in town, Billy Sansom returned from
        York. afternoon Elliston Perot and Josey Sansom, a gust to ward
        evening.

1 Day 7   Morn: mon epouse, Sally, Josey, and Sammy went to Fair Hill meet-
        ing,

2 day 8   Morn: 6 O'Clock Josey Sansom and I took a pleasent Walk to town,
        Breakfasted at Joseph Drinkers. Docter Spence dentist cleaned my
        teeth, fixed one in, that had dropped out, cost £1"10, dined at Abraham
        Mitchels, visit to Hannah Thomas, 4 O'Clock Polly Drinker, Will:
        Sansom, and I returned home. mon epouse and William had some dis-
        course conserning Elliston, I cannot find he has much other objection
        but religious oppinions. I dont remember the nick name of quaker is
        mentioned, in the scripture, but Abel tells his Brother all who offer
        meekly shall be accepted.[29]

3 day 9   Morn: mon epouse and I went to meeting, Hannah Cathrell and Owen

28. Lines cut out here.
29. Genesis 4:7.

Biddle spoke dined at home, afternoon Elliston, Josey Sansom, Polly Drinker, myself, Sammy, and Sally took a long walk

4 day 10   Morn: 6 O Clock mon epouse and Polly Drinker went to town, afternoon visit from Will: Sansom and John Head.

5 day 11   Morn: at work, afternoon, Widow & Ann Emblen, Polly Beveridge, and Sammy Howell. evening Elliston Perot. mon epouse rather uneasey, all gracious Providence favor my child, with a portion of a diserning spirit, had this man been called a quaker, I think, we all seem of one mind, that we coud as far as appears have had no objection to him.

6 day 12   Morn: at work, afternoon Kitty and Nelly Niglee our country Neighbours

7 day 13   Morn: at work, afternoon Joshua and Neddy Howell, John Head, and Will: Sansom.

1 day 14   Morn: Sally, Sammy, and I went to town, at meeting dined at Henry & Polly Drinkers, with Widow Howell, afternoon tead[30] at John and Rachel Drinkers. Polly & Josey Drinker and Hannah Thomas there, evening Ellison waited on us home.

2 day 15   Morn: at Work, afternoon Sally and I at Friend Williams, the family sick, Betsey Bass there, at our return found Thomas Lightfoot, William Millhouse, and Joshua Baldwin has passed one meeting with

3 day 16   Morn: W M went home, TL and I passed some hours in conversation on things past, afternoon Josey Sansom he walked home by moonlight, & T Lightfoot

4 day 17   Morn: 6 O'Clock, Henry and Polly Drinker, Polly and Amy Horner, and Josey Sansom, after Breakfast we were Joined from Town by Jemmy Olden, Elliston Perot, Polly Drinker, mon epouse, & Sammy. we took a walk over Schyilkill dined in the woods, passed the day pleasently, took a pleasent walk to Penns improvements. drank tea at home. part of the Company went home by moon light

5 day 18   Morn: 9 O Clock mon epouse & the two Polly Drinker's went to town. afternoon William Sansom lodged hear.

6 day 19   Morn: 6 O'Clock Billy and I rode to Friend Gibson's breakfasted with John Jackman, returned. afternoon J Jackman and Elliston Perot. returned by moon light

7 day 20   busy at Work Josey Sansom hear returned by moon light.

1 Day 21   Morn: mon epouse Sally and Sammy went to town. 11 O Clock John & Hannah Thomas with little Arthur who is sick.[31]

---

30. HCS's shorthand for "tea'd," meaning "had tea with."

31. Approximately five lines were cut from the diary.

5 day 25   afternoon Sally and Billy come home, Hannah & Arthur Thomas, and Polly Drinker

6 day 26   Morn: at work, afternoon Jemmy Olden, and William Abbot, an agreable Hibernian.

7 day 27   Morn: William Sansom, One O'Clock Sally & Billy set for Burlington & Springfeild I went to see my Neighbour Crouch who is very Ill. returned in the rain.

1 Day 28   Morn: very wet, I took the Chaise and went to Neig: Crouch found her some thing better. this day Joseph Canue left us, and John   come to live with us,

2 day 29   Morn: mon epouse and Sammy took a ride, afternoon Elliston Perot, it is not possible to think so ill of human nature, as to doubt his being a sincere man,

3 day 30   Morn: mon epouse and I went to meeting[:] Molly England, Sam: Smith, and Dorcas Lilly spoke, we dined at home, afternoon mon epouse, Sammy, and I went to Joshua Howells, Benny, Betsey, and Anne Shoemaker, and Caty Hopkins there, much talk of E P. I dont find any person has any thing to say against him but his being out of the Society. Ann Hume is dead. a woman of a superior understanding, who come from England about thirty years ago, and has led a retired life in America since, she possessed a quality of embelishing the goods of this life, to great advantage, had she been placed in a desert she would have made it smile, then immagine reader, to thyself, her house and garden and little enclosures compleat, order in miniature   yet many Cross accidents, weaned her even from the delight of our first Parents. and she is removed I hope to a better World————her dwelling was at Burlington.

4 Day 31   Morn: with Neigh: Crouch, afternoon William Sansom, he left his Sister with her Grand mother, and goes up again to morrow, Johanna Steuart walked hear with Sammy, and some more children. they had a happy time.

[September 1, 1785]

5 day 9   Mon epouse in town, inteligence of the decease of Mary Roberts the
Mo 1   wife of Hugh Roberts

6 day 2   this morn did my Neighbour Margeret Crouch a well disposed woman taken from the caresa of Old age, and wedlock with a spirit not so mild as her own! all merciful Providence even when thou givest and when thou take'st!

7 day 3   Morn: with my Neighbour, afternoon mon epouse took Johanna to town,

1 Day 4   Morn: Fair Hill meeting Mon epouse, Josey, and Sammy went, Tommy Wister come home with them, afternoon we all went to the funeral of Margeret Crouch which was ordered with decency, mon epouse rode with him to town and I staid at the house, all the poor old woman wished was to close the scene decently, her house in the heavens I believe was ready, as her hope was in her redeemer.

2 day 5   Morn: men come to Plaister some parts of the House and rough cast the side. afternoon Elliston Perot whose good humour and affability will endear him to me, Oh that he had been within our society then I am sure my friends could not blame me. first day night arrived Nicolas Waln, John Townsend, J Storer, and T Calley from England

5 day 8   afternoon Friend Thornhill and Gibson, agreable women.

6 day 9   afternoon William & Sarah Sansom returned from their Journey, [they] left mother well. Henry Drinker and Jacob Downing hear,

7 day 10   afternoon Betsey Hough and Sally Bacon hear. Josey Sansom

1 Day 11   Morn: Josey, Sammy, and I went to town, [to] marketstreet meeting John Storer and Samuel Smith spoke, dined with Mary Armitt, Nancy Emblen there. Josey Sansom went to Burlington in the boat, afternoon at meeting John Townsend spoke, drank tea at James Pemberton's, his wife is in much affliction having lost her son Samuel Morton. Susey Jones, Sally Biddle, Mary Armitt, and Sally and Nancy Pemberton there. James Pemberton read a letter from England giving an account of a small body of People near Mount Pelier in France who call themselves Quakers, and Join escactly with us in sentiment.

2 day 12   Eliza Hunt spent the day with us. Sally poorly. with a fever

3 day 14   afternoon John Head, James Olden, and Elliston Perott, Sally better by by her old friend the Bark.

4 day 15   afternoon Joshua Creson & son, Mary Armitt, [received] inteligence [that] Benjamin Franklin is arrived from France, the Bells have noted [it] fully in our ears.

7 day 19   afternoon Josey Sansom, Sally, and I [have] bad colds.

1 Day 20   Morn: mon epouse, Josey, and Sammy went to meeting, afternoon Josey Sansom and Elliston Perot

3 day 23   Morn: Sally, Sammy, and I went to meeting John Townsend, David Eaustah, Will: Savery, and Eliza Roberts spoke, being montly meeting, when the meetings separated John Storer and Sam: Hopkins come into our meeting and spoke to purpose. dined at Neigh: Warners with Friend Norton, Hannah Cathrel, Caty Howell, Sally Sansom, Molly England, and Nancy Warner, my friends spoke to me concerning Elliston Perot, I delt candidly with them, and as he has applyed to be

taken into meeting, I do sincerely hope he will be enabled to act, up to what I do believe, to be, his good Intensions, I love my friends and am fully convinced my profession is the true christian profession as any of them can be, but alas! I have not lived up to it not withstanding my jaudement is convinced! and I most fervently pray my child may never depart from the religion of the Gospel, and that the follys of youth may not lay a foundation for a repentance, whose bitterness will receive no allay, think of this Sally when I am gone. believe me nothing will be accounted triffles then that has separated thee from the good opinion of thy friends, they will be heavy as the nether mill stone. evening Josey Sammy and I come home.

6 day 26   Morn: Billy and Sally come home and with them Sally Newbold a sensible pretty young girl,

7 day 27   this day was a most violent storm, yet not without its beauties, but my poor poultry did not like it.

[In margin: "indian meal"]

1 Day 28   Morn: 7 O'Clock very fine and clear. Tommy Howard and Will: Sansom come hear in chairs, myself and Sally Newbold went to town with them at Bank meeting Isaac Potts, Ann Scoefeild, and Thomas Colly spoke, dined at William Fishers with James and Hannah Fisher, and Sammy, Taby, & Becky Fisher, afternoon, at Bank Meeting Will Savery, Molly England, and Mary Sweet spoke, visit to Neighbour Warner. mon epouse, Sammy, Josey, and I returned home. Elliston Perot there.

2 day 29   Morn: Sammy and I went to town, it being yearly meeting, we having four men rough casting the House, the rest remained at home. John Simson, Eliza Roberts, John Storer, & others spoke. we returned to dine. afternoon Sally and I paid a visit to Friend William's. Debby, Sally, & Maria Williams, Peter Lloyd, Buck Siyms there, conversation shewed some of the old party leaven left.

3 day 27   Morn: mon epouse Sammy and I went to town Women's meeting held at market street, Eliza Roberts, Mary Cox and others spoke, dined at home.

[October 2, 1785]

1 Day 10   Morn: mon epouse, Sally, Josey, & Sammy went to meeting, a visit from
Mo: 2   Debby, Sally, and Maria Williams, our folks stayed to evening meeting.

[In margin: "paid Debby Mitchel 3 dollars"]

3 day 4   a stormy day. evening William Millhouse lodged hear. we made a fire for the first [time] in the parlour down stairs

4 day 5   afternoon William and Molly Sykes, William and Sarah Sansom. the men returned and

5 day 6   Day the girls very busy at Work prepareing for Betsey Hough's wedding. afternoon William Sansom, Elliston Perot, Thomas Howard, and Edith Newbold. Peggy Dawle and Anne Shoemaker walked over to Robert Morris's improvements, and walked round the Perapet wall on top of the house, which affords a most extensive prospect. Edy lodged with us.

6 day 7   an agreable day.

7 day 8   Morn: mon epouse, myself, and the girls walked over to Springett's Bury, and Bush Hill a most delightful walk. afternoon Will:, Elliston, and Tommy come and took the girls in chairs to Grays Ferry where they enjoyed a most enchanting prospect. Edy returned to town Elliston, Sally, & Molly come home.

1 Day 9   Morn: mon epouse, Sammy, and I went to town, Market street meeting, Marget Shoemaker spoke. dined at Sam: (large ink stain or water mark) Pleasents, with Polly and Sally Pleasents and Robert Proud. afternoon at meeting, see Six or eight East india people, from China, the first I ever see of Mahomet's followers. returned home Elliston there, he confirm's me more in his Probity and Honour. and after a sufficient course of time may my child see many happy days with him,[32]

2 day 10   Morn Mon epouse, Molly, and Sally went to town, afternoon Sammy and I rode to see some of our Neighbours.

5 day 11   Morn: mon epouse and I went to town, at meeting David Eaustah spoke. dined at Friend Mitchels. paid a visit to Rachel Drinker, returned home with Ann Davis and her child, a widow woman who is come to live with me. John the dutch man left us to day.

6 day 12   afternoon. Daniel Williams paid us a visit.

6 day 14   Morn: John Grant come to live with us. Eleven O'Clock William & Sally Sansom, and Molly Sykes, return from Betsey Hough's weding.

7 day 15   afternoon Elliston come with his chaise, with Josey Sansom they took the girls [for] a fine aring, 5 O'Clock [with] Tommy Newbold and Tommy Howard, they all walked [to the] Schuilkill by a beautiful moon light. 8 O'Clock we parted with Molly Sykes and the Company.

---

32. HCS is quite confused here. East Indians would be from the Indian subcontinent or perhaps the South Pacific. Few Chinese were Muslim. Her son, William Sansom, would profit from the China trade from 1797 onward. Jean Gordon Lee, *Philadelphians and the China Trade, 1784–1844* (Philadelphia: Philadelphia Museum of Art 1984), 118–19.

1 Day 16 Morn: mon epouse Sammy and I went to meeting. William Savery a highly favored Minister of the Gospel, proclaimed in the power of the Gospel, Glad tidings unto all men a Saviour is born:[33] no partial gift, we lived in an age [that] the Patriarchs, Prophets and great men of former ages would have rejoiced to see [because of] the favors bestowed upon us, rejoice in humble gratitude to the great giver, who sent his son a man of Sorrows, and acquainted with grief to make our load of Iniquity supportable,[34] Thomas Scattergood and Hannah Cathrel spoke, it was a truly Christian gathering. SS and I dined with our good friends Joshua & Caty Howell, Betsey Howell [was] there. afternoon at meeting Thomas Scattergood spoke, drank tea with Henry & Betsey Drinker, Polly Sandwith, Bandcroft Woodcock, Tommy Irvin, Billy, Nancy, & Molly Drinker, and Susey Sweet, at our return home spent a couple of agreable hours with the family, Elliston Perot.——————

2 day 17 Morn: Sammy and I took a walk to Neigh Crouch's. very pleasant. Benny Shoemaker hear

3 day 18 Morn: mon epouse and Sally went to town, Nancy Davis walked there, lost her self in the evening, did not get hear till nine O'Clock at night

4 day 19 afternoon Thomas Scattergood hear

[In margin: "corn indian meal"]

1 Day 23 Morn: mon epouse, Sammy, and I went to town, market street meeting, James Creson spoke, Billy Sansom went to burlington, I dined with Friend Mitchell. afternoon at meeting, Sally and I paid a visit to Nancy Pemberton, John Thomas a viriginian there, Nancy is left a young Widow with Seven children, Sally and I lodged at Abraham Mitchell's

2 day 24 Morn: after breakfast Sally & Nancy Parish, Debby Mitchell, Josey & Sally Sansom, Elliston Perot, & myself, went to the Widow Norris's garden, thence to the State house walks, and to view some fine paintings in the State house[35] then after walking half way home with Sally and J we parted, afternoon Rachel Park, Anne Giles, and Sally Rawle paid us a visit. Benjamin and Isaac Horner, and Neigh Crouch hear.

3 day 25 Morn: Myself, Sammy, & Edith Hosel went to town, where I parted with her. went to meeting, Owen Biddle spoke. dined at Friend Warners with Joshua & Caty Howell, Becky Shoemaker, Molly England, Hannah Cathrell, and Nancy Warner. Hannah Cathrell and I had a serious conferance concerning Elliston and Sally, I cannot yet blame my child for her conduct, and hope I never shall have reason in the event,

33. Luke 2:10.
34. Luke 1:19, 2:11; Isaiah 53:3.
35. The beginnings of Charles Willson Peale's museum.

to do so, hitherto it has been dutiful, and she never from the first, gave the man reason to believe, she would have him in any other way, than with the consent of her friends as a body. which had not he, after repeated and sincere desires, to seek out some other companion, where the like difficulties subsisted not. uniformly persisted to think he desired, no greater temporal happiness than a union with her, and that by the full consent of her Parents, and if posible, as being a member of our society, she and I mourned together, that he had not been born within the pale of nominal Quakerism, or Birth right, for as to the true birth right as (Nicolas Waln) told us on a first day night, handed to us from Adam, to Noah, and as none but him and his decendants remained after the flood, he comes in with us, as a candidate for a seat in the Mansions, we are told, by the Son, are prepared, by the Father for all those who believe in him.[36] Bare with me my friends, think as favorably of me as you can, my childs happiness has been a tender point with me, I never expected to have been tryed in the spot I have, for my child has been kept in the company of our own society as much as most, though perhaps I am now under the censure of my friends.

4 day 26   Morn: a visit from Francis Gibson and Wife, Widow Thornhill, and Billy Sansom. the latter brought us a genteel present of foreign pickles from Elliston. evening Josey Sansom and Elliston Perot.

6 day 28   afternoon very agreable with Elliston Perot, we walked to Schuilkill

7 day 29   afternoon Sally & Sammy took a ride on Horse back, Lydia Johnson, Polly Drinker, and Josey Sansom hear, this day Benjamin Franklin was proclaimed Governor, such is the visisitude of human events yet perhaps it woud have been a greater honour to any other man than him, allredy crowned with years and litterary honour

1 Day 30   Morn: mon epouse went to meeting a very rainy day, but passed pleasently

[November 1, 1785]

3 day 11   Morn: Sammy and I went to town, Samuel Emblen at meeting Just ar-
Mo 1   rived from england, dined at Friend Warners with Widow Brogden, Molly England, and Nancy Warner. returned home Elliston Perot there.

5 day 3   Morn: walked over to see Neigh: Crouch, afternoon Betsey Brooke, Sukey Head, and William Sansom.

7 day 5   Morn busy at work, afternoon Debby and Sally Williams, James and Betsey Olden, and Josey Sansom, the latter in the evening shewed us some pretty peices of poetry, by Sam: Joseph Smith. his mother Polly

36. John 14:2.

Burling loved me and I her/the race of her mortality was short, she and the dear good woman, Betty Smith, who brought her up are now rejoiceing in the regions of bliss, how different the case, of a gay thougtless mother—Sitgreaves who has closed the last earthly scene, of her daughter, in all the glare of funeral pomp, as she had passed the short course of Eighteen years, nursed in the adulation of beauty, the glare of pomp, and contrary from her baptismal vows, indulged in all the vanitys, of this poor short lived scene! Remember thy end and let enmity cease, remember corruption and death and abide in the commandments.

1 Day 6	Morn: mon epouse, Sammy, and I went to meeting, James Thornton spoke. dined at John Head's, with mon epouse, and Sukey & Nnne Head, afternoon at meeting. evening at home, Elliston Perot.
2 day 7	Morn: 11 O Clock quarterly meeting, mon epouse and I went to town. James Thornton, Margeret Porter, and Abel Thomas spoke, the certificates of Nicolas Waln & Samuel Emblen were read, dined with friend Dawes. afternoon she and I went to meeting. I lodged at Friend Mitchels. evening Samuel Emblen and his son, Debby and Hannah Mitchel, and Elliston Perot spent very agreably.
3 day 8	Morn: Sally come to town, we went to meeting Abel Thomas, John Simpson, Dorcas Lilly, Nicolas Waln, and Thomas Scattergood spoke. Sally and I dined at John Drinkers with Thomas Wister and the family. 4 O'Clock Sally and I with Sammy returned home.
4 day 9	afternoon Benedict Dorce, John Feild, and Elliston Perot, evening very wet, the latter staid all night with us. which gave him great pleasure.
5 day 10	Morn: 11 O Clock visit from Polly Wells, Sally Drinker, and Benjamin Morris.
6 day 11	afternoon Josey Sansom, who returned in the morning of
7 day 12	and his Brother is to come tomorrow that he and I may go to Burlington. afternoon Elliston Perot, a most beautifull moonlight night.

1 Day 13	Morn: mon epouse and Sammy went to meeting. 10: O'Clock William and I set out for Burlington, crossing at Callow Hill street ferry, had a pleasent ride. found Mother and the family well. Hannah Smith and Patty Smith there. evening I related all our concern with Elliston Perot to her and have the satisfaction to see she is easey with our proceeding.
2 day 14	Morn 8 O Clock Billy went home. I was very busy all day packing up many things, which mother chose I shoud have, night wrote largely to Will: Sansom
3 day 15	afternoon Benjamin and Becky Shoemaker arrived. they are looking for a house, that our good friend Samuel Shoemaker may return home and I hope finish his days in quiet, after the storm that wrecked so

many to no purpose.[37] yet those who have acted up to there Judgements I hope will be supported to the end.

4 day 16   afternoon Abigal Martin and Mary Barker.

5 day 17   Morn: went to meeting, John Cox spoke. the new meeting house is shingling. afternoon Polly Smith and I paid a visit to John and Ann Cox, Peter Worrell, Susan Martin, and Sukey Dylvin there. they look to me a happy couple. evening a letter from William, wrote to him.

6 day 18   afternoon Sally Smith and I paid two visits to the aged and sick. Elizabeth Miller, and Sophia Lane. drank tea at John Hoskins with Molly, Lydia, Polly, Rachel, and Abby Hoskins, a fine family.

7 day 19   afternoon Sally, Polly, and Robert Smith with myself took a pleasent walk, drank tea and suped with Aunt Betty.

1 Day 20   Morn: at meeting John Cox spoke. dined with Aunt Bobby and Sally. afternoon at meeting, William Sansom and Elliston Perot come from Philadelphia. my mother received him kindly, and if her life and mine are prolonged I hope we shall have many Satisfactory hours.

[In margin: "bushel buck weat"]

2 day 21   Morn: 11 O'Clock we bid our friends adieu, crossed the ferry to Bristol and had an agreable ride home. purchased two Guiena fowles, evening a pretty large skert of snow, the men returned to town.

3 day 22   Morn: mon epouse went to meeting, afternoon Josey Sansom and Elliston Perot

4 day 23   Morn: Josey, Sammy, and our man John gone on an xpedition for ever green trees.

5 day 24   Morn: planting the ever green trees, afternoon Elliston Perot Polly Williams hear this morn. Benjamin Morris & Mary Wells were married.

1 Day 27   Morn: mon epouse, Sammy, and I went to town, William Savery spoke, dined at Robert Dawson's with his Wife and children, afternoon at meeting Samuel Emblen spoke, visit to Joshua and Caty Howel. Henry Drinker there.

2 day 29   washing day, afternoon Elliston Perot, he staid all night, spent the evening very pleasantly.

3 day 30   Morn: mon epouse and I went to town, at meeting Will: Savery spoke. dined at Abraham Mitchels, mon epouse and I at Plunket Fleeson's, returned home, Sally Dawes and two of the Jones's hear.

---

37. The Revolution.

[December 1, 1785]

4 day 12Mo 1 Morn: busy at work

5 day 12   Morn: Sally and I went to town. at meeting Dorcas Lilly spoke. dined
  Mo 1   at Samuel Shaws with his Wife and family, afternoon Hannah Mitchel
            and I paid a visit to Molly Foulk, Daniel Lofly, his Wife, and son Bet-
            sey Foulk there. lodged at Friend Mitchel's.

6 day 2   Morn: Sammy come for me and we had a pleasent ride home, after-
            noon Jonathan and Susey Jones, Dorcas Lilly, and Elliston Perot

1 Day 4   Morn: very wet. mon epouse went to town. pleasent day with Josey and
            Sammy writeing and reading.

3 day 5   Morn: Sammy and I went to town. at meeting William Savery spoke,
            dined at Friend Warners with my good Friend Becky Shoemaker,
            Peggy Rawle, and Nancy Warner, evening Sally and I come home

6 day 7   Morn: mon epouse set out for Burlington. Elliston Perot and Josey San-
            som Lodged hear

7 day 9   Morn: Sally and I at work in an agreable manner, how many such have
            I spent with my friends, that are now pure spirits, Sally Pemberton,
            Betsey Allinson, Caty Smith! evening Josey Sansom, EP, & Josey
            lodged hear

1 Day 10   Morn: Josey Sansom went to meeting. it has been very wet weather this
            three days. Elliston Perot and Josey Sansom, dined with us. and lodged
            hear.

3 day 12   a very fine day and I was very busy in the garden, and then a fine walk
            with the children, a lovely moon light night. Elliston and Josey lodged
            hear

4 day 13   a very fine day, thro' the Blessing of Providence my family seem as
            though its prospects mended, and my eve of Life may see my children
            turn out well, [there is] no greater recompence for the anxiety they cost
            us!

6 day 15   Morn: Sally Newbold and William Sansom spent the day with us. mon
            epouse returned from his Tour, Elliston and Josey Lodged hear.

1 Day 18   Morn: mon epouse and Sammy went to meeting, afternoon Elliston
            and Josey, evening spent to gether very pleasent.

3 day 20   Morn: Sammy and I went to meeting, dined at friend Mitchel's. a
            pleasent ride home the weather hitherto very open, Elliston lodged
            hear, this man seems formed for domestic happiness, and all the plea-
            sures of social Life, Sally, may thou endear his home to him so as to fix
            as a nail in a sure place, the continuance of this blessing to thee! the wis-
            est men, under all the varius dispensations of providence to man. has

found no surer road to happiness, all under different modes of speech, conclude

Reason's whole pleasures, all the Joys of sense,
Ly in three words Health Peace and Competence,
And Peace, Oh Virtue! Peace is all thine own.[38]

[In margin: "paid Debby Mitchel 6 dollars"]

5 day 22   Morn: Polly, Thomas, and Sally Newbold and William Sansom, spent the day with   evening Polly & Billy went to town. Josey Sansom lodged hear

6 day 23   afternoon myself, Sally Newbold, and Sally and Sammy Sansom had a charming excursion, the day being as mild as may, we were Joined by Elliston and Billy who staid all night.

7 day 24   Morn: after breakfast the men, set out, for town thro' a deep snow, which continued all day, we had a pleasent family day,

1 Day 25   Morn: 8 O Clock Billy come for Sally Newbold, mon epouse and Nancy Davis went to town. a beautiful day over head, afternoon Elliston Perot, I wrote to my mother

4 day 28   Morn: Dicky Vaux and Dicky Parker, afternoon Sally and I on a visit to Friend Williams's, Neddy Williams, Billy Buckly, and ——————— Patison there

6 day 30   Morn: Sally and I agreably at work. afternoon Elliston who says Billy Sansom and Sally Newbold set out for her Fathers.

7 day 31   the last of the Year 1785, and a most delightful day through out

[January 1, 1786]

1 Day of the week and first of the year and month   Morn: a very sleety day, mon epouse and Sammy went to meeting, Josey and they returned to dine, afternoon Elliston who rises in my esteem, [came here,] our man John [is] very ill, mon epouse sat up with him,

5 day 5   Morn: Sally and I pleasently at work, afternoon Samuel Pleasents and Charles Yarvois agreable

1 Day 8   Morn: mon epouse and I went to meeting, William Savery and David Eaustah spoke, we dined with James Bringhurst and his third Wife, Joseph Bringhurst, and James's five sons by Anna were the company, thus stand we on unstable ground from whence

---

38. Alexander Pope, An Essay on Man (London, 1734), 59. The second stanza is "But Health consists with Temperance alone, / And Peace, fair Virtue! Peace is all they own."

> *"Our dying friends are Pioneers, to smooth*
> *Our rug[g]ed path to death; to break those bars,*
> *Of terror, and abhorrence, nature throws*
> *Cross our obstructed Way; and, thus, to make*
> <u>Wellcome,</u> *as* <u>safe,</u> *our port from every Storm."*[39]

afternoon at meeting Samuel Emblen and Sam: Smith spoke; we returned home and spent an agreable evening, with Sally and Elliston, Josey Sansom went to evening meeting and returned to lodge.

2 day 9 Morn: at Work, afternoon Sally, Sammy, and I went to Visit Rebecca Shoemaker and Peggy Rawle, returned by moon light, found Will: Sansom at home, he has visited his grand mother

3 day 10 Morn: Mon: epouse and I went to town, at meeting James Creson, Sam: Smith, Will: Savery, and Sam: Emblen spoke. dined at John Drinkers with Rachel & Polly Drinker, and Tommy Wister. afternoon went to sea my good nurse Peggy Fleming, in the last stage of a Consumption!

4 day 11 Morn: Caty Mullen come and we began quilting Sally and myself a russel quilt. evening Elliston, Josey, and all the family went slideing

6 day 13 Afternoon: Rumford Abijiah & Sally Dawes, Samul R Fisher, Jabes Maud Fisher and Hetty Fisher, William Sykes, and Neddy Brooks, evening all the family went a slideing, Lovely moonlight nights

7 day 14 Morn: got one quilt out, and the other in, at Diner, Anthony & Josey Morris, and Henry Drinker, afternoon Debby & Sally Williams,

1 Day 15 Morn: mon epouse and Sammy went to town, Olly Gamble dined with us, afternoon Elliston, Billy, & Josey. the two latter went to evening meeting ,an agreable evening reading. 9 O'Clock mon epous and Josey returned.

2 day 16 Morn: put in Sally's mantua quilt made out of her grand mother Sansom's weding cloaths, after Sally had sufficiently worn it in a gound. my mother Sansom was a woman of a meek and quiet spirit, I have no doubt she is rejoiceing in the company of Angels and the spirits of the Just made perfect. may her name sake walk in her steps! she had an arduous path to tread in Life, which weaned her from this world, her memory is truly valueable.

3 day 17 finished the quilt, and got to curtain makeing, at which we continued
7 day 21 till 7 day when we had accomplished the full alteration of my blue camblet bed,[40] and three window curtains. evening Josey Sansom

1 Day 22 Morn: very wet, a great thaw, mon epouse went to town, afternoon Elliston Perot, come thro' extream bad roads. his perserverance, and af-

---

39. Young, *The Complaint* (1749) 99.
40. Camblet: a heavy, ribbed woolen fabric.

fection shewn to all the family give me great pleasure now, and strong presages of hope, that my child will have in him, every accomplishment of a good husband. thou hast most assuredly gained a heart. if thou guards it with female softness. it looks to me thou will keep it. many wise women, have concluded it is harder to keep a Heart than gain it. Richardson puts many beautiful expressions, in the mouth of Clarissa. in her unhappy delerium.

———*thou throwest it like a loathsom wead away!*———

6 day 27　afternoon William Atmore

7 day 29　Morn: Eliza Hunt and Hannah Walker, two orphan Girls. ——— —afternoon Caty Mullen and mon epouse went to town,

1 Day 30　Morn: mon epouse Sammy and I went to town. at meeting William Savery and Samuel Emblen spoke. dined with James and Betsey Olden yesterday died Edward Dawes a young man taken in mercy, from the snares of Fortune, and this day died the Widow Salter, favored at last to see the folly, and dreadful snares, that ly hid with beauty, and the love of Grandure and shew. strewed with thorns has the path been to her! yet the great work of forgiveness I hope was accomplished here! afternoon at meeting William Savery, Samuel Emblen, and Sarah Harrison spoke. a muddy ride home, Elliston and Josey there.

3 day　Morn: mon epouse went to town.

[February 1, 1786]

4 day 2　Mo 1 afternoon Elliston and Billy an agreable time, they lodged hear

5 day 2　Morn: Sammy and I set out for Kensington in search of a maid, hired one and returned by one O'Clock

6 day 3　Ironing up a large wash. Josey hear

1 Day 5　yesterday mild as spring, to day blustering cold and snow, appears the very depth of Winter. mon epouse and Josey went to meeting. Robert Morris walked from town to his seat, and Elliston Perot walked hear,

2 day 6　Morn: mon epouse and Ann Davis went to town, she not being to return, Sammy brought back Betty Shaw a scotswoman to live with me.

3 day 7　Mon epouse and Sally went to town, thence SS went to Kensington and returned with Hester Chester to live with us.

4 day 8　a large wash. afternoon Debby and Sally Williams an agreable visit.

1 Day 12　Morn: mon epouse Sammy and I went to meeting[:] Peter Thomas, Samuel Smith, Sam: Emblen, and Rebecca Say spoke, dined at Ann Warners, with Molly England, Nancy Warner, and Anne & Benny

Shoemaker. afternoon at meeting Samuel Emblen spoke. returned home finally. this day was well spent

2 day 13 Hetty and I tayloring, Nancy Davis come to see her child.

3 day 14 Hetty and at work, 5 O'Clock evening John Grant drove Sammy and I in a slay over the hills, for a most agreable prospect. mon epouse and Sally come from town.

4 day 15 afternoon and evening spent pleasently with Elliston and Sally. 9 O'Clock night mon epouse returned from town.

5 day 16 Morn: Hetty, Sally, and I mantua makeing

1 Day 19 Morn: mon epouse, Sammy, and I went to meeting, Sam: Smith prayed. William Savery gave a most extraordinary proof of the spirit being poured out on all flesh; in the latter day, indeed, where in God is light, and in him is no Darkness at all. when he enableth. mankind, shall be ministered unto in the light, and in the Truth. full confirmation of a living ministry this morning————. Dined with my good Friend Caty Howell, and Joshua, Neddy, and Betsey Howell. afternoon at meeting Sam: Emblen and Thomas Scattergood spoke. Becky Shoemaker and I paid visit to Friend Warner. returned home Josey and Elliston there.

2 day 20 Morn: a very bad day but agreably spent, afternoon Josey & Elliston went home. Sally turned mantua maker

3 day 21 Morn: mon epouse and I went to monthly meeting Elizabeth Drinker and Sarah Dickason spoke, poor Abel James [was] this day disunited from his friends————. dined at Friend Warners, with Molly England, Hannah Cathrell, Catherine Howell, and Nancy Warner, then mon epous, Samuel Allinson, and Will: Sansom. returned to Parlaville where we spent an agreable evening with our old Friend, with whom many pleasent hours have past————

4 day 22 Morn: our Friends left us. Sally compleated her gounds.

7 day 25 Morn: Ironing, Joshua Smith spent the day with us, wrote to Mother by him. Josey Sansom hear

1 Day 26 Morn: mon epouse, Josey, and Sammy went to town, reading John Woolman's Journal.[41] John Grant took miff[42] and walked off leaveing us to wait on ourselves

3 day 28 a series of bad weather mon epouse went to town.

---

41. John Woolman, *A Journal of the Life, Gospel Labours, and Christian Experiences of the Faithful Minister of Jesus Christ, John Woolman* (1774).

42. Took miff: was miffed or took a miss.

[March 1, 1786]

4 day 3   MO 1 a day of violent wether yet pleasently spent

7 day 4   afternoon Sammy went with Hetty to see her mother, Elliston and Josey come from town. Josey has taken down in short hand a sermon of William Savery's, the day twelve month he began to study it.

1 Day 5   a very stormy day Elliston stayed the day with us. mon epouse & Josey went to meeting. afternoon Ann Davis come for her child, she is going with a friend to live at Bergen in east Jersey, 'twas painful to part with the dear little creature, but circumstances were such 'twas indispensible.

2 day 6   Morn: Elliston went home, his character still remains the man formed for domestic happiness. poor Cephas Dawes extream ill! Hetty come home

3 day 7   Morn: Sally and I went to meeting David Eaustah and Nicolas Waln spoke. dined at Friend Mitchel's, visit to Cousin Drinkers & H Thomas bought four yards and half black Padua soy[43] to make me a cloak, 12 yards and half of buff couloured mantua to make Sally a gound and Peticoat. went home found Elliston there,

4 day 8   afternoon Sally, Sammy, and I went to Friend William's, Debby, Sally, and Maria at home. spent our time agreably, a present of Salad and Redishes from Neigh: Morris's gardner.

6 day 10 Morn: busy makeing a pair of breeches for mon epouse. afternoon John Head, Elliston Perot, and William Sansom passed some hours in agreable chat. mon epouse hired a negro man named Edward

7 day 11 Morn: finished the breeches, afternoon John Drinker and Benjamin Morgan

1 Day 12 Morn: mon epouse, Sammy, and I went to meeting, Sam: Smith, Thomas Scattergood, Sam: Hopkins, and Hannah Cathrell spoke. dined with my agreable friends Caleb Creason and Wife, afternoon at meeting Thomas Scattergood spoke. visit to Friend Warner, agreable tea at home with Elliston and the Family

2 day 13 Morn: 9 O'Clock mon epouse, Elliston, Sally, Sammy, and I had took a tour of 3 miles over Schuilkill, round the grounds of Sam: Powell. afternoon Sally, Nancy, & Henry Drinker, Sally Lydia and William Parker, Sally Williams, and Will: Sansom

3 day 14 Morn: mon epouse, Sammy, and I went to town, a distressing time———————. went to meeting, Samuel Emblen spoke, visit to Becky Fisher who is very ill, dined at Friend Mitchels, visit to Peggy Fleming, thence to Docter Parks whose Wife Rachel Park lies dead. her father—James Pemberton—has his share of affliction, in his family!

---

43. *Soi,* French for "silk."

6 day 17   afternoon Joseph Drinker tead with us. Sally rode out being poorly.

7 day 18   busy at Work Sally spent the day at Friend Williams's

1 Day 19   Morn: mon epouse and Sammy went to town, afternoon Elliston and
Josey and John Macevers hear. paid him £2"7"6

2 day 20   Morn: Betty Shaw took her departure. Josey Sansom lodged hear.

3 day 21   Morn: mon epouse and Josey went to town. Mary Macevers come to
live with us

6 day 24   afternoon Elliston Perot and William Sansom. departed our good old
Friend Peter Worrell of Burlington, full of days, like a shook of corn
fully ripe, and the real insense of a good name, sweet in the nostrils, of
that, Being! with whome I have no doubt he is now reposeing.

1 Day 26   Morn: the cow calved. Josey Sansom & myself went to Bank meeting,
John Foreman spoke, dined with Joshua and Caty Howell, Mary
Sweet, and Sally Maul. afternoon market street meeting, tead with
James and Phebe Pemberton, Friend Thomas, and John Storer, the
friend from England.[44]

3 day 28   ——mon epouse and I went to meeting[:] John Townsend from England, Joseph Moor, William Savery, and divers other spoke, it was a
good meeting, we dined at home. wrote to mother. an agreable afternoon with EP.

[In margin: "half day"]

5 day   afternoon Billy Sansom brought Cousin Sally Smith who staid with us
day 30 till

6 day 31   Morn: when Josey Sansom and she went to town. Afternoon Elliston
Perot,

[April 1, 1786]

7 day 4   Mo 1 Morn: a violent storm of Wind and snow, which continued all
day, and night

1 Day 2   Morn: very bad weather. mon epouse went to town on horse back
hardly practible for a carriage, Elliston staid with us, till,

2 day 3   Morn: mon epouse and he went to town.

3 day 4   Morn: mon epouse and I went to monthly meeting, John Storer and
Grace Beaucannon spoke. ——————Clement Remington, Sarah

44. Lines cut out from the other side of the page. End lines read:
"ishes."
"on spoke, mon"
"[qu]eens ware dishes,"

Hart, —————Barnes, and —————Tomkins passed meeting, dined at Friend Warners with Joshua and Caty Howell, Becky Shoemaker, Molly England, Sarah Harrison, Grace Beaucannon, Hannah Cathrell, and Nancy Warner. it rained pretty hard. mon epouse and I went home, found E Perot there.

4 day 5   afternoon our Neighbours Croydir come to take leave of us, an honest good old couple, going to move from the Neighbourhood.

5 day 6   afternoon Elliston Perot and William Sansom. EP and I had an interesting and satisfactory conversation, he must have a good heart. my friends delay his application. but I am not able to change my opinion of him from the first, Candour and Ingeneuity are his characteristics.

7 day 8   very busy gardning. afternoon Billy Sansom

1 Day 9   Morn: mon epouse went to meeting, Josey Sansom dined with us, and we took a pleasent walk of many miles, Elliston hear,

2 day 10   Morn: gardening, afternoon Josey Drinker, Hannah and Arthur Thomas, and Thomas, Sarah, Edith, and Benjamin Newlan, the latter staid all night.

3 day 11   Morn: the Newlan's took leave of us. mon epouse went to meeting, Sally Williams hear, afternoon Elliston hear. planting of Lealocks[45] & Alltheas

4 day 12   Morn: busy in the garden, Jemmy Steuart & Billy Turner hear, afternoon Sally & I paid a visit to Neighbour Neglee, Neddy, Debby, & Sally Williams there.

6 day 5   Morn: mending Neds cloaths, afternoon Peggy Rawle, Betsey Howell, days 14   and Elliston Perot, a pleasent walk.

7 day 15   Gardening. Josey Sansom hear. Sally & Sammy went to Friend William's, Jonathan Mifflin returned with them.

1 Day 16   Morn: mon epouse, Sammy, Polly Macevers, & Ned went to meeting

2 day 17   afternoon Henry Polly & John Drinker[46]

4 day 19   afternoon Sally, Elliston, & Sammy, took a ride.

5 day 20   Morn: Sally Sammy & I went to meeting, Dorcas Lylly, Sarah Harrison, and Samuel Emblen spoke. dined at Henry & Polly Drinker's. rain comeing on Sammy and I come home.

6 & 7 days 22[47]

2 Day 4 days 23

3 day   25 Morn: mon epouse and went to m   m: Emblen spoke, dined at Friend Warners with Joshua & Caty Howell, Molly England,

45. Lilacs.
46. Erased: "with their son John."
47. Two or three lines cut out of manuscript.

and Hannah Cathrel. afternoon Sally Sansom and I went home in the rain.

5 day 27 washing, Sally Williams hear,

6 day 28 Neddy Brooks dined hear, Sally Sansom and I paid a visit to Betsey Shoemaker, very agreable, Rachel Carpenter there

7 day 29 Josey and his father very busy makeing an arbor by the Ceders. Sally and Polly Drinker and Elliston went to Friend Williams. Henry Drinker son of Henry drank tea with us.

1 Day 5 Morn: mon epouse, Josey, Sammy, & Ned went to meeting. afternoon
days 30 Elliston and Josey

[May 1, 1786]

2 day 5 a beautifull first of may. afternoon Elliston brought his Sister Mary
Mo 1 Perot and her son Andrew to see us, She appears a sensible agreable woman.

3 day 2 Morn: Sally, Sammy, and I went to meeting, James Thornton spoke. we dined at John Drinkers with ———— Dobbins, Josey & Polly Drinker. bought Sally a brown Sattin, buff coulered Mantua, and white Marsails quilt, we drank tea with Sukey Abbington at Docter Chovets

4 day 3 afternoon: Betsey Olden, Sally Hough, and Elliston Perot, we took a pleasent ride to Robert Morris's and then tead at home a delightful day

5 day 4 Morn: Sally, Sammy, and I went to meeting, Friend Berry and Samuel Emblen spoke, it was a good meeting. Sammy and I dined at home.

6 day 5 Morn: Sammy brought his Sister home, afternoon a visit From Elliston, John, and William Perot, three amiable Brothers, who have always lived in Brotherly love, and the prospect of a nearer acquaintance with them, still carries a hope we shall be happy with it. Charles Starton and John Thomas hear.

7 day 6 a fine rainy day, pleasent to my garden.

1 Day 7 Morn: Mon epouse, Sammy, and Hetty Jester went to town, Ned
2 days mounted on horse back to see his mother about 12 miles off. Sally but poorly, afternoon Josey come and informed [us that] William Sansom was returned from Virginia. Margaret Fleming has quited this transitory Life, in full faith and firm hope of a better. Charity covers many indiscretions and Charity was hers! many acts have been done in her life, for which she will now receive the reward.

2 day 8 Morn: Sally makeing her brown Sattin gound, afternoon Henry and Polly Drinker with their son John. an agreable walk thro the woods. William Sansom hear

3 day 9 Morn: William and I went to town, at meeting William Savery,

Thomas Scattergood, and James Creson spoke, Clement Remington & Sarah Hart were married. [and I] signed the certificate. Dined with Joshua & Caty Howell. Neddy and Betsey Howell [are] looking about in search of a servant. Josey come home with me, Elliston hear, a lovely moonlight night.

4 day 10   washing, afternoon Sally and I took a pleasent ride. tead at Friend Williams, with Samuel R Fisher, Sammy come for me, left Sally with Sally William's in order to morrow morning to pay a visit to Nancy Levesey with Polly Drinker, Jonathan Mifflin, and Elliston Perot.

5 day 11   Morn: Ironing, afternoon Mary Macevers left us to return to her old place. evening Elliston, Polly, and Sally returned, had a delightful day.

7 day 13   afternoon Benny Smith and Josey Sansom

1 day 14   Morn: mon epouse and I went to town, at market street meeting, Dorcas Lyly spoke, dined with the Widow Mary Lewes, Her son, & daughter Eddy. afternoon at Pine street meeting, Polly Lewes, Hetty Eddy, and I went to Hetty Mortons, Molly Pemberton there, the child of my much loved friend Sally Pemberton. I fear she must go a different path than that, she is in at present, if her mothers footsteps, are [to be] followed, but no one knows the well timed afflictions, that are mercifully dispensed to bring us home, in time, to recollection!

2 day 15   Morn: Six O'Clock Elliston and Josey went home, Samuel and Sally Pleasents breakfasted with us, [with] Sally Williams we took a pleasent walk over to Robert Morris's, afternoon Debby & Sally Williams, William Sansom, and Sammy brought Mary Bryan to live with me.

5 day 18   afternoon Sally went to Philadelphia on a visit to William Sykes and his Wife Mary Wharton Sykes,

6 day 19   Morn: mon epouse brought Sally. home sick of glare and shew, this I hope will tend to confirm her mind, of the instability of things below! the folly! to purchase fine garments, even when Ill health assuredly confirmed the bye stander, they never should [be] ware, the undeniable warrent was gone out when, we shall say "to the Worm, thou art my Sister"[48]

7 day 2   afternoon Elliston and Josey Sansom
days 20

1 Day days 2:21   Morn: rainy mon epouse and Sammy went to town, afternoon pleasent with Elliston, Sally, Billy, and Josey,

2 day 22   Morn: they went home, Sally Williams and Sally Sansom rideing on horse back, Billy Sansom & Polly Drinker set out for Waln Ford[49] to the weding of T Wister

48. Job 17:14.
49. Wallingford, then in Chester County, Pennsylvania, now in Delaware County.

1 Day 2   a long series of wet weather, the like hardly known, during the time
days 28   Sally sick of a fever, yet part of it agreably passed with Elliston's steady
attentions,
4 day 31   Sally mending, William Sansom hear, Samuel Shoemaker arrived
from England at his House in Burlington last seventh day night. after
an absense of eight years.

[June 1, 1786]

5 day 6   Sally and I took a ride, afternoon Daniel, Sally, and Maria Williams,
MO:1   Elliston Perot, and Josey Sansom
6 day 2   Morn: Ironing. afternoon Elliston, Polly, and James Perot
7 day 3   afternoon Elliston and Josey Sansom, a delightful moonlight night.

1 Day 4   Morn: 6 O'Clock Cousin Sarah Smith and William Sansom arrived
from town, breakfasted and then we three, set out for Burlington
passed on the road with James and Ruth Bringhurst. Betsey Barker going to Rhode Island. we got to Burlington by one O'Clock. found
mother and all our dear friends well.
2 day 5   Morn: monthly meeting Sally, Polly, and I went to it. Hannah Pryor
and Betty Kerlin spoke. afternoon Sally & Polly Smith, Polly Hoskins,
and I went to Samuel Shoemakers. it is eight years. since he left
Philadelphia. he looks as well in his person, as a man can do, who had
gone thro' so many tryals, at last [I] hope safe arrived in port to a worthy wife. Rebecca Shoemaker and Sally and Peggy Rawle were there.
with the child Francis about six months old.
3 day 6   Morn: William Sansom and Molly Sykes called hear, on their way to
Parlaville. afternoon a visit from Mary Barker
4 day 7   Rainy, agreable with the family
5 day 8   afternoon Mother and I went to Aunt Betty Smiths agreable with
Robert and Sally.
7 day 10   afternoon [with] Sally and Polly Smith, Polly Allinson, and Polly
Lowry took a pleasent walk, Captain Bradford invited us on board his
Brigg Lying at Kizetmans warf, Joshua Wallace there, a new scene to
the girls. they that go down to the great deeps see the wonders of the
Almighty![50]

1 Day 11   Morn: at meeting Hannah Pryor spoke. mother and I dined with Aunt
Betty, Sally and Robert Smith, and Polly Lowry. afternoon at meeting
John Cox, Hannah Pryor, and Betty Miller spoke. tead with Samuel
and Becky Shoemaker and John & Anna Clifford. Peggy Rawle and
Neddy Shoemaker there

50. Psalms 107:23–24.

2 day 12   Morn: wrote to Billy Sansom, afternoon mother, Sally, and I went to John Hoskins, Joseph and Ruth Richardson, Molly Barker, Lydia, Molly, and Rachel, and Abbigal Hoskins there, evening Polly Smith Polly Allinson & I took a pleasent walk

3 day 13   afternoon at Andrew Craigs Molly Commins there. letter from Billy.

5 day 15   Morn: at meeting Grace Beaucannon spoke. Patty Smith and I paid a visit to Becky Shoemaker. afternoon mother, Sally, and I paid a visit to John and Nancy Cox who are a happy couple.

6 day 16   Morn 7 O Clock Anne Clifford. Peggy Rawle and I come down with Jacob Myres in his boat dined with John & Anne Clifford. William Sansom brought me to Parlaville. found Molly Sykes, Edith Newbold, Henry and Polly Drinker, and Polly and Sally Horner there

7 day 17   Morn: mon epouse took Eddy to Town, afternoon Billy Sansom and John Head. evening Josey Sansom and Elliston Perot. we had a fine supper of Stawberrys from our own garden

1 Day 18   Morn: 7 O'Clock Tommy Howard breakfasted with us. mon epouse and Sammy went to meeting. Hetty Jester set out on a Journey to the Head of Chester. William Joseph and Elliston tead with us.

2 day 19   afternoon Elliston, Sammy, Molly Sykes, Sally, and I took a ride to Harrow gate springs. a profusion of company, spent a merry afternoon [and had] a most beautiful ride home.

3 day 20   Morn: Mary Bryan took her leave of us, we seem prone to change of late, mon epouse and I went to meeting, William Savery spoke. Thomas Colly there. dined at Freind Mitchels, paid a visit to Polly Perot, tead at Freind Heads. Hannah Thomas brought a bed of her second child at John Drinkers by accident being on a visit at her mothers.

[In margin: "paid D:Mitchell L1"2"6"]

5 day 22   Morn: the girls went to town,

6 day 23   Morn: William and the girls returned, Rachel Wetherby come as a servant. afternoon Danny and Sally Williams, Elliston Perot, and Josey Sansom.

7 day 24   Morn: 6 O'Clock William, Sally, and Molly Sykes set out for Burlington and thence to spring feild. Elliston went to town.

1 Day 25   Morn: 7 O'Clock Sammy went to Burlington, mon epouse to town, Josey dined with me. afternoon Elliston Perot

3 day 27   Morn: mon epouse went to meeting William & Sammy returned from Burlington in a gust of wind.

4 day 28   afternoon George and Edith Bullock, William Sansom, and Elliston Perot. the latter goes to Burlington to morrow, I wrote to Sally Sansom

5 day 30   afternoon Joshua and Caty Howell and Benjamin and Betsey Shoemaker

[July 1, 1786]

7 day 7 Mo 1   afternoon John and Caleb Creson, Elliston Perot, and Josey Sansom

1 Day 2   Morn: mon epouse and I went to meeting Samuel Smith, Hannah
Cathrell, and Samuel Emblen spoke, it was a memorable meeting,
dined with good old friend Anna Warner, Peggy Rawle, and Nancy
Warner. afternoon at meeting. tead at John Drinkers, Hannah Thomas
very ill yet! evening at home Elliston and Josey.

2 day 3   Morn: Rachel Wetherby returned and her Sister Hannah Come.
[torn page] Morn: Sammy and I went to meeting William Savery and
Samuel Emblen spoke. the City in a tumult on account of independence ———

   day 4   ——— I dined at John Perots with Polly, Elliston, Peter Stretch, & a
french gentleman, I look forward with pleasure to a nearer conection
with this family, Elliston returned home with me.

5 day 7   afternoon William Sansom and Elliston Perot. they lodged hear and
on first day morn Josey Sansom & Elliston are to set out for Spring feild.
wrote to Sally

1 Day 8   Morn: mon epouse & Hannah Wetherby went to town, this afternoon
was intered Joice Benezet Widow of the good Anthony, they now enjoy a seat in Heaven!

2 day 9   afternoon William Millhouse and his Daughter Marcy a pretty young
girl, amiable even in uncultivated nature,

3 day 10   Morn: Sammy and I went to meeting, David Eaustah and Samuel Emblen spoke, we dined at home. afternoon mon epouse and I went to
Friend Williams. John, James, and Lydia Craxon, and Betsey Bass there,

5 day 12   afternoon: John and Polly Perot [came] with the child Andrew.
William Sansom.

7 day 14   afternoon: mon epouse and I went to Edgely. Taby and Becky Fisher
are there, the latter in bad health. Sammy Fisher, Neddy & Betsey
Howell, Katy Hopkins & her Sister there, we walked over that delightfull Leasow[51] in minature,

1 Day 15   Morn: mon epouse went to meeting, afternoon Joseph, Henry, & John
Drinker, Neddy Brooks, William Sansom, and Polly Drinker.

2 day 16   Morn Billy Sansom brought Hetty Jester up.

51. Pasture.

3 day 17   afternoon mon epouse and I took a ride to Mac Phearson's place, which
           as it was built by Privateering, ~~stayed~~ made a short stay ~~and its owner~~
           with its owner, and is now vergeing to decay! whilst he is in poverty.

4 day 18   Morn: mon epouse took Hetty home.

5 day 19   Morn: Sally Williams hear, afternoon mon epouse and I paid a visit to
           Docter Bass, a Mr: Clark and his Wife, Debby and Sally Williams, and
           Friend Bass and Betsey Bass [were there.] a pleasent pretty improved
           retreat.

6 day 20   afternoon William Sansom hear

7 day 21   Robert Valentine is dead, Billy Sansom and John and Sukey Head are
           gone to the funeral at the great Valey Yokelan Township[52]

1 Day 22   Morn: Josey brought a letter from Sally, by Elliston, mon epouse, Josey,
           & Hannah Wetherby went to meeting, afternoon Elliston Perot, ———
           ——— Hugh Roberts has departed this Life, an old Citizen, I recol-
           lect none so old but Benja Franklin, Luke Morris, and Daniel Williams.
           who have seen all the Trees of the forests Leveled before them———
           ——

2 day 23   afternoon mon epouse and I paid a visit to our Neigh Paul, a pretty
           agreable young woman, [who resides] at John Warners place, for the
           health of her child

3 day 24   afternoon Mary Foulk and Betsey Bringhurst.

4 day 25   afternoon Rachel Drinker, Hannah Thomas, and Elliston Perot.

5 day 26   afternoon mon epouse went to Burlington in the Chaise for Sally.

7 day 28   afternoon Elliston, Polly Perot, and the child Andrew, Danny & Debby
           Williams, Thomas Paschal, and William Sansom, mon epouse and
           Sally [returned] from Burlington.[53]

1 Day 29   Morn: mon epouse, Sammy, and I went to meeting, I dined at John Per-
           ots with Polly and Elliston, afternoon at meeting Samuel Emblen
           spoke. we tead at home with Elliston and Sally.

2 day 31   Rainy, Elliston stayed with us, and spoke in his manly way to mon
           epouse, sueing for [the hand of] our child [in marriage], this fall, and
           so it is, he has over come every one's difficultys by a most engageing
           perseverance. and true love for our child, I desire nothing more in this
           life, than that she may by a prudent conduct retain his affections.

---

52. Uwchlan Township, in Chester County.

53. 7 mo 28 1786. Philadelphia Monthly Meeting Minutes, 1782–89, 274. "From our last Preparative
Meeting we are informed that Elliston Perot acquainted the Overseers that he is desirous of being united
in membership with our religious Society, and the preceding Preparative Meeting having been informed
thereof, a Committee was appointed to visit him, who now reporting their Sense of his Disposition it is
agreed to lay it before our next Mo Meeting, whereupon Isaac Zane, Benedict Dorsey, Joshua Cresson &
Robert Cox are appointed to Confer with him—"

3 day 1   Morn: made Sallys Marsails coat. dull weather, afternoon Elliston, William, and Joseph, mon epouse lodged in town, fire insurance meeting.

5 day 3   Morn: Elliston and Polly Perot with the child very sick of a Dysentery

7 day 5   afternoon Sally and I went to our Friend Joshua Howels. Benjamin Shoemaker, Taby & Becky Fisher, and Caty Hopkins there

1 Day 6   Morn: mon epouse and I went to meeting Isaac Potts and Sam: Hopkins spoke. dined at home. afternoon Billy   Sansom, Polly H Drinker and her son John, and Elliston Perot.

2 day 7   an agreable day with my family

3 day 8   Morn: Sally, Sammy, and I went to Youth's meeting, James Thornton, William Savery, Eliza Roberts, Molly England, and Samuel Emblen spoke, dined with Mary Armitt, visit to Betsey Olden and her son Thomas. this day James Rogers come to live with us.

4 day 9   Morn: the Negro man Ned left us, afternoon William Sansom

5 day 10 Morn: mon epouse taken very unwell, sent Sammy to town for William and Sarah, who come after diner, Elliston's servant Thomas brought a note with an account of the death of Andrew Perot, the child of John[, who was] about 2 years of age, a pretty little innocent, who mounting on a Cherubs wing, may be supposed to say, to his afflicted Parents, and feeling Unkle: my date was short, my grief the less,

Blame not my haste to happiness.

6 day 11 Morn: 5 O Clock gave mon epouse the Bark, afternoon William Sykes and his Wife Mary, Josey Sansom.

7 day 12 afternoon Elliston who lodged hear, mon epouse better.

1 Day 13 Morn: Elliston, Sammy, and Hannah Wetherby went to meeting, afternoon Elliston and Sammy returned.

[Supplement to the Diary]

25th [day] 8th [month] 1786, Philadelphia Monthly Meeting Minutes, 1782–9, 277. "A Conference is reported to have been had with Elliston Perot on the Subject of his application to be received into Membership by the Committee appointed thereto, who mention it as their Sense, that considering how he is circumstanced, it may be right to admit thereof, it appearing that he is a person of sober conduct, measurably convinced of the principle of Truth as held by Friends to which the Meeting assents, and the said Committee are desired to give him Information thereof, and invite him to attend our next monthly Meeting."

27th [day] 10th [month] 1786, Philadelphia Monthly Meeting Minutes, 1782–9, 283. "Elliston Perot attending, request was made on his behalf for a Minute of recommendation to the Monthly Meeting of Philadelphia for the Northern district, on account of Marriage with a Member of that Meeting, Rumford Dawes & Joshua Cresson are desired to make the needful Enquiry & prepare the same for the Consideration of the next Meeting."
[Return to the diary]

[January 1, 1788]

from the last date, my Husband, had a very severe Nervous fever that held him in its effects some months, the last date is the 13 and on the 16th we moved to Philadelphia, took a house in third street between Race and Vine streets, and in great affliction, I yet had the satisfaction of proveing EP to be a man of Integrity and a feeling heart, he joined my sons, as one of my own. and on the 9th of the first Month 1787 Elliston Perot was married to Sarah Sansom. from which time We have every day more reason to be thankful for our Daughter's situation. preserve her Heaven! from the insiduous Bane that lurks beneath Prosperity's mild Bay. let not the sunshine of ease and happiness, exclude from her mind. how soon all sublunary things shall vanish like

"The baseless fabrick of a vision."

[Supplement to the diary]
[Ann Warder's diary account of the wedding of Sally Sansom and Elliston Perot.]

"1mo 9th 1787

A poring Wet night & dull Morning presentd but a sad prospect for Ellistons Perots Wedding Guests. however we having the use of George Emlems Carriage it was not of much consequence to us further then gitting into Meeting to which there is not less then a Dozen Steps from the Streets & these in bad weather so muddy as to be quite uncomfortable—met at the Door Richard & Nancy Vaux the former only returnd last evening from Varginia after seven weeks absince. when we got in found most of the Wedding company [was] there at least them who came, for the weather discouraged some from attempting I went & sat amongst them thinking one lookd so different amongst the Women which is very

much the practise, except those who are nearly related, & Brides Maids, to prevent an unecessary shew which was the reason they abolished all the company streaming in at once—Cousin Betsy Roberts first said a few words—then honest Robert Willis soon after which Betsy appeared in Supplication—then was followed with a long & fine Testimony by William Savary After which the Bride & Groom preformed[—]the latter exceeding well & the former not very bad—Meeting early closed at least when the pair had signed & Certificate was read—the woman taking upon her her husbands name—We went to Ellisons house but little distance from Meeting & I soon felt very comfortable with several of my old acquaintence amongst them Abijiah & Sally Daws and John & Anna Clifford—with many others[—] in all forty eight. we were usherd upstairs where [there] was Bed rooms in order to receive us, having fires in most part of the house. Cakes & wine was early handed [out.] the Brides Brother Joey Sanson brought the latter in two decanters and a waiter with Bitters & Glafses—his Sister going to take some [wine when] an accident happend that spilt it all over her wedding Garment for which I felt much less [for her] then for the poor young man who's embarressment was very great—our next disaster proved a discovery that the black paint on the Scurting board in every part of the house came off—some Gowns lookd almost ruined but I did not thoroly examine mine not wishing to be made uneasy about any thing of the kind—at two oclock we were summoned down to Dinner time having past till then in agreeable conversation all very sociable though some & indeed many intire strangers to me till from inquiry I found who they were & discoverd most related to some I was acquainted with—all the company set down at one horse shoe Table except Cousin John Head, Jacob Downing & Billy Sanson who were Groomsmen & waited off us the Brides maids were Sally Drinker—her Cousin Polly Drinker & a young Woman named Skyes—Jacob Downing has long courted the former & it is now likely to be a match in the spring report say—she is a very chearfull cleavour Girl & he an agreeable young Man—We had a plenty full plain entertainment almost all things that the season produced . . . after being all satified we adjorned up Stairs again & chatted away the afternoon moving from one room to another as Inclination took us—the young Folks were innocently chearfull & old ones not less so They made Tea in another room & sent too us—about Nine we were calld to Supper which was mostly the fragments with addition of a few hot partridges &c—but less Pastry and such like then I ever saw upon such occation indeed we have had more at many private entertainments—after all had sufficuntly satisfied themselves a general remove took place & the house seemd soon cleard. Sally Daws went with us in Sally Emlens Carriage & so to her home—we set down & related some particulars of our visist & then retired to bed—————
[Return to diary.]

Philadelphia First Month 9th 1788
EP and Sally were married, and now live in the house we moved from
in Front Street between Market and Arch Streets and on the 16th of
the eighth month 1787, we moved to Second street near Arch street, in
a House of our own. our family [consists of] mon epouse, three sons,
Hester Jester, a little negro boy Abram Pee. and my pretty little dog
Clara, My Mother come to Philadelphia, 11 Month 10th, 1787. and lives
at Elliston's in a comfortable maner.

[January 1, 1788]

3 day 1   Morn: at meeting William Savery, Thomas Scattergood, and Samuel
Emblen spoke. afternoon at Home finished a pair of breeches for Josey,
he and some more young men are learning German of of John De Brahm

4 day 2   chief of the day at Sallys, she dined at John Perots with a gentleman
called — Nibbs

5 day 3   Morn: at Sallys dined with them, Nibbs called and took Sally in the
chariot airing, Sammy Sansom and I teed with Nancy Warner, and
Molly England, our worthy old Friend Ann Warner, departed this life
some months past, having been for near a year before struck with the
Palsey in her tongue which grew gradually worse till she closed the
scene! she had always been a lively worthy woman blest with affluence,
and a spirit to distribute, her charity and compasion for her fellow mortals in distress, was much, and her works will follow her, she did as
young says,

> ~~put good works on board, and wait the wind, which shortly b~~
> *"Age should fly concourse, cover in retreat,*
> *"Defects of Judgement, and the will subdue,*
> *Put good works on board, and wait the wind.*
> *Which shortly blows us, into worlds unknown:*[54]

I weept for her as my mothers friend, and mine own, but all tears are
wiped from her!

6 day 4   Morn: at home fitting up an old garment. afternon Edith Bullock, mon
epouse, and I tead with Mother & Sally

7 day 5   Caty Mullen and I put up Sallys bed. I was at J Perots. little James Perot
very poorly

1 Day 6   Morn: at meeting Samuel Smith and Thomas Scattergood spoke. the latter read the London Epistle, Rebecka Scattergood dined with mother,
afternoon at meeting. Susanna Sweet tead with me. evening at meeting.

---

54. Young, *The Complaint* (1749), 145–46. HCS deleted two middle lines: "walk thoughtful on the
silent, solemn Shore. / Of that vast Ocean it must sail so soon.

2 day 7   Caty Mullen and I at S Perots makeing curtains, covering arm chair.

3 day 8   makeing a petecoat for Sally's girl Caty

4 day 9   Morn: at home Thomas Metair dined with us. afternoon the Aniversary of Sarah's marriage, Anne Clifford, Jacob & Sarah Downing, Hannah Thomas, Polly & Nancy Drinker, John Perot, and mon epouse.

5 day 10   Morn: at Sallys afternoon John Rachel and Polly Drinker, John Debby & Molly Feild, Danny & Sally Williams, and Elliston & Sarah Perot.

6 day 11   Morn: Peggy Wharton had a son last night. I spent the day with mother.

7 Day   evening, I was taken very ill, first day Elliston brought Sally to see me, in the carriage, we sent for Abby Siddens to nurse me, and on third day growing much worse, [we sent] For Docter Abraham Chovet a man of great skill in his profession, I was confined a month during the time Billy Sansom and Sammy Sansom were sick! my illness appeared so sharp, I was ready to conclude my time was come, but the providence of God has spared me a little longer to my family, for which I am thankful, as my mother is aged, and [my] Daughter young, I may be of some little service yet! on and the first day four weeks, I went in Nibb's carriage to Elliston's and on the 19th day of the 2 Month 1788 and third of the week, six O'Clock evening, Sarah Perot had a son born, and called Samuel. Lydia Derraw[55] was the midwife, Rachel Drinker, Polly Perot, Caty Mullen, and her Nurse Olen Gamble [were] present, my mother an anxious spectator! third day week, in the morning went to meeting, paid the collection for 1788, and asked for a minuet of the meeting, to be recommended to the middle district, Catherine Howel & Mary England are appointed for enquirers.

[March 11, 1788]

1 Day   Morn: Josey Sansom come to me at Elliston's, and we went to meeting, at bank [Street], William Savery preached an extraordinary sermon reaching the witness! Thomas Scattergood prayed and we had a solemn meeting. Josey Sammy and I dined at home

2 Day   at Sally's [nurse] Olin and the maids makeing cake. lodged at home.

3 day   Morn: Sarah Fisher and Nancy Vaux—Nibbs who sets off to morrow for Tortola, afternoon. Sally Parker, Polly H Drinker, and Susan & Anne Head, lodged at home.

5 day   at Sally's. afternoon Anne Clifford, Peggy Wharton, Sally Rawle, Nancy Vaux, Sally Lippincut, Nancy Lynn, —————Montgomery, Polly Perot, Caty Hopkins, and Betsey Howell.

---

55. Lydia Darrah or Derrach, according to legend, risked her life to forewarn George Washington of an impending attack by the British in 1777. Elizabeth F. Ellet, *The Women of the American Revolution* (New York: Baker and Scribner, 1848), I:171–77.

6 day 14   at Sally's. Sarah Downing was delivered of a son, after a very critical time.

7 day 15   at Sally's. Polly Sykes there, a morning visit, Mon epouse, Josey, Sammy, and I tead at home.

1 Day 16   Morn: Josey and I went to meeting, Thomas Scattergood spoke. an alarum of fire at the Widow Hoods. dined at home with Josey, Sammy, and Alexander Reynear the son of the worthy old french woman. afternoon at meeting. tead at home [with] mon epouse and Sam:

[In margin: "note the other side"]

2 day 17   at Sally's. her child is a fine hearty babe, that will occasion his mother the less trouble for it

3 day 18   at Sally's, afternoon Polly Wister, Sally Pleasents, Molly Rhoades, Lydia & Ellenor Parker, and Polly & Debby Foulk
A Counterpart of the following lines, was put into the Coffin, with the Remains of my old French Mistress Maria Jeanne Reynier.

Altho' no Sculptor shall my lines retrace—
Should Time or Chance recall these Bones to view,
This Script may tell, in Whom each Christian grace
Fell in good Ground, and tow'r'd perfection grew:
The praise be thine, great Husband man to whom alone 'tis due.—

What matter, tho' through life, Misfortune frown,
If Christ with faith and hope the gloom but chear?
She can't with hold from an immortal Crown,
She could not, from its certain earnest Here,
A meek and quiet Spirit, Maria Jeanne Reynier.

Born in one of the Cantons of Switserland—died in the House of Employment, at Philadelphia in 1787 aged about 75 years, having submited, with Christian patience and resignation, to afflicting dispensations, from that all supporting Providence in whose wisdom and goodness she confided, during a series of near Forty Years, in different parts of Pennsylvania. she was known and respected during cheif part of the time by Anthony Benezet.

4 & 5 day 20   at Sally's. Polly Perot has inoculated her little Susan.

6 day 21   Elliston, Sarah, little Samuel, and Nurse Olin Gamble dined with us. the child is a lovely hearty baby. if he gives the same pleasure thro' life [as] he now does, it will recompence all cares! poor Sally Downing has lost her Baby and has been very ill herself all along.

7 day 22   began a coat for my man Abraham. Sally walked hear for exercise

1 Day 23 Morn: at meeting several Country friends spoke, it being the spring meeting, Hannah Millhouse and John Roberts dined with us. afternoon at meeting —————————Gascon spoke, a friend who has been deprived of his sight for some time, and no probability of [its] return. in a lively manner, clearly proveing himself not deprived of the light within.

2 day 24 Morn at meeting Thomas Loydd &c spoke Benny & Danny Smith dined with us, afternoon Joshua Baldwin and his Wife.

3 day 25 Morn: at meeting James Thornton spoke, it was our monthly meeting & my minute[56] was prepared. the worthy old friend Mary Cox spoke and Sarah Chambers, Rebecca Wright, Danny & Polly Smith, and Polly Allison dined with us. afternoon Benjamin & Mary Sweet, Caty Howell, and Ann Cox called, and we adjourned to mothers at Elliston's, had a satisfactory afternoon. Benny & Polly to ward the close appeared in the ministry,

4 day 26 at work on my coat, our folks began to dig a celler at Parlaville for a Kitchen,

5 day 27 at work Sally hear,

6 day 28 Morn: at meeting which was the largest I have ever known, William Savery spoke, John Foulk & Ellen Parker, Howell & Betsey Burge, and Docter Wistar and Annabella Marshall passed meeting. my minute was received. afternoon at Sally's Neigh: Dawes, Patty Whitelock, and Hannah Wood there. evening mon epouse & Billy [had] an oyster supper.

7 day 29 I at my work, and the men at the place. Sally hear.

1 Day 30 Morn: at meeting, Susanna Sweet dined with me, afternoon at home, evening Josey and I went to meeting, Daniel Lofly preached an excellent sermon calling to us, on whom the shadows of the evening had taken place—[57]

2 day 31 at work on the coat afternoon Sally called hear, and I returned with her to see mother and the dear little child.

[April 1, 1788]

3 day 4 Morn: at meeting, an Honest worthy man named James Simpson
Mo: 1 spoke, a Presbetyrian turned quaker, filled with much charity for the christian reformers, as they come on step by step till friends see the necssity of awful silent Worship! afternoon at work.

4 day 2 Morn: at work, Sarah and her son hear, Edward Callender, son of Benja Callender of Barbados, dined with us, poor Barbados, not much can be said for thy Inhabitents, slavery has been your bane.

---

56. Testimony from her old meeting for business to her new meeting that she is in good standing.
57. Jeremiah 6:4.

5 day 3   finished my boys coat, riped up one of Williams. Sally hear,

6 day 4   at work but not very well. a visit from little Sam with maid Caty

7 day 5   Edward Callender and Billy took a ride.

1 Day 6   Morn: went to Sally[']s, not quite well, mon epouse, Billy, Josey, and
            Sammy dined there. Edward tead with us,

2 day 7   Docter Shovet called hear and was paid his account for William and
            I[—] £7"15. he advised me to be bled. Martha Wharton is dead.

3 day 8   I was bled. the docter called to see the blood and advised [me]

4 day 9   at work on the coat. Edward dined with us

5 day 10   finished my coat. a rainy day.

6 day 11   Morn: William brought mother hear in a chaise, Elliston, Sally, & the
            child and Edward Callender dined with us. afternoon Polly Perot was
            hear. evening we took a walk.

7 day 12   morn: at work, afternoon at Sallys

1 Day 13   Morn: (missing) Docter called hear, and left a recipe. Joseph Sansom
            went to Plymouth meeting, Sally and the child come hear. ————————
            — James Nailor's last testimony said to be delivered by him about two
            hours before his departure out of this life; several friends being present.
            There is a spirit which I feel, that delights to do no evil, nor to revenge
            any wrong, but delights to endure all things, in hope to enjoy its own
            in the end: Its hope is to outlive all wrath and contension, and to weary
            out all Exaltation and cruelty, or what ever is of a nature contrary to its
            self, so it conceives none in thought to any other: If it be betrayed it
            bears it; for its ground and spring is the mercies and forgiveness of
            God. Its crown is meekness, its life is everlasting love unfeigned, and
            takes its Kingdom with entreaty and not with contension, and keeps it
            by lowlyness of mind. In God alone it can rejoice, though none else re-
            gard it, or can own its life. Its conceived in sorrow, and brought forth
            without any to pity it; nor doth it murmer at grief and oppression It
            never rejoiceth, but through sufferings; for with the worlds Joy it is
            murthered. I found it alone, being forsaken, I have fellowship there in,
            with them who lived in dens, and desolate places in the Earth, who
            through death obtained this resurrection and eternal holy life. such was
            the great Mercy of God to a man who saw his errors, repented and suf-
            fered deeply for them!

2 day 14   a rainy day pleasently at work

3 day 15   wet allso and at work

4 day 16   morn: at work, afternoon a visit to Nurse Nailor poor woman————
            ————tead with mother. Elliston & Sally, & dear little Samuel.

5 day 17   Morn: at meeting Isaac Potts spoke. invitation to the funeral of H Cas-
            sel. afternoon Sally & I on a visit]t to Debby and Hannah Mitchell, the

worthy good old people Abraham and Sarah Mitchell having departed this life within two weeks of each other, in the second month last, they lived in love and died in the same! Sally Parish there.

6 day 18   mon epouse & William very busy shelveing the store, & checking the seller stairs, Docter called in passing.

7 day 19   Morn at work. afternoon at Sallys. Molly Foulk and Sally Williams there

1 Day 20   Morn: Josey and I went to meeting, Thomas Scattergood spoke, Josey, Samy, and I dined at home, the rest at Elliston's, afternoon Josey and I tead at Ellistons. he has a violent pain in his face. evening at meeting Arthur Howell and Lydia Cracson spoke.

2 day 21   Morn: at Sally's. afternoon visit to Neighbour Jacob Shoemaker & Wife

3 day 22   Morn: Sally Perot and I at monthly meeting, Sally asked for a minute of removel to the Philadelphia meeting, Sarah Fisher and Catherine Howell are appointed to prepare one, she paid Catherine Howell a Guine[58] for her Monthly & quarterly collection for the two last years, I staid at EP['s] in the afternoon, Polly Drinker there

4 day 23   Morn: took my work to EP's our two Cousin Sarah Smiths from Burlington also little John and Joseph Smith,

5 day 24   Morn: Sally Smith and I went to meeting, the two Sarah's and Eliza Barker dined with us, afternoon we all went to visit Molly England and Nancy Warner, Caty Howell there, evening at Ellistons. our good old friend Grace Fisher has departed this Life for a better and Kitty Swingler, accompanied by Elliston, William, and Joseph Sansom in a stage waggon arrived there 5 O'Clock afternoon,

4 day 26   very busy in adjusting house matters. mon epouse lodged hear, Elliston is our constant lodger, my men by turns [are lodgers], as all are fond the place.

5 day 27   very busy washing ceilings, afternoon mon epouse, and Polly Perot

6 day 28   Morn: Sally and I went to town, being monthly meeting, Sarah Fisher and Mary Smith brought in her minute of removal from the Southern district, it was received. Daniel Lofly and James Ceason spoke

7 day 29   Morn: cuting out Jaket for John Louden, drawers for Elliston. afternoon ————————Bird and his Wife, Thomas Paschall mon epouse, and Will Sansom lodged hear.

1 Day 30   Morn: mon epouse & I Elliston & Sally went to town, at bank [Street] meeting. Sam: Smith spoke, Elliston & Sally dined with us. afternoon at meeting. thence returned. John Perot tead with us. Sammy Sansom lodged hear

58. Guinea, twenty-one shillings.

2 day 31 Morn: a large wash in hand, Polly Perot, her son James, maid Charlotte, mon epouse, and Josey Sansom.——————

[July 1, 1788]

3 day 7   Morn: Ironing, Polly Perot, her child Susan and Nurse, Edward
Mo 1   Brooks, and Josey Drinker.

4 day to   afternoon Sally and I took a ride, at night Sally had a violent oppres-
day 2   sion and continued poorly all the next day,

5 day 3   in the afternoon Polly Perot, Rachel Tybout, and William Sansom,

6 day 4   Morn: Elliston, Sally, & Josey Sansom went to town, Josey to mind
house, and they to see the grand prosession for the Federal goverment,
mon epouse come to me, and we let the whole family go to the place of
destination, union green, at bush hill. I was well pleased with dear little Sam thinking myself better employed to raise I hope a good and
happy subject, to a constitution built on a stable foundation.——————
Elliston & Sally and Polly Perot and her son James tead hear, mon
epouse and Polly returned to town.

7 day 5   Morn: Kitty washed rooms, mon epouse, Josey Sansom, Sally & her father took a ride,

1 day 6   Morn: mon epouse & Josey and Elliston & Sally went to fair hill meeting, Sam: Coates, & his two sons John Reynolds Coates & Joseph Saunders Coates, Will: & Sam: Sansom dined hear.

2 day 7   morn at work. afternoon Polly Perot, her children James & Susan,
Nurse

3 day 8   Morn: Sally and I went to meeting. afternoon Elliston & Sally, Josey
and I returned home pleasently,

4 day 9   Morn: Ironing, afternoon pleasently at work, mon epouse, Elliston,
and Josey.

5 day 10 afternoon Polly Perot [with] her children & Nurse, we took a walk to
Neigh Warners

6 day 11 at work pleasently. Elliston and mon epouse.

7 day 12 William Sansom come up, with a bad boil.

1 Day 13 Morn: mon epouse Elliston & Sammy went to meeeting, poltiseing
Billys boil, Polly Perot her nurse and two children, Andrew Tybout
Samuel Spolding, and John Perot dined hear. a dreadfull frecaw[59] with
Nurse Betty, all things will have there alloy.

2 day 14 William with us, a pleasent farmer's day. Christian Riffe & sons geting
in his Barly,

59. Fracas.

3 day 15   intended to have gone to meeting but the morning rainy, chair broke with Elliston & Sammy [in it. They] got along at last.

4 day 16   Morn: at work. afternoon Neddy Compton & Charles Cooper, two of Robert Prouds latin schollers, they enjoyed the time with all the happiness of youth, evening Elliston, Josey, and Sammy.

5 day 17   Morn Ironing, afternoon mon epouse, Sally, and I took a walk. lovely moonlight nights

6 day 18   at work. Elliston, Josey, & Sammy

7 day 19   Morn: 8 O Clock Buckingham to drive Sally. Sammy & I took a ride to Germantown, thence to Philadelphia, afternoon tead at John Perots. mon epouse, Elliston & Sally, and Josey & Sammy went to Parlaville, I staid

1 Day 20   morn: Billy Sansom, Capt Basden, & Spolding went to Parlaville. meeting at fair hill to day, I went to bank [Street] meeting, John Webb spoke, I dined with Nancy Warner and Molly England. Betsey Mecom and Josey Sansom tead with me. evening at meeting William Savery spoke.

2 day 21   Morn: 7 O'Clock they all returned and Billy took me back. Polly & James Perot and Lydia Tybout dined with us. afternoon Polly & Sally went to Germantown on a visit to Hannah Haines, Josey Sansom, Lydia, & I took an agreable walk. evening mon epouse & Elliston

3 day 22   Thomas Lane and his son with William Sansom dined hear. the Stangers are English merchants

4 day 23   Sally and I bysy at the needle. Elliston & mon epouse

5 day 24   quite a storm but passed pleasantly.

6 day 25   at work

7 day 26   at work. all the men of the family hear,

1 Day 27   Morn: mon epouse, Elliston, Josey, Sammy, and I went to meeting. John Webb, William Savery, and Hannah Cathrell spoke it was a good meeting! Sarah Fisher and I called at John Cliffords. afternoon at meeting. tead at home. mon epouse, Sammy, and I returned to Parlaville, Capt Craig, Sam: Spolding, and Will: Sansom there.

2 day 28   mon epouse Sammy & Philip mending the road, dull weather. evening Josey & Elliston

3 day 29   Morn: large wash. afternoon John and Rachel Drinker, mon epouse, Elliston

4 day 30   Morn at work. evening mon epouse, Elliston, Josey, this morn died William Double a great stroke to his family! and short warning to himself.

5 day 31   Morn: 5 O Clock Elliston set out to Double's funeral at Mount Benger a mile from Bristol where he is to be intered. Afternoon mon epose and

Josey Drinker. 8 O Clock Elliston returned: the deceas'd left a Wife, 6 children, and a Brother & Sister' in the deepest distress, he being an affectionate family man, Sally Perot could not help realiseing the poor woman's loss, how should I support such a dreadful separation, avert it thou supreme, pass the bitter cup from me! or enable me to bear, what thou may see meet to inflict.

[August 1, 1788]

6 day 1   Morn: at work. afternoon Sally and I took a ride

7 day 2   Ironing. afternoon Josey Drinker, mon epouse, Polly Perot, Josey & Sam

1 Day 3   Morn the men went to fair hill meeting after diner Josey Sansom & I went to town, evening at meeting Mark Reeve spoke.

[Supplement to the diary]

The only surviving letter of HCS is dated this day

Dear Mother   8 Mo 3 1788

And thee thinks we have forgot thee, no, we often tell Samuel if his grand mother had him a little, how pleased she would be, he is as hearty & grows as finely as heart need wish, and we often think how happy a thing it is, that thou enjoys the summer so charmed visiting and being visited by the good Burlington family. Thee has paid Nancy Cox a visit, and her little one, with whom I make no doubt, they [are] well pleased, thy note of the uncertainty of all things has been and wil   assuredly continue on all things here below! William Doubles sudan departure is a recent instance, of deep affliction to his family.

myself and Sarah are engaged with the child, it being a rainy day. The men are gone to meeting some to town, others to fair hill. Becky Shoemaker has been very ill but is now mending, what with our own child and Bettys too, we go very little out. Do let me tel thee, the little hand bason is alive yet, and he is washed in it from head to foot every day, cold from the pump till he shuddrs again, he wears no cap, his hair grows a little, and he is so saucy as to distinguish those he does see byt seldom, he looks a squint at his Aunt Pollys cap. Saucy as Clara, he distinguishes fine folk. All our loves to thee & the family

HSansom[60]

[Return to diary]

---

60. Morris Family Papers, Box 17, Quaker Collection, Haverford College Library.

2 day 4   Morn quarterly meeting. Sarah Fisher and I went to meeting, Samuel Emblen and Mark Reeve spoke, among the Women Elizabeth Drinker and Lydia Star, evening Elliston and I rode home,

3 day 5   Morn: Elliston & Sally went to town, Betty and I Ironing. afternoon Josey & Sammy Sansom, myself & dear little Sam, Betty Louden and Kitty Spangler took a pleasent walk to Shylkill, set on the rocks where about this time three years Elliston was for the first time. and now behold I am looking on his dear little likeness: Bless and make him such another man; who delighteth to give pleasure Virtuously to every female heart, pitying our infirmitys, and casting a vail over our faults,

4 day 6   Morn: at work Josey Sansom furbished our yard with gravel &c. afternoon Thomas & Nancy Morgan, Jacob & Sally Downing, Polly Howel Drinker, Nancy Drinker, Micheal & Mark Prager, strangers.

5 day 7   Morn: Sally and I took a ride, afternoon Jacob Shoemaker & Wife, mon epouse & Sammy. we took a pleasent walk.

6 day 8   Morn: Sally and I took an agreable ride to Joshua Howells, my good friend Caty & her daughter at home, we took a walk to Samuel Shoemakers, my old friend Becky at home, Nancy Warner, Anne Clifford, and her children Becky & Tommy. the habitations of my friends are a little Elizeam[61] afternoon Elliston & Josey.

7 day 9   morn: at work, afternoon Josey and I crossed Britton's bridge rode 4 miles along the Schylkill to Denny's ferry very pleasent. Sammy gone to burlington

1 Day 10   Morn: Elliston, Josey and I went to meeting. John Webb and ——— ———Williams spoke. Becky Scattergood, Danny Smith, and Betsey Mecom dined with us. mon epouse & Sally come from Parlaville, I returned with them back, John Perot with us. 8 O Clock Elliston returned from a visit to William Double's family. this evening, was intered Sarah Moor———————

2 day 11   Morn: Mon epouse Elliston went to town. mon epouse returned with Caty Mullen. afternoon John & Polly Perot.

3 day 12   Morn: went to town with Elliston, at meeting John Webb, Samuel Emblen, and Sarah Williams spoke, Polly Drinker measured me for a pair of stays

4 day 13   Morn: at work. afternoon Capt Barre's Wife Dolly Crathorn

5 day 14   Morn: the two Polly Drinkers, Edy Newbold, Josey & George Drink. afternoon Hannah Anne & Thomazine Clifford, Anne Giles, Sarah, Tabitha, & Becky Fisher, and Nancy Warner. this day was intered the Widow Banton. a great loss to her daughters.

6 day 15   Morn: at work. afternoon Edward Stiles, letter from mother.

61. Elysium.

7 day to day 16   Morn: at work. afternoon Thomas Morris, mon epouse, and Elliston.

1 Day 17   Morn: mon epouse and Elliston went to Fair Hill meeting. myself &
Sally not very well, excellent converse with young, afternoon John
Polly and James Perot, Rachel Tybout, Edward Shoemaker, and Sammy
Sansom

2 day 18   very wet day, mon epouse and Sammy staid with us.

3 day 19   Morn: mon epouse set out for Potts grove, afternoon William Sansom
and Sally Perot took a very pleasent ride, save our foritide was called
in question, being in eminent danger. of overseting.

4 day 20   at work. afternoon a pleasent walk

5 day 21   Caty, the washerwoman, come and we had a tite days work. evening
mon epouse [came back] from his Journey.

6 day 22   Caty with us Ironing. afternoon myself, Sally Perot, Polly Mongomery,
and Polly Perot on a visit to Capt Barre's Wife, living a place beauti-
fully situated on Frankford road. Betsey Kean and Susan Josiah [were]
there. evening Elliston & Joseph Sansom.

7 day 23   Morn: busy, Polly & James Perot, Captains Mac'Coy & Burrows dined
hear. Elliston, mon epouse & Sammy

1 Day 24   Morn mon epouse & I, Elliston & Sally, and Josey & Sammy went to
town, a good meeting at the bank [Street meeting.] William Savery
spoke. afternoon at meeting Josey Sansom & I went to John Heads on
a visit to Susan Head, young John & Anne at home, Janny was there.
evening we all went to meeting, Samuel Smith spoke.

2 day 25   Morn: Barbary began to white wash Sallys house,

3 day 26   Morn: rainy went to meeting, afternoon Sally & her father went home

4 day 27   Morn: Barbary white washing, Caty scowering, Betsey Foulk called
and desired me to accompany Debby Foulk on sixth day, to pass

5 day 28   Sally in town. very busy at the house, afternoon she went home. Docter Wister and his wife, Sally Downing, Nancy Drinker, and Neighbour Lee and his Wife. William Sansom returned from New york.

6 day 29   Morn: Jane Foulk and I went to meeting as orderly women, with James
Pearson & Debby Foulk,[62] Warner Mifflin and Ann Emblen passed
also, evening I returned with Elliston, Josey & Sammy

3 day 30   Morn: at work, dear little Sam gives us greatt pleasure.

[September 1, 1788]

1 Day 9 Mo 1   Morn: Elliston, mon epouse & Sammy went to fair hill meeting

2 day 2   Caty, the washer woman, come. a busy day.

---

62. They were the committee that had cleared this couple for an orderly marriage.

3 day 3   afternoon Thomas Paschal & William Sansom, and Sally and I took a ride

4 day 4   Morn Ironing. afternoon Polly Perot and James, Rachel Tybout, Abram Dubois, William, Sarah & Joshua Lippincut, and mon epouse.

5 day 5   Morn: concluded to move to town, William Sansom come out. & by noon we packed Sarah and her goods and chattles of Sally & her son, Betty Lowden and her two sons in the Pheaeton, Will: Sansom, Betty Riffe, sundry milk pails and other moveables in the chaise, —Parlaville—George and Philip with three Cart loads of goods, thus we leave this pleasent place, after having enjoyed many agreable hours, and full confirmation that Sally is well married! thanks to the great disposer of all things, mayst thou read this and take the full sense of the favor bestowed on thee, thou art favored among women there fore remember what thou owest to Church and State! evening mon epouse and Josey,

6 day 6   busy in the family, Leah Jones very poorly,

7 day 7   William and I went after a maid, engaged one for second day, afternoon Mon epouse & I, Elliston & Sally went to the funeral of Hannah Morton, Widow of Robert Morton, and daughter of James and Hannah Pemberton, a woman seasoned by affliction!

1 Day 8   Morn: rainy, at meeting seasonable service by Samuel Emblen, afternoon at meeting Samuel Emblen spoke, tead at home [with] Betsey Mecom. evening at meeting divers young hands.

2 Day 9   Morn: at work, afternoon[63] and I took a ride to Parlaville

3 day 10   Morn: at meeting, afternoon Nancy Warner and I took a walk to some shops, tead with her, and Mary Smith and Molly England.

4 day 11   Morn: at shops bought some muslin for [This first line is overwritten.] ~~all day Elliston & Sally~~[64] Morn: at shops bought some muslin for neckcoaths & stock 4 yards very fine for 5/6 p yd. afternoon Polly Howell Drinker and I went to Docter Chovets, Susan Abbington and Polly Beveridge there, the poor Docter is in what is generally the last stage; of men who will not submit their genius to the gospel, they are too wise to be come fools, for which reason the Talents bestowed on them are Towering talents, with Terestial aims!

5 day 12   Morn: Barbary come and we began white washing. afternoon Elliston and Sally, poor Sarah is worried with the tooth ake, afternoon happence drew the tooth.

6 day 13   Morn: at work. afternoon at Sallys

7 day 14   at Work. paid Polly Drinker for makeing and materials for a pair of stays 32/5 a pound of knitting thread 7/ Nancy Carlisle very ill.

---

63. Illegible name follows.
64. Erased in margin: "5 Day 12."

1 Day 15　Morn: 6 O Clock William and Elliston went to burlington on a visit to mother, 8 O Clock Ann Carlisle is dead, thus has she finished a course of affliction, heavy both before and after the decease of her husband, Abram Carlisle, he being one of the unhappy sufferers in the late commotion,[65] I went to the house and staid with her son till 12 O Clock, dined with Sally, Josey Drinker & Sammy Sansom, afternoon at meeting, tead with Sally, 8 O Clock E P & W S returned. mother well. an insolent letter from Ned Pole. Philadelphia

2 day 16　Morn: 9 O Clock Rachel Drinker and I at the funeral of Ann Carlisle, Samuel Emblen spoke. dined at Sallys and staid the rest of the day.

3 day 17　Morn at Sally & I at meeting, visit to Neighbour Foulk & Debby, afternoon Visit to Hannah Drinker. Jenny Plankinhorn, Sally Hart, and Polly Drinker there

4 day 18　Morn: at work for the poor, the ship Alliance arrived this morn from Canton in China, Caty, the washer woman, brought home the wash of Cloaths, having taken them on second day for the first time. on the same lay with Betsey Riffe, afternoon mon epouse & I on a visit to John & Rachel Drinker. John, Hannah, Arthur, & John Thomas there, the two latter sweet children well tutored.

5 day 19　Morn: mending shirts, afternoon at Sally's. evening Josey and I to see Abram Carlisle

6 day 20　Morn: at work. went with William to look at a house for him to live in, afternoon Sally and I on a visit to Sally & Molly Pemberton, [with] James Logan. Polly Pleasents, Hannah Cathrell, and Sally Lane there

7 day 21　very busy mending. evening Docter Griffits and Elliston Perot.

1 Day 22　Morn: at meeting. Samuel Emblen and William Savery spoke, afternoon at meeting, Lydia Noble, George & Edy Bullock, Robert Stevenson, and Elliston & Sally tead with us, paid the girl Polly 10[66] for the 2 weeks

2 day 23　Morn: at work, sent the wash, afternoon Sally Perot and I on a visit to Cousins James and Phebe Pemberton, he feels the many losses his life has been checquered with sensibly,

3 day 24　Morn: at meeting Lydia Star spoke, afternoon Sally and I on a visit to Sarah, Tabitha, & Becky Fisher, [with] Robert & Phebe Waln, Susan Hartshorn, Elliston there, a melancholy night———————

4 day 25　busy in the family evening Sammy & I took a run to Sally's.

---

65. Abraham Carlisle collaborated with the British during the occupation of the city and was tried and executed in 1778 after the Americans reassumed control. Crane, Drinker Diary, 2123. Carlisle was one of the witnesses to the will of William Callender; the families remained close. Philadelphia Wills, William Callender, May 17, 1763, M518, HSP.

66. Illegible word follows.

5 day 26   Mon: Ironing. John Macevers puting up my curtains, evening at M
Foulks

6 day 27   Morn: at monthly meeting, Warner & Nancy William & Debby,
Samuel Mickle Fox and Sarah Pleasents, John Todd and (space) passed
meeting, Nicolas Waln, Eliza Drinker, and Lydia Star spoke, much
good advice from William Savery and James Creson, to keep our meetings for dicipline among ourselves, and have patience to set them out
that we might receive the benefitt as many scattered hear and there in
their lonely cottages would be glad to do, Sarah Harrison's certificate
from Georgia in Carolina was read, and thro' thee meetings home,
having been gone almost a year, passed thro' many Perils. a dreadful
night—

7 day 28   Morn: busy in the family afternoon with Sally she has the Asma, Polly
Perot and Caty Mullen there, evening Owen Biddle brought us a cir-
cular epistle from friends as a body, [At] night rather better but in
much affliction. Danny Smith lodged hear

1 Day 29   Morn: begining of the yearly meeting, went to Bank [Street Meeting,
where] divers [people] spoke, dined with us, William Millhouse and
wife, Daniel Smith & Wife, and Sally, Polly, and Benny Smith, afternoon at bank [Street Meeting] Thomas Loyold & others spoke. Joshua
Baldwin and wife tead with us, evening at bank [Street Meeting],
William Mathews spoke

[October 7, 1788]

3 day 7   a very wet day spent pleasently at work. 4 day also,

5 day 9   Morn: at meeting Thomas Scattergood, Eliza Roberts, and Lydia
Gracson spoke, Warner Mifflin and Ann Emblen were married, afternoon on a Visit at Cousin John Drinkers

6 day 10   Morn: Visit to Sally Newlen. afternoon at Sally Perots.

7 day 11   at Elliston Perot's the company at diner Cheif Justice Georgies, and his
son, from St Christophers, —————Molleneuse, —————El-
der, —————Smith, the two Pragers, and Charles Starton

1 Day 12   Morn: at meeting. Josey & I dined together, the rest of the family at
EP['s.] afternoon at meeting. Samuel R Fisher tead with us, evening at
meeting Daniel Lofly and Hewson Langthstrogth spoke,

2 day 13   Morn: shoping bought Billy 4 pair of stockings. afternoon Sally Williams. evening Sammy and I took a long walk by moonlight

3 day 14   Morn: turning my long cloak. 10 O Clock went to meeting Lydia Star
spoke

4 day 15   Ironing and at work on my Cloak

5 day 16 Morn: at meeting, Samuel Emblen, Lydia Star, and Nicolas Waln spoke, William Pearson and Deborah Foulk were married, Jane Foulke and I went to the wedeing, the company was about forty persons and we spent an agreable day,

6 day 17 at home busy at work,

7 day 18 afternoon Sally and Elliston

1 Day 19 Morn: 8 O Clock William, Samuel, and I out for Burlington in Ellistons Pheaton, arrived there between 1 & 2 O Clock, found mother and the good family well, Sally Polly & I went to meeting, afterward tead with John & Nancy Cox, their child Susan and my mother, Sally Smith, Peggy Smith, William Sansom, and Benny & Sally Smith.

2 day 20 Very rainy. William returned to Philadelphia, got to kniting a pair of stockings for my self spent the day agreably.

3 day 21 dined with Aunt Betty Robert & Sally, then we adjourned to Dannys, William Sansom & Polly Hoskins arrived from Philadelphia.

4 day 22 Morn: we shiped mothers goods on board Capt Myers boat with Caty   and Samuel Sansom. 9 O Clock mother, William, and I set out in the Pheaton, a very boisterous passage over dunks ferry, other ways a pleasent Journey home to Elliston Perots, where I lodged that night that I mought settle mother comfortably in her lodgeing.

5 day 23 Morn: Caty and I put up mothers curtains.

6 day 24 busy at work, Sally Perot and I took a ride to Parlaville.

7 day 25 Morn: at home, afternoon with mother,

1 Day 26 Morn: at meeting, William Savery, Samuel Emblen, and Becky Jones spoke. it was a good meeting to me, Becky Jones being opined in a feeling manner to me, Joseph and Samuel were at fair hill meeting, mon epouse William and I dined at Elliston's, afternoon at meeting Samuel Smith spoke, Becky Jones called on us,

2 day 27 Morn: myself and Sally Perot paid a visit to Susan and Anne Head, at their fathers, Susan is the worthy choice of our son William for a Wife and they are to pass meeting on sixth day next, afternoon Sally and I at the Funeral of Molly Rhoades a young girl of 20 years of age, who has fallen a sacrifice to pride and vanity, and at whose shrines no more victims fall:

3 day 28 Morn: at monthly meeting, —————Star and Betsey West, and Philip Bunting & ————— Tomkins passed meeting, our friend Becky Jones produced three certificates from Ireland and England, also mentioning in a very agreable manner, the Joy she felt in returning to her native land! in which we cordially joined her, Sarah Harrison prayed, it was a good meeting.

4 day 29   Morn: at work. afternoon myself and Sally went to John Heads, to see the girls Hannah Wood, John Janny, and mon epouse there,

5 day 30   Morn: at work. afternoon with my mother;

6 day 31   Morn: 8 O Clock Sally & I went to John Heads, from whence Susan & Anne Head, Betsey Baker, Lydia Parker, Anne Dawson, and Becky Scattergood went to the fourth street meeting, Owen Biddle, Elizabeth Drinker, Hewson Langthsrogth[, and] Lydia Star spoke, Jane Foulk & I gave a good account of Debby Pearson['s] marriage, S M Fox & Sally Pleasents, John Todd & Alice Poultney, and William Sansom and Susan Head passed, Sarah Harrison & friend Willson went with us to the men's meeting, in the afternoon we all tead with Susan, allso mon epouse, Elliston, Josey & John Head & his sons John & Joseph

[November 1, 1788]

7 dya 11 Mo 1   Morn at work, also at home in the family agreably.

1 Day 2   Morn: William went to Darby, 10 O Clock went to meeting. Thomas Scattergood and William Savery spoke, Hannah Williams dined with me afternoon at meeting Arthur Howell and Samuel Emblen spoke. mon epous, Joseph & I tead at home, evening Joseph & I went to meeting. Arthur Howell and William Savery spoke, Cousin John Drinker paid us a visit.

2 day 3   Morn: quarterly meeting at fourth street went to it, William Savery Becky Jones divers others spoke, meeting adjourned to 5 O Clock afternoon, at which I attended, Rebecca has returned from Europe a lively minister and serviceable servant of the church

3 day 4   Morn: went to mothers and staid with her and the child, while Caty went to meeting, afternoon Sally Perot and I went to visit Sarah Rhoades on the death of her daughter Molly, Molly Pemberton the fortune, was there, and Betsey Rhoades,

4 day 5   Morn: Nelly Shirly   come to live with me, Leah being too infirm for my work,

5 day 6   Morn: at meeting, Phebe & Molly Pemberton, Susan Dylvin & I paid a visit to mother, afternoon Nancy Warner and I went to Benjamin Shoemaker's, Rachel Carpenter there,

6 day 7   Morn: Mother and I took a ride up Point road, round by Frankford stoped at James Pemberton's and dined with James & Phebe, Mary Armitt, Sally & Molly Pemberton, the only remaining children of that stripped family, Molly the daughter of my cousin Sarah Smith Pemberton.

7 day 8   Morn: busy at work, afternoon with mother

1 Day 9   Morn: Anthony Van Manyerk and Josey Sansom went to fair hill meeting, we went to the Bank [Street Meeting where] Samuel Taylor spoke, mon epouse William & Samuel with myself dined at Elliston's, after-

noon at meeting, Betsey Drinker and I went to Jacob Downings tead with Sally Downing

2 day 10   Morn: makeing stocks, afternoon myself & Sally Perot on a visit to Hannah Thomas, our respective husbands Joined us at tea,

3 day 11   a very stormy, rainy day. William Savery hear,

4 day 12   Morn: William took mother in a chaise to see Becky Scattergood, afternoon I went to her, Sally Scattergood there. a pleasent afternoon.

5 day 13   Morn: at meeting William Savery preached an excellent sermon, on the benefit of silent worship, branching out on many subjects[:] the grace of God, the universal Gift, the spark of vital fire! John Todd and Alice Poultney were married.

1 Day 16   Morn: at meeting. Susanna Sweet dined with me, afternoon at meeting, evening at mothers, Sally poorly,

2 day 17   a very wet day. Caty Mullen hear makeing me a cotton gound

3 day 18   Morn: at meeting, Samuel Hopkins spoke, Cousin Sally Smith dined with us. afternoon and evening with mother and Sally. kniting.

4&5 day   Morn: at meeting, Hugh Judge and Eliza Roberts spoke, mon epouse
20   & I dined at Elliston's, afternoon ——————Lee and his Wife, Rachel Drinker, and Polly Perot tead there

6&7 day   Nelly, Shirly and I at William Sansom's house in third street between
22   New street and Vine street, fitting it for there abode.

1 Day 23   Morn: at meeting William Savery spoke, mon epouse, self and the children dined at Elliston's, afternoon and evening staid with mother. Caty went to meeting

2 day 24   Morn: Warville breakfasted with us. Kitty Gamble and I began a dozen Shirts for William

5 day 26   Morn: at meeting Eliza Roberts and William Savery spoke, Samuel Mickle Fox and Sarah Pleasents were married. not much appearance of the quaker in the Company, time may bring back the spirit of their fore fathers,

6 day 27   Morn: having been a long series of wet weather myself and Sally Perot went to meeting in Hannah Pembertons Chariot, William Sansom & Susan Head passed, afternoon and evening passed with Sally Perot.

7 day 28   Kitty & I finshed four shirts.

1 Day 29   Morn: at bank meeting Becky Jones preached and prayed, a good meeting, mon epouse, William Sansom, Jacob Downing & I dined at Elliston's, little Sam & his nurse come home with me.

An Afterword

Hannah Callender Sansom lived for another dozen years after she finished writing her diary. She became more active in the meeting and in charitable work, but never as heavily involved as her mother had been. The domestic concerns of an engaged grandmother no doubt continued to absorb her time and attention, as did the new standards of comfort and decoration that required so much shopping, sewing, cleaning, planting, and weeding. As her son Joseph anticipated in a note to his wife, after he promised to bring his mother for a visit, "if weather, inclination, Family circumstances, and every other Female uncertainty combined shall permit."[1] Women's lives, ideally dedicated to the service of others, were filled with interruptions.[2] It is perhaps not surprising that she could not continue her journal.

Many tragedies marred HCS's last years. Her mother died in 1789 on the same day that her second grandson was born. Sarah and Elliston Perot had borne five children by 1793, but four had died at a young age. Two sons, including their first-born, Sammy, had died of the "putrid sore throat" (diphtheria), a daughter was suffocated accidentally by her wet nurse,[3] and another son died during the yellow fever epidemic of 1793, although perhaps of another cause.[4] Their surviving

1. Joseph Sansom to Beulah Sansom, June 11, 1794, Morris Family Papers, Box 17, Quaker Collection, Haverford College.
2. See Felicity A. Nussbaum, "Eighteenth-Century Women's Autobiographical Commonplaces," in *The Private Self: Theory and Practice of Women's Autobiographical Writings* (Chapel Hill: University of North Carolina Press, 1988), 147–71.
3. It was common for infants to sleep with adults. Such deaths were commonly assigned to adults rolling over in their sleep onto the child. Recent work has suggested that these were not suffocations but Sudden Infant Death Syndrome (SIDS).
4. Crane, Drinker Diary, I:511.

Figure 11 A silhouette of Hannah Callender, probably from the 1790s, by her son Joseph Sansom. Note that the caption refers to her by her maiden name only—very unusual for a married woman in the eighteenth century. Courtesy American Philosophical Society.

child, Hannah, was joined in 1794 by Sansom Perot; followed by Francis Perot, born in 1796; Joseph Perot in 1799; and William S. Perot in 1800. Three of the children married Morrises. Hannah wed Samuel Buckley Morris; Francis married Elizabeth Marshall Morris; and Joseph, Sarah Morris. HCS's quilt was kept and treasured in the Morris family until it was donated to Independence National Park.

In January 1799, HCS had a bad fall. Then in early March 1801, she fell ill of a pleurisy or putrid sore throat (modern diagnoses might be pneumonia, diphtheria, or scarlet fever) and died on March 8. She was buried next to her parents in Burlington.[5] Hannah's old friend, Mary Penry, wrote to Elizabeth Drinker after learning of the death, "You tell me our Friend Hannah Sansom is gone to Rest—happy she is, after having gone thro' her share of trouble—Is her Husband living or did he go before her? She lived to see her children settled in the

---

5. Crane, Drinker Diary, II:1391–92.

World and then had leave to *Retire.*"[6] Obviously, both HCS's marital difficulties and the relative successes of her children were well known.

THE CHILDREN

Sarah Sansom Perot spent most of her married life pregnant or nursing, unlike her mother, perhaps continuing to bear children because she feared a repetition of the epidemics and accidents that afflicted nearly all of her children born in the early 1790s. If Sarah and Elliston's lives were not always happy, by all accounts the marriage was, as HCS had hoped, mutually supportive. They lived quietly and privately. Sarah died of a persistent and long painful inflammation of her hand and arm in 1806. "Poor Sally!" exclaimed Elizabeth Drinker, "She has long been in a suffering state."[7] Elliston never remarried, even though he lived until 1834.

William was the only one of the children who exhibited a desire to get away from the domestic life of home and family and Philadelphia. HCS recorded approvingly that a speaker at Meeting had addressed Quaker youth that "a people might always remain in this place for the Lord and his Truth" (January 16, 1785). Nonetheless, three months later, "Will: Sansom set out for Virginia" with an intention to live there (April 18, 1785). Only three weeks later, however, he was back: "Will: Sansom returned from Virginia, likes Pennsylvania best" (May 10, 1785). It was a relief. Within three years he was settled, married, and in business for himself. William Sansom married Susanna Head and had two daughters. Daughter Hannah never married. Eliza married George Vaux, the son of her grandfather's apprentice. (The Vaux family preserved the diary.) William did very well, although he nearly died during the yellow fever epidemic of 1793 and was briefly ostracized by his close friends the Drinkers, who feared contagion. Even weeks after his recovery, Billy was denied entrance to the Drinker household.[8] But despite several health problems, he prospered. In 1798 he could write to a business associate that "As I have come forward in the theatre of Life in some measure since thee left this state it may be necessary to say that Providence hath indulged me with an ample fortune."[9] His fortune came primarily from trade, but he also carried out his mother's domestic ideals by building row houses, most famously a series of twenty-two identical, affordable, mass-produced houses on what is now known as Sansom Street. They embodied many of the new ideas of

6. Mary Penry to Elizabeth Drinker, April 3, 1801, copied by Jonathan W. Jordan, January 12, 1889, and bound into the diary.

7. Crane, Drinker Diary, III:1,957.

8. Crane, Drinker Diary, I:505, 516, 518.

9. Quoted in Elva Tooker, *Nathan Trotter: Philadelphia Merchant, 1787–1853* (Cambridge, MA: Harvard University Press, 1955), 239.

privacy and comfort and were originally situated away from the congestion and bustle of the commercial district—ideals that had been so important to his mother. Sansom Commons, a commercial block at the University of Pennsylvania, is a recent development that also perpetuates the family name.[10] His brother characterized William's business as "the usual round of Scantling and Lumber, Bricks, Lime and Sand, wound up with complaints and alterations, Bill and Receipts."[11] Billy enjoyed it, Josey did not.

Joseph Sansom married Beulah Biddle and had little of his brother's interest in business. "I prefer the enjoyment of domestic quiet, and the satisfaction of useful industry, to the unceasing round of pleasure, or business, for the sake of living in splendor, or amassing riches," he wrote.[12] Literature, art, and history, especially of a sentimental cast, fascinated Josey. The love letters and poems of Joseph and Beulah survive in the Quaker Collection at Haverford College, where an anonymous cataloguer remarks in the finding guide that they contain "fine expression of feelings—much more open than most Quakers."[13] Josey lived out many of the ideals of his mother's life. He and Beulah traveled widely. He published his letters from Europe.[14] He published an antislavery poem[15] and assisted in negotiations with the Iroquois. His description of Canada has become a classic of Canadiana.[16] He dabbled in the arts, made silhouettes of the family and of prominent Philadelphians and politicians, sketched, and had his portrait painted by Charles Willson Peale, pushing the boundaries of what was acceptable among Quakers.[17] He was an early member of the Historical Society of Pennsylvania. He served in the state assembly as a Federalist. What he could not do was support himself as a writer, artist, or silhouettist, much to his chagrin, so he engaged in just enough business to support his avocations. He and his wife had no children.

Little is known of the later life of HCS's youngest son. Sammy Samson had a brief career as a printer in the 1790s, publishing some short pamphlets on Quaker business matters and a couple of anti-Democratic, pro-Federalist tracts by Peter

10. Donna Rilling, *Making Houses, Crafting Capitalism: Builders in Philadelphia, 1790–1850* (Philadelphia: University of Pennsylvania Press, 2001), 79.

11. Joseph Sansom to Beulah Sansom, June, 11, 1794, Morris Family Papers, Box 17, Quaker Collection, Haverford College.

12. Joseph Sansom to Beulah Biddle, April 26, 1792, Morris Family Papers, Box 17, Quaker Collection, Haverford College.

13. Finders Guide, 1008, Morris Family Papers, Quaker Collection, Box 17, Haverford College, 36.

14. [Joseph Sansom], *Letters from Europe During a Tour through Switzerland and Italy in the Years 1801 and 1802. Written by a Native of Pennsylvania,* 2 vols. (1805 and subsequent editions).

15. [Joseph Sansom], "A Poetical Epistle to the Enslaved Africans: in the character of an ancient Negro, born a slave in Pennsylvania" (1790). Excerpts are available in James G. Barker, ed., *Amazing Grace: An Anthology of Poems about Slavery, 1660–1810* (New Haven: Yale University Press, 2002).

16. Joseph Sansom, *Sketches of Lower Canada* (1817 and subsequent editions).

17. Charles Coleman Sellers, "Joseph Sansom, Philadelphia Silhouettist," *Pennsylvania Magazine of History and Biography* 88:4 (1964), 395–438; and Anna Cox Brinton, "Quaker Profiles," *Bulletin of the Friends Historical Association* 29, no. 1 (1940), 7–17.

Porcupine. His major effort was a 292-page book by "A Friend to the Sex [Women]," *Sketches of the History, Genius, Disposition, Accomplishments, Employments, Customs and Importance of the Fair Sex in all Parts of the World,* published in 1796. His last publication was in 1800. Sammy then followed the family into mercantile trade and real estate investment, working with his brother William.[18] Like many Quakers at the time, he never married, and he died in 1828.

The three oldest children married for love and for the mutuality in marriage that love promised. HCS thought that "a man must ask his wife if he shall be rich." Sammy Sr. did not care to listen to HCS, but her sons and son-in-law did. They not only appreciated the private, comfortable, domestic, suburban realm created by their wives, where the men could engage in conversation, go for walks, buy presents, play with the children and the pet dogs, or plant trees—when they were spared from the workaday world of the city, that is—but they found that this new female domesticity was capable of commodification and profit. Elliston Perot developed a popular family summer resort at the seashore; William became a major real estate developer, with some help from his younger brother, and is credited with inventing the Philadelphia row house. Joseph also dabbled: in housing, in writing romanticized poems and travel accounts suitable for family leisure hours, and in cutting silhouettes, providing the masses with cheap, quick portraits of family and friends. All three sons also helped supply the consumer goods that fed these newly sentimental family ties. They were all successful, William spectacularly so. And despite the tragedies of sickness and early death, about which little could be done, HCS could not have written a happier ending.

For historians of the early twenty-first century, that happy ending must be mitigated by the other side of loving family lives, especially for women. The requirement of strictly enforced female sexual virtue became even more rigid in the nineteenth century, as women's economic opportunities shrank and the house often becoming more a prison than a refuge. While emotional fulfillment might have enhanced and equalized marriage relationships, the laws remained one-sided and masculinist. The revolution in women's lives continued well beyond HCS's struggle to overcome the unhappiness in her own life and her successful campaign to improve her daughter's fortunes in love and marriage.

18. Abraham Ritter, *Philadelphia and Her Merchants as Constituted Fifty @ Seventy Years Ago* (Philadelphia: Published by the author, 1860), 144.

Index

This index only hints at the wealth of information contained within the diary. No attempt has been made to index all of the hundreds of names in the diary or to provide a universal notation of subjects broached. Selected individuals and subjects are listed as a beginning approach to this rich document.